Presidential Party Building

Dwight D. Eisenhower to George W. Bush

Princeton Studies in American Politics

Ira Katznelson, Martin Shefter, and Theda Skocpol, eds.

A list of titles in this series appears at the back of the book

Presidential Party Building

Dwight D. Eisenhower to George W. Bush

Daniel J. Galvin

PRINCETON UNIVERSITY PRESS

Princeton and Oxford

Requests for permission to reproduce material from this work should be sent to
Permissions, Princeton University Press

Published by Princeton University Press, 41 William Street,
Princeton, New Jersey 08540
In the United Kingdom: Princeton University Press, 6 Oxford Street, Woodstock, Oxfordshire
OX20 1TW

Library of Congress Cataloging-in-Publication Data

Galvin, Daniel.
    Presidential party building : Dwight D. Eisenhower to George W. Bush / Daniel J. Galvin.
        p.   cm. — (Princeton studies in american politics)
    Includes bibliographical references and index.
    ISBN 978-0-691-13692-9 (hardcover : alk. paper) — ISBN 978-0-691-13693-6 (pbk. : alk.
paper)   1. Political parties—United States—History—20th century.   2. Political leadership—
United States—History—20th century.   3. Presidents—United States—History—20th
century.   4. United States—Politics and government—1945-1989.   5. Eisenhower, Dwight D.
(Dwight David), 1890–1969   6. Bush, George W. (George Walker), 1946–   I. Title.
    JK2261.G35   2010
    324.27309′045—dc22   2009020971

British Library Cataloging-in-Publication Data is available

This book has been composed in Minion and Myriad

Printed on acid-free paper. ∞

press.princeton.edu

Printed in the United States of America

10 9 8 7 6 5 4 3 2 1

For my family

Contents |

Preface |

Political parties have long been viewed as vital to democracy in America. But they have also been a perennial source of disappointment for small-d democrats: rarely have they proven capable of performing the many functions that are ascribed to them. In the latter half of the twentieth century, as the partisan attachments of voters began to loosen and party organizations seemed to fade in importance relative to interest groups, the mass media, and candidate-centered campaigns, frustrated scholars and concerned citizens began to search for the causes of party failure and decline. There were many culprits to be found: some were deeply rooted, like the peculiar design of the constitutional system. Others were more recent developments, such as technological change and the rise of the national administrative state. But a good deal of the blame was also placed on our modern American presidents—those notoriously ambitious, self-aggrandizing figures—who, scholars said, had abdicated their roles as party leaders.

Recent presidents, scholars observed, had willfully exploited their parties in pursuit of their self-interests. Rather than support their parties and promote collective responsibility, they took what they needed and gave little, if anything, back. What's more, modern presidential practices—such as speaking directly to the people, relying on independent campaign committees, and building a partylike apparatus within the White House—only served to push the parties further to the sidelines of national politics and undercut their traditional functions. Modern presidents were not party leaders, scholars argued, they were party predators.

Despite the fact that this observation lacked clear empirical referents, the notion that the president-party relationship was deeply problematic soon became conventional wisdom. Reinforced over the years by the repetition of familiar anecdotes and theoretical claims, it repeatedly escaped critical scrutiny.

In this book, I seek to reopen this question of long-standing interest. How, exactly, do presidents interact with their parties? Why do they do what they do, and with what effect? In my investigation of every presidential administration since Dwight D. Eisenhower, I find that the president-party relationship has not, in fact, been all of a piece. Contrary to conventional wisdom, modern presidents have not acted in a uniform manner toward their parties. Democratic and Republican presidents approached their parties quite differently, for different reasons, and with very different consequences.

Republican presidents, I find, worked persistently to build their party into a stronger and more durable political organization. Motivated by their party's minority status to build a new Republican majority that would reflect and perpetuate their political purposes after they left office, they made forward-looking investments in their party's organizational capacities. More often than not, they failed to build the new majority they envisioned, and their personal brand of politics faded into history. But through their party-building efforts, they made incremental contributions to their party's cumulative organizational development and encouraged their successors to do the same.

The notion of the president as party predator, I argue, is best viewed as an exclusively Democratic phenomenon. Since John F. Kennedy's presidency—until Bill Clinton's second term—Democratic presidents neglected their party, exploited it for short-term gain, or undercut its organizational capacities. Though they were often presented with the opportunity to make constructive investments in their party organization, they repeatedly refused. With deep and durable Democratic majorities in the electorate and at the congressional, state, and local levels, they had little reason to believe that their exploitation of the party apparatus in the short run would make much of a difference in the long run. They were not out to build a new majority, but to make use of the one they had. But by keeping their party's resources scarce and its operational capacities inchoate, they made cumulative organizational development in their party more difficult.

When the Democrats lost their long-standing majorities during the 1990s, their approach to organizational matters began to change. Bill Clinton and his team made a number of targeted investments in the party organization, and subsequent party leaders followed suit. But as we have seen in recent years, though new electoral uncertainties created new incentives for party building, translating those incentives into change at the organizational level happened only gradually, in a piecemeal fashion. Incremental investments led to cumulative gains over time as party leaders from Terry McAuliffe to Howard Dean to Barack Obama inherited an increasingly robust party apparatus upon which they could continue to build. As the following chapters demonstrate, this is precisely what characterized the process of organizational change in the Republican Party over the last half-century as well.

By missing out on these patterns of presidential behavior over the last fifty-plus years, not only have our normative concerns been largely misguided, but we have turned a blind eye to an important dynamic of modern American political development that has clearly shaped the politics of our day. Whether by building his party or by standing in its way, each modern president helped to push his party along a unique organizational trajectory. Indeed, the contemporary political landscape can now be characterized by the different speed and rhythm of each party's development; future political contests will undoubtedly be animated by the different challenges each party now faces. For all these reasons and more, the following pages seek to bring the president-party relationship into sharper relief.

Many people have helped me with this project, and it gives me great pleasure to acknowledge them. First thanks go to Stephen Skowronek, chair of my dissertation committee and adviser through six years of graduate school. Every step of the way, he offered penetrating criticism, invaluable guidance, and un-wavering encouragement. Steve is the best kind of mentor because even as he engages with your work as if it were his own, his goal is to teach you the importance of following your own lights. I was also fortunate to have benefited from the dedicated counsel of David Mayhew, whose keen insights and encyclopedic knowledge of American political history made this project much stronger and the author more confident. My thanks also to Gregory Huber, whose feedback, advice, and support were indispensable during the dissertation phase. I owe a debt of gratitude, as well, to my undergraduate mentor from Brandeis University, Sidney Milkis, who also served as my adviser at the Miller Center of Public Affairs. Sid's scholarship and teaching continue to be a great source of inspiration to me, and his comments and suggestions on this project were of tremendous help. Three former teachers were also critical to my development as a scholar, and it is an honor to acknowledge them as well: Todd Feldman, Richard Gaskins, and Rosabeth Moss Kanter.

I am especially grateful to Peri Arnold, William Howell, Philip Klinkner, Benjamin Page, and Steven Teles for going over my manuscript with a fine-tooth comb and for coming to Northwestern University to participate in an intensive one-day workshop on it. Their suggestions for improvement, coming at a critical time, made this book much stronger, and I thank them for engaging so seriously with it. The workshop was entirely thanks to Dennis Chong, whose helpful suggestions I also gratefully acknowledge. Jamie Druckman, Jacob Hacker, Scott James, and Byron Shafer also read all or parts of the manuscript at different stages, and I am grateful to them for offering their incisive and constructive comments.

I also wish to thank Rafaela Dancygier, Matthew Glassman, Stephen Engel, Stephen Kosack, Colleen Shogan, Julia Azari, Thomas Pepinsky, Reuel Rogers, Brian Balogh, Kathleen Thelen, Edward Gibson, Fred Greenstein, Tyll van Geel, Caroline Lee, Karen Alter, James Mahoney, and Bonnie Honig for sharing their insights, suggestions, and comments on different parts of this project as it developed. I am grateful also to Kenneth Janda for generously sharing his invaluable collection of party documents and correspondences, and to Christopher Mann for sharing his elections data. I would also like to acknowledge the helpful feedback I received from workshop participants at Yale University and the Miller Center. Of course, none of the above-mentioned scholars bear any responsibility for the faults that surely remain in this book; they do, however, get credit for helping to make it much better than it would have been otherwise.

I wish to extend my deepest thanks to the former party chairmen, White House officials, party professionals, and other participants who agreed to be interviewed for this book. I also thank my two anonymous reviewers, my supportive editor Chuck Myers and his team at Princeton University Press, and Richard Isomaki. I am fortunate to have received generous research support from the National Science Foundation, the Miller Center of Public Affairs, the Harry Middleton Fellowship at the LBJ Library, the Eisenhower Foundation, the Institution for Social and Policy Studies at Yale University, and Northwestern University. Over the course of my research, I received valuable assistance from archivists at the Eisenhower Library in Abilene, Kansas; the Kennedy Library in Boston, Massachusetts; the Johnson Library in Austin, Texas; the Nixon Library in Yorba Linda, California; the National Archives in College Park, Maryland; the Ford Library in Ann Arbor, Michigan; the Carter Library in Atlanta, Georgia; the Reagan Library in Simi Valley, California; and the Bush Library in College Station, Texas. I also received assistance from special collections librarians from Dartmouth College, Clemson University, the Iowa Women's Archives at the University of Iowa, the Bentley Historical Library at the University of Michigan, the University of Kentucky, Yale University, Northwestern University, and the National Conference of State Legislatures.

My greatest debts, however, are to my extraordinary family. I thank my parents, Irene and Tom, and my sister Rachel, for their rock-solid support and love, as well as for their eager consumption of my ideas every step of the way. I am especially grateful to my mother, who, lucky for me, doubles as a professional copyeditor. She scrutinized the entire manuscript and saved me from countless embarrassments (though all remaining errors are mine alone). And I thank the rest of my family for their steadfast encouragement and confidence in my abilities, especially my grandparents Joseph and Libby Flum, my mother-in-law Pat Glassmyer and late father-in-law Steve Glassmyer, Isabelle Gordon, and my great Uncle Louis Flum. My thanks also to Jeff Hellman and Sean and Jackie Whitney for their humor and moral support. Finally, I thank my wonderful wife and "secret weapon," Katie Glassmyer, who is perhaps not so secret a weapon. She is irrepressibly brilliant, as all who know her know well. She read every word of this book and sharpened every idea; the dull ones that remain undoubtedly escaped her gaze. But beyond this, I thank her for her constant encouragement and love, and, of course, for Eliza, the greatest blessing we share together.

1

Introduction | A Common Half-Truth

Dramatic differences in the organizational capacities of the Democratic and Republican parties were on full display during George W. Bush's presidency. The Republican Party was revealed to be a vertically integrated, technologically sophisticated national political machine with impressive capacities to activate local grassroots networks in coordinated, "microtargeted," get-out-the-vote campaigns.[1] This durable, versatile organization was a source of great pride for Republican leaders: irrespective of the ebb and flow of election outcomes, they remained steadfast in their determination to develop and enhance its structures and operations. After he won reelection in 2004, for example, Bush's deputies at the Republican National Committee (RNC) launched a four-year plan to "internalize the mechanics" of the successful presidential campaign in the formal party apparatus.[2] And when Republicans lost control of Congress only two years later, party leaders saw an opportunity to measure the organization's performance, make incremental improvements to its operations, and rededicate the party to organizational development—to "expand and perfect what we did well, and identify and correct what we didn't."[3] Bush reminded party leaders that the story remained the same: "You win votes by organizing and turning out the vote."[4] This commitment to GOP party building remained unchanged in the final years of Bush's presidency.[5]

The situation on the other side of the aisle could hardly have looked more different. Although the Democratic Party was raising money more efficiently and effectively than ever before over the Internet, its electoral apparatus was seen as "decades behind the Republicans organizationally."[6] Democrats had become accustomed to outsourcing their get-out-the-vote activities to largely uncoordinated advocacy groups, for-profit canvassing firms, tax-exempt 527 organizations, and other allies operating outside the formal party structure.[7] Such an approach was not without consequence: "At the end of the campaign," the Democratic National Committee's (DNC) field director remarked, "you're left with nothing, basically."[8] Inside the formal party umbrella, national party leaders played tug-of-war over scarce institutional resources. DNC chairman Howard Dean's ambitious "fifty-state strategy" to make long-term investments in state parties was met with fierce resistance from a hostile congressional party leadership accustomed to pursuing quick wins in swing districts.[9] Dean also faced high start-up costs: state and local parties were in a state of organizational disrepair and required a significant investment of time and resources. Most needed financial resources and more staff, and some also needed legal assistance, technological upgrades, public relations support, and campaign expertise.[10]

How and why the two parties developed such asymmetrical structures and strategies has become the subject of increasing scrutiny. In most accounts, however, credit and blame are assigned in a seemingly indiscriminate fashion: elite "power brokers," special interest networks, policy choices, marketing strategies, rhetorical frames, and even contrasting ideological commitments are offered as explanations for the divergent paths taken by the two parties.[11] Undoubtedly, each of these factors played a role. But oddly, American presidents—the party leaders who have had, arguably, the greatest stake in their party's current and future operations—have not made much of an appearance.

American presidents are perhaps the political actors most closely associated with major historical changes in the parties, but precisely what role they played in pushing these developments along is not at all clear. Six different Republicans occupied the White House for thirty-six of the fifty-six years between 1953 and 2009, yet the extent to which they were involved in building the new Republican Party organization of which we speak is not known. If anything, Republican presidents are seen as the beneficiaries of a party built by others, but are not, themselves, seen as integral to the GOP party-building project. Was this, in fact, how things developed? And did the four Democratic presidents of this period try to build their party organization and simply fail, or were they, too, peripheral to the currents of party change?

Remarkably, most existing scholarship has passed over these questions and focused instead on the characteristic party-building activities of "out parties"— that is, those parties that do not hold the White House. In the wake of defeat in a presidential election, the losing party's leaders and activists are depicted as the real party builders, the primary actors who build new organizational capacities and develop new methods of reaching out to new groups of voters and recruit new candidates.[12] Party building, in this frame, is the work of the underdog, the labor of the losing party. Presidents are nowhere in view.

In fact, when presidents do come into the picture, they are usually depicted as party predators, not party builders. There is a strong consensus in the literature that all modern presidents—Democrats and Republicans alike—view their parties as "at best a drag," and more commonly as "a nuisance."[13] They are portrayed as agents of party decline, as party antagonists whose approach ranges from "simple neglect" to "outright hostility."[14] Whether they treat their parties "with contempt" or mere indifference, modern presidents are said to "undermine the development and maintenance of a strong national party organization."[15]

This prevailing view results from the assumption that all presidents are driven by self-interest and short-term calculations, and are more concerned with their own problems than those of collective leadership. Especially in the modern context of "rampant pluralism," where presidents face "unnegotiable demands, political stagnation, and stalemate," they are compelled to break free from the centrifugal force of their traditionally decentralized party organizations and develop their own capacities for independent leadership.[16] They are said to have disengaged from their parties, transcended them, subordinated them, exploited them, or ignored them.

Modern presidential practices, we are told, have only made matters worse. By "running alone"—that is, by relying on independent, highly personalized campaign committees whose sole purpose is "to get them into office"—presidents are said to undercut their parties' core electoral functions.[17] Likewise, by creating offices for political affairs and public liaison inside the White House, they build "the equivalent of a presidential party for governing" inside the White House and short-circuit the party as a mechanism for representation.[18] And by employing common strategies such as "going public," presidents push their parties further "to the periphery of national politics."[19] Meanwhile, they "appoint a nonentity" to serve as national committee chairman, "downgrade the job, and humiliate the incumbent."[20] "The development of the modern presidency," Sidney M. Milkis summarizes, "clearly weakened party organizations by preempting many of the tasks they performed prior to the New Deal."[21]

If all modern presidents do indeed adopt a predatory relationship toward their parties, if they seek not to strengthen and expand their organizations but to marginalize or debilitate them, then Howard Dean and the Democrats might have done better simply to save their money and wait for President Bush to sap the strength of the organization that defeated them.

But what if the conventional wisdom is wrong? In my investigation of every presidential administration from Dwight D. Eisenhower to George W. Bush, I find that at best only half the story is in view. Drawing upon a wealth of primary source materials, including internal White House memos, letters, strategy papers, personal notes, party documents and publications, oral histories, memoirs, White House tape recordings, and personal interviews, I find that modern presidents did not act in a uniform manner with respect to their parties; in fact, the full scope of their party interactions reveals striking contrasts between them.[22] While it is true that all modern presidents sought to "presidentialize" their parties and use them instrumentally to pursue their independent purposes, Republican presidents did something more. Since Eisenhower, Republican presidents persistently and purposefully worked to *build* their party, to expand and develop it into a stronger, more durable, and more capable organization. Their instrumental use of the Republican Party organization did not prevent them from simultaneously investing in new organizational capacities to expand the party's reach and enhance its electoral competitiveness.

The conventional wisdom, it turns out, is more accurate as an exclusively Democratic phenomenon. Democratic presidents worked assiduously to personalize their party, altering and reconfiguring it to maximize the immediate political benefit to their administrations, but took few steps, if any, to leave behind a more robust party organization able to persevere over the long term. Whether they ignored their party, exploited it, or purposefully sought to undercut its organizational capacities, their actions had a debilitating effect on its organizational development. This Democratic pattern of behavior remained remarkably stable until Bill Clinton's second term. As Clinton's competitive environment changed, so too did his approach to his party organization; as discussed below, his presidency thus offers critical insights into *why* Republican and Democratic presidents acted so differently over the course of more than forty years.

But before we get ahead of ourselves, it is worth dwelling a bit more on this variation in presidential behavior. Partly because we have assumed that all presidents act in fundamentally the same ways, and partly because of the methods we have used to research such questions, we have long missed out on this striking pattern. But this has been no minor oversight: the different approaches taken by Republican and Democratic presidents clearly contributed to the divergent historical trajectories taken by the two parties over the course of the modern period and helped to create the uneven—and unsettled—political landscape of the early twenty-first century.

My aim in this book is neither to champion nor indict presidents for how they interact with their parties, nor is it to elevate Republicans for their efforts or denigrate Democrats for theirs. It is to show that the president-party relationship has not been all of a piece. Some modern presidents have acted more constructively with regard to their parties than others; my objective is to consider why this might be so and to bring *presidential party building* into view as a variable component of modern American political development whose significance is clearly evident in politics today.

I do not go so far as to claim that the lack of presidential party building explains all of the Democrats' organizational woes over the second half of the twentieth century or that the Republican Party's organizational strength, as observed in the Bush administration, was only due to presidential party-building efforts. No doubt a host of factors are at work. Nor do I claim that every Republican presidential party-building effort over the past sixty years was pursued with a vision of the contemporary Republican Party in mind. Quite the contrary: each Republican president pursued different visions of what a new Republican majority would look like, and each met with at least as many disappointments as successes. However, I do argue that in the course of pursuing their own distinctive purposes, each Republican president made incremental contributions to his party's cumulative organizational development. Likewise, I aim to show that the Democrats' persistent inattention to their party organization and their relative indifference to the long-term impact of their actions prevented the Democratic Party from capitalizing on the potential benefits of presidential power and made cumulative organizational development in their party more difficult.

What Is Presidential Party Building?

Clarifying terms and setting definitions up front is critical, because the heart of the problem, and the objective of this study, is to make precise what has thus far been obscured. While all modern presidents have tried in some way to change their party organizations to better suit their purposes, some have taken additional steps to develop their party's organizational capacities, strengthen its foundations, and expand its reach. Their party building has not been incompatible with the instrumental party-changing acts all presidents routinely undertake for their own immediate benefit. In fact, I will argue that the very essence of the thing—that which makes it an interesting and significant political phenomenon—is that presidential party building is *both* instrumental and developmental at the same time.

What it means "to build" is, admittedly, not self-evident. In the first place, presidents never create parties from scratch.[23] Even Jefferson, the first and perhaps greatest of presidential party builders, was acting upon an existing organization.[24] Presidential party building always entails rebuilding, recasting, or reconstituting an existing structure. Second, presidents frequently work to build electoral coalitions, but often do so without ever interacting with their party apparatus. "Going public," stumping for fellow partisans, promoting carefully tailored policy programs, staging symbolic spectacles, and other such strategies are often designed to mobilize electoral support for presidents and their fellow partisans, but they are not necessarily meant to "build" the party per se. Third, everything a president does in the course of his official duties—every speech, every policy proposal, every local visit, every dinner party, every foreign initiative—will reflect on his party and may even be undertaken to some extent with partisan political gain in view; most presidential actions have an impact on their party's public standing, even if only incidentally so. But the incidental effects of presidential action cannot possibly "count" as party building. One of the reasons we have had difficulty coming to terms with the president-party relationship—one of the reasons the subject has collapsed into a purely predatory perspective—is that it seems to be synonymous with whatever presidents do.

To shed some light on this relationship, we need to take a narrower view. In this study, I focus attention on what is at the heart of party building. Presidential party building will be distinguished here from everything else presidents do by its organizational focus and its explicitly constructive aims. Presidential party building aims to enhance the party's capacity to

1. Provide campaign services
2. Develop human capital
3. Recruit candidates
4. Mobilize voters
5. Finance party operations
6. Support internal activities

Decision rules, data sources, and other methodological issues are elaborated in the appendix. For now, it suffices to say that concrete evidence of efforts undertaken by the president to endow the party organization with enhanced capacities on these six dimensions is what counts as presidential party building. Actions that are indifferent, exploitative, or meant to undercut the party's organizational capacities along these dimensions count as confirmation of the conventional image of the president as party predator. As this specification suggests, presidential party building aims to bolster the party's operational wherewithal, both now and in the future. It is an intentional effort to foster party development: it is aimed at creating durable improvements to the party's organizational capacities. To be sure, presidential party-building efforts are meant to redound to the immediate benefit of the sitting president as well, and are usually designed with this goal in view. But they are constructive rather than exploitative and look as much to the future as to immediate political gain.

As this definition suggests, it is the party's organizational capacity that takes center stage in this study. Sometimes the term *party building* is used differently, so it is important to be clear. Sometimes it refers to discipline building in Congress, coalition building in the electorate, policy agenda building, party brand building, ideology building, and sometimes even giving campaign stump-speeches for fellow partisans.[25] Sometimes a president's expressed feelings of partisanship—his willingness to identify with and speak well of his party—are treated as evidence of his overall approach to his party, no more or less significant than purposeful organizational changes. Sometimes "party building" is meant to encompass multiple notions of party leadership at once.[26]

Organizational capacity, however, must be the starting point if we are to gain a fuller and more precise understanding of the relationship between presidential action and party development. Without organizational capacity, after all, parties cannot possibly perform any of the functions we ascribe to them. As Frank Sorauf has written: "A meaningful approach to political parties must be concerned with parties as organizations or structures performing activities, processes, roles, or functions. . . . The logical intellectual and analytical point of reference is the party as a structure. Activity (or function) is certainly important, but one must begin by knowing who or what is acting."[27] Organizational capacity can be built, it can be ignored, it can be undermined, it can be altered. It can grow, diminish, stay the same, or be transformed; it is where durable party change is executed. The party organization—its structures, processes, and operations—is thus the principal site for observing, measuring, and evaluating purposive president-party interactions.

Just as there are reasons for focusing on the party's organizational capacity, there are reasons for moving *presidential* party building to the center of the analysis.[28] While other actors surely have a hand in building the party's organizational capacities, the party-building efforts of presidents stand out as particularly portentous for the party's development. To be sure, some "out-party" national committee chairmen have been formidable party builders: former RNC chairmen Ray Bliss, Bill Brock, and Haley Barbour, for example, were critical agents of the GOP's organizational development in the modern period.[29] And former DNC leaders, including Charles Manatt, Paul Kirk, Ron Brown, and Howard Dean, have also received attention for their organization-building initiatives.[30] Congressional party leaders, too, have sought to strengthen their party through various means: consider Newt Gingrich's efforts to recruit and train candidates through GOPAC and other initiatives in the 1980s and early 1990s, Tom DeLay's redistricting efforts in the early years of this century, or the McGovern-Fraser reforms in the Democratic Party in the early 1970s. Extrapartisan outfits such as think tanks, advocacy groups, and nonprofit organizations are also sometimes credited with affecting a party's capacity to contest elections, recruit personnel, and so on.[31]

But in contrast to these nonpresidential party builders, presidents possess unusually potent resources to effect significant party change. In addition to their usual sources of leverage (appointments, endorsements, and so on), they can also draw upon the administrative muscle and unparalleled prestige of the presidency. For example, their West Wing teams can marshal considerable administrative resources to plan extensive party activities; presidents can raise more money with a single appearance or signed letter than any other political figure; and a simple call from the White House can inspire reluctant candidates to stand for office or rouse a complacent local leader to action. Whatever resources they choose to use in any given instance, presidents also tend to be skilled political actors, and should be expected to bring their own personal touch to the project at hand.

Presidents are also set apart from other party leaders by their unique position of authority in their parties. Though formally independent from them, modern presidents assume their parties' "titular" leadership, handpick the national chairperson and other leaders at the national committee, and exercise decisive authority over the party's national activities. Perhaps most important, their actions effectively define the parties' political purposes, a fact that by itself can induce concerted organizational action. For all of these reasons and more, modern presidents possess unusual capacities to effect party change.[32]

But the importance of presidential party building is not simply a matter of resources and authority. It is also a matter of the opportunity costs that are incurred when presidents choose *not* to involve themselves in party building. Squandering the opportunity to leverage presidential power and prestige on behalf of constructive party change during periods when the party holds the White House may be more detrimental to the party's long-term development than is often realized. For instance, we know that some ambitious Democratic "out-party" chairmen took pains to launch new party-building initiatives, but in the absence of continued presidential support during subsequent "in-party" periods, there was little that these chairmen could do to effect long-term change in the party. Their periodic attempts at party building became isolated events.[33] Eschewing party building, Democratic presidents not only set their party's organizational development back, but they made it more costly for future party leaders to launch new programs.

On the Republican side, in contrast, persistent investments in the party organization fostered the continuous, cumulative growth of the GOP's organizational capacities. Each new round of party building not only carried forward past successes, but built on them and fostered conditions amenable for further party building in the future. Investments and reinvestments in human resources, technological capacities, and strategic operations made for durable, self-reinforcing processes that helped to carry forward constructive, party-building purposes over time despite personnel changes in party leadership; such stability and continuity in party activities also helped the Republican organization withstand fluctuations in its electoral fortunes. With ongoing programs on which to build and low start-up costs, future presidents were more likely to find it in their interest to continue down the party-building path. As this contrast makes clear, presidents can either be a boon to party development or they can stop it dead in its tracks—either way, they are formidable political actors whose actions cannot help but shape the course of party change.

Presidential party building, it should be noted, also speaks to those activities that party "functionalists" have long argued are the core "constituent" or "integrative" functions parties play (or should play) in the United States.[34] When presidents engage in party building, they seek to enhance the party's capacity to engage with voters, register them, and mobilize them to vote; to attract new volunteers and activists and involve them in politics; to encourage citizens to stand for elected office and serve in appointed office; to adapt to meet changing conditions; and to pace the opposition in electoral politics. To the extent that the necessary starting point for assessing party functions must be the structural, procedural, and operational wherewithal of the party to implement these activities, presidential party building becomes an important factor in how we evaluate the "proper" functioning of the political system and how we assess different functional trade-offs under different conditions.[35] These questions are addressed further in the concluding chapter. Suffice it to say, unpacking the president-party relationship promises to address long-standing concerns about the representative process in America and the variable role presidents play.

Lest I overstate the case, I hasten to repeat that the interesting thing about presidential party building is that it is never fully about building "the party" per se, as an independent political entity separate from the president, or as a responsible or functional instrument of democracy. This is not "altruistic" behavior. All president-party interactions are undertaken with the president's best interests in view, and all party-building actions should be expected to serve the president's interest as well. The peculiarity of the phenomenon, and perhaps one of the reasons it has long passed under the radar, is that presidential party building involves both the personal and the collective, the instrumental and the developmental. As this book aims to make clear, instrumental action need not always be predatory; indeed, while it is safe to assume that the president's relationship to his party is always instrumental, it might at times also be directed toward building something stronger and more durable.

Herein lie the two literal alternatives suggested by the term *presidential party building*. One might take the term to mean "party building, undertaken by the president," or, alternatively, "building a presidential party." The first reading implies that the president helps to build a durable electoral organization with the wherewithal to operate continuously and independently of his administration; the second implies that the president sidelines the regular party organization and builds an alternative wholly dependent on himself.[36] While the range of the concept may be encompassed by these two alternatives, much of this book is meant to elaborate upon the possibilities that lie between. We will see some of each, but more importantly, we will see that neither tells the whole story.

Republican presidents did not seek to sacrifice their party's independent capabilities at the altar of their personal interests, but neither did they try to build their party to operate without regard for their personal purposes. Instead, their efforts were geared toward creating a new and different kind of party. They aimed to "presidentialize" their party, to make it more responsive to their leadership and more reflective of their personal brand of politics, but at the same time, they sought to strengthen its organizational foundations and enhance its capacities to expand and improve in the future. Though they hoped to benefit personally from their party interactions in the short term, they did not exploit or debilitate their party organizations in order to do so. On the contrary, they perceived that a constructive approach promised a higher political payoff than an antagonistic approach. Republican presidents treated the GOP as central and consequential, not peripheral or detrimental, for themselves and others.

Whether their party-building efforts helped to create a normatively desirable party—one that might, for example, judiciously balance the president's interest with the collective interest—is an important matter for debate. The Republican Party under George W. Bush, for example, was by most accounts a robust organization that was also highly subordinate to the White House. With this combination of attributes, it may well have sacrificed some of the capacities of earlier American parties to hold presidents accountable to a collective interest; as we will discuss, variations in the president-party relationship have entailed some rather unexpected trade-offs in party "functions."[37] But my primary aim is not to adjudicate the results so much as it is to account for them and to clarify the political dynamic at the heart of this modern political development. By conflating presidential instrumentalism with the notion of the party predator who ignores or weakens the regular party organization, existing scholarship has missed out on critical variation in the president-party relationship and obscured an integral component in the development of modern American politics. Republican presidents in the modern period did not perceive their party as irrelevant or as an obstacle to their leadership: rather, they saw it as a useful and beneficial resource. In their persistent attempts to fortify their party organization, these presidents created new, potent resources for presidential power and also new, durable organizational capacities in their party to last well beyond the moment.

Pressing the Limits of Current Scholarship

As I have noted, political scientists have had next to nothing to say about presidential party building as a general phenomenon. We have a vague notion that most "great" presidents—Jefferson, Jackson, Lincoln, FDR—were also great party builders, but virtually everything we know about that connection comes from historians and remains scattered and anecdotal.[38] The relationship has been squeezed out of discussion. In early years, it lost out to the Progressives' celebration of a presidency-centered government as an alternative to the perceived corruptions of party government, and in later years it fell victim to the normative critique of the modern presidency, especially as this critique was tied to a lament for the decline of parties.[39] But there is an analytic as well as a normative component to this remarkable lacuna: the approach most political scientists have taken to studying the presidency for almost fifty years has given us only limited purchase on presidents as agents of systemic political change.

Presidents are usually evaluated and compared in terms of how much of their agendas they can accomplish within the bounds of a tightly constricted political system and a short time frame. In the standard accounts, the contours of the political system are essentially given; the president faces a fixed environment that, although different for each incumbent in its particulars and different perhaps even from one biennial election to the next, is treated as largely external to the leadership problem the president confronts. The environment is, in this sense, a "deal of the cards" in an ongoing game over which the president exerts little control. Because presidents are seen as confined to working with their political environments as they find them, their own capacities to *change* the existing configuration of political forces, including their parties, seldom receive direct attention. What escapes investigation is the possibility that presidents are out to change the rules of the game itself, and that party building is one of the instruments at their disposal to do that.

The typical finding of work that proceeds on these assumptions is that presidents have no durable effect on the political environment in which they act. George C. Edwards III, for example, casts his investigation along these lines and finds that "there is little evidence that presidents can restructure the political landscape to pave the way for change. Although not prisoners of their environment, they are likely to be highly constrained by it."[40] I do not mean to suggest that all party-building presidents successfully or permanently change their parties and restructure the political landscape according to their own designs. Most do not; nor do they all try to the same extent. But findings such as Edwards's must be understood in relation to the premise of their research questions. Indeed, if the George W. Bush presidency does not conclusively refute the standard conclusion, it certainly does raise questions about it and about the methods by which it was reached.

The dominant frame of presidential scholarship might be described as "man against the system." The assumption is that if the president does not dominate the system, it will dominate him; that its component parts will smother him with their demands, if not their own special interests. Presidents are more or less able to get things done depending on the given configuration of political forces in play and their own individual leadership styles, strategies, and skills.[41] The behavioral school of presidential studies ushered in by Richard Neustadt in 1960 inaugurated a debate about whether the individual or the contextual configuration was most important in determining how much a president could get done, and Edwards, for one, has weighed in heavily on the side of context.[42] Either way, the predominant assumption that the president must subdue his party before it subdues him is implicit in these analyses.

A more dynamic and interactive sensibility might be teased out of the new rational choice scholarship. Terry Moe, for example, finds the impulse to alter, politicize, and control the president's governing environment to be inherent in his leadership position and particularly consequential for the development of American political institutions. Presidents, he says, take "aggressive action within their own sphere of authority to shift the structure of politics for themselves and everyone else."[43] Suggestive as such insights are, however, rational choice scholars have not thus far followed through to consider whether the institution-controlling efforts of presidents have any effects more durable than those realized in the moment at hand; subsequently, the terms of analysis have not been fundamentally altered. Notwithstanding its critical thrust, work in the rational choice tradition remains very much preoccupied with a Neustadtian understanding that the problems to be addressed in presidential politics are framed by the structural limits of presidential power and the strategies available for presidents to get more done. Presidential unilateral action, legislative bargaining, executive branch management, and legislative policymaking are usually examined for the purpose of learning how much the president can extract from a system stacked against him.[44]

What, then, if we assume that the contours of the system are not given, but are, in each instance, a main object of contestation? It is hardly a stretch to think that presidents see it this way, that they are not just interested in realizing particular policy objectives but also in restructuring the political landscape and tilting the competitive balance in their favor, and that their actions are, more often than not, undertaken with these larger ends in view. Getting at this would require an analysis that treats presidents as constitutive of the political system, as actors who can affect their political environment just as surely as their political environment affects them. It would require a more protean view of the system in which some basic structural features remain unsettled and open to presidential manipulation. What such an approach would offer is a fuller accounting of presidents as agents of political change, as engines of party development, as potential party *builders*, and not just transient party actors.

There are a few studies that proceed along these lines, enough to suggest that presidents do have unique capacities to bring about dramatic change in the political landscape. Benjamin Ginsberg and Martin Shefter, for example, have argued that presidents are capable of rearranging the configuration of social groups. In their view, presidents are "not in fact limited to dealing with some predefined or fixed constellation of forces." Rather, they can "reorganize interests, destroy established centers of power, and even call new groups into being." They can "attempt to enhance their own power and promote their own policy aims by constructing a new, more congenial configuration of social forces."[45] Similarly, Sidney M. Milkis shows that, in seeking to enhance the administrative capacities of the executive branch, successive presidents since FDR have contributed to the emergence of a modern executive establishment and a more national and programmatic party system. Changes in the party system and changes in executive administrative capacity have been inextricably linked—each one implicates the other, with presidents as the main facilitators of these developments.[46]

And in Stephen Skowronek's study of presidential leadership, the president is depicted as a "blunt disruptive force" who always shakes up, and sometimes reorders, "basic commitments of ideology and interest" in the course of exercising power.[47] Along the way to fulfilling their constitutional duties as national representatives, Skowronek's presidents routinely "make" politics and leave an altered political landscape in their wake. What these and a few other like studies aim to show is that presidents are powerful agents of change, capable of redrawing the lines of political contestation and restructuring political power, authority, and influence.[48]

Mainstream presidential scholarship, however, has yet to heed the call of these scholars and follow up in earnest on their theoretical and empirical insights. How, precisely, presidents interact with their political environments and shape the structures of which they are a part remains far too underspecified in most studies. Presidential rhetoric, policy promotion, unilateral action, coalition building, and even symbolic action are presumed to cause political change; the outstanding challenge is to test these assumptions by specifying how each factor does so. As too often happens with an endogenous view of change, we run the risk of leaving a thick composite of determining factors where everything of significance appears to be bound up with everything else. The task at hand for anyone interrogating the system-altering potential of presidential action is to clarify the relationship between action, circumstance, and effect. Presidential party building is ripe for scrutiny in this manner.

But a new analytic approach that relies on the same data will not do. One of the reasons the received wisdom regarding the president-party relationship has remained intact for so long is that we have been too willing to rely on secondary sources and recycle familiar stories.[49] As burgeoning work in the traditions of American political development and historical institutionalism demonstrate, there is no substitute for going directly to the primary sources to investigate pressing conceptual and temporal political puzzles.[50] Immersing oneself in the archives may not be the most glamorous of undertakings, but it does allow for new findings to emerge that can cast old assumptions in new light, generate new questions, and open up new lines of investigation.

Considering the Variation

The tendency to view modern presidents as party predators is encouraged and reinforced by some of our most deeply rooted assumptions about American political parties, how they are structured, and how they operate. Most theories of the parties rest on the assumption that, except for their policy proposals, the Democratic and Republican parties are essentially symmetrical organizations that face the same imperatives to structure their operations and activities to appeal to the median voter and construct majorities throughout the constitutional system.[51] Regardless of the period of American history we are concerned with, scholars usually assume that both parties are structured and operate in fundamentally the same ways. Especially within demarcated party "periods" or "systems," both parties are presumed to exhibit organizational isomorphism.[52] While this assumption of party symmetry has been widely useful as a theoretical device in political science, it has led to a chronic failure to observe evidence of party asymmetry in reality.

Despite the pervasiveness of these assumptions, the existing literature does not go so far as to portray the president-party relationship as wholly static. Variation, however, is usually presumed to be historical—change is thought to occur around historical breakpoints, at least four of which can be readily identified:

1. *Assumption:* Each incumbent acts differently toward his party on account of his individual personality, skills, and style.[53]
   Expected variation: Every four or eight years, with every new administration.
2. *Assumption:* John F. Kennedy's "going public" strategy ushered in a new era of president-party interactions in the television age.[54]
   Expected variation: Before and after Kennedy's presidency.
3. *Assumption:* The presidential primary system and campaign finance reforms altered how presidents approached their party organizations.[55]
   Expected variation: Before and after the reforms of the 1970s.[56]
4. *Assumption:* The growing use of independent presidential campaign organizations had a deleterious effect on the parties.
   Expected variation: A gradual increase in party subordination culminating in 1972, followed by an "established pattern" thereafter.[57]

As we shall see, these presumed sources of variation, especially changes in the campaign finance regime in the 1970s, did significantly alter the institutional environment in which presidents operated, and presidential practices changed as a result. But these historical junctures do not represent the critical pivot-points in the president-party relationship. When the data is assembled

		Party Building						Party Predation					
		C	H	R	V	F	I	C	H	R	V	F	I
Republicans	Eisenhower	•	•	•	•	•	•						
	Nixon	•	•	•	•	•	•	•				•	
	Ford	•	•	•	•	•	•						
	Reagan	•	•	•	•	•	•						
	Bush	•	•	•		•	•						
Democrats	Kennedy				•	•		•	•		•	•	•
	Johnson							•	•		•	•	•
	Carter							•	•	•	•	•	•
	Clinton (1st term)							•	•	•	•	•	•
	Clinton (2nd term)	•	•		•	•	•						

C=Provide campaign services, H=Build human capital, R=Recruit candidates,
V=Mobilize voters, F=Finance party operations, I=Support internal activities

Figure 1.1. Variation in President-Party Interactions

and the comparisons are made, an altogether different pattern emerges: for a quarter of American history, *which party* the president belonged to was the best predictor of how he would approach his party. Figure 1.1 illustrates this rather striking partisan pattern across the six dimensions of party activity listed above.[58]

This partisan pattern was not, however, a simple matter of inherent differences between the parties. As we will see, it resulted from the very different competitive environments in which Democratic and Republican presidents found themselves throughout this period. With their party in the ostensible minority, Republican presidents engaged in party building as a means of building a new majority. With deep and durable majorities, Democratic presidents faced different challenges, and the condition of their party apparatus did not figure as a prominent concern. Both impulses came into play during Bill Clinton's presidency, which helps to explain the mixed bag of party interactions over the course of his two terms in office. This "competitive standing" theory of presidential party building, and the assumptions and expectations it entails, is elaborated in detail in chapter 2. For now, brief comparisons along two different dimensions of party activity suffice to introduce the basic contrast between party building and party predation.

First, consider how Presidents Lyndon B. Johnson and Gerald R. Ford altered their parties' capacities to *finance party operations*. As I have noted, fund-raising capability is a major advantage presidents can bring to their parties. But if presidents can raise money quickly and easily, they can also do so for a variety of specific purposes; and on that count, the fund-raising activities of Johnson and Ford were markedly different. While both presidents broke fund-raising records, the money Johnson raised remained tightly controlled by the White House, while most of the money Ford raised went directly to state parties. The contributions Johnson raised were spent at his sole discretion—some were disbursed to members of Congress and other officials deemed particularly useful to the president, and the rest were used to build up his campaign war chest. The money Ford raised went directly into state party treasuries to help them get out of debt, develop improved local campaign operations, recruit new candidates, and register and mobilize voters.

Second, consider how John F. Kennedy and Ronald Reagan influenced their parties' capacities to *provide campaign services*. In preparation for his 1964 reelection campaign, Kennedy refused to seize upon the opportunity provided by his presidential campaign to enhance the Democratic Party's organizational capacities. Instead he established a highly personalized campaign network that bypassed the existing party apparatus. Largely an ad hoc arrangement of gentlemen's agreements, fragile deals, and personal loyalties, Kennedy's evolving campaign offered little help to his fellow Democratic candidates and proved to be useless for his successor. In contrast, Ronald Reagan integrated the RNC into his 1984 reelection campaign as an equal partner. The RNC, the Reagan-Bush '84 campaign committee, and several other groups divided the labor of registering and mobilizing voters. Taking advantage of Reagan's popularity and the prime-time event of a presidential campaign, Republican activists, volunteers, and party members were able to develop their campaign skills; millions of new Republicans were registered and brought into politics as volunteers; and a voter information database was developed for use in future campaigns. Reagan's reelection campaign, in short, was turned into a comprehensive party-building affair.

Johnson, Ford, Kennedy, and Reagan all had similar interests in securing reelection, achieving policy successes, and leaving personal legacies, and each found that he could use his party to assist in these purposes: but the nature and extent of their interactions with their party organizations were qualitatively different. They were different in their aims: Republicans sought to bolster the independent organizational capacities of their party down to the local volunteer; Democrats exploited their party organization for their own purposes and diverted resources away from local party organizations. Republicans seized the opportunities afforded by presidential politics to enhance their party's operations; Democrats either ignored or eliminated those opportunities. And they were different in their time horizons: the Republicans' efforts were geared toward strengthening their party as it looked toward the future; Democrats aimed to maximize their immediate benefit and assumed that their party's future would take care of itself.

The story does not end with this bifurcated partisan pattern, however. Variations can be found within each partisan grouping; indeed, variations can even be found within individual presidencies. The richness of the data proves to be indispensable to the analysis: it offers important lessons about why and when presidents act the way they do, and it strengthens the conceptual framework elaborated in the next chapter. Each of the following chapters, therefore, provides a means of probing the explanation from different angles and subjecting it to very different tests in each instance.

First, however, we need to consider more fully the question of why Democrats and Republicans acted so differently over such a long stretch of time. What was it about their competitive environment that motivated Republican presidents to adopt a more constructive approach to their party than Democratic presidents? And how should we think about enduring differences between the parties, and the relationship of those differences to patterns of presidential behavior? These questions are taken up in detail in chapter 2.

Organization of the Book

After chapter 2 presents a theory of presidential party building, the book divides into two parts. Part I, "The Republicans," examines the presidencies of Dwight D. Eisenhower (chapter 3), Richard Nixon (chapter 4), Gerald R. Ford (chapter 5), Ronald Reagan (chapter 6), and George H. W. Bush (chapter 7). Part II, "The Democrats," then examines the presidencies of John F. Kennedy (chapter 8), Lyndon B. Johnson (chapter 9), Jimmy Carter (chapter 10), and Bill Clinton (chapter 11). The conclusion summarizes the findings and the explanatory framework, elaborates upon them, and takes up long-standing questions about the role of the presidency and the parties in the American constitutional system. The afterword then discusses the presidency of George W. Bush and offers an update on the Democrats' organizational development through Barack Obama's election.

All of the case study chapters follow the same organizational schema. Each begins with a brief summary of the president's competitive political environment and the condition of the party apparatus he inherited—the two factors that I argue are critical to explaining the variation in presidential behavior (see chapter 2). The discussion of each presidency is then structured around three or four "lessons"—or general observations—about the relationship presidents tend to establish with their parties under different conditions. The lessons are derived from the case study in which they appear, but they are not tied to that case; they are meant to be applicable to every presidency within each part and freely interchangeable therein. The historical material then cuts through these lessons in mostly chronological fashion. The goal, however, is not to provide a step-by-step historical account—it is rather to explicate the more general phenomenon of presidential party building as it is revealed in each episode of president-party interaction under consideration. Finally, each chapter concludes with a brief discussion and summary table that locates these episodes along the six dimensions of party activities.

The case studies are divided by party, rather than presented chronologically, in order to draw attention to the carryover effect of each president's actions from one administration to the next and to provide a better sense of the different organizational trajectories taken by each party. By starting with Eisenhower and finishing with Clinton and his successors, this organizational structure is meant to provide the semblance of chronology while also bringing the analysis full circle. The hope, in any case, is that this organization will accommodate readers with historical and theoretical interests in equal measure.

2

A Theory of Presidential Party Building

The pattern of presidential party building introduced in the last chapter challenges some of our most prominent theories of presidential behavior, party organizations, and American political development. It also raises a critical question we never before knew to ask: Why did Republican presidents act constructively toward their party organizations while Democratic presidents did not, at least not until late in Clinton's presidency? What sets these two groups of presidents apart?

In this chapter, I argue that Republican and Democratic presidents acted differently on account of the different competitive political environments they faced as well as the different organizational arrangements they inherited from their predecessors. In the first part, I elaborate the "competitive standing" theory and discuss how institutional inheritances, timing, and sequence come into play. Then I consider two alternative explanations, both having to do with deeply rooted differences between the parties, and use the discussion to further explicate the theory. Finally, I consider the relationship between competitive standing, party differences, and the two parties' trajectories of organizational development.

Competitive Standing

One of the hallmarks of the American political system is that a president can (and often does) get elected while his party remains in the minority in other branches and levels of government. Between 1953 and 2009, Republicans held the White House 64 percent of the time but were in the minority in Congress, at the state level, and in terms of party identification throughout most of this period (see figure 2.1). The Democratic Party, in contrast, controlled both houses of Congress 64 percent of the time (and at least one house 78 percent of the time), controlled most statehouses and governors' mansions, and claimed a majority of self-identified partisans in the electorate—but held the White House only 36 percent of the time.

Formally, there is no such thing as a "majority" or "minority" party in the United States, as these split decisions attest. But presidents do not care to be so precise; they know it when they see it. As we will see in the following chapters, as far as every president from Eisenhower to Clinton was concerned, the Democratic Party was the majority party and the Republican Party the minority party for all practical purposes.[1] In any given election, of course, Democrats could lose seats and voter support. But a steady Democratic advantage in partisan identification, a large Democratic "farm team" at the state and local level, and a Democratic ideological advantage carrying over from the New

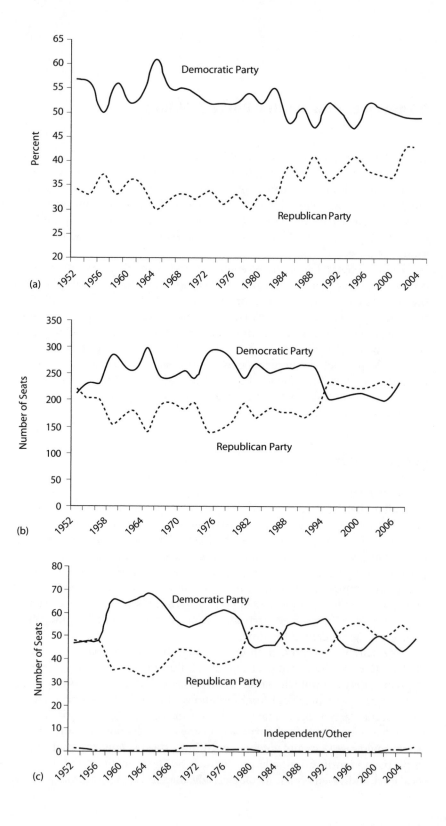

(a)

(b)

(c)

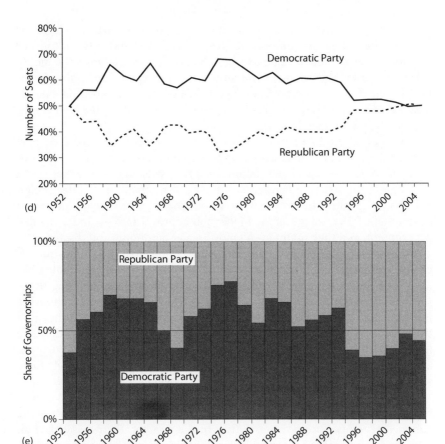

Figure 2.1. Competitive Imbalance between the Democratic and Republican Parties, 1952–2004: (a) Partisan Identification in the Electorate (3-pt scale); (b) Partisan Composition of House of Representatives; (c) Partisan Composition of Senate; (d) State Legislative Seats Held By Party; (e) Governorships By Party

Deal / Fair Deal period meant that all else equal, Democrats could be expected to win more congressional, state, and local elections than Republicans.[2]

This competitive imbalance was more than a mere inconvenience for Republicans and an agreeable state of affairs for Democrats: it also had important implications for how presidents pursued their ambitions. Presidents, after all, are notorious for their oversized ambitions; their sights are set higher and their purviews far wider than other political actors. They want to make the system work for them, but more than that, they want to have a lasting impact on that system. They do not just want to ride the currents of history, they want to steer them as well: they want to establish a historical legacy of their own designs. As presidents probe for opportunities to vent these grand ambitions, the different competitive political environments in which they find themselves should be expected to open some doors while closing others.

The way we normally expect presidents to pursue a historical legacy is through the policy instruments of government. Alexander Hamilton, for example, expected that presidents would be driven by their "love of fame" to "plan and undertake extensive and arduous enterprises for the public benefit."[3] To one degree or another, every president seeks to leave behind a policy legacy that bears his imprint: this holds true for Republicans and Democrats, conservatives and liberals alike.

But not all presidents will find the policy route sufficient for their purposes. Minority-party presidents who face a Congress controlled by the opposition, for example, are likely to find it less than satisfying. While they might sign significant pieces of legislation into law, the content of that legislation will almost certainly differ from what it would have looked like under unified government.[4] They might enjoy higher job approval ratings under divided government, and they might even enjoy greater autonomy and discretion to create administrative changes, but they can accomplish only so much durable change unilaterally.[5] Indeed, whatever it is they seek—reelection, policy accomplishments, a reputation for statesmanship, popularity, or anything else— the likelihood that they will leave behind a durable legacy of their choosing is diminished by the disadvantaged competitive position in which they find their party. Without durable political majorities—in Congress, at the state level, and in the electorate—to support and sustain their political purposes after they leave the White House, their accomplishments appear likely to be short-lived.[6] Their historical footprint looks to be light.

Under such conditions, minority-party presidents will be driven to change their political environment. They will not remain content to work within the confines of the political system as they find it—rather, their dissatisfaction with the current state of affairs will propel them to try to alter the competitive landscape and tilt the balance in their favor. Party building will thus emerge as a particularly attractive strategy. It offers a different line of approach from the familiar one anticipated by Hamilton: by investing in their party's organizational capacities, reaching out to new groups of voters, and cultivating the party leaders of the future, party building affords minority-party presidents an opportunity to effect systemic political change through nonpolicy means. While it can certainly benefit the president in the short term and will, to some extent, be undertaken for that purpose, the primary attraction of party building is its potential to reshape the contours of the political universe.

Constrained on other fronts, party building offers minority-party presidents a chance to construct a new political majority in their image and secure for themselves a place in the history books as the one who led his party out of the wilderness. As we will see, Republican presidents saw party building in precisely this way. Winning a numerical majority in Congress figured prominently in their efforts, and in most cases it was the proximate goal; it certainly offered the most expedient rationale for party building. But these presidents were also after something more. They aimed to establish themselves as the founders of a durable new political majority that would bear their stamp and perpetuate their policy purposes long after they left the White House.

Dwight Eisenhower, for example, aimed to transfer his enormous personal popularity onto the Republican Party, remake it into a "Modern" Republican Party, and give it the wherewithal to promote his "middle of the road" principles in the future. Richard Nixon sought to use the Republican Party to build his own vision of a "New Majority" based on his 1972 electoral coalition, and despite his short-lived second term, he successfully launched a broad-based party-building program at the RNC to recruit new candidates, teach new campaign management techniques, and reach out to "New Majority" groups. In the wake of Watergate, Gerald Ford found the Republican Party operationally active but politically destitute. Picking up where Nixon left off, he sponsored grassroots party-building programs to get the "New Majority" ball rolling again. Ronald Reagan sought to translate his popularity among Republicans, independents, and "Reagan Democrats" into an enduring majority for the Republican Party. He leveraged his prestige to strengthen his party's local organizational capacities and expand the rolls of registered Republicans. Hoping to build on Reagan's gains and capitalize on reapportionment to level the playing field in 1991, George H. W. Bush redoubled the party's commitment to strengthening state parties and winning state legislative and gubernatorial elections. Party building, for Bush, was how the Republican Party would "become the majority party in America" within a decade.[7] Despite the party's improved competitive position in the early twenty-first century, George W. Bush and his team similarly viewed party building as a means of creating a "permanent Republican majority" that would finally "reverse the course set 70 years ago by President Franklin D. Roosevelt."[8]

It is not inevitable, of course, that minority-party presidents will always view their party organization as the best vehicle for building the new majority they envision. As we will see, on several occasions the Republican minority seemed so permanent and irreversible that Republican presidents considered starting third parties or using alternative vehicles to construct their envisioned new majority. Their primary impulse was to build a new political majority, not to redeem the Republican Party per se. Yet in each case, they concluded that their formal party apparatus was the most efficient and broadly useful vehicle for their purposes.[9] In part, their decisions were influenced by prior rounds of party building: each successive Republican president inherited an apparatus that was increasingly organizationally robust and ripe for further party building.

Similarly, though the impulse to build a new majority will motivate minority-party presidents to undertake party building, they will not do so at any cost. At times, they may perceive party building to work at cross-purposes with their larger majority-building goals. In such circumstances, they will find it necessary to put their party-building plans temporarily on hold. Nixon, for example, believed that building his "New Majority" depended upon his ability to win a second term *and* rebuild his party. But based on his assessment of his political environment in 1972, he did not believe he could do both at the same time. The Republican Party was significantly less popular than he: in June of that year, he read in a Gallup Poll that only 24 percent of the public chose to identify with the GOP. He wrote: "If the Republican Party, weak as it is, is to be rebuilt, it cannot be done so at the expense of risking losing the Presidential election. The time to do it will be after the election."[10] As we will see in chapter 4, Nixon ultimately followed this plan; his first-term party-building efforts were put on hold until the election was over, whereupon he launched a broad new program to rebuild the Republican Party organization.

This majority-building impulse will also encourage minority-party presidents to become innovative. As old practices become associated with the party's competitive problems, new techniques will be deemed necessary to build a new majority. The notion that competition drives the minority party to adapt, innovate, and rebuild is not new to political science. Scholars have long identified the political "losers" as "the desperate ones; they are the ones whose survival is at stake; they are the ones driven by their despair to seek ways to triumph; they are, therefore, the inventors. Defeat is the mother of invention."[11] Of course, by virtue of their election, all presidents are "winners," not "losers." But with their historical significance inextricably bound to their party's disadvantaged competitive standing, minority-party presidents will be motivated to become institutional entrepreneurs, to make speculative investments in their party's physical assets, in its human capital, and in its strategic operations.[12] Republican presidents, we will see, did not simply strengthen the party organization they inherited: they also experimented with new ways to cut into the Democratic coalition, tap new sources of support, and awaken their "silent" majority.

Just as the GOP's competitive standing was the catalyst for the innovative, forward-looking approach Republican presidents took toward their party, relatively stable Democratic majorities prompted inconsistent and decidedly noninnovative actions on the part of Democratic presidents. Because the Democratic Party's competitive advantage appeared to be deep and durable, these presidents simply saw no urgent need to make long-term investments in their party.

Since the incumbents of their own party had already secured control of a solid majority of offices, Democratic presidents had little reason to be concerned with their party's processes of recruiting candidates, with the campaign services it could provide, or with its other organizational capacities. Their priorities were elsewhere. Their primary challenge was to persuade their fellow incumbents to support their policy goals—a task that required more of a personal touch than a long-term organizational strategy. Indeed, a long tradition of scholarship has defined presidential leadership in precisely this way, as the struggle to enhance the president's "personal capacity to influence the conduct of the men who make up government."[13] More often than not, of course, Democratic presidents found their party's friendly majorities less friendly, and unified government less unified, than they had hoped. Yet the prospect of unified government working in concert under their leadership proved to be irresistible: rather than dismantle an imperfect majority and build a new one in its place, they tried to make the best of the majority they inherited.

Indeed, rather than seek out new groups of voters to join the Democratic coalition, Democratic presidents from Kennedy to Clinton worked to poke and prod the "natural" Democratic majority and activate it at election time. For this they relied more on policy appeals and publicity campaigns than organizational renovations; their challenge was simply to keep step with changing conditions. They were not out to build a new majority, but to put the current Democratic majority to work.

Democratic presidents occasionally sought to influence the composition of their party and tinker with its operations, but they were not interested in developing new organizational capacities. Instead, their party interactions were aimed at controlling their party and making it more responsive to their administrations. When they did not neglect their party organization, they exploited it; and when it was perceived to be an obstacle in the path of their larger objectives, their approach became antagonistic. Kennedy sidelined his party; Johnson undercut it; Carter ignored it; in Clinton's first term, he exploited it; and each offered something of the other's approach.

Investing in the organizational capacities of a party already firmly in the majority simply ranked low on their list of priorities. On occasion, they enlisted their party to help publicize policy initiatives, to help induce members of Congress to fall in line behind the administration, or to collect contributions for their reelection campaigns. But without simultaneous investments in the party organization, these initiatives supplanted existing party functions and siphoned away critical party resources. As we will see, Democratic presidents routinely traded off their party's organizational future for the prospect of short-term gain.

To summarize, the competitive imbalance between the parties created different challenges for Republicans and Democrats, and these challenges produced correspondingly different types of president-party interactions. With their party in the ostensible minority, Republican presidents were driven to act in an innovative, constructive, and forward-looking fashion with respect to their party organization; with their party in the ostensible majority, Democratic presidents perceived no need for such an approach.

The Importance of Presidential Perception

Sometimes, of course, it is difficult to determine whether a given president should be considered a "minority party president" or a "majority party president." Bill Clinton, for example, would seem to have been a "majority party president" during the 1993–94 period, but a "minority party president" after the Republicans' dramatic gains in the 1994 elections. During George W. Bush's two terms, the Democratic Party maintained its advantage in terms of partisan identification in the electorate, but for almost six years the Republican Party was in the majority in Congress and reached parity or better in state-level elections: by these measures, the competitive standing of the Republican Party would seem to have been decidedly mixed during Bush's tenure.

At issue, therefore, is not how we evaluate the president's competitive environment from afar; it is how the president perceives it from where he sits. In any given moment, how does he evaluate his party's trajectory? When he considers past events, evaluates the current state of politics, and estimates the possibilities for the future, how strong does he perceive his party's competitive standing to be? In most of the cases examined here, the president's perceptions are clear: letters, memos, reports, speeches, tape recordings, and other primary sources provide invaluable information. For example, we know that Kennedy, Johnson, and Carter inherited a party with deep and durable majorities, and despite experiencing many difficulties in trying to manage their heterogeneous and internally divided coalition, they always expected their party's majorities to last. We also know that Eisenhower, Nixon, and Ford perceived their party's competitive standing to be weak—even a liability in their own reelection campaigns—and that Reagan and George H. W. Bush consistently referred to their party as the "minority party," even though Republican presidents occupied the White House for twenty out of the twenty-four years between 1969 and 1993.

When we do not have access to such evidence—as is currently the case for the Clinton and George W. Bush presidencies—we must make our best assessment of how the president perceives his competitive environment based on available evidence, state our expectations, and then use observations of his behavior as a provisional test of those expectations. Though the conclusions we draw will necessarily be tentative, we can use the exercise to test the more general proposition that when the president's party is in a relatively strong position, he should act more like our archetypal "majority–party presidents," and when it is in a relatively weak position, he should act more like our archetypal "minority–party presidents."

And yet it is worth emphasizing that presidents are hardly automatons who change in lockstep with alterations in their competitive environment. Fluctuations in their party's numerical status should not be expected to translate automatically into changes in their behavior. What they choose to do in any instance will turn more on their subjective appraisal of their party's competitive standing—on their interpretation of historical trends, election returns in bellwether states, public opinion polls, and the like—than on anything else. Presidents will take stock of their party's standing today, as well as its expected standing in the future, and tailor their approach accordingly.

In the Eisenhower, Clinton, and George W. Bush presidencies, for example, each president's perception of his party's long-term trajectory shaped the timing and type of the party building he pursued, irrespective of his party's current standing in Congress. Eisenhower's appraisal of his party's long-term problems prompted unusual haste in his party building; Clinton's uncertainty about his competitive environment prompted a "lag" in his; and

Bush's belief in his unusual opportunity to solidify a durable Republican majority prompted unyielding resolve in his. Each president's behavior ultimately conformed to general expectations, but it did not automatically follow from changes in the parties' electoral fortunes.

To formalize these considerations and expectations a bit, we might say that the president's party-building incentive will be *strongest* when he perceives his party's overall competitive standing to be *weakest,* and it will be *weakest* when he perceives his party's overall competitive standing to be *strongest.* Presidents will therefore be most likely to undertake party-building activities in the former scenario and least likely to do so in the latter.

Inherited Institutional Conditions, Timing, and Sequence

We have thus far considered the conditions under which presidents will be more or less likely to adopt a constructive approach to their party organization. But the competitive standing of the party is not, by itself, sufficient to explain why a president chooses to adopt one strategy over another. After all, no president walks on untrodden ground: the condition of the party he inherits and the timing of when he inherits it are also critically important factors. Just as surely as the competitive environment will encourage certain behaviors over others, the state of the party organization he inherits will make him more likely to pursue certain types of activities over others.

Timing, as they say, is of the essence: a president who inherits a party organization with few capacities on which to build is in a very different position from a president who inherits a party organization already buzzing with organizational activity. The biggest challenge facing a president in the former position is to summon the motivation and resources to pay the start-up costs associated with launching new party-building programs from scratch. Eisenhower, for example, found little to build on in the Republican organization he inherited, but because he perceived his party's competitive status to be an urgent problem requiring his personal attention, he summoned the resources to start new party-building initiatives from scratch. Bill Clinton faced even higher start-up costs, but when he recognized that his party's newfound minority status was not likely to be reversed anytime soon, he worked to bring his party out of debt and get a number of new initiatives off the ground before he left office. Both presidents' efforts were complicated, but not thwarted, by the organizationally decrepit parties they inherited.

The "downstream" effects of persistent party building over the course of many years tend to exert a stronger influence on presidential behavior. This is particularly evident in the type of party-building initiatives presidents choose to pursue in later rounds. Presidents who inherit a relatively robust party organization, for example, tend to emphasize continuity over change. Why stop collecting voter data or terminate activist training programs when data files already exist and training programs are already in operation? It is relatively cheap and easy to upgrade existing capacities and expand upon existing arrangements; up-and-running programs offer a discount, as it were, on further party building.

Continuity is also encouraged by the political costs associated with terminating party-building operations already in motion. How to dismantle a division dedicated to reaching a specific minority population, for example, without offending large groups of people and setting off a public relations backlash in the process? Once such commitments are established, presidents are unlikely to find it worth the cost of discontinuing them. Finally, there are internal pressures that tend to encourage further party building downstream. Party professionals who have grown accustomed to organization building may agitate for the president's continued assistance. The influence of Ed Gillespie and Karl Rove (both products of GOP party-building programs themselves) on George W. Bush's efforts offers a case in point.[14]

The *sequence* of party building also matters in shaping downstream party-building efforts. The amount of time elapsed between administrations and the operational emphasis of the most recent round of party building is of particular import. Gerald Ford and George H. W. Bush, for example, took the reins of leadership directly from Republican presidents who were deeply engaged in party building. Both were able to continue the party-building programs they inherited while making only minor adjustments. Richard Nixon and George W. Bush, in contrast, assumed office after eight years of Democratic administrations. They built upon the operations they inherited from the "out-party" chairmen who preceded them, but they perceived a greater need to refashion the party apparatus to be more responsive to the White House and more vertically integrated in its operations. All four presidents engaged in party building, but the types of initiatives they pursued—and the operational changes they emphasized—were shaped by the timing and sequence of their presidencies.

In all of these ways, prior rounds of party building shaped the expectations and calculations of subsequent presidents and party actors. One president's party building did not guarantee that the next would follow directly in his footsteps, but it did ensure that future presidents and party leaders would be in a favorable position to protect the party's developing infrastructure, capitalize on it for short-term gain, and make further organizational investments in pursuit of a new majority. Most Republican presidents entered the White House with no particular commitment to building their party's organizational capacities, but soon found that they had good reasons to continue in their predecessors' footsteps. Party building bred more party building, if only because the existence of party-building operations created incentives for their further use.[15]

While the timing and sequence of organizational investments in the Republican Party shaped the GOP's trajectory of development, the lack of such investments in the Democratic Party had an equally important effect on its organizational trajectory. The persistent refusal of Democratic presidents to build new party structures or sponsor new party-building activities kept their party's resources scarce and its operational capacities inchoate. Their successors repeatedly found little to build upon, little reason to begin party building anew, and few resources with which to proceed. Consequently, they directed their attention to nonorganizational priorities, which sapped the time and resources that might have otherwise been devoted to making organizational repairs.[16] Repeated over time, this dynamic stunted the growth of the Democratic Party organization. When competitive conditions changed in the mid-1990s, Clinton's attention began to turn to organization; yet a lingering debt, weak state parties, and a cadre of party professionals committed to timeworn strategies slowed his party-building efforts and continued to frustrate the party chairmen who succeeded him (see chapter 11).

In sum, changes in the competitive environment produce new behavioral incentives, but presidents cannot respond to those incentives without confronting the institutional legacies of the past. What presidents inherit from their predecessors—and when they inherit it—delimits their range of choices, encourages certain types of behaviors over others, and forces them to negotiate with the very organizational arrangements they hope to change. As it should now be clear, presidents are not the "prime movers" whose actions automatically result in new party forms; they are formidable actors, but they are also historical actors whose efforts are rooted in their particular historical moment. Their actions shape the condition of their party, but the condition of their party shapes their actions in equal measure: the organizational arrangements they produce are not mere reflections of their intent.

Democrats versus Republicans

As the following chapters aim to demonstrate, for over fifty years, the best predictor of how a president would approach his party organization was his perception of its competitive standing and the condition of the apparatus he inherited. This conceptual framework, I argue, can explain more of the variance than any other alternative. Yet it is worth noting that two other factors—both involving deeply rooted differences between the two parties—come quite close. Until Bill Clinton's second term, after all, every party builder was a Republican and every party predator was a Democrat. The following discussion explores these party-specific factors, weighs them against the evidence, and uses them to further explicate the "competitive standing" theory. At the end of the day, I find that deeply rooted differences between the parties are very real—and very helpful in framing much of what we will observe throughout this book—but they do not get us very far in understanding *why* different presidents chose to act so differently toward their parties.

Inherent Party Differences

At first glance, presidents seem to act differently simply on account of the different parties from which they come. The two parties, after all, constitute veritably distinct social organizations unto themselves: each tends to draw from different socioeconomic populations, observe different operating norms, and pursue different purposes in government. Each party is also composed of different configurations of interests and groups. Whereas the modern GOP tends to enjoy a relatively more harmonious blend of interests and a more homogeneous constituency, the Democratic Party has been home to a coalition of opposed "types": liberals and conservatives, regulars and amateurs, rich and poor, whites and minorities, urban and rural dwellers, northerners and southerners. Operationally, the Republican Party is more organizationally inclined than the Democratic Party: it functions in a more businesslike, hierarchical, and disciplined fashion. The Democratic Party tends to reject formalism and instead values a fluidity of roles, procedural democracy, and diversity. A number of studies have found these characteristics to be deeply rooted in each party's history and evident in a wide range of political arenas.[17]

For example, in presidential nomination contests, Republicans tend to follow a more orderly, predictable process that is biased toward establishment candidates; Democrats tend to have a more wide-open free-for-all.[18] In staffing and operating the White House, Republican administrations tend to run in a more hierarchical, orderly, and formalistic manner than Democratic administrations, which are more likely to follow a "spokes-of-the-wheel" approach to White House governance.[19] In Congress, the Republican Conference tends be more centralized and disciplinarian than the Democratic Caucus, which has traditionally been more individualistic and contentious.[20] Ideological cleavages are evident as well, both in terms of the party leaders' public philosophies and the motivations of each party's activists.[21] And the list goes on.

Most importantly for our purposes, the parties' different organizational cultures also appear in president-party interactions. At least since Eisenhower, Republican presidents have enjoyed a close partnership with the business community, recruited staff from among their ranks, and leveraged their networks for fund-raising and other party activities. Their party-building initiatives are often drawn up as business plans with long-term strategic objectives and concrete organizational schemas. Borrowing organizational templates from the business world, they establish chains of command, evaluate and enforce performance standards, and aim to maximize efficiencies. Democratic presidents, in contrast, tend to approach their party with trepidation or reluctance: they anticipate having to broker deals with party factions and run interference to avoid embarrassments to their administrations. Other times their approach is more peremptory—they seize control over party processes, restrict the flow of information and resources, and try to suppress dissent within their diverse party coalition. In these and many other ways, the two parties' inherent differences can be observed in how Republican and Democratic presidents interact with their party organizations.

But can these party differences explain *why* Republican presidents worked to enhance their party's organizational capacities and Democratic presidents did not? Setting aside for the moment Clinton's late-breaking party building, might these inherent differences explain a fair portion of the variance we observe over the course of the modern period?

Perhaps, one might argue, Republican presidents perceived party building to be relatively easy, cheap, and more likely to yield a payoff, given their more organizationally minded party. Democratic presidents, for their part, might have calculated that party-building initiatives would be too costly and too unlikely to yield results, given what they perceived to be a change-resistant and cumbersome party. They might have viewed other routes of building political support to be more effective and less likely to provoke conflict within their party.

While this surely seems like a plausible explanation, little evidence exists in the archives to support it. But then again, why would cost-benefit calculations of this kind be spelled out on paper? Perhaps such considerations are too obvious to mention; perhaps presidents are unaware of the determinants of their choices even as they make them. Insofar as the president "comes from" his party and shares its culture, his behavior might simply be a reflection of its inherent characteristics. Does the fish notice the water in which it swims?

If we cannot confirm or deny this hypothesis with archival documents, perhaps we can find confirmatory evidence in other places. The experience of presidents, after all, would seem to offer only one case with which to test it, and a rather unusual one at that. Most presidential candidates have found it advantageous to run as party "outsiders" since at least 1972, when popular primaries became determinative in both parties' nomination processes: long gone are the days when presidents could be described as creatures of their party organizations.[22] Thus, if inherent party differences can explain the behavior of presidents—who have *minimal* attachments and formal obligations to their parties—then surely they should explain the behavior of those party leaders who are closest to the party, most accountable to its membership, and most familiar with its inner workings: the national party chairmen. Elected to their position of leadership by the national party committee membership, national party chairmen ostensibly embody the multiple interests in their party. Embedded within the party structure, they should have a better understanding of their party's liabilities and capabilities than anyone—especially presidents. Considering the actions of national party chairmen, then, offers a "most likely" case with which to test the hypothesis of inherent differences.[23]

As hinted at in the last chapter, however, no such similar partisan pattern emerges when we survey the behavior of national chairmen. With his impressive dataset of primary-source documents and personal interviews, Philip Klinkner demonstrates that as long as the resources were available to them, Democratic out-party chairmen—including Robert Strauss in the early 1970s and Charles Manatt, Paul Kirk, and Ron Brown in the 1980s—periodically launched new party-building programs for the purpose of keeping pace with the Republicans' efforts.[24] Their initiatives were not always successful—and they evidenced little staying-power—but this was not for a lack of trying.[25]

Howard Dean's ambitious "fifty-state" party-building program, launched despite fierce resistance from congressional party leaders, further suggests that DNC chairmen have not perceived the costs of trying to develop their party's organizational capacities to outweigh the benefits. Nor have the idiosyncrasies of the Democratic Party deterred them from trying.

As we will see in Part II, even "in-party" DNC leaders proposed new party-building plans on their own initiative. John Bailey (DNC chair under Kennedy), John Criswell (DNC director under Johnson), Kenneth Curtis (DNC chair under Carter), and Donald Fowler (DNC chair under Clinton) all drew up concrete organizational programs and presented them to the White House for the president's approval and support, only to be dismissed or rejected. The main obstacle to their party-building plans was not the party's heterogeneous interests, its tradition of antiformalism, or its resistance to authority—it was the president. Those in the best position to determine what kinds of organizational changes the party could or could not handle clearly deemed party building to be possible and prudent.

In- and out-party chairmen offer two alternative tests of the assumptions and implications of the "inherent differences" hypothesis. A third and perhaps even better test involves the experience of presidents located just outside the period examined here. Studies have shown that the Democratic Party's relatively more heterogeneous constituency and greater commitment to diversity and procedural democracy can be traced back to the Jacksonian period.[26] If these deeply rooted characteristics were the cause of the modern Democratic presidents' aversion to party building, then presumably they would have also deterred Franklin Roosevelt, Harry Truman, and every earlier Democratic president from party building as well. In the same way, continuities in the internal characteristics of the Republican Party over the years should have made Republicans Calvin Coolidge and Herbert Hoover in the 1920s more likely to engage in party building. While conducting equivalent archival research on these and other earlier presidents falls outside the purview of this study, a review of the secondary literature can offer some useful clues.

Assumptions about modern presidents as party "predators" may have obscured significant party building undertaken by Republican presidents in the postwar period, but they have not concealed the party-building activities of Franklin D. Roosevelt and Harry Truman. In two prominent studies of Roosevelt's party leadership, for example, Sidney M. Milkis and Sean J. Savage demonstrate that FDR and his team set out to ensure the durability of the Democratic Party's electoral advantages in the 1930s by enhancing its organizational capacities (albeit en route to making "party politics less important").[27] Otis L. Graham argues that FDR ultimately succeeded in his party-building project: "As an institution the party had been expected to recruit able leaders, nominate them to office, mobilize a majority, win elections, and enjoy power. This the party accomplished, beyond its fondest dreams."[28]

Similarly, it is quite clear that Truman and his team worked to strengthen the organizational capacities of the Democratic Party at precisely the same time that the durability of the Democratic majority was thrown into doubt during the 1947–48 period. In the face of a Republican-controlled Congress and a widely anticipated Republican sweep in the upcoming presidential election, Truman and his team turned their attention, albeit briefly, to building new organizational capacities in the Democratic Party apparatus.[29]

Yet even more important than the FDR and Truman cases is the Democratic presidential party building we observe *within* the period under investigation here. As we shall see in chapter 11, when his competitive environment changed, so too did Bill Clinton's approach to his party. In his final two years, Clinton and his team sponsored a series of party-building initiatives aimed at enhancing precisely the same organizational capacities targeted by Republican presidents in previous years. Suffice it to say, Democratic presidents have not *always* eschewed party building.

On the Republican side, studies suggest that despite strong continuities in the Republican Party's operating norms and sociocultural attributes from the 1920s to today, Hoover and Coolidge did not engage in party building. Coolidge was evidently content to maintain the Republican National Committee "in skeleton form" only, and no new organizational development programs appear to have been initiated on his watch; Hoover conspicuously avoided his national chairmen. While both presidents supported efforts to "crack" the "solid" Democratic South, they evidently preferred to rely on symbolic appointments and policy appeals rather than organizational investments in the southern states.[30]

Additional research is clearly needed to confirm these observations and make them commensurate with my findings from the modern period. But the fact that the secondary literature picks up on Democratic presidential party building in the 1930s and 1940s but fails to observe any significant Republican presidential party building in the 1920s and early 1930s is particularly noteworthy, and gives us further reason to doubt the explanatory power of inherent party differences. While the Republican Party may be more naturally amenable to collective organizational undertakings than the Democratic Party, that difference has not prevented Democratic presidents and party chairmen from periodically hazarding the attempt, and it has not reliably predicted when Republican presidents will undertake such initiatives either.

We might do well, therefore, to reconsider the assumption that organizational party building operates on the same plane as other types of party-changing efforts. Some dimensions of party politics are bound to be more sensitive, controversial, and difficult to change than others, and there is reason to believe that organizational party building is a significantly less contentious proposition. Consider a Democratic president who wants to redefine his party's ideological commitments, reorder its policy agenda, reshape its cadre of elected officials, or alter its traditional rules and procedures. On these more sensitive fronts, he will almost surely encounter resistance from his party's more heterogeneous interests and multiple standard-bearers. A Republican president, in contrast, might be expected to have somewhat less difficulty pushing his party in new directions on these ideological, programmatic, co-alitional, or procedural dimensions, on account of his party's more homogeneous constituency and hierarchical traditions.

Building the party's organizational capacities, however, is likely to receive a warmer welcome from inside either party. Insofar as party-building initiatives seek to repair the party's infrastructure, enhance its campaign-service capacities, and develop improved fund-raising methods, why would any faction of the party resist? So long as sufficient resources are available to invest in organizational capacities without trading off other party priorities in more sensitive realms, all factions stand to gain. Cherished traditions, norms, commitments, and relationships need not be challenged by party-building activities.

To be sure, the availability of financial resources is critical: so long as there is enough cash to go around, resource-allocation decisions need not be contentious. And here again we observe another party asymmetry: the Republican Party has traditionally been more adept at raising money than the Democratic Party. But this has not been a matter of inherent party differences.[31] Both parties' bank accounts have ebbed and flowed from period to period. During those times when the Democratic Party was flush with cash (at various points during the Kennedy, Johnson, and Clinton presidencies), Democratic presidents still opted not to undertake party building. On the rare occasion when Republicans found their coffers running low, they still persisted in party building (at points in the Eisenhower and Ford presidencies). Thus, while it clearly matters, the relationship between financial resources and party building does not appear to be determinative.

The point is that organizational party building may fly under the radar in ways that other efforts to change the party simply cannot. After all, there is much room for creativity in crafting party-building initiatives. Republican presidents did many of the same things, but they also experimented with new approaches and tailored their initiatives to meet the changing needs of their party. Enterprising Democratic party leaders, too, were capable of periodically designing party-building initiatives that suited the peculiarities of their party and accommodated its traditions and norms. Top-down party building might be a more natural fit in the Republican Party, but investments in organizational capacity need not imply centralized control, as was evident in Howard Dean's decentralized and individualized investments in state parties and the support Clinton offered to state parties in his final years.[32] Inherent differences, in other words, certainly shape *how* Democratic presidents and party leaders interact with their organizational apparatus, but they do not seem to have much bearing on *why* a given president would choose to engage in party building.

Different Party Partners

Just as the Democratic and Republican parties can be distinguished by their internal characteristics, they can also be set apart by their different networks of "partners." These networks, located primarily outside the formal party structure, have provided critical financial, intellectual, and organizational support over the years: a full accounting of the place of parties in American politics cannot ignore the influence and importance of such outside groups.[33] But the nature and extent of the support that the Democratic and Republican parties have received from their partner networks has not been equivalent; the question is how far the variation in their partner networks goes toward explaining the patterns of presidential behavior we observe.

The post–New Deal Democratic Party, for example, has been described as a party with "three distinct organizational bases—machines, unions, and liberal activist groups."[34] Centralized urban party "machines" and machinelike "traditional party organizations" in rural areas provided reliable organizational support for local and national Democratic candidates. Organized labor, for its part, "supplied critical campaign money to Democratic candidates, mobilized voters," and performed other important electoral functions on behalf of the Democratic Party.[35] By the 1960s, liberal activist ("amateur") groups and civil rights groups began to play a significant role in Democratic electoral activities as well; in recent years, tax-exempt groups, for-profit firms, and single-issue advocacy groups have continued to play this role.[36] These important partners were represented in formal party councils, but their strength lay in the organizational capacities they commanded outside the formal party umbrella.

In addition, Democratic incumbents in Congress could be counted on to run their own reelection campaigns, oversee the party operations in their localities, and help support one another's campaigns through the congressional campaign committees.[37] The power of incumbency proved especially critical in the "Solid South," where the Democratic Party apparatus was weak in most places and nonexistent in others.[38] It fell to incumbents to perpetuate the Democratic majority in that important region. In sum, Democratic presidents and party leaders could rely on organized labor, urban and rural machines, activist groups, and incumbents to perform essential organizational activities in the electoral sphere.

The Republican Party, in contrast, did not have a comparable network of partnerships on which to rely. The Chamber of Commerce and other networks of business leaders, for example, could not conduct massive voter registration drives, get-out-the-vote campaigns, training schools, or other campaign operations. The "managerial elite" brought significant fund-raising capacities to bear in elections on behalf of Republican candidates, but it was "an elite without a mass," and hardly represented an organizational juggernaut on par with the Democrats' partners.[39] Despite the impressive growth of the intellectual conservative movement beginning in the 1950s and 1960s— which founded powerful think tanks, foundations, leadership training programs, media outlets, and other organizations—conservatives outside the party structure lacked the kind of organizational capacities brought by Democratic partners. The closest thing to organized labor on the Republican side was evangelical Protestant groups, but these well-organized partners did not fully enter the political fray until the 1980s.[40]

The Democratic advantage in external partners might therefore seem to explain why Republican presidents worked assiduously to build their organizational capacities inside their party while Democratic presidents turned their attention to other things: Republican presidents *had* to build those party capacities in-house to compensate for what they lacked in outside partnerships. Democratic presidents, meanwhile, could keep their formal party apparatus in a kind of "caretaker status," use it periodically as an instrument for their personal purposes (policy promotion, public relations, etc.), and rest assured that organized labor, local party machines, "movement" groups, and incumbents would provide an organizational foundation of support both for their own reelections and for their fellow partisans across the country.

This accounting, however, has several faults. First, setting aside for a moment its inability to explain those instances of Democratic party building discussed above, it assumes that Democratic presidents were generally satisfied to leave in the hands of their external partners critical funding, mobilization, recruitment, and other campaign-related tasks. Yet this does not appear to have been the case. Rather than rest comfortably with their extrapartisan organizational support, most Democratic presidents and their political teams perceived their many partners to be major thorns in their sides. Take organized labor, the Democrats' biggest and most powerful ally. Whereas its assistance and support was widely coveted in local Democratic campaigns, in the eyes of Democratic presidents its partnership was often perceived to be burdensome. Labor leaders were seen as excessively demanding and ultimately self-interested.[41] Presidents never like to be dependent upon forces beyond their control, and their reliance upon organized labor and other outside groups was no exception. If anything, Democratic presidents would seem to have had an incentive to build organizational capacities inside their party apparatus as a means of counterbalancing the power of their more problematic allies.

Second, the "party partners" hypothesis cannot account for variation in partner strength over time. It posits an inverse relationship between partner organizational strength and the party-building incentive: the stronger the external partners, the less incentive there will be for a president to build his party's organizational capacities, and vice versa. Over the course of the modern period, as union membership declined and the Democratic Party's firm grip on the South and urban centers loosened, Democratic presidential incentives to build organizational capacities in-house would be expected to increase. But as we will see, this was not borne out in how they acted. In the 1950s, the power of urban machines began to decline; in the 1960s, the party's hold on the South began to loosen; and in the late 1970s and early 1980s, union membership entered a steep decline.[42] Yet Democratic presidents did not take steps to compensate for these developments at any of these junctures, in any of those specific geographic areas, or with any increased intensity over time.[43] In fact, Jimmy Carter was even less inclined toward party building than his predecessors; and despite the confluence of these developments in the early 1990s—the weakest Democratic showing in the South, the lowest percentage of union membership, and probably the weakest traditional party organizations in the twentieth century—Bill Clinton's first term offered the most extreme case of party predation to date.[44] If the party-building incentive was present, these presidents did not respond to it.

The inverse relationship between partner strength and party-building incentives does not appear to hold on the Republican side, either. As organized evangelical groups began to deliver increasingly reliable electoral support for GOP candidates in the 1980s, 1990s, and 2000s, Republican presidents continued party building in much the same way and with the same degree of intensity as their predecessors. When, for example, the evangelical organization Focus on the Family reached the "height of its political power" and took credit for reelecting George W. Bush in 2004, Bush and his team embarked on an ambitious new party-building plan at the RNC.[45] In fact, the Bush team decided it had better "take evangelical mobilization into its own hands" during the reelection campaign rather than outsource its outreach efforts to the movement's prickly leaders, as it had done in 2000.[46] As we will see, this was the approach adopted by Reagan and the elder Bush as well. Despite the growing strength of their external partners, Republican presidents built a stronger and more responsive Republican Party apparatus. Yet when Democratic presidents perceived their partners to be rival political powers, they continued to eschew party building. In short, there does not appear to be much of a relationship between the variable strength of party partners and the party-building incentive.

If presidents are generally uncomfortable relying on outside partners, and if the party-building incentive does not increase as partner strength declines over time, then perhaps the explanation is a matter of time and resources. Perhaps the time and resources presidents must spend placating their external partners reduce the energies they have to devote to party building. Time, energy, staff, and other such resources are finite quantities, and even the most efficient White House must make trade-offs. Perhaps in tending to all of their needy partners, Democrats simply spent whatever capacity they might have had for party building. While this explanation certainly sounds plausible, it does not hold up very well against the evidence, either. Democratic presidents did not lack the ability, time, or resources to engage with their party: they simply lacked the desire to build it.

Consider Lyndon Johnson. His party partner network was particularly large and active, and required considerable attention and nurturing. It included labor union leaders, party "bosses," amateur groups, civil rights activists, and many other interest groups. Yet Johnson still found time to micromanage the activities of his loyalists installed at the DNC. He expended a great deal of his and his staff's time and resources eliminating party programs, ensuring that individual party officials were fired or reassigned, and tightly controlling the party's remaining activities. Jimmy Carter and his team, too, spent enormous amounts of time and effort placating a restless party membership and preparing for a midterm party conference in 1978 in an attempt to forestall any embarrassments to the president. Democratic presidents repeatedly found the time to engage with the DNC and use it for their political purposes, but they simply chose not to invest in or cultivate it.

Indeed, one might argue that the party would have been better off if Democratic presidents had simply ignored it. It would have been easier, cheaper, and more beneficial for the party in the long run, for example, if Johnson had allowed a DNC voter registration program to continue operating when he succeeded to the presidency. Instead, he took great care to strip the DNC of its staff and minimize its activities. He could have turned these party interactions toward constructive purposes, but he elected not to do so. With his party in the comfortable majority, he had no compelling reason to undertake party building.

Neither Johnson nor any other Democratic president was prevented from party building or deterred from engaging forcefully with his party on account of its heterogeneous constituency, its traditional operating style, or its expansive and cumbersome partner network. The party's strong competitive standing simply did not make party building seem worthwhile or particularly useful.

Two Paths of Development

While the variation we observe in presidential behavior cannot be easily reduced to the distinctive internal characteristics or partner networks of each party, it is still worth taking stock of these important party differences. As we will see in the ensuing chapters, each president contended with a party that had its own norms of appropriateness, drew from different organizational templates, and worked with different allies. These differences suggest that all else equal, Democrats and Republicans will tend to make decisions differently, develop different models of organization, and deal with unanticipated problems and challenges in different ways.

But so long as they are sufficiently motivated to do so, there is no reason to assume that their distinctive operating styles will make Democrats or Republicans any more or less able to customize party-building programs to suit their different party organizations. Indeed, at issue is not the president's operating style, per se, but his decision to adopt a more or less constructive approach to the party organization. And on this score, "competitive standing" still seems to offer the most explanatory power.

Our object of inquiry, however, extends beyond questions of presidential decision-making. We are also interested in how the president-party relationship contributes to the changing shape of American politics. In this regard, it is worth noting that differences between the two parties are not merely contextual factors that frame the analysis; they are also, to some extent, produced and reproduced by the persistence of party-building efforts on the Republican side and the absence of such efforts on the Democratic side. The preferences of party actors, after all, are not simply derived exogenously: their interests, commitments, and expectations are shaped by the institution of which they are a part. To the extent that presidential party building (or lack thereof) shapes the party's institutional environment, it should be seen as a contributing factor in the evolving character and identity of the parties themselves.

Consider the Republican Party. Driven by their majority-building ambitions to build new structures, operations, and strategic commitments in their party, Republican presidents influenced the institutional environment in which other party actors operated. Shared experiences in "campaign colleges," for example—launched at Eisenhower's behest and routinized by his successors—helped to develop a culture of party building within the GOP. A rite of passage for the many thousands of activists who went through them, these campaign training programs reinforced the commitment of party workers to developing long-term strategic plans, building internal operating cohesion, growing new talent in-house, and promoting a sense of "mission" to become the new majority. Over the years, these party-building commitments became insinuated into the Republican Party itself and permeated its organizational culture, operating norms, and political interests. As party-building activities claimed more human and material support, they came to be seen as increasingly institutionally legitimate, and their persistent reproduction over time only served to reinforce that legitimacy.[47] Presidential party building thus contributed to the GOP's distinctive organizational culture and helped to reinforce its operational orientation by persistently orchestrating concerted action on behalf of organizational development.

The absence of presidential party building in the Democratic Party had a similar effect on its distinctive organizational style and norms of behavior. To a certain extent, of course, any majority party—especially one found in a federal two-party system—will be a heterogeneous aggregation of diverse and unwieldy interests. But the absence of presidential leadership on behalf of organizational party-building programs only served to perpetuate the Democrats' lack of internal cohesion and to reinforce its nonorganizational priorities. Over time, such a dynamic took on a life of its own: procedural democracy became a goal unto itself; brokering alliances with external groups became routine; *dis*organization around election time came to be expected. With resilient majorities, Democratic presidents had no compelling reason to emphasize a different approach; and without such leadership, existing patterns of organizational behavior had no impetus for change.

The tendency of Democratic presidents to view *policies* as the primary instruments for nurturing their party coalition was an integral part of this dynamic. This was, in part, a legacy of the New Deal: the modern Democratic Party was conceived under FDR as the "party of administration," and its original rationale was to put government to work on behalf of the majority of interests it represented.[48] But the party's emphasis on policy was also a product of its deep and durable majorities: its virtual lock on Congress and its resilient appeal in the electorate made the prioritization of policymaking over organization building an entirely rational and continually attractive strategy. The Democratic Party's long-standing majorities were thus a contributing factor in the reproduction of its governing priorities, its distinctive attributes, and its relatively deficient organizational capacities.

The catalyst for the Democrats' newfound interest in organizational party building during the very late twentieth and early twenty-first centuries was not an ideological transformation, a loss of faith in government, or even a change in the party's diverse constituencies: it was the decline in the party's competitive standing. At the tail end of Clinton's presidency and during the "out-party" period under George W. Bush, the Democrats' emphasis on organizational party building grew in direct proportion to their electoral uncertainty (see chapter 11).

In sum, president-party interactions contributed to the distinctiveness of the two parties as political institutions and helped shape their divergent paths of development. Whether we fold these effects into the "competitive standing" framework or view them as significant drivers of American political development in their own right, it is clear that every president contributed to the particular historical trajectory taken by his party over the course of the modern period.

PART I The Republicans

3

Building a Modern Republican Party | Dwight D. Eisenhower

I am by no means yet a politician—but I do know that the revamping of the Party must come from the very basis of the organization. There must be precinct workers who believe in our principles and policies; there must be district workers who will fight for them—and so on. . . . I am willing to devote every energy I can in the effort, as I have time and again said.

—President Dwight D. Eisenhower[1]

Dwight D. Eisenhower was the first Republican president to be elected in twenty-four years. He won with an impressive 55 percent of the popular vote and 83 percent of the electoral votes in 1952, but like every minority-party president, he was much stronger than his party: he received a higher share of the vote than the Republican congressional candidate in 79 percent of all districts. A mere 34 percent of the American public identified with the GOP in 1952, and while his election helped to carry new Republican majorities to Congress, they were slim majorities: a one-seat edge in the Senate and an eight-seat edge in the House.[2] Despite Eisenhower's strong popular support, the Republican Party was still at a competitive disadvantage vis-à-vis the Democratic Party, and Eisenhower knew it.[3]

At the level of party organization, Eisenhower inherited few ongoing activities: little had been done to build the party's organizational capacities in recent years. During the late 1940s and early 1950s, the RNC suffered from a lack of funds and was mired in internecine feuds between the party's liberal and conservative factions. Outgoing RNC chairman Guy Gabrielson launched a few constructive initiatives to prepare the party for the 1950 midterm campaigns, but they proved to be isolated events; he did not follow through in the 1951–52 period. Once attention turned to the contentious battle for the party's nomination in 1952, the condition of the party machinery became a decidedly second-order concern.[4] If Eisenhower were to begin party building, he would be starting largely from scratch.

A review of the scholarly literature on Eisenhower's presidency would lead one to believe he did no such thing. According to the received wisdom, Eisenhower was uninterested in party politics and disengaged from the Republican Party. Despite a wave of revisionist scholarship showing him to be a more active and engaged leader than his contemporaries thought, scholars still tend to view him as a president "above party."[5] Ralph Ketcham, for example, argues that Eisenhower hearkened back to the patrician statesmen of the founding generation; he was an "exception" to the "rule" that modern presidents eagerly engage in partisan politics.[6] Other prominent works draw similar conclusions: John Bibby and Robert Huckshorn argue that Eisenhower was "generally oblivious to party affairs"; James Sundquist concludes that "there is no evidence that the Eisenhower administration gave any appreciable support to party-building."[7] Philip Klinkner writes that "Eisenhower never made a serious attempt to recast the GOP in his own image of 'Modern (read moderate) Republicanism.'"[8]

Analysts often draw attention to the fact that Eisenhower had little need for the Republican Party. A military general who had been recruited by both parties, Eisenhower's appeal was, after all, nonpartisan. The assumption is that he must have "recognized that his own popularity was so much greater than his party's that he could only damage his position by too strong an association with it."[9] What's more, Eisenhower always had an "out": the Citizens for Eisenhower groups who ran his 1952 campaign offered an extrapartisan vehicle for building his personal political support throughout his presidency.[10] Eisenhower's contemporaries certainly assumed that he would remain disengaged from his party. Writing in the *Washington Post* the day after Eisenhower's election, Walter Lippmann summarized popular expectations: "His true role, if the general was to become a President, was that of a man who in the style of George Washington was above party and above faction."[11] Eisenhower was hardly expected to don the role of party leader, much less party builder.

Yet Eisenhower did work to build the Republican Party. While many of his efforts were not publicly known, Eisenhower worked tirelessly behind the scenes to build a new Republican Party that could appeal to a majority in the electorate and serve as a durable testament to his presidency. Indeed, he did not simply dabble in party building here and there—his efforts were persistent, aggressive, and often large in scope; they were commensurate with what Eisenhower perceived to be severe competitive problems facing his party.

After twenty years of Democratic dominance, Eisenhower believed his adopted party had a long way to go before it regained parity with the Democratic Party, its slim (and brief) congressional majorities in the fifty-third Congress notwithstanding. Indeed, if his presidency was to be anything more than an interregnum between periods of Democratic dominance—if he was to have anything more than a fleeting impact on the course of American political development—he believed he would have to redress the competitive imbalance between the parties. The GOP would need to be recast in his image and its organizational capacities significantly strengthened. Under the banner of Modern Republicanism, Eisenhower hoped to lead his party out of the wilderness, equip it to compete with the Democrats, and enable it to perpetuate his political vision long after he left the White House.

If Eisenhower is wrongly cast as a throwback to the patrician ideal of a president "above party," he is an equally bad fit with the image of the modern president as a party predator. Though he did seek to control the Republican Party and shape it to be more responsive to his leadership and reflective of his own politics, Eisenhower worked at the same time to develop its organizational capacities. He did not use his party without giving something back; he made investments in his party organization as a matter of course.

The party predator's quest for political independence has a certain resonance with the presidential office as the Founders created it. Not so, the stance of the president as party builder. It is a conflicted posture in which the inherent incongruity between the president and the party, between the individual and the collective, is often laid bare. Eisenhower, for example, gave his party-building project a name—and in so doing, he made the awkward juxtaposition of the personal and the collective obvious for all to see. Ike's public championing of Modern Republicanism spoke volumes to existing members of his party, whose own versions of Republicanism were identified as different and inadequate and who were now placed on the defensive. Eisenhower never managed to resolve the incongruity between his Modern Republicanism and the growing conservative sentiment in his party. To the contrary, his efforts served to light a fire under the conservative insurgency.

The more resistance he encountered, the more attention Eisenhower gave to the nuts and bolts of party building. But nuts and bolts could not, by themselves, build a new Modern Republican consensus among the rank and file. At the end of the day, Eisenhower built a more centralized, modern, and reliable party organization that was responsive to the White House, but one that did not reflect his political principles. By 1961, Modern Republican ideas had not spread to the state parties, the local parties, the congressional party, or the activist base; he had not built a new ideological consensus.[12]

While party building cannot by itself create a new party consensus, and though it does not always produce the outcomes the president desires, it does consistently make an impact on the political landscape. New organizational forms directly shape the political calculations and expectations of other party actors, both in the present and in the future. The consequences of party building, however, can diverge widely from the president's purposes: it can even work against the president's objectives and lead to outcomes wholly different from those intended. On more than one occasion, Eisenhower unwittingly gave his opponents the instruments through which to sound their grievances, develop alternative formulations, and move the party in directions he never intended for it to travel.

Perhaps the reason Eisenhower's party building has been lost to history has to do with the methodological approach typically used. Too often historians begin with an observed outcome of interest and then trace backward the factors that were important in producing it.[13] A recent review of Eisenhower scholarship, for example, dismisses his efforts because "notwithstanding his own electoral appeal, Eisenhower failed as a party leader."[14] Similarly, a popular synoptic history of the Republican Party overlooks Eisenhower's party building because he is said to have "largely failed to make any impression on the GOP."[15] This claim would surely have surprised Eisenhower's conservative adversaries in the 1950s who decried Ike's *harmful* effect on the party and pointed to congressional Republican losses in 1954, 1956, and 1958. Nevertheless, because Eisenhower failed to remake the party according to his own designs, it is not terribly surprising that his party-building efforts have received

		Party Building						Party Predation					
		C	H	R	V	F	I	C	H	R	V	F	I
Republicans	Eisenhower	•	•	•	•	•	•						
	Nixon	•	•	•	•	•	•	•				•	
	Ford	•	•	•	•	•	•						
	Reagan	•	•	•	•	•	•						
	Bush	•	•	•		•	•						
Democrats	Kennedy				•	•		•	•		•	•	•
	Johnson							•	•		•	•	•
	Carter							•	•	•	•	•	•
	Clinton (1st term)							•	•	•	•	•	•
	Clinton (2nd term)	•	•		•	•	•						

C=Provide campaign services, H=Build human capital, R=Recruit candidates,
V=Mobilize voters, F=Finance party operations, I=Support internal activities

Figure 3.1. Eisenhower's Party Interactions

scant attention.[16] But the measure of a president's personal success and his political significance are two very different things. While Eisenhower was not "successful" in the sense that he did not produce the new Modern Republican consensus he sought, his party-building efforts proved to be of real consequence for the Republican Party's organizational development.

As we will see, in his quest to build a new majority around his political principles, Eisenhower sought to strengthen his largely dormant party organization along each of the six spheres of party activity presented in chapter 1 (see figure 3.1). While examining these activities, this chapter also elaborates upon four essential characteristics of presidential party building as a more general phenomenon: (1) presidents can "personalize" their parties without debilitating their organizational capacities; (2) while they have other options, minority-party presidents consistently choose to work with their party organization because of its unusual durability; (3) investments in party organization cannot by themselves create a new political consensus; (4) presidential party building can produce unintended consequences that shape the party's future trajectory in unpredictable ways.

Personalization without Predation

Over the course of the modern period, every president used his party organization as an instrument with which to pursue his personal political objectives. But whereas majority-party presidents tended to use their party to help resolve their short-term problems without simultaneously helping to strengthen its organizational capacities, minority-party presidents consistently made forward-looking investments in their party organization an integral part of their broader leadership projects. Their initiatives were surely meant to benefit their administrations in the short term, but they were also aimed at leaving behind something more durable.

For the first six months of his presidency, Eisenhower shied away from major party-changing moves. He developed a surprisingly amicable rapport with his former rival for the Republican nomination, majority leader Senator Robert Taft of Ohio, and concentrated on making united government work for the Republican Party. But Taft died in July 1953 and Eisenhower was unable to forge a similar working relationship with his successor, Senator William Knowland of California. Throughout the summer of 1953, Eisenhower became increasingly frustrated with recalcitrant members of his own party and with the constant need to line up the support of Senate Democrats in order to pass measures of importance to him; these frustrations led him to begin thinking more concretely about how he might effect a change in his political environment.[17] By the fall, he determined that the Republican Party should be revitalized, brought into the service of building support for his administration, and made more attractive to the median voter.

In November 1953, he told RNC Chairman Leonard Hall: "The Republican National Committee must be in a very definite sense the 'selling' organization for the Administration and the entire Party."[18] But for it to play a central role in Eisenhower's political projects, it had to be firmly committed to the administration's agenda. Eisenhower told Hall to root out those who would not work enthusiastically on behalf of the administration by taking the "Administration program in all its phases" and placing it "before your committeemen and women as the Administration's 'Bible.' In this way you could uncover those who are not going to support you fully and energetically."[19] Ensuring responsiveness from the party rank-and-file was an important first step to entrusting his party with important political tasks: but it was only a first step. Following up his correspondence with Hall, Eisenhower assembled a team of experienced Republican Party leaders and charged them with improving the liaison process between the RNC and the Cabinet, streamlining patronage processes, building unity among the rank and file, and ensuring the "revitalization of the party through the appointment of young, energetic precinct, county, and state officials and committee members."[20]

Eisenhower's reasons for embracing his party organization were simple. Despite his "remarkably high level of popularity with the people," a trusted adviser wrote, he had no guarantee that his political purposes would survive beyond the moment at hand. It was critical, therefore, to swell the ranks of the Republican Party "as an insurance for the future public support of the Administration's programs and policies."[21] Eisenhower agreed with this assessment and set out to build new structures and operations to strengthen his party and broaden its appeal.[22] He signed off on a plan to establish a Board of Strategy that would generate long-term plans—a "more than excellent" idea that "describes an imperative. . . . I do hope that the committee will be promptly organized and will operate effectively," he wrote to his political team.[23] One adviser suggested that Eisenhower appoint a new public relations director at the RNC to oversee five new administrative divisions. Within three months, the new position was created at the RNC, given the title of director of public relations, and filled by James Bassett, who quickly became a member of Eisenhower's team of political advisers.[24]

Zeroing in on improving the party's public standing was a logical starting point under the circumstances: Eisenhower's popularity represented perhaps the best opportunity in a generation to enhance the Republican Party's public appeal. But this was not simply an act of generosity on Eisenhower's part: he hoped that his party, once revitalized, would help to sustain support for his personal brand of politics well into the future. The last thing any president wants is for his presidency to be remembered as a historical interlude; for Eisenhower, party building promised to create something durable under conditions of impermanence. His early efforts to strengthen his party organization were thus instrumental in the pursuit of his personal political objectives while constructive for his party at the same time.

The GOP Campaign School

In the 1954 midterm elections, Republicans lost eighteen seats in the House and one seat in the Senate, and returned control of both chambers to the Democrats. For Eisenhower, the new competitive environment only served to reinforce his interest in party building. He redoubled his efforts to strengthen the organizational capacities of the Republican Party while making it a more reliable instrument for his administration. This dual purpose was evident in the party's primary organizational undertaking of 1955, a campaign school designed to train state chairmen and party activists in campaign techniques. Hosted by the RNC but designed in conjunction with the White House, the school was "the first time in the history of either party that the 48 state chairmen have been brought together as a single group" for training.[25] Eisenhower agreed to speak at the four-day event, host the participants at the White House, and lend his vice president, members of his Cabinet, and the White House staff to the effort.[26] The school held workshops on the subjects of "fundamentals of campaign organization," "organizing the rural vote," the "techniques of door-to-door fund raising," "methods of reaching non-Republican voters," "effective utilization of advance men," "use of direct mail," "press, radio, and TV," and so on.[27]

Participants spent four days in Washington, D.C., attending workshops, classes, and presentations on campaign techniques. The state chairmen were encouraged to replicate the conference two weeks later for their county chairmen, and county chairmen were then encouraged to replicate the conference for their precinct workers. The *New York Times* reported that "the hope" was that "there soon will spread down through the party into all its working levels the enthusiasm and unity of purpose needed to cement the whole structure together into an effective whole."[28] At the opening session, Hall announced that the school was undertaken on Eisenhower's initiative:

> This meeting was called because many times—many times—in talk-ing with the President he spoke of precinct organization . . . it is close to his heart to see to it that the party of his choice is organized right down to the precinct level . . . [he has] a keen interest in our party, and I think the happiest moment in his life would be to see our party in the Nation the majority party, and the only way he can do that is by getting our precincts better organized.[29]

Eisenhower's keynote address to the forty-eight state party chairmen was reproduced and 425,000 copies were distributed "to every segment of the Party structure—finance, all committeemen, right down to the precinct worker level."[30] The speech took place amid speculation over whether Eisenhower would seek a second term; disappointing the state chairmen, Eisenhower did not announce his decision. Instead he focused on the nonpersonal nature of GOP party building and stressed the importance of the Republican Party as a collective organization: "We don't believe for a minute that the Republican Party is so lacking in inspiration, high quality personnel and leadership that we are dependent on one man," he said. Humans, he said, "are frail—and they are mortal." While expressing the importance of collective action and col-laboration across party organizational spheres, Eisenhower also called for the "reconstruction of the party in the philosophical image of Abraham Lincoln," and suggested that its theme ought to be "progress, peace, and prosperity."[31] In addition to receiving a copy of the president's speech, each state chairman received complete transcripts as well as audio and "motion picture versions of the outstanding presentations."[32]

The school was complemented by a new initiative called Republican Recruit, which sent RNC "field men" to help state and county conferences replicate the conferences effectively. These field men were also available to help state parties establish activist-recruitment programs to attract new, young Republican volunteers at the local level. Hall directed them "to develop the effective working force of the Republican Party at all levels by bringing in people under the age of 30."[33] The GOP Campaign School and the Republican Recruit program thus constituted major undertakings through which Eisen-hower and his team sought to enhance the party organization's capacity to provide campaign services and build human capital.

Eisenhower's interest in such activities was not sporadic: he repeatedly stressed the importance of building the party organization down to the pre-cinct level. For example, in a personal letter the following year, he wrote:

> Leadership alone cannot do the job. . . . I am by no means yet a politician—but I do know that the revamping of the Party must come from the very basis of the organization. There must be precinct

workers who believe in our principles and policies; there must be district workers who will fight for them—and so on. . . . I am willing to devote every energy I can in the effort, as I have time and again said.[34]

The GOP Campaign School was repeated in 1958 with the same programmatic emphases: "the problem of organization," "recruitment of volunteers," "sustaining membership fund raising," "organizing a telephone campaign," and so on.[35] Building on the success of the first school, which the RNC explained "was the outgrowth of a suggestion by President Eisenhower," the second session aimed to make incremental improvements to the program and "carry this basic project ahead further."[36] The centerpiece of the event was a speech called "How to Overcome a Democrat Majority," delivered by a county chairman from Ohio. The answer, of course, was to build the local party's organizational capacities.[37] With the party at a decided competitive disadvantage heading into the 1958 midterm elections, Eisenhower spoke at the conference and again emphasized the importance of local organizational activities: "No matter how good the organization is at the top, it won't be effective without organization down at the voter level, too."[38]

The same emphasis on "convert[ing] Republican voters into Republican workers, and through that medium get[ting] your new voters" characterized the party's efforts heading into the 1960 elections as well.[39] A program called Recruit for '60, for example, was launched for the purpose of developing an "ever-expanding army of new Republican workers recruited by other Republican workers" and enlisting two million new party activists before 1960.[40] These recruitment and training programs thus sought to promote the administration's agenda and build unity around Eisenhower's program—but not without making concomitant investments in the party's human capital and campaign-services capacities. The initiatives were both instrumental for Eisenhower *and* constructive for the party at the same time.

Fund-Raising for the Party

Leveraging his celebrity status, Eisenhower raised unprecedented amounts of money for the GOP. But in contrast to his Democratic successors, whose fund-raising efforts also resulted in unprecedented sums but who purposefully diverted resources away from their party organization, Eisenhower insisted that the proceeds be widely shared across the party. A full 50 percent of the funds remained in the state in which they were raised.[41] The other half was not set aside for the president's own purposes—as was the tradition followed by JFK and LBJ (chapters 8 and 9)—but was rather distributed equally between the RNC, the House campaign committee, and the Senate campaign committee. Eisenhower's fund-raising thereby infused badly needed cash into every level of the party organization.

To ensure his party's long-lasting "solvency and virility," Eisenhower often drew upon his personal network of friends in the business community.[42] He also participated in numerous fund-raising dinners, including several Salute to Eisenhower events, over the course of his presidency. The Salute dinners exploited the new medium of television to maximize the impact of the president's personal appearance. The first Salute dinner, held on January 20, 1956, broadcast Eisenhower's live keynote address through closed-circuit television to fifty-three large rallies across the country, netting $5.5 million for the party in a single evening.[43] The Salute dinners were replicated in 1958 and again in 1960, and both times the amount of funds raised was considered astronomical.[44] Eisenhower thus simultaneously sought to spread his message and publicize his accomplishments while helping to replenish the party's coffers.

Eisenhower also supported the RNC's Neighbor-to-Neighbor program, which was a multistate "precinct canvass" held in October 1957, a full year ahead of the 1958 midterm elections, where volunteers performed "door-to-door fund solicitation to broaden the base of contributions."[45] The project was designed to leverage Eisenhower's popularity and inspire workers on the ground; it culminated on October 14, Eisenhower's birthday, with a celebration and TV broadcast in honor of the president.[46] The objective was four-fold: expand the GOP's donor pool, enroll new activists and volunteers, make early "personal contact" with voters, and "compile precinct records" for later use.[47] The data-collection and human-capital-building exercise thus offers a good illustration of the typically incremental, iterative process of party building. Once the "pilot project" was complete in 1957, the RNC sought to identify strengths and weaknesses and make adjustments and improvements before the midterm elections of 1958. Neighbor-to-Neighbor was implemented in twenty-one states in 1957; the following year it was repeated in all forty-eight states.[48]

Eisenhower called the effort "positive action of which I heartily approve . . . the only way the job can be done successfully is to enlist a sufficiently large number of volunteer workers in every community to call on their neighbors."[49] While the state-by-state results were mixed, the program's leaders were gratified to have carried out "the pioneering phase of this great national program." New canvassing manuals were produced and distributed, critical voter data was collected, and more activists—particularly women—were signed up to participate in party operations. Almost $2 million was raised, and operational mistakes were flagged for improvement next time.[50]

Thus, from creating new divisions and strategy boards at the RNC to the GOP Campaign School and Republican Recruit programs to the Salute to Eisenhower dinners and the Neighbor-to-Neighbor campaign, Eisenhower helped to fortify the Republican Party's organizational capacities while simultaneously trying to use the party apparatus for his own purposes. These initiatives sought to make the party more responsive to the White House *and* more capable, efficient, and effective in its operations. Responsiveness and competence were treated as complementary, not mutually exclusive, goals.

Choosing Party Organization over Extrapartisan Groups

Minority-party presidents are sometimes tempted to eschew the work of party building and instead take the easier route of using extrapartisan organizations to build support for their goals. Such alternatives always seem to exist: Eisenhower had Citizens for Eisenhower groups; Nixon considered starting a new third party; and every modern president has had the option of bypassing the formal party apparatus entirely during their reelection campaigns. Yet time and again, minority-party presidents reject these alternatives and choose to work with their party organization. Eisenhower chose to integrate Citizens groups into the formal party apparatus, Nixon decided to build a new majority by adding to the Republican Party, and almost every Republican president sought to use the opportunity of their reelection campaigns to benefit their party.

This dedication to party organization, even in the face of potentially more attractive alternatives, can be explained by the unusual durability of the party organization. Unlike many other types of political organizations, the formal party organization is certain to outlast the president's term in office; its longevity makes it a particularly attractive option for those presidents seeking to create durable change through nonpolicy instruments. And it is fairly malleable; given the president's authority over the national committee, he is in a strong position to effect real changes in the party organization. As we will see, the extrapartisan groups nurtured by Democratic presidents were so personalized that they proved to be ephemeral. They left no lasting impact on the political landscape. Because Republican presidents consistently perceived their party to be the entity that would be best able to build a new majority and persevere over the long run, they bypassed very real—and often very attractive—opportunities to use extrapartisan vehicles.

For Eisenhower, Citizens for Eisenhower committees constituted a genuine alternative to his party organization. Throughout his presidency, Ike had multiple opportunities to encourage these extrapartisan groups and mobilize them to work on his behalf. Pursuing this course certainly would have been easier than trying to reconstruct his cumbersome party. But Eisenhower made the conscious and often difficult decision to rebuild the organizational foundations of his party and confront its ideological cleavages instead. He consistently exhorted Citizens and other young up-and-comers to join the Republican Party so as to change it from the inside.

Infiltrating the Republican Party with Citizens for Eisenhower

In 1954, Eisenhower became increasingly frustrated that Joseph McCarthy's anti-Communist witch hunt was being associated with the Republican Party as a whole: "The worst thing about this McCarthy business," Ike said, "is that the newspapers are all saying that the leadership in the Republican Party has switched to McCarthy and that we are all dancing to his tune."[51] During the

Army-McCarthy hearings in the spring of 1954, Eisenhower wrote that he essentially agreed with Adlai Stevenson, who called the GOP "half Eisenhower, half McCarthy."[52] He said: "The Republican Party has got for once and for all to make up its mind whether to follow the ludicrous partnership of the Old Guarders and the McCarthyites (one of my friends has called it a 'marriage of convenience'), or whether it is going to stand behind the program of the Administration."[53] Rather than leave the outcome to chance, Eisenhower worked to undermine McCarthy in a delayed but crucial behind-the-scenes campaign.[54]

His party remained divided, however, and when polls indicated that the Democrats would likely regain control of both houses of Congress in the midterm elections of 1954, Eisenhower worried that GOP losses would give the "extreme right wing" an opening for "recapturing the leadership of the party." And "if the Right Wing really recaptures the Republican Party, there simply isn't going to be any Republican influence in this country within a matter of a few brief years," he wrote. The party would surely split, and "a new Party will be inevitable."[55]

Eisenhower thus perceived the midterm elections as a critical juncture for his party. Consequently, during the last three weeks of the campaign, Eisenhower traveled more than 10,000 miles and made nearly forty speeches on behalf of Republican candidates, despite his wavering health.[56] More importantly for his party organization, he decided to seize the opportunity to begin integrating Citizens for Eisenhower into the GOP. In the final weeks of the campaign, he exhorted former Citizens to set aside their antipathy for the formalities of party and go to work "electing a Republican majority to the Congress."[57] The speech in which he urged Citizens to work for Republican campaigns was broadcast on 471 radio stations and 218 television stations, designed to reach every congressional district in which there was a Citizens for Eisenhower Committee still in existence.[58]

When Republicans lost control of both houses of Congress and reverted to minority status at the state level, Eisenhower became even more determined to transform his party from the inside-out. He wrote: "The Republican Party must be completely reformed and revitalized . . . the Republican Party must be known as a progressive organization or it is sunk."[59] His concern for his party's newfound minority status seemed to light a fire under him. As he laid out a political strategy for the remainder of his first term, Eisenhower made party building a top priority:

> If there is one thing that I am going to try to do during the next two years, I have just one purpose, outside the job of keeping this world at peace, and that is to build up a strong progressive Republican Party in this country. . . . If the right wing wants a fight, they're going to get it. If they want to leave the Republican Party and form a third party, that's their business, but before I end up, either this Republican Party will reflect progressivism or I won't be with them anymore.[60]

The best way to remake the GOP into a "progressive" party—one that would presumably represent a majority of the electorate—was, he concluded, to bring Citizens leaders and activists into the party fold.

Immediately following the disappointing midterm elections, Eisenhower began a concerted effort to persuade the Citizens to officially join the ranks of the party organization. To Paul Hoffman, a friend and former Citizens leader, Eisenhower indicated that he intended to reshape the Republican Party, not through a "revolution," but "more surely by the evolution of infiltrating the organization with people who thoroughly believe in the President's political philosophy."[61] This transformation of the formal party apparatus would be helped enormously by "volunteers" such as Hoffman and his fellow Citizens, Ike said, whose "heroic efforts" would surely "obtain results." Sherman Adams, writing at Eisenhower's urging, encouraged Citizens activists to "devote all the time and effort they have to contribute" to remaking the party.[62]

As a first step, Eisenhower directed Adams to create a Civilian Committee that would serve in an advisory role to the RNC and the White House. The committee would serve as an official entry point into Republican Party politics for Eisenhower's many friends in the business community, most of whom were active in the Citizens groups. In their new capacity as "Civilian" advisers to the RNC, Ike wanted these men to survey "local and national issues in each state" and recruit "fine young men and women both for party work and for candidates."[63]

Because of its strong ties to the business community, the Civilian Committee also promised a new way to help finance Republican Party activities. Eisenhower therefore also directed Adams to form an adjunct Finance Committee that would draw upon Eisenhower's connections to raise money for the Republican Party. Rather than establish the group as a wholly separate entity operating at the expense of the party apparatus (a common practice among Democratic presidents), the new Finance Committee was established for the explicit purpose of providing funding for party operations.[64]

Eisenhower also wanted former Citizens leaders to be embedded within the RNC leadership structure. "For help in the work of the National Committee," Ike directed, "I would like to see Len Hall . . . secure as his two principal deputies people like Walter Williams and Mary Lord."[65] Williams and Lord were the cochairmen of the Citizens for Eisenhower in 1952.[66] Hoffman expressed his doubts to Eisenhower that Hall was sufficiently progressive to push for important changes in the political character of the party, as Hall was still popular with conservative Republicans. But Eisenhower clearly believed that sticking with Hall and adding deputies of his own choosing would allow him to change the character of the national party organization without causing too much of a stir.[67]

In the winter and spring of 1955, Eisenhower pushed his political advisers to begin to "develop a program which would show the country that the Republican National Committee was sincerely endeavoring to bring Citizens for Eisenhower and other supporters of the President into Party organization."[68]

To achieve "the President's desire to see that Citizens become new working Republicans," Citizens leaders and party leaders began to hash out the details of "merging" the two entities at the state and national levels.[69] By May, plans were set to bring Clancy Adamy, a thirty-eight-year-old former Citizens leader into the RNC as an assistant to the chairman and director of a new Division for the Enrollment of New Republicans within the RNC headquarters.[70] The new division would emphasize the recruitment of "younger members of communities," Hall announced.[71]

The objective could not have been clearer: it was "to expand the base of the Republican Party by encouraging former Citizens for Eisenhower workers to come into the party framework."[72] Indeed, the new advisory committees and the new Division for the Enrollment of New Republicans were explicitly designed to "dramatize the open-door policy, i.e., that there is room for every American in the political activities carried on by the Republican Party."[73] Along with other organizational efforts, these programs aimed to implement Eisenhower's "overall plan for the changing of the Republican Party from a minority to a majority party."[74] By establishing a new formal division within the RNC framework and dedicating it to Citizens recruitment and youth outreach, Eisenhower institutionalized his efforts to grow the Republican Party and swell its ranks with his own supporters.

Eisenhower also worked to remake the party from the inside out through less formal methods. Many young businessmen were attracted to Eisenhower's personality and to his "middle way" approach; he frequently received letters from young supporters who expressed their displeasure with the congressional GOP leadership. Though Eisenhower recognized that his support among young people was personal and not partisan, he persistently tried to translate that support into support for the Republican Party. For example, he frequently encouraged his friends in the business community to promote young Republicans in their public events and to search their personal networks for quality young candidates to stand for office as Republicans. By encouraging young men to assume positions of leadership in Republican Party politics, Eisenhower hoped to plant the seeds for the party's future. For example, in December 1953, Eisenhower asked the president of Rocky Mountain Oil and Gas Association, a golfing buddy, to "take advantage of every opportunity to put in a word, in any locality, in favor of virile, forward-looking, energetic, Republican candidates as opposed to the 'party-hack' type."[75] In 1958, he sent suggested lists of names of young men whom he recommended: "To my mind they should ask for the 'comers' . . . meaning the kind I have just named. If they can't place such a person in the primary slot, at least they should get their secondary speaker from this group and he would, on the average, steal the show."[76]

Though he met with mixed success, Eisenhower consistently sought to remake the Republican Party by infusing it with the "fire and energy" of young people. He continually directed his party chairmen to place these types of men "in critical positions" in the party, to involve them in new activities, and let them "start a cult of optimism and work" to carry the party forward.

Integrating new networks of young, energetic, moderate Republicans into the party apparatus, Ike thought, would provide the "necessary horse power" for progress.[77]

Citizens leaders repeatedly sought Eisenhower's advice and support for their plans to build and sustain their extrapartisan network. But Eisenhower consistently declined their overtures and instead recruited them to join the Republican Party. On a few occasions, Eisenhower was tempted to strengthen the Citizens groups and leave the Republican Party behind. But he always revised his thoughts and encouraged Citizens to devote their efforts to strengthening and "revitalizing" the Republican Party instead. After the second round of midterm GOP defeats in 1958, for example, Eisenhower was clearly struggling with the issue. Two Citizens leaders in California asked him for advice about what their organization ought to do in the future. In an original draft that he never sent, Eisenhower revealed that he seriously considered giving the two leaders his explicit approval for their extrapartisan activities. In his draft, he wrote: "I would hope that your present organization might not only be kept alive, but strengthened. . . . As the titale [sic] implies, 'Citizens for Eisenhower-Nixon' are not formally incorporated into any party. They choose to cast their votes, and, to win other votes, for candidates of their own choice, rather than any party label." He considered encouraging the Citizens leaders to maintain their independence: "Citizens can build for itself a permanent organization of real strength that is in sympathy with the regular Republican Party but is also able to attract Independsn [sic] and like-minded Democrats."[78]

This letter, however, was never sent. In his final draft, instead of sending words of encouragement, Ike exhorted the Citizens leaders to devote their energies to helping him rebuild the GOP. He knew they would not disband their organization, but he asked them to "suggest to your people that they work with the regular Republican Party in an effort to reinvigorate and rebuild it."[79] This final draft reduced his enthusiastic six-page draft letter to a short three-paragraph note. Eisenhower had weighed his options and elected to focus on building the Republican Party over other alternatives.

Indeed, as we will see, a recurring characteristic of minority-party presidents is that they tend to consider (and discard) the possibility of starting a new party. Their ultimate goal, after all, is to build a new majority, not to revive their party for its own sake. When their efforts are met with resistance from some corner of the party, their frustration often leads them to explore other options. Contemplating the third-party alternative—giving up—is a natural response to that resistance. For example, after nominating moderate California Republican governor Earl Warren to the Supreme Court, Eisenhower anticipated resistance from congressional leaders of his own party and imagined that it might cause him to abandon the GOP once and for all. He wrote that on the basis of Warren's eminent qualifications, his "confirmation should be immediate and overwhelming. If the Republicans as a body should try to repudiate him, I shall leave the Republican Party and try to organize an intelligent group of Independents, no matter how small."[80]

Though Ike was never serious about pursuing the idea, Adams explained that he did weigh the pluses and minuses of such a strategy:

> Eisenhower's thoughts about a new political party . . . were confined to a few thinking-aloud sessions with me in the privacy of his office. . . . He was well aware of the dangerous confusion that might come from breaking up the two-party system. He recalled, too, how the third parties launched by Theodore Roosevelt and the elder Robert M. La Follette became one-man ventures rather than popular movements. Eisenhower decided to go on hoping that the Republican Party could be changed by younger blood into a broader and more effective political force.[81]

When Citizens leader Lucius Clay pushed Eisenhower to make a decisive break with his party, Eisenhower argued that a reconstituted Republican Party offered a source of longevity for his political purposes that a thoroughly personalized party would not. He recorded in his diary: "Admittedly it was probably easier to personalize such an effort and therefore to use my name as an adjective in describing it. But I pointed out that if we focused the whole effort on me as an individual then it would follow that in the event of my disability or death, the whole effort would collapse. This, I pointed out, was absurd. The idea is far bigger than any one individual."[82]

Building Party Organization Cannot, by Itself, Create a New Consensus

The hope of building a new ideological consensus lies at the heart of the party-building posture. But organizational initiatives cannot, by themselves, create that consensus. New organizational initiatives can create structured opportunities for party members to come together and deliberate; they can reach out to new groups of voters and activists, from whom new ideas and principles can be culled; and they can help to cultivate an organization that is primed to germinate new ideas. But they cannot guarantee that a consensus will form around those ideas.

Eisenhower campaigned in 1956 on the claim that he had transformed the Republican Party into a vehicle for progress, a Modern Republican party. But when put to the test, his claims came up empty. After his reelection, his party remained bitterly divided: many local party leaders were becoming more attracted to unabashedly conservative alternatives, and Eisenhower's lack of coattails in 1956 did not help matters. As discussed below, in 1957 and again in 1959, Eisenhower launched a series of highly publicized party forums to rally his party around Modern Republicanism, but in each case he failed to build support for his ideas. Instead, his forums revealed the fragility of Modern Republican ideas and galvanized a more ideologically robust conservative movement in opposition. When Eisenhower proposed broad, ambiguous principles in order to offend none and include all, his efforts only invited his challengers to expose his vagueness, sharpen their own claims, and clarify the differences they had with the administration. Eisenhower's organizational forums, ironically, provided a place for more doctrinal conservatism to grow.

The following episodes should not be read to suggest that presidential party building is always ineffective, for it is easy to imagine how these same actions might generate a stronger consensus when the president's ideas are more congruent with those held by a majority of his party membership. As the case of Ronald Reagan shows, under such conditions, presidential party building can help to build a robust organization *and* forge new ideological commitments. Eisenhower did not face such favorable conditions, however, and instead learned the hard lesson that organization does not necessarily create consensus.

Party builders often seek to put a name to their outward-reaching party-building efforts. Characteristically, they use metaphors like the "big tent" or the "open door." As noted above, the new Division for the Enrollment of New Republicans was described in precisely these terms. Interestingly, the very same "open door" theme was repeated in the presidencies of Nixon, Ford, and Reagan. Eisenhower's Modern Republican label was similarly meant to express the inclusive thrust of his party-building efforts. Eisenhower was not wedded to that appellation—he was, however, committed to the overall theme of inclusiveness. In August 1957 he told new RNC chairman Meade Alcorn he was willing to try "'Republicanism of the 20th Century' or '20th Century Republicanism,' or any other appropriate designation."[83] More than a year later he was still toying with different names, telling a friend that he entertained using "'Party of justice for all the people,'" but it was not "quite catchy or short enough, but it does indicate what I think should be our basic 'selling' effort."[84]

He never settled on a title with which he was comfortable. But his effort to differentiate his brand of Republicanism did motivate conservative activists to elaborate the distinctiveness of their own principles—to distinguish conservatism from both New Deal liberalism and the "wrong direction" of "Progressive Moderation."[85] What was at the core of their conservative ideas that was so abhorrent, they asked? As Eisenhower's reelection campaign picked up steam in 1956, conservatives began to work toward a "rebirth of ideological conviction," toward a positive affirmation of the "right principles" rather than simply offering a "negative response to Liberalism."[86] The *National Review* wrote in June 1956 that Eisenhower "contributed" to the "chaos" of the Republican Party by "abjuring all theory, and personalizing his leadership of the party to the point of blurring beyond distinct recognition the principles on which Republicanism rests." Conservatives must begin, the magazine prompted, to "infuse a coherent set of principles into the Republican Party, and permit ourselves to look around" for a real conservative to lead the party after Eisenhower retired in 1961.[87]

To be sure, the conservative movement had been searching for clear distinctions, unequivocal beliefs, and sharp definitions of its political principles long before Eisenhower took office.[88] But in the eyes of conservatives, Eisenhower's Modern Republicanism was a rallying point, an offense to be remedied. "The stillness at San Francisco," noted one observer of the surprisingly harmonious 1956 Republican National Convention, "was less that of an enemy vanquished or even cowed than of one patiently biding its time."[89] Confessed one conservative: "I won't give a damn about Ike the day after the election. He's our meal ticket now. Once we're in, the hell with him."[90] Despite this dissent, Eisenhower met with great success in repopulating the RNC with "Eisenhower men." By mid-1956, Republican state party chairmen in forty-one states and two-thirds of the official membership of the Republican National Committee self-identified as Modern Republicans.[91]

By the fall of 1956, Eisenhower felt comfortable entrusting the RNC with total responsibility for running his reelection campaign.[92] Indeed, his integrated campaign was everything party regulars could have hoped for. In Harold Bass's study of the relationship between presidential campaigns and the national party committees, Eisenhower's reelection campaign receives "by far the highest score for integration [of the president's campaign with the party apparatus] of any incumbent president."[93] But instead of providing a set of ideas around which Republicans of all stripes could rally, Eisenhower's Modern Republicanism created resentments and hardened ideological divisions within the party membership. It was against this backdrop that Eisenhower began a series of new organizational initiatives in his second term.

Regional Conferences

As his second term began, Eisenhower was determined to push his organizational efforts to new heights. As the first constitutionally mandated lame duck president, his time was short, and yet he wrote, "I still have a job of re-forming and re-vamping the Republican Party."[94] If the party was to be remade into a majority party that could promote his brand of politics after he left office, Eisenhower believed, two things were necessary. First, the party would need to "adopt and live by" his Modern Republicanism philosophy, and second, "It must organize itself far better than it has in the past, particularly at the precinct, district and county levels. We have had a Party that I am afraid wanted to have too many generals and too few fighting men."[95] Building an organizational foundation for sustained party activity at the local level was essential:

> I firmly believe that to have a strong basis for the Modern Republicanism that will best represent the interests of all the people, the Party must build upward from the precinct, to the district, to the county and to the state level. Only on such a firm foundation can there be a permanent change. If people will work together, at all levels, the job can be done.[96]

In 1957, Eisenhower worked with Alcorn to design and implement a series of regional conferences for precisely these purposes. Unlike the GOP

Campaign School of 1955, they did not teach campaign techniques, but as a first order of business, they encouraged local party leaders to discuss "Republican Organization," including

> how to increase Republican membership in Senate and House . . . in State and local governments . . . [how to] strengthen Party organization and structure at state levels; Discussion of the value of a unified plan to be carried out on a national basis such as a salute dinner, door-to-door campaign, poll takers, precinct day.[97]

In addition to subcommittees dedicated to organization, the regional conferences discussed "Republican Goals," "Democrat Weaknesses," "Formulation of State, Congressional District, or County Conferences," and "Specific Senate and House Races."[98] Eisenhower hoped that these conferences would be the foundation for a new Modern Republican party, a structural means of involving all party members in a common discussion about what the party stood for and what it was equipped to do. Held in April 1957, the conferences were followed up with parallel state conferences, county conferences, and a national wrap-up conference in June. Alcorn was responsible for coordinating the massive organizational undertaking, but it was all done under Eisenhower's watchful eye. "As a matter of fact," Alcorn told the RNC Executive Committee, "It was upon his insistence that the idea of carrying these conferences down to the county levels was put in . . . he said: 'This has my complete approval if you will go down to the county level and make them do the same thing there.'"[99]

Although Alcorn said he believed there was "a common denominator of belief running throughout the thinking of all Republicans," he still feared a rupture from inside the party. It would be a "catastrophe," Alcorn said, if "we let the discussion get to the point where we say, 'Well, there is one group over here and another group over here, and we have two parties within one.' . . . I hope it never happens."[100]

Ironically, Alcorn and Eisenhower unwittingly brought the "catastrophe" upon themselves. Operationally, the regional conferences were an unqualified success; held in all six regions of the United States, they brought together party leaders and members who, in many cases, had never before sat down together to discuss their problems and share their goals and ideas.[101] But they did not build the consensus Eisenhower had hoped. Instead of unifying the party in support of the administration, the conferences provided an opportunity for opponents to come together, hone their message, and challenge the president to move toward their more conservative positions. They vented their shared dissatisfaction with Eisenhower's budget proposal, farm policy, and other legislative initiatives. Newspapers reported the dissent with headlines such as "Party Heads Tell Alcorn of Unrest," "Alcorn Asks for Criticism and He Gets It," "Midwest GOP Snubs Eisenhower Plea," and "GOP Rift 'Approved.'" The *Washington Post* said the conferences evidenced the "obvious resistance" of local party leaders to the administration's moderation and encouraged the further organization of the opposition. The conferences brought "strong criticism" of Eisenhower's budget, "strong opposition" to federal school aid and grants-in-aid to the states, and "hostility" to farm-benefit limits.[102]

Senator Barry Goldwater's public break with the administration on April 8, 1957, did not help matters; on the floor of the Senate, Goldwater assailed Eisenhower's failure to produce a balanced budget and declared that Eisenhower had perpetrated a "betrayal of the people's trust" by submitting a $71.8 billion budget. He reminded his audience of Eisenhower's pledge to cut spending, lower taxes, reduce the debt, and balance the budget. "It is curious," Goldwater said, "that the Administration's departure from its pledges to the American people should occur during what I believe will be the rather brief tenure of this splinterized concept of Republican philosophy."[103] Old Guard Republicans and McCarthyites noted admiringly that Goldwater "did not hesitate to stand up for his beliefs."[104] The grassroots conservative discontent evident in the regional conferences, coupled with Goldwater's emergence as the "most articulate spokesman" for the conservative ideology, created the impression that "the prospects of conservatives capturing power are brighter today than at any time since 1952."[105]

Alcorn tried to make the best of the situation at the wrap-up conference in Washington: "We asked you folks to let your hair down, and you were just wonderful. . . . You talked frankly. You told us what was the matter with us. . . . Out of that criticism and that self-examination ought to come a more united and stronger party."[106] But the regional conferences were clearly a consensus-building failure. They exposed the deep philosophical divisions in the party and left Eisenhower and Alcorn "in the position of trying to equate party division with party strength—a job that calls for more than an ordinary amount of political rationalization."[107] Though Eisenhower had successfully implemented a large party-building program to develop and articulate consensus party principles, by the end of the regional conferences the GOP seemed to be more divided than ever before. Organizational effectiveness proved to be no substitute for ideological consensus.

Percy Committee

Eisenhower's second major initiative to forge a new ideological consensus was called the Committee on Program and Progress, also known as the Percy Committee. The committee was charged with articulating the party's principles and designing coordinated party activities for the long term, but its unintended effect was to create more dissension within the party and to stimulate a series of public rebukes from increasingly organized and articulate conservative groups. The committee was publicly presented as an RNC-initiated program, but it was Eisenhower, in fact, who was personally responsible for founding the committee. When Meade Alcorn sent Eisenhower a copy of his opening remarks delivered at the committee's commencement, Eisenhower's secretary recorded that "the President pointed out that Meade took full credit for something he, the President, originated."[108]

The idea for the committee occurred to Eisenhower after the GOP's second consecutive midterm losses in 1958. The depths of his party's losses suggested that something fundamental had gone wrong; Eisenhower was determined to redress the problem and put his party back on solid footing. He resolved to rebuild his party from the bottom up before he left office and prepare it to meet the challenges that lay ahead. In a confidential memo, he wrote that he was committed to getting "a broadly based committee to analyze Republican difficulties and failures and to work out the finest possible plan we could develop for their correction . . . time is of the essence because we have to do a lot of rebuilding."[109] The party organization, he thought, would need to be overhauled and rebuilt "up from the grass roots." It would have to emphasize "youth, vigor and progress so that as it develops upward there will be elected as county and state chairmen the finest young leaders that we can find." The existing congressional campaign committees would either need to be "eliminated or drastically reduced" or replaced by a new advisory committee, composed of six senators and congressmen, to "advise" the RNC chairman. The RNC chairman would, of course, remain "the alter ego on Party matters of the President. This means that the proclamations and policies and plans of the National Committee must, under the President's leadership, provide the guide lines for Party effort."[110]

The president believed that a more centralized and responsive party apparatus that emphasized its "grass roots" could help to strengthen one of the party's most critical activities, namely candidate recruitment:

> With this kind of an organization developed we must have, in addition to a clear understanding of our problems and policies and programs, the finest possible candidates. Again these people—men and women—should be young and vigorous and intelligent. If the preliminary organizational steps are properly accomplished, the result in terms of good candidates will be almost automatic. However, nothing can be taken for granted and we believe that it would be a good move to have in the National Committee two or three "travelling salesmen" who are clear headed people looking out for this type of candidate and able to get the local people to carry out the necessary measures.[111]

In early 1959 Eisenhower discussed his ideas with a dozen top Republican strategists. He emerged from the meeting with a decision: the rebuilding process would begin with a new strategy committee chaired by moderate Republican Charles Percy.[112] Eisenhower sent a telegram to the RNC meeting later that month to convey his enthusiasm for the party-building work that lay ahead:

I deeply regret that some people look upon our party as a kind of hibernating elephant who wakes with a mighty trumpet blast at election time and then rests calmly until the next campaign. Political activity must be a matter of unremitting effort. It must go on 365 days a year. . . . Immediately we must give the millions of Americans who look to the Republican Party for progressive leadership a clear understanding of our long-range objectives. . . . This demands constant attention to organization, to cooperation at all levels, to assuring that candidates are capable, vigorous, personable and dedicated; that finances are secured on a continuing and satisfactory basis; and that every Republican and every friend of Republicanism keep everlastingly at the job of recruiting for the party.[113]

At the same meeting, Senator Barry Goldwater made his own suggestion for how to rebuild the party after the devastation of 1958: "Let the Party quit copying the New Deal." Goldwater challenged Eisenhower to explain exactly what the GOP stood for.[114] Representative Richard Simpson, the chairman of the Republican Congressional Campaign Committee, also called on Ike to "give us a statement of principles for which we can stand."[115]

The ambitious Committee on Program and Progress set out to meet the conservatives' challenges by identifying the most pressing political, social, and economic challenges likely to emerge between 1959 and 1976, and articulating a new set of consensus principles for the party to follow.[116] Alcorn reminded the Committee of Eisenhower's personal enthusiasm for the initiative: "The President, as I have said, is extremely anxious that this be done. . . . I don't think I have seen the President in the two years I have been working very closely with him more vigorous on any subject I have ever talked with him about than on this."[117]

The committee conducted a poll of 1,200 "of the Nation's leaders in business, labor and the professions" and asked questions such as "What are the greatest problems [and opportunities] facing the United States in the next 15 years." It then spent most of the year analyzing the results of the poll, meeting with experts and opinion leaders, and hammering out a new party strategy.[118] Its final report was issued to the press on September 27, 1959, published in paperback, and sold around the country.[119] The report aimed to give the party guideposts for the future, standards to follow, purposes to pursue: it was meant as a blueprint for how the Republican Party might again become the majority party in America. Alcorn's successor, Thruston Morton, announced that the Percy Committee report reflected the sentiments of "a latent majority-ship among the people." All that remained was for the Republican Party to summon the "intellectual and organizational force to awaken that underlying majorityship and translate it into political victory."[120] Once Republicans rallied around the principles articulated in the report, Eisenhower's bottom-up organization-building plans would follow naturally.

But the Percy Committee report did not have its intended effect. Stephen Shadegg, who served as a campaign manager for Goldwater's early senatorial bids and sat on the Percy Committee, initially reported that the first few sessions were "thrilling and productive," and that the committee seemed likely to avoid supporting "'Me-tooism.'"[121] But the final report produced by the committee was, he thought, a disappointment: it was too vague and ambiguous. As author John Andrew points out, the report aimed to please everyone, declaring at once that the "federal government has a role to play only when individuals, communities or states cannot by themselves do the things that must be done," but also that the "Republican Party stands for a strong, responsive federal government . . . using its strength to ward off inflation and depression . . . regulating wisely where the national interest demands it." While it literally spoke to both conservative and liberal views, it did not create a set of principles around which the whole party might coalesce.[122]

Liberal Republican senator Jacob Javits praised the report, saying it "demonstrates again when a composite of our Party is taken, the thinking is Eisenhower (modern) thinking." Eisenhower, perhaps not surprisingly, also lauded the report, calling it a "real accomplishment" that "should certainly incite the interest of everybody."[123] But one conservative commentator had a slightly different take: "May the devil take you, Eisenhower, and all the rest of the gang that are involved in this criminal operation."[124]

Conservatives used the Percy Committee to mobilize their supporters and develop an alternative of their own. Conservative Republicans in the House delivered a series of speeches entitled "Meeting the Challenges of the Sixties"—an imitation of the theme of the Percy Committee—released it to the press, and introduced it into the *Congressional Record.* Their goal was to "clarify the differences in party responses to the challenges of the 1960s."[125] Goldwater and Bozell's *The Conscience of a Conservative* was published in April 1960 and quickly became a best-selling title; the articulation of conservative ideas and values had taken off, thanks in part to the ambiguously worded Percy Committee report.

Indeed, the period between 1958 and 1961 witnessed the blossoming of conservative organizations that were motivated by the chance, at long last, to repudiate Modern Republicanism and nominate a conservative presidential candidate of their choosing. They rejected Nixon, whose overtures to Nelson Rockefeller and Henry Cabot Lodge (Nixon's vice presidential pick) seemed to demonstrate his inability to dissociate from the "New Deal imitators." Many hoped to nominate Goldwater for either president or vice president. Succeed or fail, they wanted to ensure that in 1960 "their ideological position is preserved as a recognizable political alternative." After the 1960 election, Goldwater proclaimed that Nixon lost to John F. Kennedy because he was "not Republican enough."[126] Conservative groups rushed the demoralized party structure, consolidated their support, and took control of the national party apparatus.

The Unintended Consequences of Presidential Party Building

While presidents may intend for their party-building initiatives to produce certain outcomes, they cannot know in advance how their efforts will shape the future course of politics or how their organizational innovations will be put to use by the party leaders of the future. By creating new structures, processes, and activities in their party, their innovations become susceptible to what Kathleen Thelen has termed "functional conversion," whereby organizational forms are used to promote different purposes by future party actors.[127] Indeed, the inclusive, party-expanding thrust of most party-building initiatives magnifies such a possibility by welcoming a greater diversity of interests into the party structure and giving them a stake in the party's current and future operations. A poignant example of this can be found in Eisenhower's efforts to build the Republican Party in the South.

Operation Dixie

After the Civil War, the South remained solidly Democratic; the Republican Party was essentially a "shadow organization that existed solely for the purpose of providing delegates."[128] Yet Eisenhower won four southern states in 1952 and five in 1956. His campaigns "attracted strong support from the rising urban and suburban middle class"—more than 70 percent of southern upper-income urban whites voted for Ike in 1952—and gave the Republican Party a "precarious beachhead" in the metropolitan areas of the South from which to expand.[129] Eisenhower believed he was well positioned to reach out to his moderate southern Democratic supporters—the most promising "pool of potential converts"—and convince them to join the ranks of the Republican Party.[130] Ike's close friend Robert Anderson of Texas, a high-profile convert to the Republican Party, gave the president even more confidence that such conversions were possible.[131]

Eisenhower did not waste any time: as president-elect in November 1952, he met with his political advisers and authorized them to draw up a "long range program for expanding the Republican party in the South."[132] In February 1953 he appointed John Minor Wisdom, an RNC member and campaign leader for Eisenhower in Louisiana, to chair the new Committee on the South. The committee's task was clear: to "organize for the development of the Republican Party in the entire south."[133]

But because the Republican "name [was] still not a vote lure" in the South, the committee was "established as a civic foundation" that would "cooperate closely with the President's advisors, the Republican National Committee, and regular organizations in the states." Its primary aim was to vigorously promote the idea of a "two-party system" in the South—because "any argument for a two-party system," Eisenhower's team argued, "is automatically an argument for the Republican Party."[134]

A struggle for authority over the committee ensued between Wisdom and Hall, however, and little progress was made through most of 1953.[135] This lack of expeditiousness irritated Eisenhower. He recorded the sense of urgency with which he viewed the party-building operation in the South:

> This morning I called the National Chairman (Len Hall) to tell him of my intense personal interest in the objectives of this Committee. I have little concern as to whether the Committee is formal, informal, or anything else—I am simply interested in finding out from intelligent and experienced people what should be our next and succeeding moves in that region. Chairman Hall is to see Mr. Wisdom tomorrow and will try to get this whole matter straightened out and the whole project on the rails.[136]

By November, the RNC had asserted its control over the operation and begun to survey state laws and meet with local activists. Its goal was to install new party leaders in the state committees by the end of 1954.[137]

Eisenhower was keenly aware that the desegregation cases pending before the Supreme Court could "forever defeat any possibility of developing a real Republican or 'Opposition' Party in the South."[138] But he vowed that his "convictions would not be formed by political expediency," and continued to reach out to his supporters in the South.[139] He encouraged the committee to make its appeals to moderates like Anderson and young urban-dwellers who shared Eisenhower's political philosophy. Republicanism in the South, Eisenhower and his team argued, "had to be based on the separation of conservatism from racism." This was best accomplished "by building organizational strength in the cities," where African Americans would "vote in increasing numbers, and in the suburbs, where the new generation of voters may have fading memories of the racially conscious southern rural culture."[140] By May 1957, Eisenhower proudly announced that the GOP was "in the South to stay," because its appeal was strongest among the fastest-growing areas of the region—"in urban areas and among younger voters."[141] The *Wall Street Journal* agreed, reporting that the organizational legwork undertaken through Operation Dixie promised to pay dividends later as the South continued to evolve: "The insistence on distant gains means something. The predictions of long-term progress are based largely on continuing urbanization of the South."[142]

The progress of organizational party building in the South proved to be slow, however. When Meade Alcorn assumed the RNC chairmanship in the spring of 1957, he found that in most southern states, there was still "no Republican organization. . . . No office, no staff, no telephone, no program of party action, no effort to develop candidates, no effort to do anything" except to provide delegates to the quadrennial national convention.[143] After "a series of talks with the President and with the Vice-President," Alcorn was charged with redoubling the RNC's efforts in the region and launching a more aggressive party-building program called Operation Dixie. The president's support for such an operation was critical, Alcorn recalled, because "if this thing were undertaken, it would more likely succeed if he endorsed it, and . . . never could get off the ground if he didn't."[144]

I. Lee Potter, former state party chairman of Virginia and current RNC staff member, was tapped to lead the new Southern Division at the RNC and was directed to give "his entire attention to working with our Party organization in the Southern states."[145] The new division was given a budget of $20,960 in the second half of 1957, which represented the third-highest budget of any special division within the RNC, trailing only Young Republicans and Women.[146] Potter traveled across the South throughout 1957 and 1958, meeting with state central committees, finance committees, and state federations of Republican women. He attended state party conventions, consulted with local leaders, and offered the RNC's assistance in selecting new organization leaders and setting up new state party headquarters.[147]

The principal objective of Operation Dixie was to lay an organizational foundation in the South. It would begin with investments in infrastructure and new organizational capacities; once an organizational presence was established, new headquarters were set up, new leaders were installed, and new strategic plans were designed, a "feeling of respectability about being a Republican" was expected to gradually emerge.[148] Prospective candidates would be lured by the promise of campaign assistance from the state party organization and would be increasingly willing to run for governor, for Congress, for the Senate, and so on. Those campaigns would then spur further party growth. "Even if, at first, [the candidate] gets only a small percent of the vote," Eisenhower explained, "he helps to encourage the growth of the two-party idea. He becomes known in his community, and the next time he runs he probably will increase his vote."[149] This was how Operation Dixie sought to build the Republican Party in the South: one organization and one candidate at a time.

But when Eisenhower sent federal troops to Little Rock, Arkansas, to enforce the Supreme Court's school desegregation ruling in *Brown v. Board of Education* in September 1957, the administration found that its organization-building campaign could not compensate for the ire he had raised among states-rights southerners. The "Little Rock situation," Potter reported, "threw us into quite a tailspin . . . . I have been into every one of the Southern States and I can tell you that there has been severe damage done." Potter reported that forced desegregation set the Republican Party's expansion plans for the South back fifty years. It had eroded the movement of southern Democrats into the GOP and slowed their financial contributions to a crawl—they had been "contributing to the Republican Party" but "have now said no. They feel that this is an invasion of the rights of the States."[150]

Rather than hope to gain congressional seats in 1958, Potter now simply hoped the party could "hold the nine seats we have got." For the sake of the nascent GOP in the South, he argued that Eisenhower ought to "pull the last semblance of Federal Intervention out of Little Rock" and "turn it back over to the states." This was the only way of "getting candidates and raising money in 1958." As it was, "We have lost at least the enthusiasm and as things stand it appears we have lost the votes."[151] Potter was not the only one who was frustrated: Alcorn began to receive calls from the most "stalwart" supporters of Operation Dixie "saying, 'I guess we've had it. We might just as well forget it.'" But "to the everlasting credit of the President," Alcorn recalled, Eisenhower insisted on staying the course.[152]

By 1960, Operation Dixie's funding had been doubled and more Democrats were becoming Republicans than ever before. Alcorn recalled that "we had an office in every one of those states, and a program, and we were starting to nominate candidates."[153] Though it was still "unfashionable and sometimes unprofitable to be a Republican publicly" in the South, Operation Dixie had successfully "brought forth a bumper crop of GOP candidates" to stand for Congress in 1960.[154]

After Eisenhower stepped down, Operation Dixie lived on. In fact, it became the central front in the GOP's "out-party" party-building efforts during the early 1960s.[155] But new RNC chairman William E. Miller believed that Operation Dixie's focus on recruiting young urban professionals was shortsighted: although forty-two of the South's fifty-three biggest cities went for Nixon in 1960, this concentrated urban support had not translated into significant gains for the GOP in Congress. Miller believed that a broader-based strategy could cut deeper into the Democrats' congressional majorities. Consequently, he poured more resources into Operation Dixie and extended its operational reach. By 1964, the RNC was spending almost a third of its total expenditures on Operation Dixie; more than 87 percent of the counties in the South now had a Republican chair and vice-chair; its newsletter *Republican Southern Challenge* was being circulated to 39,000 people (up from 5,000 in 1962); and regional conferences were being held to train southern party activists in campaign techniques. The Southern Division of the RNC was described by *Congressional Quarterly* as more fully funded and active than "any other division."[156]

Miller had built upon the organizational foundation laid by Eisenhower and his team, but used it to pursue very different political purposes. Under Eisenhower, Operation Dixie primarily sought to recruit candidates and activists who emphasized fiscal conservatism and federalism but shied away from hot-button civil rights topics. In 1958, for example, most Republican candidates in the South reportedly tried to "avoid taking a stand on touchy race questions. When they do speak out, it's usually a veiled attempt to lure what they hope is a growing body of moderates."[157] Under Miller, in contrast, the new recruits tended to be extremely conservative and very often made "distinctly conservative and segregationist appeals."[158]

Alcorn regretted the political conversion of Operation Dixie under Miller and then Barry Goldwater in his 1964 presidential campaign. "Its whole purpose was perverted," he said.[159] The Goldwater/Miller group, he said, had exploited the organizational gains made under Eisenhower to pursue antithetical objectives. "Through our efforts to mold a modern, forward-looking, progressive Republican organization in those Southern states . . . we had set up headquarters," hired "staff people," and developed processes for recruiting new candidates. The new party leaders simply "took over the Operation Dixie machinery and attempted to convert it into a lily-white Republican organization. They did succeed in some states, I'm sorry to say."[160] Whereas the Eisenhower approach aimed "to obliterate any semblance of division, segregation, between white Republicans and Negro Republicans," the new party leaders made explicitly segregationist appeals.[161] The operational success of Operation Dixie, in short, had unwittingly laid the groundwork for Eisenhower's more conservative successors to move the party in a direction he never intended for it to go.

Eisenhower's activities as an ex-president further demonstrated that he did not favor these developments. From his farm in Gettysburg, Eisenhower launched a Republican Citizens Committee to "broaden and moderate the increasingly conservative GOP" in 1962. Despite its lukewarm reception, in 1963 he established a Critical Issues Council (run by brother Milton Eisenhower) to infuse the party with "modern" ideas. Unfortunately for Eisenhower, the entire initiative was told to "drop dead" by a member of the RNC, and Barry Goldwater insisted that "the same people who have caused most of our trouble" should not be "given another opportunity" to pervert the party with moderate ideas.[162]

■

Contrary to conventional wisdom, Eisenhower persistently sought to build his party into a stronger, more effective, and more attractive political organization. Along each of the dimensions of party activity introduced in chapter 1, Eisenhower undertook decidedly constructive organization-building initiatives (see table 3.1). His efforts also illuminate some of the more distinctive characteristics of presidential party building as a general phenomenon: (1) presidents can *build* their party while simultaneously *personalizing* it; (2) minority-party presidents consistently choose their party organization over extrapartisan groups because of its unusual durability; (3) bringing about ideological change requires more than successful organizational ventures; (4) presidential party building can produce unintended consequences. In Eisenhower's case, his party-building efforts led to long-term political developments that he did not favor.

The minority status of the Republican Party served as a strong motivation for Eisenhower's party building from the earliest days of his presidency to his years as an ex-president. As early as the 1952 campaign, Eisenhower's campaign manager recorded that "Ike's goal" was not just to win, but to "build as we go" and "reinstitute the GOP as majority party."[163] This competitive impulse propelled each and every one of Eisenhower's party-building efforts.

Indeed, the strength of Eisenhower's majority-building incentive also helps to explain why he was not deterred by the dearth of organizational capacities he inherited from his predecessors. One might expect that the absence of

Table 3.1   Eisenhower's Party Building

Provide campaign services	Build human capital	Recruit candidates	Mobilize voters	Finance party operations	Support internal activities
Committee on the South (1953+)	Appoint young local party leaders (1953+)	Committee on the South (1953+)	Committee on the South (1953+)	Finance Committee (1954+)	Liaison and patronage processes (1953)
GOP Campaign School (1955, 1958)	Committee on the South (1953+)	Civilian Committee (1954+)	Support young Republican groups (1955+)	GOP Campaign School (1955, 1958)	RNC Public Relations Division (1953)
Regional conferences (1957)	Infiltrating Citizens into RNC (1954+)	Support young Republican groups (1955+)	GOP Campaign School (1955, 1958)	Salute to Eisenhower (1956+)	Board of Strategy (1953)
Operation Dixie (1957+)	Civilian Committee (1954+)	Regional conferences (1957)	Neighbor-to-Neighbor (1957+)	Fund-raising for party organizations (1956+)	Committee on the South (1953+)
	Division for the Enrollment of New Republicans (1955+)	Operation Dixie (1957+)	Regional conferences (1957)	Neighbor-to-Neighbor (1957+)	Civilian Committee (1954+)
	Support young Republican groups (1955+)	Traveling salesmen (1958+)	Operation Dixie (1957+)	Regional conferences (1957)	Williams and Lord appointments (1954)
	GOP Campaign School (1955, 1958)		Recruit for '60 (1959+)	Operation Dixie (1957+)	Regional conferences (1957)
	Republican Recruit (1955)			Solicit funds from business community (1958)	Neighbor-to-Neighbor (1957+)
	Regional conferences (1957)				Operation Dixie (1957+)
	Neighbor-to-Neighbor (1957+)				
	Operation Dixie (1957+)				
	Reinvigorate RNC with Citizens (1958)				
	Recruit for '60 (1959+)				

ongoing party-building programs on which to build would discourage presidents from launching wholly new initiatives. With high start-up costs and a party membership accustomed to old ways of doing business, why would any president engage in party building? As we have seen, Eisenhower had to summon the will and the resources to begin party building from scratch, and he was not always successful in his endeavors. But his desire to build a new majority remained a powerful motivator of his behavior. In fact, the higher the start-up cost, the more forcefully Eisenhower pushed his party-building initiatives. Party building in the South, for example, proved extremely tricky in the early 1950s, and became even more difficult after "the Little Rock situation" —yet Eisenhower persevered. When finances became tight in his second term, Eisenhower remained steadfast in his determination to find new sources of funds, rebuild his party organization, and improve its competitive standing.[164] When he experienced difficulty recruiting young, energetic Republicans and former Citizens to join the party, he only pushed his organizational initiatives harder. And the more dissent he heard from conservatives, the more he sought to influence the party's future trajectory. In other words, with the Republican Party at a severe competitive disadvantage, the costs of launching brand new party-building programs were not perceived by Eisenhower to outweigh their potential benefits.

At the end of the day, Eisenhower failed to build a new majority in his image or create a consensus around his Modern Republicanism. But his party-building efforts did alter the political landscape and make it more likely that future party leaders would follow in his footsteps. His successors continued to centralize operations in the RNC, build up the party's organizational presence in the South, and invest in its "nuts and bolts." Indeed, as the next chapter demonstrates, by the time Richard Nixon was elected to the presidency in 1968, the GOP had become accustomed to organizational party building and was primed for further growth.

4

Building the New Majority | Richard Nixon

I intended to revitalize the Republican Party along New Majority lines....
I was going to build a new Republican Party and a new majority.

—President Richard M. Nixon[1]

Richard Nixon was elected in 1968 with only 43 percent of the popular vote and 56 percent of the electoral votes.[2] Yet like all minority-party presidents, he still ran ahead of a majority of Republican congressional candidates. Only 33 percent of the public identified with the GOP in 1968, and while Republicans made modest gains in Congress—five seats in the House and seven seats in the Senate—they still held under 44 percent of the seats in both chambers and only 43 percent of state legislative seats. Even Nixon's landslide reelection victory in 1972 (61 percent of the vote, 97 percent of electoral votes) did little to change his party's competitive standing, as I will discuss later. Throughout his presidency, Nixon perceived the Republican Party to be the clear minority party in American politics.[3]

The party organization Nixon inherited in 1969 was significantly more active than the one inherited by Eisenhower in 1953. Between 1961 and 1968, RNC chairmen continued to emphasize the same organizational priorities that Eisenhower had emphasized in the 1950s: strengthening state parties down to the precinct level, teaching campaign management techniques, building new fund-raising capabilities, and expanding candidate and activist recruitment efforts. Operation Dixie was but one of the organizational initiatives that benefited from the foundation laid by Eisenhower; new small-donor lists and new templates for training seminars and field-worker programs also gave the "out-party" chairmen of the 1960s a head start on further party building.[4] RNC chairman Ray Bliss, in particular, received great acclaim for his unwavering faith in the party's "nuts and bolts" between 1965 and 1969. His tenure was marked by his multiple investments in the party's physical infrastructure, in its human capital, and in its capacity to provide candidate services.[5] The party organization Nixon inherited, in short, was primed for further growth.

According to the received wisdom, Nixon did not follow up on these organizational developments. In fact, Nixon is usually seen as the most predatory of all the modern presidents in his approach to, and in his effect on, his party. His behavior is said to represent the "culmination" or "logical extension" of the pattern of presidential party predation in the modern period.[6] Two sets of claims usually underlie this view. First is that Nixon evidenced a "callous disregard for his party" during the 1972 reelection campaign when he centralized authority in his Committee to Re-Elect the President (CREEP), let loose an aggressive "Democrats for Nixon" campaign, offered little support to down-ticket Republicans, and diverted resources away from state and local parties.[7] Arthur Schlesinger Jr., for example, argues that

> Nixon cut loose from his party, ran his campaign through the Committee for the Re-election of the President rather than through the Republican National Committee, abandoned Republican governors, senators and congressmen to their fate and concentrated on collecting the largest possible majority for himself.[8]

Walter Dean Burnham agrees that Nixon's reelection campaign "reflected an aggrandizement of the president's personal power at the direct expense of the continuing electoral viability of his own party."[9]

The second type of claim refers to Nixon's detrimental *effect* on the Republican Party. Heading into the 1974 elections, the Watergate scandal cast a giant shadow, and Republican candidates suffered dramatic, across-the-board losses.[10] The American public disassociated from the Republican Party, and only about a fifth of the electorate identified with the GOP (by 1975, only 18 percent were registered as Republicans).[11] "The Watergate scandal and the political fate of President Richard M. Nixon defined the Republican Party in the 1970s," writes noted historian Lewis Gould.[12]

The "party" of concern, however, is not usually well defined. Insofar as it refers to partisan identification in the electorate, the detrimental effect of Nixon's Watergate scandal seems incontrovertible, whatever Nixon's intentions may have been. If the "party" refers to elected Republican officials, then here, too, Nixon's indifference to their fortunes in 1972 and the political fallout from Watergate clearly had a devastating effect. But what of Nixon's approach to, and effect on, the Republican Party organization? On this score, we have yet to develop a clear picture.

Rarely do scholars attempt to interrogate the extent of the party predation they ascribe to Nixon. Most do not reopen the question or venture to explore the voluminous documentary evidence of the Nixon years to determine whether Nixon had any other kinds of interactions with, or effects on, the Republican Party.[13] In consequence, this neglect has served to recycle the received wisdom rather than to use the Nixon case more productively to probe the dynamics of the president-party relationship.

Thus, it may be somewhat surprising to observe that Nixon worked to strengthen his party along each of the six dimensions of party activity examined here. In fact, his party-building efforts appear in many different shapes and sizes over the course of his five-plus years in office. In his first term, Nixon advanced a variety of organization-building initiatives in the South, and brought the full weight of the White House to bear on behalf of these efforts. He also charged his national chairmen with remaking the RNC into a more streamlined "service organization" with enhanced capacities to assist state parties and support campaigns. His most ambitious and comprehensive party-building efforts, however, are to be found in his second term: after securing reelection, Nixon sought to usher in a durable partisan realignment and build a new

		Party Building						Party Predation					
		C	H	R	V	F	I	C	H	R	V	F	I
Republicans	Eisenhower	•	•	•	•	•	•						
	Nixon	•	•	•	•	•	•	•				•	
	Ford	•	•	•	•	•	•						
	Reagan	•	•	•	•	•	•						
	Bush	•	•	•		•	•						
Democrats	Kennedy				•	•		•	•		•	•	•
	Johnson							•	•		•	•	•
	Carter							•	•	•	•	•	•
	Clinton (1st term)							•	•	•	•	•	•
	Clinton (2nd term)	•	•		•	•	•						

C=Provide campaign services, H=Build human capital, R=Recruit candidates,
V=Mobilize voters, F=Finance party operations, I=Support internal activities

Figure 4.1. Nixon's Party Interactions

electoral majority for the Republican Party—to "revitalize the Republican Party along New Majority lines," as he later wrote.[14] He elevated the stature of the RNC and directed its new chairman (future president George H. W. Bush) to launch new campaign-management and candidate-recruitment initiatives, implement multiple programs to build human capital, and establish new divisions and activities to reach out to new electoral groups. The Watergate scandal cut short Nixon's second term and overshadowed his party-building initiatives, but these episodes demonstrate that even when a president is rendered politically impotent, his party-building efforts can have a dramatic impact on his party's course of organizational development.

As indicated in figure 4.1, however, his efforts were not all of a piece. In two instances (Operation Townhouse and CREEP), I find that he did, indeed, pursue strategies to divert resources and manpower away from his party organization. These count as "predatory" acts, and cannot be dismissed. Yet as we will see, this within-case variation reveals important lessons about why minority-party presidents pursue party building in the first place. Nixon's party interactions were a varied lot, but they were always geared toward the same purpose: building a new majority in his image. He never lost sight of this larger goal, but was willing to mix and match strategies to achieve it.[15]

Regrettably, our preoccupation with these episodes—CREEP, in particular —has obscured the many constructive ways in which Nixon interacted with his party organization. In consequence, we have not only developed an image of Nixon as party predator that rests on only a small portion of the data, but we have been left with an incomplete and misleading conception of the president-party relationship as a whole. By examining the full record of Nixon's interactions with his party organization, this chapter aims to demonstrate that Nixon did more, and different, things to his party than we previously thought.

While discussing Nixon's various party interactions, this chapter also elaborates upon four characteristics of presidential party building as a more general phenomenon: (1) the unique resources of the White House are a major asset in presidential party building; (2) by strengthening the national committee's organizational capacities while prioritizing electoral activities at the local level, presidential party building vertically integrates the party's operations; (3) minority-party presidents will not engage in party building at all times or at any cost, and occasionally their larger majority-building purposes will dictate different strategies in the short term; (4) presidential party building aims to use organization-building initiatives to transfer the president's broader base of support onto the party.

Leveraging Presidential Resources and Prerogatives

The institutional and administrative resources available to presidents set them apart from other party actors and give them an advantage in party building. For example, the appointment power can be used to "politicize" the bureaucracy and reward or punish fellow partisans, thereby inducing cooperation and generating enthusiasm for organization-building projects within the party structure.[16] Presidents can also leverage the unparalleled informational resources and administrative capacities of the executive branch on behalf of party-building projects; within limits, they can reshape administrative procedures and employ the expertise of the executive departments to their party's advantage. Finally, the prestige of the presidency and the largess of the White House can be used to create favorable conditions for party building. An invitation to a White House dinner, a strategic announcement by the president, or an offer of fund-raising assistance, for example, can marshal support for the president's party-building objectives. Nixon leveraged all three of these prerogatives— the patronage power, the administrative advantage, and the prestige of the presidency—to create a climate conducive to party building.

Party Building in the South

After his election in November 1968, Nixon indicated that he was committed to revitalizing his party. According to his new director of communications, Nixon intended "to strengthen the Republican National Committee and the state committees in an effort to increase the number of registered Republicans and to bring the party to 'the strength it needs if it is going to survive.'"[17] Once he assumed the presidency, Nixon followed up on these promises and gravitated toward the biggest prize: the South. For more than ten years, party leaders had labored to develop a stronger organizational presence in the southern states. But Nixon could finally do what Goldwater, Miller, and Bliss could not: bring the unique resources and advantages of the presidency to bear on party building.

There was no more important party-building deputy in Nixon's first term than Harry Dent, a former political adviser to Senator Strom Thurmond of South Carolina. Dent had helped the Republican Party grow into a political force in South Carolina, and Nixon hired him to replicate those efforts on a national scale.[18] As Nixon's chief political assistant in the White House, Dent's main responsibility was to improve the president's political position while leveraging the resources of the presidency to help the Republican Party grow in the South. He was charged with responding to local party leaders when they sought White House support: to "provide speakers, make contributor contacts, get statements and endorsements, pictures with the President, and provide advice." By supporting "National Party leaders and leaders in the field," Dent would "keep Party leaders and contributors happy and working for the President and the Party" and "make them feel they have access to White House and Administration." Dent also gave the president unfiltered political advice and relayed day-to-day briefings from RNC chair Rogers Morton "on what the political situation is, what the party machinery is doing to improve it, and what the White House can do to help."[19]

The first order of business was to establish strong ties with Republican state party leaders: to "lubricate these Southern Chairmen" and "make good troopers out of them."[20] Capitalizing on the prestige of his new Cabinet, Nixon directed each Cabinet member to make "four visits through the Republican Party organization" in the southern states to give the state party organizations a publicity boost and demonstrate the administration's commitment to southern interests.[21]

One major difficulty was that the administration was caught between southern congressional Democrats, whose support the administration needed for its legislative initiatives, and southern Republican Party chairmen, who were trying to build their local organizations. GOP chairmen resisted any overtures the administration made to southern Democrats: how could they build their state parties if it still paid to be a Democrat in the South?[22] Patronage proved to be the key mollifying agent; at an RNC meeting in June 1969, Dent gave the disgruntled party leaders his personal assurances that appointments would be forthcoming.[23]

"There was revolt in the air," Dent said. "I had to win their confidence right off or I was finished. I brought the 'plum books' with me, which listed all the jobs and commissions and honorary posts we were going to fill, and I started off by saying that party people were going to get every one. After that it was easy."[24] But Dent did more than simply promise jobs to spoils-hungry Republicans. He explained that these appointments were to be used in service of a larger purpose: to build the Republican Party in the South. Nixon's goal, Dent told them, was "to help us build this Party and transform it from a minority party into a majority party."[25]

Dent said that "directly on the orders of the president," he had developed a new system for handling patronage requests that would "help you build and extend the roots of the Republican Party." Requests would go through the

RNC to Dent so that appointments could be strategically distributed across the South to "make this into a majority party." Nixon, Dent said, "is determined to see that his friends are not forgotten and that his Party is built and that we win greater victories in 1970 and on into the future . . . we think that this is the best way that you can use patronage, and the best way you can build your Party."[26] In the first year alone, Dent coordinated the replacement of approximately 2,000 Democrats from the federal bureaucracy. He also ensured that an additional 3,000 Republicans were appointed to "honorary" positions (such as the American Battle Monuments Commission and the Bi-Centennial Commission).[27]

Of greater concern than patronage, however, was the speed and thoroughness of school desegregation. State chairmen were unsure how to tread on the issue, as any change in the administration's position was certain to affect their ability to organize in their localities. Dent found that by giving southern GOP chairmen talking points with up-to-date facts and figures, the administration could aid their party-building efforts even in that difficult climate; the state chairmen believed they could "make gains" if the administration could give them "something on schools they can sell rather than have to defend."[28] Sharing information from the attorney general and secretary of health, education, and welfare was an indirect but still useful way for the administration to promote the GOP party-building project in the South; another was to coordinate a "continuing pilgrimage" for southern party leaders to visit the White House and greet the president. Such initiatives facilitated local party leaders' efforts and even helped to raise money for the GOP.[29]

Dent's efforts to leverage presidential resources and prerogatives on behalf of party building began to foster a cooperative relationship between Nixon and southern party leaders. After the RNC meeting, Dent reported to Nixon that he had dutifully conveyed "the President's strong interest in helping to build the party and see that the President's supporters are given an attentive ear and full cooperation"; he also showed Nixon a copy of a letter he had received from Clarke Reed, Mississippi state party chairman and chairman of the Southern Association of State Chairmen, showing a "complete switch from southern griping to southern praise for the President."[30] The letter noted: "The vast majority of our people are pleased with the overall performance of the Administration." Nixon scribbled back to Dent: "Harry, Good work."[31]

The changing economic and social conditions of the South and Nixon's vigorously debated "southern strategy" during the 1968 election were the hot political topics of the day. Kevin Phillips's *The Emerging Republican Majority* (and related articles), for example, attracted a great deal of attention, and required a strategic response from the White House.[32] Phillips appeared to be correct, Dent noted, that a "clearly discernible white reaction has begun to take shape" in response to "a decade of extremely rapid social and economic progress by American Negroes." This "white reaction" combined a fear of "the Negroes' progress" with a frustration with integration. Racial conflict would continue to persist, Dent believed, "especially over those issues where the races are in intimate competition (e.g., housing, schools, blue-collar jobs)." These social, economic, and political changes had important implications for how the administration would orient its party-building projects, Dent wrote. It had to tread cautiously through "the mine field of race relations," while realizing that "old political loyalties have been dissolved by the racial situation and that we have an unprecedented opportunity to garner votes in large blocks. To capitalize on this opportunity we need a carefully conceived 'master plan' for the Administration to implement."[33]

The master plan was to "disavow Phillips's book as party policy," avoid using divisive rhetoric, and instead focus on building the state parties' organizational capacities—a constructive goal that seemed likely to fly under the radar. The president approved Dent's plan to have "a coordinated effort by the White House, the Hill Committees and the RNC especially in the critical areas of candidate recruitment, financing and campaign management."[34] Nixon soon began to echo these party-building priorities back to Dent: in October, Dent recorded that "our problem, as the President says, is candidate recruitment and campaign management."[35] Continually hammering away on these themes, Nixon directed the RNC to "undertake an effort to guide campaign managers in the future on the need of maintaining a candidate at peak fighting trim."[36] The administration's decision to concentrate its "southern strategy" on building organizational capacities for candidate recruitment, financing party operations, and campaign management made perfect sense in a volatile political climate; in a confidential memo to the president, Dent explained that conditions were actually quite favorable "to get more switchovers throughout the South" if "our people" began "working quietly and effectively" to recruit them.[37]

To encourage southern Republican Party leaders to focus on developing new outreach programs, Dent led a delegation of administration officials to the Southern Republican Conference in late 1969, the first-ever region-wide GOP conference in the South.[38] At the conference, Dent read a letter from Nixon that stressed the president's "conviction" that "our Party will become the majority party in the United States." Some progress had already been made, Nixon said, but much organization-building work remained:

> By holding the Republican Party's strength at its present level; by recruiting attractive, articulate candidates; by strengthening the Party's manpower in the precincts; by implementing programs of involvement with people beyond party lines ... and by adequately financing our Party's candidates and organizations, you can make sure that the Republicans gain for their Party its rightful place in American political affairs.[39]

Dent told southern Republican leaders to "forget the idea of trying to build a party on the basis of patronage" and instead to "go out and start a grassroots campaign to register more Republicans, switch local and statewide office holders, and proclaim the message and accomplishments of this Administration."[40]

By the end of 1969, Nixon's southern party-building strategy had thus evolved from the less direct approach of using patronage, informational resources, and presidential prestige to boost morale to a more explicitly organizational approach. Going forward, local organizations would receive the RNC's direct assistance with campaign management, fund-raising, activist enrollment, candidate recruitment (including the conversion of Democrats), and voter mobilization.[41]

This emphasis on building party organization complemented Nixon's carefully crafted response to questions about his "so-called Southern strategy." Nixon told Dent to use this statement: "This Administration has no Southern strategy but rather a national strategy which, for the first time in modern times, *includes* the South, rather than *excludes* the South from full and equal participation in national affairs . . . the Democrats seem to have written the South out of the Union, but the Republican Party is writing the South into the Union on an equal basis."[42] Nixon noted that this was "a good line to hit continually. Get this out—*Democratic* pols throwing the South away."[43]

A lesser-known component of Nixon's "southern strategy" was a short-lived effort to reach out to African Americans in southern states. In February 1969, Nixon told Dent to develop a comprehensive, balanced strategy for the South that would "keep the Negroes and the white South happy."[44] Dent directed RNC chairman Rogers Morton to "intensify [the RNC's] efforts to enlist Negro leaders and, in fact, develop Negro leaders to work for our Party." The RNC should "hire part-time workers all through the South" where "the attainment of 10 to 20% of the Negro vote would mean victory. I really do not believe any national money could be better spent than through such a project."[45] The plan was evidently implemented, as Morton continued "subsidizing Negro Republican recruiters in the South" in conjunction with state and local parties throughout 1969.[46] By the end of the year, Nixon reflected on his team's efforts to "make inroads into the Negro community." In a confidential memo to chief of staff H. R. Haldeman, the president wrote: "Just as we are trying to appeal to our own constituency among the whites, we should remember that there is a similar constituency, although eminently smaller, among Negroes. Let's not overlook them in attempting to pander to the radicals—black or white."[47]

Paul Frymer and John Skrentny have ably argued that Nixon's efforts to reach out to African Americans through policies, appointments, and other initiatives were part and parcel of a larger strategy to "counter potentially severe and damaging criticism that he was a racist and not a legitimate national leader in the post-civil rights era." By mid-1970, however, they find that the administration had moved "away from blacks and black interests on a national scale" and expressed "regret that attempts were ever made to support 'black' policies" within the Nixon administration.[48] This shift away from African-American outreach was also evident in Nixon's party-building efforts. In 1972 Haldeman wrote that "we should forget about a massive effort with the Blacks. It's okay to talk about it and cover it on a general public basis, but it is not something that we should put any effort against, because it is counter-productive."[49]

Nixon was willing to recalibrate his strategies as political conditions changed; but the tie that bound these early initiatives together was Nixon's desire to build the Republican Party's presence in the South. In each instance, Nixon and his team leveraged the resources of the White House to support the Republican state parties as they worked to grow their operations, expand their reach, and swell their ranks.

Building a "Service Organization"

At the RNC, Nixon's top priority during his first term was to develop its institutional capacity to provide campaign services to local party units and to candidates directly. Nixon's contributions in this area were, in this way, constitutive of a broader historical trend toward the development of more "nationalized" and "institutionalized" party organizations in American politics.[50] The parties began to move in this direction during the 1920s and 1930s; by the late 1940s and early 1950s, both parties' national committees operated continuously and maintained a permanent staff and headquarters; and by the 1960s "the basic organizational functions and duties of the Democratic and Republican national committees, chairmen, and headquarters were fairly well defined and stabilized."[51] Eisenhower's efforts in the 1950s, as we have seen, were constitutive of these changes. These developments fundamentally altered the way the parties did business: in the Republican Party, in particular, where Republican presidents consistently relied upon their RNC chairmen to implement large party-building programs, the national committee became the locus of planning, coordination, and implementation of party activities.

But because the objective of most party-building programs was to expand the Republican Party's electoral reach, recruit more activists and candidates, mobilize more voters, and enhance the party's campaign services, only so much could be accomplished from the RNC headquarters in Washington, D.C. The thrust of Nixon's efforts, therefore, was to vertically integrate party operations by strengthening the RNC's capacity to provide services to local parties and assist in campaigns. With centralized planning and coordination, it was possible to create an economy of scale, as it were: to offer services to every party unit, make local party activities more efficient, share best practices across the organization, and improve coordination all around. Nixon's support for these changes thus helped to create a new kind of national party: one that had new mechanisms of coordination and efficiency, that emphasized grassroots organizational capacities, and that focused on helping candidates with their campaigns.

First, however, Nixon wanted to ensure that the RNC leadership was responsive to the White House. Demanding loyalty from national committee leaders, as we will see, is the first step every modern president—Democratic and Republican alike—took when he entered office. Yet their insistence upon loyalty did not predict what kind of changes they would ultimately try to make to their party's organizational capacities. Nixon, for example, showed little hesitation in removing the widely respected Ray Bliss in early 1969 in favor of someone who would be more responsive and loyal to him.[52] He selected Congressman Rogers Morton of Maryland, his skilled floor manager at the 1968 convention, as his new chairman.[53] Morton may not have had Bliss's reputation as an adept party builder, but, as we will see, his selection was hardly a repudiation of Bliss's programmatic emphasis on "nuts and bolts."

Asserting control over the RNC is not the same thing as undercutting its operations or diminishing its organizational capacities. Nixon wanted a loyal and responsive RNC, but that did not mean he had no interest in party building. Unlike the Democratic presidents we will consider later—but like each of his fellow Republican presidents—Nixon empowered his party chairmen to undertake extensive party-building initiatives.

Mission '70s Party Organization Program

In his inaugural address, Morton praised the "strong and smoothly functioning organization" he inherited from Ray Bliss and promised to "build on it— this time with the full muscle of a Republican Administration going for us." Nixon's election offered a "fantastic opportunity" to build the Republican Party, he said. But because times had changed, the RNC would need to adapt its operations to meet new conditions. "Today the emphasis is on the individual, rather than on his party label," Morton said. "We must recognize this fact." Therefore, the task of the RNC was "to perfect our Party machinery for candidate selection, so as to bring forth men and women who can win public office."[54] This rededication to electoral activities reflected more than the changing times, however—it also illustrated Nixon's priority of building a new majority. Morton explained that the "mission of our Party is to grow. We cannot be resigned to being a political minority."[55]

The centerpiece of the RNC's first party-building effort, called Mission '70s Party Organization Program, aimed to bring into closer contact precinct, county, state, and national party chairmen and to coordinate their campaign efforts through uses of new technology.[56] Mission '70s set up task forces to evaluate party organizations on a state-by-state basis and "shore up" their weaknesses in preparation for upcoming campaigns and redistricting efforts. "We'll be flexible," Morton said. "The idea is to develop programs that fit the local need."[57] The RNC invested in "advanced systems of computer software" and used the new technologies to help with the "management of the party." RNC specialists were assigned to help state parties use new computer surveys to identify likely Republican voters and design programs for voter registration, get-out-the-vote, and redistricting in 1971.[58]

But the key was to make investments in human capital. In preparation for the 1970 campaigns, the RNC studied the 1968 campaigns, identified the best campaign managers, and placed them in "interim jobs from which they can break free for next year's Congressional and state races."[59] These moves "brought the proposition of training professionals into an actual, living, continuing process. . . . this is our job: continual education, not crash programs before a campaign, but trying to establish a network of campaign managers available when the time comes whom we know have the professional confidence to do the job," Morton explained.[60]

The "requirement for the '70s and beyond," Morton told the southern state chairmen, is to turn the RNC into "a service organization." The motto, he said, was "We can do very little for you but a great deal with you."[61] Combining this service-based approach with accountability and "performance standards," the program aimed to vertically integrate the party's operations. Mission '70s provided manuals with job descriptions for every level of the political organization down to each "block worker." The manuals were "designed so each county chairman can train his own precinct workers and provide a method to follow up on all activities." What's more, in thirty-seven workshop sessions held in as many states over the course of 1970, Mission '70s trained local party leaders on how to recruit and train grassroots activists.[62] The efforts were deemed to be operational successes. Because the programs "succeeded in involving literally hundreds of Party activists" and "have been pretty well pushed into the states," Morton wrote to Nixon, they did not "require more than a very modest investment of our time, energy, and money."[63]

Work still remained, however, to bring the RNC's operations "into a perfected working relationship with the Presidency and its senior staff."[64] Part of Morton's challenge, therefore, was to "evaluate the working relationship between the Presidency and the Committee" and "jointly determine the priorities for the investment of our resources." Nixon's White House political team kept close tabs on Morton and encouraged him to continue streamlining party operations, reduce redundancies in the RNC's operations, develop processes to ensure greater responsiveness to the White House, and do more "innovative thinking" on issues ranging from fund-raising to special-group outreach.[65]

Nixon thus encouraged Morton's efforts at the RNC and occasionally gave him additional party-building responsibilities.[66] But Nixon became increasingly displeased with Morton's public speaking style. He wanted him to be more hard-hitting and aggressive in defense of the administration, to play hardball politics so the president could appear above the fray.[67] "Morton just isn't the type for attack," Haldeman recorded in his diary, though he was "really tops on the positive side" of things.[68] After the disappointing midterm elections of 1970, in which Republicans lost twelve House seats, eleven governorships, and control of four state legislatures, Nixon decided he wanted an RNC chairman who was more comfortable in an attack-dog role. He had no interest in terminating the useful party-building programs launched under Morton, but he did want more responsiveness from the RNC. Haldeman recorded: "P[resident Nixon] really got into gear on future planning. Decided major personnel changes."[69] Morton would have to resign, and a "nut-cutter" would have to be brought in to make the RNC more aggressive.[70] After some discussion, the president settled on Senator Bob Dole from Kansas, a strong Nixon supporter.[71]

The Dole-Evans RNC

Contemporaries inferred from Dole's appointment that Nixon intended to downgrade the RNC and cut its operations; after all, Dole would be a part-time chairman while he served in the Senate. But because of the secretive manner in which Nixon operated, contemporaries were unaware of what the president had in mind. Specifically, confusion surrounded Nixon's decision to appoint Thomas B. Evans Jr., a national committeeman from Delaware and friend of Attorney General John Mitchell, as cochairman of the committee. Having two cochairmen was unprecedented. But Nixon did not want to choose between using the RNC for his own political purposes and building its organizational capacities; he wanted to do both. Nixon thus became innovative, and established a novel division of labor between Dole and Evans.

Nixon explained that Evans would be the "day-to-day" operating chief of the RNC and Dole would assume the role of "party spokesman around the country."[72] Evans was a young, moderate Republican who was an excellent organizer and fund-raiser; Dole was a "staunch conservative and a forceful speaker."[73] The two men would play to their strengths. Dole wanted full control of the RNC, but Nixon refused: the organizational work, he insisted, must be left to the more experienced Evans.[74] On the president's marching orders, Dole proceeded to tour the country as the mouthpiece of the administration while Evans worked to revitalize the party organization in the wake of its midterm election losses.

Like Morton, Evans was firmly committed to the proposition that "the only way to build a strong national party is by building strong state parties."[75] To that end, he concentrated his efforts on providing "assistance and coordination to the federation of state parties." He frequently sent task forces into states to provide assistance and support, an initiative that built directly upon Morton's task force programs.[76] Whenever a state elected a new executive director, for example, Evans would send in a "team of staff professionals" to help the new leader get his or her organization up and running and reduce start-up costs.[77] Since Republican losses in 1970 had created bitter factional conflicts in key battleground states like Illinois, Ohio, and Texas, Evans directed an "expanded and upgraded" special Field Force to aid these state parties with their education, training, and fund-raising efforts.[78] The "Fieldmen" also helped state parties create "sustaining membership" programs to generate small contributions within their states. Evans also launched a "regional concept" at the RNC in 1972, and opened small offices in Atlanta and Salt Lake City to "provide better liaison with the state parties" in the South and West.[79]

Building on Morton's efforts to invest in the party's human capital, Evans ran several "Campaign Management Seminars" in 1971 and 1972 to create a "reservoir of professionally trained talent at its disposal." A set of "Professional Staff Conferences" were also held on a national basis.[80] And Project Blitz, a program to register new Republicans to vote, was implemented successfully: by August 1972, Evans announced that 400,000 new voters had been enrolled through the program.[81]

These new programs helped to improve the mutual "responsiveness" of the state and national party committees, Evans said. But other initiatives helped as well. Prior to Evans's arrival at the RNC, state parties were instructed to pay a 10 percent commission fee to get members of the administration to speak in their states: Evans eliminated it. Additionally, the profits from lucrative "Salute to the President" dinners were equally divided between the national and state parties.[82]

Nixon was determined to "get the politics out of the White House" and avoid too close an association with his less popular party as he geared up for his reelection campaign. In a strategy memo to Haldeman, Nixon wrote: "Under no circumstances will I do the big Republican fundraiser in 1971."[83] Despite these vows, he ultimately changed his mind: the benefits of his participation in the event were evidently deemed to be worth the political costs.[84] He spoke at the "Salute" event, and like Eisenhower, his speech was simulcast to twenty different locations and viewed by 9,000 supporters who paid $500 per person: the RNC grossed a whopping $4.3 million in that single evening and distributed half of the proceeds to the state parties with the rest going to the RNC. Evans explained that the effort did more than help raise money: the Salute dinners helped him to identify those individuals who were adept fund-raisers and "test their performance under fire." The event also tested the state parties and enabled Evans to measure their "effectiveness."[85]

Nevertheless, during the two-year period before his 1972 reelection campaign, the Republican Party's weak competitive standing weighed heavily upon Nixon. Despite his desire to appear "above" partisanship, he continually found himself exploring new ways to remake his party and improve its electoral fortunes. In early 1971, for example, Nixon stumbled upon a new concept for the Republican Party: the GOP, he decided, ought to be known as the "party of the open door." In what were partially "off the cuff" remarks delivered at the dedication of the RNC's new national headquarters building on Capitol Hill on January 15, Nixon warned that "the great danger of any party organization" or "of any club" is to organize "fewer and fewer better and better" rather than to create "something bigger than itself." He then made a connection between his own majority-building goals and those of his predecessor, Dwight Eisenhower, more than a decade earlier:

> [Eisenhower] used to emphasize the necessity for the party to expand, to get more people, more troops to join with us. . . . In order to win, it is necessary to pick up enough independents and enough members of the other party to get a majority. . . . I would like the Republican Party to be the party of the open door, a party with its doors open to all people of all races and of all parties, those who share our

great ideals . . . our party will not grow unless it is the party of the open door.[86]

Nixon called Haldeman immediately after the RNC speech and conveyed his enthusiasm for the new theme. The "open door" concept, after all, captured the essence of Nixon's party-building project: to use the Republican Party as the starting point and add to it, to create a new majority that reflected Nixon's broader support. Nixon directed Haldeman and Dole to be sure to emphasize the theme in public statements.[87] Though such rhetoric does not count as a party-building action in our tally, it does illustrate the motivation behind Nixon's various organizational party-building initiatives rather nicely.

Indeed, Nixon used the "open door" theme to explain his goals for the Republican Party. In February, he spoke at a Young Republicans Reception and encouraged the activists to go out and mobilize the 55 percent of young people who were "up for grabs" with "no party allegiance." The Republican Party's "spirit of reform and positive change could win them over," he told them.[88] Presidential adviser John Ehrlichman wrote in his notes that Nixon explained his goal as building "an edifice for future. 55% of 12mm new voters not Rep or Dem or [philosophy] committed—up for grabs—must be *for* building, not destroy; this is a chance to build."[89]

Nixon's party-building efforts in this period must be seen in this light: the president was looking for mechanisms through which to build a new majority in his image and found his party organization to be a useful, though not perfect, mechanism for doing so. He believed it to be politically imprudent to associate himself too closely with his party in the public eye; but behind the scenes, he lent the full support, resources, and prestige of the presidency on behalf of the endeavor.

Within two months of Evans's appointment, the president was delighted to receive rave reviews of his party-building efforts at the RNC. Herbert Klein, the president's director of communications, wrote to Nixon: "I am impressed by the way Tom Evans is taking hold and moving into building both organization and morale. Lyn Nofziger [deputy chairman] is doing a good job also. Our new team is much stronger than the old one."[90] Dole disagreed, and later revealed his low opinion of Evans and his abilities; a rivalry had clearly formed between Evans and himself during their joint chairmanship.[91] But Nixon evidently did not agree with Dole's assessment of Evans's work. He met with Evans and his two deputy chairmen and told them how "pleased" he was with their work and asked what he could do to help; he also volunteered to host the Republican state chairmen at the White House to facilitate Evans's efforts.[92]

Majority-Building Trade-offs

Minority-party presidents seek to construct a new majority in American politics that will reflect and perpetuate their personal brand of politics, and party building offers a particularly attractive strategy for pursuing that objective.

But on occasion, these presidents will perceive their majority-building purposes to be better served, in the short run, by alternative strategies; in these instances, they may find it necessary to put their party-building plans temporarily on hold and adopt a decidedly nonconstructive approach until the exigency has passed. This is precisely what we observe with Nixon's subterranean, illegal funding operation to channel money directly to specific congressional campaigns in 1970 (Operation Townhouse) and with his 1972 reelection campaign (CREEP). In both cases, Nixon calculated that he had a better chance of building a new majority in the long run if he adopted "party predator" strategies in the short run.

The Democratic presidents examined in Part II conducted similar financing operations and established similar campaign committees. But their efforts were part and parcel of a larger strategy to squeeze what they could out of the existing Democratic majority without taking steps to expand that majority, and their predatory acts were unaccompanied by additional efforts to develop their party's organizational capacities. In contrast, while Operation Townhouse and CREEP worked at cross-purposes with Nixon's party-building programs in the short term, they were viewed by Nixon as part and parcel of his larger majority-building objectives. Indeed, it is telling that once the urgency of the 1970 and 1972 elections had passed, Nixon returned to his party-building approach; after the 1972 election, he even sought to extract organizational benefits for his party from the remnants of CREEP.

In other words, rather than characterize Nixon's whole approach, these two predatory episodes stand alone. Because previous scholarship has tended to focus exclusively on these efforts in isolation from everything else Nixon did, it is not surprising that Nixon has long been viewed as a party predator. But when we view these episodes alongside his many more constructive party interactions and in light of his larger majority-building purposes, it is easier to see why he was willing to mix and match strategies. Let us examine each of these episodes in turn.

Operation Townhouse

As we have seen, Nixon's party-building efforts were meant to produce long-term political change. Programs to recruit new candidates, invest in local party infrastructure, and improve the party's campaign-service offerings aimed to build a new "farm team" that would someday rise to challenge incumbent Democrats and recapture a congressional majority for the Republican Party. These same majority-building goals even characterized Nixon's nonconstructive party interactions.

In September 1969, Nixon began privately to urge several Republican candidates to challenge incumbent Democratic senators in 1970. He showed special attention to Representative George Bush in Texas, Representative William Cramer of Florida, Governor Paul Laxalt of Nevada, and Governor James Rhodes of Ohio.[93] Because most of these men would be sacrificing their current positions to run, the president reassured them that "we'll be here," suggesting that government appointments would be forthcoming in case of a loss.[94] But Nixon also went much further than this, and established an illegal fund-raising and fund-disbursement system that replicated Lyndon Johnson's "direct assistance" program (chapter 9) in an uncanny fashion. Hoarding cash in a private account, Nixon channeled large contributions to his favored candidates, compliments of the president and his friends. Nixon believed that, in addition to building loyalty among the candidates, such an effort would begin to reshape his congressional party coalition in his image.

In early December 1969, Haldeman met with Commerce secretary Maurice Stans, Harry Dent, and presidential aide Jack A. Gleason at the president's request to discuss "setting up our own funding for backing the good candidates in hot races." There were several Republican candidates running in 1970 that "were not considered 'good' and P[resident] felt we should do what we could to help those who would be most likely to support the Administration when elected," Haldeman wrote. The concept was simple. The administration would develop its own process for raising and distributing funds to its favored candidates outside normal party channels. "A little tricky to handle outside the RNC," Haldeman noted, "but looks pretty good."[95]

Haldeman and Dent enlisted Herbert Kalmbach, Nixon's personal attorney and fund-raiser, along with Gleason, to run Operation Townhouse. Named after its office location in a town house on Nineteenth Street in Washington, D.C., the operation followed a general pattern: Kalmbach would solicit contributions from Nixon's network of friends and former donors by offering them "expert advice" and telling them that if they contributed large sums of money, they could "join 'the privileged few that would have the honor of raising funds for the President.'"[96] Gleason would then explain to the donors which campaigns needed the money the most; he would receive their contributions and distribute them accordingly. Gleason reportedly bragged that the operation raised more than $12 million for the 1970 elections.[97]

But as Dent explained to a judge reviewing the illegal operation in 1974, "what evidently occurred is that it finally didn't work that way." Enough enormous donations were made from single donors that "they weren't easy to funnel, being in checks of $150,000."[98] Dent said the funds were instead deposited in a secret bank account, from which certain sums were distributed "directly to candidates."[99] Those funds were "personally earmarked for candidates by President Nixon."[100]

As would prove to be the case with their other covert efforts, Nixon and Haldeman overestimated their ability to pull it off. It was later revealed that Operation Townhouse was illegal because it was not organized with a formal chairman and treasurer under the Anti-Corrupt Practices Act, and Dent, Kalmbach, and Gleason were convicted of crimes associated with the operation. In Dent's statement, he told the judge that he was unaware that the operation was a crime: after all, the entire program was undertaken "under the direction of the President of the United States," Dent said.[101]

The operation must be counted as "predatory" because it was designed to circumvent normal party finance channels, and hypothetically, it could have sapped the party organization of the resources it needed to finance party operations. Yet so far as we can tell, Operation Townhouse did not ultimately detract from the party's operations: by 1970, the RNC had established a relatively stable financial footing, with its direct-mail operations and large-donor, medium-donor, and small-donor sustaining membership programs in full swing.[102] Campaign management training sessions continued unabated, leadership schools continued to be held, manuals and guides continued to be printed, and the RNC chairman reported lucrative fund-raising for the party throughout 1970.[103] Nevertheless, Operation Townhouse had the potential to undercut the party organization, and this is what makes it stand out from Nixon's otherwise constructive approach to his party organization.

Though it was consistent with Nixon's majority-building objectives, Operation Townhouse serves as a useful reminder that while party building is usually perceived to be a promising strategy for majority building, it is not always. Depending on the president's perception of his competitive environment and the strategies available to him to effect a change in that environment, he may calculate that a nonconstructive approach serves his purposes better in the short run, even if party building is the favored strategy in the long run. As we will see in Part II, Democrats who undertook Operation Townhouse–like activities did not have the same incentive to build a new majority, and therefore did not design any long-term party-building strategies: their party predation was unaccompanied by any more constructive efforts. In contrast, as we have seen, following the 1970 elections, Nixon turned his attention back to party building, hired Tom Evans at the RNC, and lent his support to a number of important organization-building efforts.

CREEP

The same short-term benefit that Nixon hoped to receive from Operation Townhouse was again pursued during his 1972 reelection campaign. CREEP (sometimes CRP or CREP) is probably the most infamous acronym in campaign finance history; its story is already notorious.[104] We have long known, for example, that CREEP was run separately from the party organization and that its operations undercut the Republican Party when necessary. But we have not known exactly why Nixon was willing to run such a campaign. Indeed, in light of his more typically constructive approach to his party organization, CREEP seems especially out of place.

Newly released documents from the Nixon Library in Yorba Linda, California, reveal much more about Nixon's thought process. While Nixon knew his campaign committee would be "predatory," he also knew it would be temporary. In June 1972, he read a Gallup poll that found only 24 percent of the public identifying with the GOP; under the circumstances, he believed that he would need to disassociate from his party for the duration of the campaign.

To build his party—indeed, to build his new majority—he would need to secure his reelection first: he did not believe he could do both at the same time. In a confidential memo to Attorney General John Mitchell, Nixon explained:

> We must "leave the door open" for Democrats and Independents not only to join us but to have positions of real leadership in the Nixon campaign. I can't emphasize too strongly how much I agree with this position. You will get squeals of outrage from the National Committee and from State Chairmen, but we must remember that if the Republican Party, weak as it is, is to be rebuilt it cannot be done so [sic] at the expense of risking losing the Presidential election. The time to do it will be after the election.[105]

CREEP would be used to secure reelection in the near term, and his long-term party-building plans would recommence in November.

Another good reason for establishing CREEP as an independent entity involved the Federal Election Campaign Act of 1971. Limiting campaign expenditures and placing a ceiling on contributions, the act was passed in February 1971 but was not scheduled to go into effect until April 7, 1972, thus practically guaranteeing that candidates would try to raise as much unregulated money as possible before the deadline. Maurice Stans, the head of the new Finance Committee to Re-Elect the President, began raising enormous sums of money (in what Theodore White calls nearly a "manic glee") and distributing them to different adjuncts of the Finance Committee. In advance of April 7, the Committee raised about $20 million, $6 million of which came in the final days before the deadline. The committee later went on to raise approximately $60 million, dwarfing McGovern's otherwise impressive $38 million effort.[106]

Ultimately, for Nixon, the biggest political problem stemming from this frenetic fund-raising was the money trail it left for Watergate investigators. From the perspective of the Republican Party in 1972, the main problem was that CREEP sapped the party of its resources and diverted funds and manpower away from Republican candidates down the ticket.[107]

In June 1971, the precursor to CREEP, called Citizens for the Re-Election of the President (led by future CREEP director Jeb Magruder), began to recruit campaign workers. David Broder reported that Nixon's campaign managers were "touring the country, checking the degree of preparedness or unpreparedness of state and local Republican organizations and lining up prospects to head the 'Nixon committees' that will burgeon early next year," which Broder assumed would "supplement the work of the regular GOP units."[108] Of course, as Broder and others would soon discover, rather than *supplement* the regular party apparatus, CREEP intentionally circumvented state party committees and disassociated the Nixon campaign from the Republican Party in order to attract conservative southern Democrats and George Wallace supporters.[109] CREEP units were eventually established in the battleground states (Nixon would not repeat his inefficient visit to all fifty states as in 1968), and volunteers and activists were organized under the direction of CREEP managers, not state Republican Party leaders.

It is worth noting, however, that CREEP did integrate the RNC's much-vaunted Target '72 voter registration program into its campaign operations. Target '72 was the name given to a series of pilot projects earlier in the year that were regarded as operational successes; in the fall, it became the primary collaborative effort between CREEP and the Republican Party.[110] CREEP's manual for state campaign chairmen, for example, explained that in states where "the Republican Party has an organized [voter registration] program underway, it is the job of the Nixon campaign organization to work closely with the Party, providing manpower, etc., so that the program will be an overwhelming success."[111] The joint venture was said to have helped "resolve whatever differences" existed between "the Re-election and Party committees at the local level."[112] After the election, the RNC's political director noted that the party benefited greatly from being "adopted" by CREEP "for the nationwide canvass."[113]

Despite collaborating with the party on voter registration and mobilization, the Nixon reelection campaign otherwise operated with little concern for the Republican Party. This was especially true with regard to Republican candidates running for office in 1972. Nixon explicitly told his reelection chairman Clark MacGregor not to waste any resources on weak Republicans down the ticket: he should "be sure we're not pissing away support for candidates who can't win," Haldeman recorded.[114] After the election, the president claimed to be angry about the lack of support given to GOP congressional candidates. Whether his complaints were disingenuous or not, the fact remains that Nixon's campaign supplanted state party operations, diverted financial resources and manpower away from other Republican campaign efforts, and hoarded those resources for his reelection campaign. It was no great surprise, therefore, that Nixon lacked significant coattails, despite his landslide victory: Republicans lost two Senate seats, two governorships, and gained only twelve House seats, while Democrats took control of two more statehouses. CREEP also ended the campaign with a surplus balance of $4.9 million, clearly indicating that Nixon's campaign did not do what it could to help Republican candidates.[115]

In the mainstream literature, CREEP has come to characterize the whole of Nixon's party relations. While it is clearly true that Nixon's 1972 campaign was all too willing to bypass the regular party structure and denigrate the GOP's image for Nixon's personal benefit, this episode has obscured his efforts to build the party in the South and strengthen the coordinative capacities at the RNC, and as we will see, it has obscured his most comprehensive and ambitious party-building effort, launched at the start of his second term. When CREEP is viewed alongside these more constructive efforts, it becomes clear that the campaign only temporarily put Nixon's party-building programs on hold; in fact, as discussed below, the remnants of CREEP were earmarked for constructive party-building purposes after the election. Indeed, if we are interested in developing an accurate picture of the approach Nixon adopted with his party, his predatory actions must be viewed as portions of a much larger story. Throughout, Nixon never lost his focus on expanding his party's reach and building a new majority in his image.

Building the New Majority

Immediately following the 1972 election, Nixon began an intensive period of planning for his second term.[116] The question of the hour was how to turn his enormous electoral support into something more durable. Because his own electoral support was so much greater than his party's, Nixon began to question the usefulness of continuing to work with a party for which he felt little personal enthusiasm. Perhaps, he considered, he should build a brand new party from scratch. As we have seen with Eisenhower, the difficulties involved in grafting the president's broader support onto his party often lead to third-party ruminations. Nixon entertained such considerations with his characteristic shrewdness and eventually dropped the idea with his characteristic pragmatism.

A New Party?

As early as April 1972, Nixon began to toy with the idea of anointing his Treasury secretary, Texas Democrat John Connally, as his successor. He began discussing with Haldeman and Ehrlichman the idea that "the P[resident] and Connally, after the election, could move to build a new party, the Independent Conservative Party, or something of that sort, that would bring in a coalition of southern Democrats and other conservative Democrats, along with the middle road to conservative Republicans." But there were practical difficulties in starting a third party: for example, any new party would need to include both "Rockefeller and Reagan on the Republican spectrum" as well as many Democrats. "By structuring it right," however, Nixon might "develop a new majority party. Under a new name. Get control of the Congress without an election, simply by the realignment, and make a truly historic change in the entire American political structure." Connally would clearly "emerge as the candidate for the new party in '76, and the P[resident] would strongly back him in that."[117]

Conversations with Connally continued through the summer, and by September, the president was meeting with CREEP's youth vote director, Ken Rietz, to discuss "some post-election ideas in the area of wanting to mobilize a new majority and a new establishment. [Nixon] was counting on [Rietz] for a plan to lead the development of that kind of a thing," Haldeman wrote.[118] Though Nixon had indicated his openness to a new party, Rietz came back to the president in November with a "reorganization plan for the RNC," drawn up in collaboration with Senator Bill Brock. This proposal became the blueprint for the ambitious and wide-ranging party-building program of Nixon's second term.

Rietz and Brock suggested that the RNC was, in fact, the best available vehicle for building the new majority, so long as it became entirely focused on "achieving a national 'New Majority' identification" and "follow[ed] the creativity and pragmatism of Richard Nixon." This would involve some re-structuring of the party organization, beginning with the chairman's office. The new RNC chairman should become the president's "full-time political staff director," and all national political activities—including those of the con-gressional campaign committees—should fall under the chairman's leadership. The chairman would take the lead in changing the philosophy of the party "from a smaller, well-organized elite group to an open organization that wel-comes all and questions none," and he "must have access to the President, for without that there will be no power, and of course, no respect."[119]

The key to building the New Majority through the party was to strengthen the RNC's organizational capacities and equip it to focus on candidate re-cruitment and campaign management. Electing "new majority" candidates was the paramount goal: once they were elected as Republicans, "the Amer-ican people will respond naturally by increasing their identification with the party." To be absolutely clear, Brock and Rietz emphasized: "*the road to ma-jority status for the Republican Party is through the electoral process, not the identification process . . . the new majority will become the Republican Party only after the individual candidates are elected with the support of the new majority.*"[120]

Nixon's team, they suggested, should draw up a two-year plan to win control of the House and Senate by targeting "75 winnable House and 10 winnable Senate campaigns." To win those races, the RNC should "prepare campaign plans for those races, recruit the candidates, train campaign di-rectors and supervise the campaigns." The keys to victory involved basic or-ganizational techniques: "candidate selection; developing a plan; efficient organization; recruitment of volunteers; identifying the vote; registering fa-vorable voters; turning out the vote." If the RNC were restructured to be wholly "candidate-oriented," they wrote, the GOP could become "the majority party" in 1974.[121]

This practical, down-to-earth plan to win more public offices turned Nixon away from his flirtation with starting a third party and toward the question of "how to implement it."[122] Talk of starting a "new party" continued, but with a concrete plan in the works to build the New Majority for and with the Republican Party, Nixon's conversations became increasingly centered on how to "use the Republican Party as a base, but add to it the New Majority."[123] The problem of how to graft the president's personal majority of support onto his minority party seemed to have resolved itself simply through Nixon's ac-knowledgment that Rietz and Brock's party-building program offered the best chance of achieving his goal.

Remaking the RNC

Nixon immodestly hoped to initiate a full-scale partisan realignment, and now believed that this grand vision began with the "nuts and bolts" of his party. To be sure, he also pursued this objective through other means as well, including the establishment of new programs for public liaison at the White House, the initiation of new policies, the use of new rhetoric, and the appointment of new personnel.[124] Yet Nixon was keenly aware that without a strong organizational foundation, his New Majority coalition would evaporate once he left office. He needed to establish a secure party structure in order to perpetuate the new majority in the future.

As Nixon contemplated his place in history, he acknowledged the inherent limits of policy accomplishments, in and of themselves. The kind of historical legacy he sought went beyond changes in government policy. He told his close advisors that a great deal had already been accomplished, and yet it was not enough. His secret Oval Office taping system recorded him saying, sarcastically: "We've done China, we've done Russia. We've done the campaign. So what's next? Huh? What's next? Well we're going to solve the black-white problem, right? Or maybe the transportation problem? Or maybe we'll find an answer to welfare? And everybody's going to jump up and down and say isn't that just, just great?" Nixon doubted that such second-term policy accomplishments—even in the important areas of race relations and welfare—would secure the place in history he desired. He continued: "See, we've just gotta realize we're looking at a very different kind of a game here, you know. . . . That's why your idea of maybe a new, different party structure becomes important."[125]

The first move, as Brock and Rietz suggested, was to install the right chairman. Whereas Harry Dent was Nixon's chief party-building deputy during his first term, the president now intended to follow Rietz and Brock's plan and establish that role inside the National Committee itself. Nixon wanted a chairman who was young, well-respected by all segments of the party, and capable of spearheading the entire party-building effort. His first choice was George Bush, then ambassador to the United Nations. He invited Bush to Camp David and explained his objectives: he had a "New concept re: RNC," he said. According to Ehrlichman's point-by-point notes, Nixon told Bush they had "2 yrs to build Rep pty nationwide." Dent was going to be leaving the White House, and now the "RNC ch[airman] will be president's . . . top political advisor." As RNC chair, Bush would be included in Cabinet meetings, and the congressional campaign committees would "pull close to Natl Chrmn."[126]

Nixon explained that he "care[d] a great deal re: future of Rep Pty." Nixon received almost 61 percent of the vote and Republican members of Congress only 38.2 percent, while only 24 percent of the electorate identified themselves as Republicans: the "president never higher, RNC never lower," Nixon said. Nixon wanted to transfer his majority onto the party; but to "fold RNC

& [presiden]cy" together for this purpose, the party needed someone like Bush to lead the effort.[127] The Republican Party had been fielding "poor candidates," Nixon believed, and he wanted his new chairman to focus primarily on "cand[idate] search." Bush had his sights set on a higher government appointment—such as deputy secretary of state or undersecretary of the Treasury—but he agreed to take the RNC chairmanship if it was what Nixon wanted.[128] Nixon told Bush to explain in his acceptance speech: "You should say yes . . . you've discussed it with the president, and with great reluctance in one sense you leave, on the other hand, this is a great challenge, you want to undertake it. You particularly like the emphasis on the need to build, to broaden the base of our party, and for the greatest candidate search in history, okay?"[129]

The conversation continued over several days, as Nixon "talked about putting together for the Republicans the new majority, mentioning specifically Sons of Italy, Knights of Columbus, Labor leaders, teamsters, seafarers, and many other groups," Bush recorded in his diary. The president also "spent some time dwelling on his aspirations for getting the South together," and noted the difficulty of being a Republican in that region.[130]

Once Bush accepted, Nixon spread the word to other party leaders. He invited Gerald Ford, a strong ally in the House, to Camp David to share his plans. Nixon's aide recorded:

> The President discussed his view of a new RNC dedicated to campaign management and candidate recruitment. The President expressed his wish that there be Republican candidates in every single District in 1974, and that the GOP should concentrate on very young challengers. He indicated that no candidate should run for the House the first time who is over age 40, or for the Senate over 50. Ford agreed. . . . The President emphasized the need for the GOP to build upon the "new majority."[131]

Throughout the transition period, Nixon continued to emphasize to his assistants that the way to build "the new majority" must be through "candidate development" and better techniques for campaign management.[132] In a private meeting with RNC cochairman Anne Armstrong, for example, Nixon explained that the RNC during his second term should devote all of its attention to supporting state party organizations and recruiting quality "New Majority" candidates. By necessity, the party had been wholly focused in the previous year on the presidential election, he said. But going forward, its attention could shift completely to emphasize party building:

> Right now, this is the beauty of it now, you see—during last [year], naturally you had the election. Everything had to be concentrated on that. . . . But now, all they've got to do is to try to elect members—not just to the House and Senate, but even State Legislatures—that, of course, is a matter of state organizations. But it all gets down to a

new spirit. They can't go with the old hats anymore. Isn't that it? They can't go with the old hats. And they can't go with people who don't know how to talk . . . to the Democrats.[133]

In his inaugural chairman's address at the RNC, Bush explained that he would have a close partnership with the president. "We need a strong Republican National Committee working closely with the President as head of the party," Bush said, "and I am going to try to be that kind of Chairman." His strong relationship with Nixon, Bush explained, offered a critical advantage in the quest to build the new majority for the party. "The $64 question," Bush noted, is "how do we encourage this new majority that voted so overwhelmingly for President Nixon" to support Republican candidates? The answer, as Nixon had said, was to improve candidate recruitment and enhance the organizational support the RNC could provide to campaigns, Bush explained:

> The President's magnificent majority must welcome in a broader and broader-based Party. . . . We must identify good, articulate candidates; then we have to support them—support them by having strong organizations working, support with money. The RNC is going to continue to help the States with programs. We must provide the States with a wide range of research and demographic data, financing, election support. And we must offer the States the very best in candidate recruitment techniques.[134]

Nixon lived up to his promise to make Bush a prominent figure in his second administration by giving him a seat at Cabinet meetings and singing his praises. Bush noted in his diary that he was now "sharing the reception room with the President in the EOB. There is great symbolism for this . . . there is a great message in 'proximity'"[135] Thus, the first constructive move of Nixon's second term was appointing George Bush to the RNC, elevating his stature, and empowering him to reorient the operational focus of the RNC.

Using CREEP for Party Building

In early February 1973, Nixon and Bush began to discuss how "excess" CREEP funds could, legally and strategically, be transferred to the RNC and put "toward building on the new majority to elect GOP candidates."[136] In addition to using the funds for party-building purposes, Nixon wanted Bush to restore harmony with the party's regular activist base and ensure their continued assistance in party building at the local level. In particular, he was told to keep in touch with field men and to continue to build relationships with state chairmen.[137] Nixon also wanted to lend a hand himself, and asked Bush to create a list of key party leaders who he could "be in touch with periodically, either in meetings or by phone," to support the party-building efforts.[138]

Watergate revelations began to pour in during March 1973.[139] On April 19, Bush noted in his diary that the "grassroots" of the party had begun to "stir," and the "level of concern had mounted considerably."[140] By May 1973, the Watergate investigation had rendered the CREEP funds tainted, and it was becoming increasingly clear that CREEP's accounts should "go out of business as soon as possible."[141] Though it was possible to transfer about $650,000 to the RNC, Bush decided that such a move would infect the RNC with the Watergate scandal and was therefore not a good idea.[142] "The President has told me that he wants the assets at CRP to be used to help elect Republicans to office in 1974 (and, I presume, 1976). He specifically stated that he wanted the money to be used to help elect non-incumbents to Congress in '74," Bush wrote. But under the circumstances, the transfer could not be accomplished "without getting the RNC involved in several of the lawsuits pending against the CREP." Thus, Bush proposed to "lay claim" to the money and indicate that the funds would go to the RNC "*after* the lawsuits are cleared up."[143] Nixon agreed with the plan.[144]

Watergate cast a shadow over important fund-raising initiatives planned for 1973 as well. Bush proposed another "Salute to the President"–style dinner to highlight the New Majority project and raise funds for the national and state parties. The dinners would benefit the party in several ways, Bush said: in addition to publicizing "the concept of 'New Majority Campaign '74' . . . it would be a vehicle for the RNC to provide a service to the participating states . . . it would provide the states with much needed cash well in advance of the campaigns next year . . . [and] build a new bridge of mutual trust and support between the RNC and the individual state committees."[145] The president's prestige soon plummeted, however, and the dinners were never held.

Nevertheless, Bush proceeded to develop new systems of accounting, fund-raising, and fund expenditures for the RNC to "save some [money] in '73 for the 'New Majority' push in '74." He hired Ken Rietz to focus exclusively on developing a "master 'New Majority' plan including budget." Thanks to his efforts to streamline communications and administrative processes across the various Republican campaign committees, he was confident that going into 1974, the party would have a "well coordinated, non-overlapping, central campaign using resources of House and Senate Committees and RNC."[146] Despite the unfavorable political climate, Bush felt he was able to make constructive changes at an organizational level.

Watergate may have slowed the flow of resources into the RNC, but it did not prevent the party from benefiting from the voter lists compiled by CREEP over the course of the 1972 campaign. When he left the RNC, Tom Evans recommended to Bush that the "computer lists compiled by the Committee for the Re-election of the President should be utilized as a tool to help build the Republican Party," and Bush had scribbled "Yes" as if to remind himself for later.[147] Though the CREEP funds were now tainted, the CREP Voter Registration Data Base, with magnetic tapes with data on over 30 million registered voters in eleven states, was not. This data storage project was extensive and quite valuable: it contained sophisticated maps and individual-level voter data replete with socioeconomic characteristics and historical data available in different formats.[148] The RNC took hold of the database, updated it, and made it available to any state chairman who was willing to work with the RNC on a "list maintenance program."[149] The voter lists were thus put toward enhancing the Republican Party's voter mobilization efforts in future elections: CREEP, the ultimate example of presidential party predation, was thus turned to constructive party-building purposes.

An Altered Institutional Context

Though Nixon was obviously quite distracted with the Watergate scandal during most of 1973 and 1974, the strong push he had given to the New Majority party-building program in late 1972 and early 1973 began to produce real organizational changes by the time he left office. By setting constructive party-building priorities, choosing talented people like Bush, and empowering them to execute his vision, Nixon ensured that party building would continue even as his presidency unraveled; indeed, he set in motion a sequence of organizational developments that would outlast his presidency.

In the 1973–74 period, Nixon's team at the RNC began to make critical investments in the party's human capital, in its campaign services capacities, and in its outreach programs. The RNC's new political director, Eddie Mahe Jr., for example, took responsibility for running a dozen weeklong sessions to train 150 future campaign managers in 1973.[150] Called the "RNC Campaign Management College," the effort was said to be "longer, more intense, and more complete than any previous program of its type." Campaign management experts took attendees on field trips and trained them in a wide range of campaign management issues, including campaign finance, using computer technology in campaigns, media relations, and so on. Upon graduation, the students were paired up with congressional, senatorial, or gubernatorial campaigns.[151]

In 1974, the emphasis on cultivating the party's "foot soldiers" was intensified under the leadership of new RNC cochair Mary Louise Smith of Iowa.[152] Smith's main project was "Grassroots '74," a series of thirteen one-day training seminars held across the country throughout the summer to teach the basics of identifying, registering, and turning out voters.[153] The program brought in almost 2,000 attendees, more than 80 percent "active workers within the Republican Party structure." The initiative, in other words, built the party's "in-house" human capital: those attending were the very people who, in the coming elections, would "implement the techniques gained." The response to Grassroots '74 was "outstanding," Smith said: "Press coverage, excellent; enthusiasm, high; determination, solid."[154]

Campaign management training was a primary emphasis of the New Majority party-building program at the RNC, but so was providing direct assistance to local party organizations and candidates. Bush encouraged party leaders to be proactive and "make maximum use of our RNC resources. We must build this party in an organizational sense to unprecedented heights," he said.[155] The RNC offered "task forces" for state parties that requested them, and promised to "bring the most specialized kind of expertise available into your state to deal specifically with your problems."[156]

Other programs aimed to strengthen the party's capacity to recruit activists and mobilize New Majority voters. A series of New Majority Workshops explicitly set out to consolidate the party's gains among those "who came over to us in such great numbers in support of President Nixon last year." The workshops were designed to share best practices among those Republican activists who had successfully worked with "the ethnic voters, Spanish speaking voters, senior citizens, youths, blacks, and the blue collar laborers" in the past and to discuss methods of "involving them in party activities." Held across the country in November and December 1973, the workshops were thus designed to teach the "effective use of issues and techniques" to appeal to the "special voter groups."[157]

The decision to turn away from the African American community in 1972 was evidently reversed after Nixon secured his reelection: now, reaching out to black voters was envisioned as an important part of the New Majority strategy. In February 1974, Nixon met with Bush and the head of the RNC's Black Political Division to discuss how to "secure more Black participation in the Republican Party." Nixon was pleased to see that the participation of blacks in the party "is being sought after and that they are being welcomed into the 'New Majority' as equal participants."[158]

Despite his many obvious distractions during this period, Nixon continued to emphasize the importance of recruiting strong candidates. After a meeting with Nixon in the spring of 1974, for example, Bush wrote that "he is tremendously candidate-oriented. He kept talking about it. At that meeting there was no chance to point out that some of our candidate problems were related to Watergate." Nevertheless, "the president felt that I was doing a good job."[159]

The cumulative effects of such party-building efforts are nicely illustrated in the transitionless transition from Nixon to Ford. As we will see in the next chapter, because of Nixon's party building, Ford did not have to start from scratch or overturn his predecessor's handiwork: he could take the leaders, organizations, and party-building initiatives he inherited and expand upon them during his new administration.

■

The preceding pages have demonstrated that Nixon engaged in a wide range of party-building activities throughout the course of his five-plus years in the White House. Along each of six dimensions of party activity, he either personally initiated or lent his direct support to a wide variety of constructive organization-building initiatives (see table 4.1). His efforts also illuminate some of the more distinctive characteristics of presidential party building as a general phenomenon: (1) the powers and resources of the White House are invaluable when put to use on behalf of party-building efforts; (2) by

Table 4.1   Nixon's Party Building

Provide campaign services	Build human capital	Recruit candidates	Mobilize voters	Finance party operations	Support internal activities
Southern strategy (1969+)	Southern strategy (1969+)	Southern strategy (1969+)	Southern strategy (1969+)	"Continuing pilgrimage" (1969)	Elevate stature of southern state party chairmen (1969+)
Mission '70s (1969+)	Subsidize African-American recruiters (1969–1970)	Mission '70s (1969+)	Mission '70s (1969+)	Southern Strategy (1969+)	Mission '70s (1969+)
New Majority Campaign '74 (1973+)	Mission '70s (1969+)	New Majority Campaign '74 (1973+)	Subsidize African-American recruiters (1969–70)	Direct mail and sustaining member programs (1969+)	Morton's task forces (1969–70)
Grassroots '74 (1974)	Evans's field forces (1971–72)		Project Blitz (1971–72)	Salute to the President (1971)	Evans's task forces (1971–72)
	Campaign management seminars (1971–72)		Outreach to young Republicans (1971)	Evans's field forces (1971–72)	Regional liaisons (1971–72)
	Field recruiting (1973)		Target '72 (1972)	CREEP funds for party building (1973)	Bush's organizational changes (1973+)
	RNC Campaign Management College (1973+)		CREEP voter registration database (1973–74)	Salute '73 (1973)	New Majority Campaign '74 (1973+)
	Grassroots '74 (1974)		New Majority Workshops (1973–74)	New Majority budget (1973+)	Bush's task forces (1973+)
			Grassroots '74 (1974)		
			RNC Black Political Division (1974)		

Table 4.2   Nixon's Party Predation

Provide campaign services	Build human capital	Recruit candidates	Mobilize voters	Finance party operations	Support internal activities
CREEP (1972)				Operation Townhouse (1970)	
				CREEP (1972)	

strengthening the RNC's coordinative capacities, presidential party building has contributed to the transformation of the Republican Party into a vertically integrated "service" organization; (3) minority-party presidents will not engage in party building at all times or at any cost, and occasionally their larger majority-building purposes will dictate different strategies in the short term; (4) presidential party building aims to use organization-building initiatives to transfer the president's broader base of support onto the party.

The weak competitive standing of the Republican Party served as a strong motivation for Nixon's party building throughout his time in office. Indeed, the impulse to alter his competitive political environment in a durable way—to build a veritably new political majority—propelled each and every one of his party interactions, including Operation Townhouse and CREEP (see table 4.2). With respect to his many party-building initiatives, Nixon did not seek to strengthen the Republican Party for its own sake; in fact, he felt ambivalent, at best, about his party. His primary goal was to expand his party's coalition along the lines of what he called the New Majority that supported him, so that he might leave a historical legacy of his own designs. The Republican Party organization was simply deemed to be the best vehicle through which to build that new majority and ensure its longevity after he left the White House.

Ultimately, Nixon failed to realize his vision of the new Republican majority, and his party-building initiatives failed to prevent major Republican losses in the 1974 elections. No amount of party building, it seemed, could compensate for the electoral devastation wrought by Watergate. Yet Nixon's party building did leave an important organizational legacy. The people, programs, and structures did not disappear when Nixon resigned; in fact, their very existence made it more likely that Nixon's successor would find it in his interest to continue party building.

5

The Politics of Addition | Gerald R. Ford

It can be argued by some that because our national problems are so serious we should not be wasting time on the problems of our party—or any other party—yet it is precisely because of our national problems that it is essential to look to our party and its revitalization everywhere.

—President Gerald R. Ford[1]

When Gerald Ford took the oath of office on August 9, 1974, the Republican Party's competitive standing was at an all-time low. In the party's worst show-ing in the history of the Gallup poll, less than a quarter of the American public identified with the GOP.[2] In the November 1974 midterm elections, Republicans lost forty-three House seats and six Senate seats, leaving them with a mere 33 percent of House seats and thirty-eight Senate seats. The Re-publican "farm team" at the state level nearly disappeared: Republicans lost control of fifteen statehouses and six governorships and held only 32 percent of legislative seats and 24 percent of governorships nationwide, their lowest share in modern history. Some Republicans worried that their party was on the verge of becoming "extinct."[3] The party's weak competitive position was of particular concern for Ford: as the first unelected president, he had no electoral base of his own. More than any other minority-party president, his party's problems were his problems.[4]

The Republican Party may have been stuck in the "perpetual minority," but at an organizational level, it was on the move.[5] Though party workers felt on the "defense" rather than on the "offense" during the tumultuous summer of 1974, New Majority party-building programs continued apace.[6] When Ford assumed the presidency, campaign management training seminars, outreach efforts, candidate recruitment programs, activist enrollment initiatives, field operations, and voter mobilization drives were in full swing. Even as Nixon resigned in disgrace, the party-building initiatives he had launched over a year and a half earlier continued without interruption. Ford immediately proclaimed his support for these programs, insisted upon their continuation, and launched a number of new party-building innovations. By the end of his brief stint in the White House, Ford had not only bridged the party-building work of the past with the party building of the future, but he had made im-portant contributions of his own to his party's organizational development.

Ford had many reasons to continue party building. Some were specific to him as an individual, and others he shared with all minority-party presi-dents. Whereas Eisenhower and Nixon had few personal reasons for engag-ing in party building, Ford had many. First, his political identity, as well as his legitimacy as president, rested on his many years of dedicated, disinterested service to the Republican Party: whether viewed as a "party hack" or as an "orthodox Republican politician," Ford clearly had a deep and abiding commitment to the Republican Party.[7] Second, nurturing his party organization was consistent with a pledge he made in the spring of 1974 to revitalize the party in the wake of CREEP; and third, party building offered a means of building support among party chairmen, particularly in the South, whose support Ford needed to fend off Reagan's challenge for the nomination in 1976.[8]

Yet even if Ford did not have so many personal reasons for engaging in party building, the Republican Party's unusually weak competitive standing likely would have motivated him to act in precisely the same ways. Notwithstanding the shadow of Watergate, his party's deep minorities suggested that his presidency was likely to be temporary. Whatever he managed to accomplish while in office looked to be a historical aberration—a mere interlude between periods of Democratic dominance—unless he took steps to improve his party's competitive standing. With little chance to leave a policy legacy of his own design, party building offered Ford a particularly promising way to establish a meaningful political legacy for himself.

As we have seen, neither Eisenhower nor Nixon shared Ford's deep personal commitment to the Republican Party. In fact, their proximate motivations for party building were as different from one another's as they were from Ford's. But the tie that binds these three very different men together is that they all shared an interest in reviving their party's flagging electoral fortunes. They all wanted to build a new majority for the Republican Party that bore their imprint. In truth, Ford's partisan background was probably more similar to Lyndon Johnson's or John F. Kennedy's than to his fellow Republican presidents, yet neither Johnson nor Kennedy adopted a constructive approach to their party organization. With deep and durable party majorities, neither Democrat perceived a need to strengthen his party's organizational capacities. In contrast, every minority-party president, irrespective of his personal background or proximate motivations, was drawn to party building.

In this chapter, we also observe the emergence of another factor—inherited institutional conditions—that exerts an increasingly powerful influence on presidential behavior over time. In this and subsequent chapters, we will see that repeated rounds of party building incrementally and cumulatively created the institutional conditions in which successive Republican presidents would find it in their interest to continue party building. For Ford, the Republican Party's unusually weak competitive standing was probably enough to motivate his party-building behavior. But more than his predecessors, the condition of his inherited organization shaped the choices he made. In the Reagan and George H. W. Bush presidencies, we will see this factor become increasingly significant. By the time George W. Bush assumed the presidency in 2001, the legacies of past party-building efforts could be seen to exert a direct influence on the president's behavior.

		Party Building						Party Predation					
		C	H	R	V	F	I	C	H	R	V	F	I
Republicans	Eisenhower	•	•	•	•	•	•						
	Nixon	•	•	•	•	•	•	•				•	
	Ford	•	•	•	•	•	•						
	Reagan	•	•	•	•	•	•						
	Bush	•	•	•		•	•						
Democrats	Kennedy			•	•			•	•		•	•	•
	Johnson							•	•		•	•	•
	Carter							•	•	•	•	•	•
	Clinton (1st term)							•	•	•	•	•	•
	Clinton (2nd term)	•	•		•	•	•						

C=Provide campaign services, H=Build human capital, R=Recruit candidates,
V=Mobilize voters, F=Finance party operations, I=Support internal activities

Figure 5.1. Ford's Party Interactions

The following pages emphasize the competitive environmental and institutional factors that shaped Ford's behavior while examining his many efforts to strengthen the GOP along each of the six dimensions of party activity (see figure 5.1). In the course of this examination, this chapter also aims to elaborate upon four characteristics of presidential party building as a more general phenomenon: (1) presidential party building is shaped by the "carryover" effect of institutional structures, human capital, and strategic priorities from one period to the next; (2) fund-raising is one of the primary ways presidents can help to build their party; (3) presidents can make an important contribution to the institutional development of their party by integrating it into their campaigns; (4) presidential party building is fundamentally geared toward the expansion of the party and the addition of new groups to the coalition: it is, at its core, the "politics of addition," not subtraction.

Institutional Reproduction in the GOP

Thanks to Ford's transitionless transition to the presidency, the mechanisms of institutional reproduction in the Republican Party—the pieces that "carry over" from one round of party building to the next and shape each new president's menu of choices—are on prominent display. What we observe as more subtle continuities in the longer transitions between other administrations is much more obvious and striking in the sudden transition from Nixon to Ford. As we will see, the party's *institutional structures,* its *human capital,* and its *strategic priorities* were transferred wholesale from Nixon to Ford; they shaped Ford's choices and were then reshaped by his incremental contributions in each area. He did not start with a blank slate, nor did he finish the job; but he did help to further institutionalize the Republican Party's "service" capacities, develop its human capital, and reinforce its strategic priorities.

The first continuity involved the leadership team at the RNC. After the Watergate debacle, Bush was eager to leave his post. But before he resigned, he recommended Mary Louise Smith, his cochairman, as his replacement.[9] Smith had a sterling reputation as a dedicated and effective nuts-and-bolts party builder. Before becoming RNC cochairman and directing the successful Grassroots '74 initiative, she founded Iowa's Woman's Political Caucus and served as a member of the RNC for ten years. She was viewed as a "grassroots specialist" who believed in the organizational side of politics; she was also well liked and widely respected within national party circles.

When Ford selected Smith as the new chairman, he emphasized that he wanted her to continue leading initiatives like Grassroots '74 (described in the previous chapter) that would "provide people at the local level with the knowledge and techniques to run their own campaigns."[10] He promised Smith unprecedented access to the White House and committed himself to working closely with his party:[11]

> Among all my responsibilities to the American people, none is more important to me than the leadership of my Party. . . . I intend to work closely with the leadership of the Republican Party, to involve myself in its affairs to the extent I can, and to delegate to the Republican National Committee the principal role in all future campaigns—which may just possibly include one of my own in 1976.[12]

He instructed his staff to be open and accessible to provide whatever assistance Smith asked for.[13] Smith took him up on his offer and met with him on a monthly basis; a long paper trail evidences their frequent communications.[14]

The close working relationship established between Ford and Smith illustrates an important distinction between the typical Republican and Democratic approach to matters of party politics. Ford established the same collaborative relationship with Smith that Eisenhower and Nixon established with their chairmen; all three empowered their chairmen to leverage the White House in the service of their party-building projects. As we shall see, Reagan and Bush treated their chairmen in precisely the same way. By authorizing their chairmen to act on their behalf and charging them with expansive party-building responsibilities, Republican presidents enhanced the stature, authority, and independent operating capacities of the RNC. Democrats, in contrast, either isolated their chairmen or kept them on a tight leash. Kennedy and Johnson had a distant relationship with John Bailey, their DNC chairman, and gave him little, if any, support; Carter and Clinton were personally closer to their chairmen but did not authorize them to undertake party-building projects.[15] The strong relationship Ford established with Smith in the fall of 1974, in contrast, was critical to the many party-building activities that followed.

Investing in Institutional Structures

In October 1974, Ford's top assistants Dean Burch and Donald Rumsfeld began a series of meetings with Smith to discuss a long-range "party-building program" to continue enhancing the party's "service" functions.[16] In an editorial for the RNC publication *First Monday*, Ford offered his full-throated endorsement:

> I have reviewed the program, and I have talked with Mary Louise about her plans for the RNC and the entire Republican Party over the next two years. I am confident that this is the kind of approach we need to bring about a resurgence of Republicanism. . . . Mary Louise has focused on the nuts and bolts of politics. Our emphasis must be on organization and person-to-person contact. These are the surest ways I know to build a winning party. I congratulate Mary Louise on this initiative and offer her my total support as we work together toward 1976.[17]

The first step involved reorganizing the National Committee staff structure and appointing a new executive director to handle the day-to-day tasks of running the committee. For this role Smith looked no further than to Bush's political director, Eddie Mahe Jr., who had coordinated the Campaign Management College and New Majority Workshops in 1973–74.[18] Like Ford's promotion of Smith, Mahe's promotion literally embodied the carryover effect of prior rounds of party building. Not only did the party-building programs and their objectives transfer over from Nixon's administration to Ford's, but so did Eddie Mahe Jr., Mary Louise Smith, and most of their staff.

Ford's party-building team continued to emphasize the importance of building institutional structures that could vertically integrate party operations. These were the same priorities that Nixon's party-building team had emphasized during the 1969–74 period; indeed, Smith wrote that "most of the above represents a reactivation or intensification" of what was already under way.[19] The idea was to equip the national committee to provide institutional support and services to state and local party organizations and to candidates directly, thus becoming a veritable "party in service," as political scientist John Aldrich has called it.[20]

The centerpiece of the effort involved hiring ten full-time regional field directors, each of whom would be responsible for approximately five different states.[21] Employed by the RNC, these directors would be the main points of contact between the national committee and "party organizations, candidate organizations, Republican office-holders, special voter groups and Party auxiliaries." They would work closely with state party officials to design and implement new organizational development programs and provide hands-on assistance to campaigns.[22] The program was "aimed at helping every one of the 50 states build a strong, aggressive party organization."[23] In 1976, the RNC's regional field director program claimed to have helped 192 campaigns nationwide.[24]

In her opening remarks as chairman of the RNC, Smith stressed that the effectiveness of the support-service model of the Republican Party depended on its application at the local level. This model respected the autonomy of local party leaders but also asked much of them:

> From the national level, we can and will develop and offer programs. We can recommend, we can suggest, we can support, we can encourage, we can instruct, and we can lead, but just as we cannot tell states how to elect their delegates, or how to run their business, neither can we mandate more active and effective precinct, county, city, and state organizations. This is up to you.[25]

From Ford's standpoint, vertically integrating the party's operations served a dual purpose. Because Ford intended to rely in large part on the RNC for his own presidential bid in 1976, his party-building programs simultaneously developed "the management and support capability necessary to undertake the 1976 presidential campaign while continuing to provide services to candidates at other levels."[26] Ford's "solid program of party building" was thus designed both to bring the Republican Party out of the minority and to further his own election prospects; like Eisenhower and Nixon before him, Ford's party-building efforts were instrumental and developmental at the same time.

Investing in the party's infrastructure also served the all-important goal of recruiting strong candidates. While Nixon prioritized candidate recruitment, Watergate had made strong candidates hesitant to run. Ford recognized that one of his most pressing tasks was to make the idea of running for office as a Republican attractive again. Ford invited the RNC membership to the White House and offered his personal help:

> We have to find good candidates for local office, for State office and for national office, and the Congress particularly. Let me assure you that in the months ahead I will help in any way I can to get good candidates locally or statewide or for the Congress, and once you have selected them in whatever way you do in your respective States, I will be proud to campaign with them. This is the way we build a party.[27]

But Ford also did more than offer his personal support. He recognized that an effective candidate recruitment program required a strong party infrastructure: if Republican organizations could demonstrate to prospective candidates that well-trained campaign managers were ready to assist them, that plenty of campaign funds were flowing through the organization and were ready to be applied to their campaigns, that sophisticated issue research and voter information would be easily accessible to them, and that an RNC-sponsored field force was already implementing programs to register and mobilize voters in the area, then recruiting those candidates would become much easier. Investing in the party's organizational capacities, in short, would help to attract potential candidates to the GOP.[28]

Ford's party-building team thus set out to develop new technologies and service capabilities to assist candidates with their campaigns. Thanks to Bush's efforts to bring CREEP's 1972 precinct-by-precinct election data file to the RNC, party leaders were now able to add to it 1974 election return data "from every precinct in the nation." Merging election data from the past two cycles with Census Bureau data, lists of registered voters, telephone lists, and even motor vehicle registration lists, the RNC aimed to provide useful, accessible data for all Republican candidates and GOP state parties. By making new investments in technologies and research capabilities, analyses of "ticket-splitting, voter turnout and other studies can be produced for any county, city, and Congressional district within the nation," the RNC announced. These voter lists were made available for campaigns to "communicate personally with large numbers of voters by mail, door-to-door, or by telephone."[29]

Smith also made investments in the party's survey research capabilities, building directly upon a "pilot-project" Bush had conducted in 1974. The idea, she explained, was to offer polling data as a "new service" for the 1975–76 campaigns—to provide "professional quality research to candidates and party organizations at a fraction of the cost of professional polls." Together, new research data, individual voter data, and new polling data could be offered to candidates and party organizations at a whopping 90 percent discount.[30] While the new investments in research, polling, and data collection would cost the RNC a pretty penny, candidates could not afford such services on their own: by leveraging the president's fund-raising muscle, the RNC could make the primary investment and create savings across the whole party organization.[31] This effort to share sophisticated research and data with Republican candidates stands in stark contrast to a similar DNC program, which was designed under Carter to make money off of Democratic candidates rather than to save them money (see chapter 10). Nevertheless, by investing in the party's infrastructure, Ford's team found that it could develop a platform from which to support a wide variety of activities, from candidate recruitment to campaign assistance to fund-raising to opposition research. Investments in the party's human capital had a similarly wide-ranging impact.

Developing Human Capital

A major carryover effect of party building involves the development of human capital in the party. Whereas infrastructural investments have an inherent "stickiness" (computer terminals and data files, for example, once created, do not tend to go anywhere), developing human capital—investing in the skills, expertise, and experiences of party workers—requires the persistent effort of party leaders to repeatedly conduct training programs and hold educational seminars. Yet investments in human capital also contain the seeds of their own reproduction: once trained, party professionals tend to stick around, assume positions of leadership, and reinforce the party's commitments in the future.

Ford made an important contribution to the development of human capital in the Republican Party by sponsoring multiple training programs. Most prominently, his party-building team expanded upon the Campaign Management College (CMC) spearheaded by Mahe in 1973–74. By training dozens of capable campaign managers in 1974, the College's first run was credited with helping to prevent the GOP's midterm "rout" from being worse that it might have been.[32] In 1975, the basic structure of the college was kept the same, but those who were trained in earlier rounds now became the new teachers. Under Ford, the college was able to reduce its use of outside consultants and instead began to rely on the party's "in-house" expertise. Instructors were primarily drawn from the National Committee's political staff, who averaged eight years of campaign management experience; consultants were only brought in for specialized training sessions.[33] Far from a lecture course, the college was a "workshop where the students can develop their own strategies, plans, and schedules" and review the "latest techniques and tools available."[34] The core curriculum remained the same as it was under Nixon, covering "campaign strategy, planning, tactics and organization, targeting, and press relations, advertising, and direct mail . . . candidate scheduling, fundraising, budgeting and cash management, opposition research, issues research and polling."[35] Graduates became "a cadre of qualified campaign managers" ready to be placed in congressional or gubernatorial elections in 1976.[36]

The CMC was expanded with a new session, called Advanced Campaign Management, for graduates from the previous year's college who had "effectively functioned" in 1974 campaigns. A third innovation involved a program focused exclusively on winning majorities in state legislatures. Representing the "middle portion" of the yearlong training program, the additional seminars stressed that while the national party could "design and offer programs, provide guidance and leadership," the "real job of rebuilding the party" happened at the local level.[37]

College Republicans also ran parallel training school programs on "youth organization and middle-to-upper level campaign management"—and the College Republicans Fieldmen School, founded in 1971, claimed to have trained 850 students since its commencement. Karl Rove, later chief political strategist for President George W. Bush, was the chairman of the College Republican National Committee and a noted teacher at its seminars. The young Republicans emphasized "nuts-and-bolts political work, including scheduling and advance, press relations, research."[38] Ford met with the College Republicans as well as the Teen Age Republicans to encourage their efforts to grow the Republican "farm team."[39]

The flagship CMC received such overwhelming interest from party activists that its initial plan to hold ten sessions could not satisfy demand: Smith added five additional sessions in the spring of 1976. The National Republican Congressional Committee (NRCC) funded additional instructors and sponsored scholarships to pay the travel, room, and board expenses of the students. Representative Guy Vander Jagt, chairman of the NRCC, noted that the college had established itself as a "fundamental part of the overall effort to gain control of the House of Representatives." The college continued to develop its curriculum, and by the middle of 1976 it was running an intensive campaign simulation where each student ran the hypothetical campaign of "Bob Warwick for Congress." The students learned to deal with "constant harassment from the press, a steering committee which could not be satisfied, fundraising difficulties—all on only two to three hours of sleep a night."[40] By October 1976, more than 150 graduates of the CMC were "in the field" running campaigns.[41]

These human-capital building initiatives replicated earlier efforts launched under Nixon, fine-tuned them, and expanded them. In this way, despite his short time in office, Ford managed to link together in a continuous stream earlier rounds of party building with later rounds of party building. These trained party activists and professionals were not only available to help with Ford's 1976 election campaign, but they remained in the party, assumed positions of leadership, and continued party building after Ford left the White House. During the period between 1977 and 1981, RNC chairman Bill Brock continued to invest in these very same human-capital building initiatives.[42]

Reaffirming Strategic Priorities

Ford also continued to emphasize many of the strategic party-building priorities that he inherited from his predecessors. One such priority involved the ongoing effort to register new Republicans: Ford's contribution was a national registration drive called Register '75.[43] Another involved making continued gains in the South. Let us discuss each in turn.

Register '75. In May 1975, the RNC launched a multipart thirty-minute network television program to provide "information, perspectives, and viewpoints of the Republican Party" in the hopes of rebuilding the public's "shattered perception" of the GOP. The program ran through the summer months and was followed by Register '75, which aimed to capture those who were swayed by the programs.[44]

Ford personally encouraged local party leaders to participate in the program by sending a letter to 3,000 Republican county chairmen asking for their help. He offered his "strong support" and "personally urge[d]" the state chairmen to participate.[45] By November 1975, thirty states had either already completed or were currently in the midst of running their programs.[46]

The secondary purpose of Register '75 was "to help the state and local organizations identify their strengths and weaknesses and generally tune up for the campaigns in 1976."[47] It had five basic objectives: "to develop and strengthen our organizations, particularly at the local level; to recruit, train and motivate new volunteers and Party workers; to measure the readiness of local organizations for the 1976 campaign . . . [and] to help recruit top candidates, and to identify and register Republicans."[48] In these ways, the registration drive became, effectively, a dress rehearsal for the 1976 general election campaign.

Party building in the South. Investing in southern state party organizations served Ford's dual purposes of building upon the gains made in the region during Nixon's tenure and of building relationships with southern state party chairmen, whose support he needed to secure the nomination. Ford's first move in this direction was to appoint conservative Richard Obenshain, Virginia's state chairman, as cochairman of the RNC.[49] Obenshain was widely credited with helping to build the Republican Party in Virginia, and his task was to continue growing the GOP in the South during Ford's presidency.[50] Ford also appointed conservative southerner Dean Burch, Goldwater's choice for RNC chairman in 1965, to serve as the administration's top liaison to the state party organizations. These appointments, as well as his own statements to the RNC, signaled Ford's commitment to continuing to build the party in the South:

> We have been a long time working on trying to make the Republican Party a viable, effective party in all fifty States. When I came to the Congress 26 years ago, the Republican Party was practically prohibited from having an impact politically in a number of our States in the South. Patiently, constructively, and effectively, today the Republican Party is viable. It is constructive in every one of our fifty states. And the Republican Party can only expand and broaden that total effort by making certain that the voices in that area of our country are heard, and heard at the highest level.[51]

Ford made sure that the southern chairmen understood that his service-oriented party-building programs were aimed at helping them build their organizations. He invited them to the White House in late 1974 to discuss his "rebuilding efforts in the Southern States," and in early 1975 Smith laid out her plans to provide state chairmen with expanded services and resources in the coming year.[52] Clarke Reed of Mississippi, the influential chair of the Southern State Chairmen's Association, expressed the chairmen's enthusiasm for Ford's party-building program: "It's the best program to come out of the National Committee since I've been on the scene. . . . It's a real quantum jump for the RNC in the area of services to the states . . . it really puts the states on the spot to do their job."[53]

Yet enthusiasm for Ford's party building was not enough to win the allegiance of the southern chairmen: many still hoped that the more conservative Reagan would emerge as the party's nominee in 1976. In mid-April 1975, Reed let Ford's top assistants know that "under today's conditions, Ronald Reagan would sweep delegates from the 13 southern and border states against Gerald R. Ford in a race for the Republican nomination." In his "sincere effort to help the President," Reed explained that the South needed more of the president's attention.[54]

In June, Ford announced that southern conservative Howard "Bo" Callaway of Georgia would be the chairman of his campaign organization, the President Ford Committee (PFC), an appointment that was "carefully designed to keep Southern Republicans from lusting after a golden ox from California named Ronald Reagan," Ford's former press secretary wrote.[55] At the end of the day, Ford managed to secure the Republican nomination, but not before the contest with Reagan reached the convention in August 1976. His party-building efforts could not, it turned out, prevent a long, bitter fight. It can hardly be doubted, however, that his investments in state parties—and perhaps even more important, his indefatigable efforts to raise money for state parties—helped him in his quest to defeat his more conservative, and arguably more popular, opponent for the nomination.

The Fund-raising "Star Power" of the President

Every modern president has proven to be an adept fund-raiser. Even Gerald Ford, an unelected president, managed to command significant attention and raise large sums of money. Our interest, however, is not whether the president raised a lot of money, but whether he used it to build his party. Ford, like every other minority-party president, turned his fund-raising "star power" toward constructive, party-building purposes.

The organizational investments described above were unusually ambitious and large in scope, and consequently very costly. In 1975 alone, the RNC's programs cost upwards of $12 million. Because this budget doubled the 1974 budget (and 1974 was an election year), Ford's fund-raising for the RNC was essential.[56] The state parties also looked to Ford for his help: in early 1975, twenty state party treasuries were in debt and reeling from the 1974 debacle.[57] These debts were preventing them from taking advantage of the RNC's new service operations, which was hindering their ability to recruit strong candidates. In early 1975, the administration worked to develop a fund-raising strategy to maximize the unique fund-raising capacity of the president and make the best of the new campaign finance laws.[58]

Under the Federal Election Campaign Act (FECA) of 1971 and its amendments in 1974, presidents could no longer raise unlimited sums of money from undisclosed donors for their independent campaigns, but they could raise unlimited, unregulated contributions for their national and state party organizations. Their party could then use those funds to assist the president's campaign through legally defined "party building" activities such as get-out-the-vote and voter education campaigns, and later, television campaign advertisements. These uncapped donations to party organizations became known as "soft money." The new regulations thus gave presidents a strong incentive to raise money for their parties, as such an effort would clearly redound to their benefit as well. Ford certainly responded to this incentive: he raised impressive sums of money for his national and state party organizations.

But Ford's approach was not wholly instrumental: it was also aimed at building his party. Indeed, when faced with the same conditions—multiple state parties in debt and the same incentive to raise "soft money" for their party—the two Democratic presidents of the FECA era, Jimmy Carter and

Bill Clinton, pursued a very different course. Rather than raise money for the state and local parties' use, Democratic presidents insisted that funds *pass through* the state parties and be spent entirely on behalf of their presidential campaigns: no money was reserved for state party-building purposes.

In contrast, Ford and his FECA-era Republican successors, Reagan and Bush, put the money they raised toward constructive party-building purposes; they encouraged state and local parties to enhance their capacities to recruit new candidates, run campaigns, register voters, and so on. Indeed, Ford's RNC even supplied finance directors for twenty-one state parties in 1975 to assist in making party-building expenditures and offered "year-round help" on "every phase of campaign organization, from recruiting viable candidates to getting Republican voters to the polls on Election Day."[59] While the FECA regime did incentivize presidents to raise large sums of "soft money" for their parties, only Republican presidents devoted this money to the development of their party's organizational capacities.

Ford's fund-raising assistance came in a variety of forms. First, he helped the RNC launch a new direct-mail sustaining membership program by lending his signature to solicitations and by meeting with a random selection of donors during his travels as part of an incentive program for donors.[60] The goal was to bring in a steady stream of small contributions to fund ongoing operations. This goal was accomplished, as the sustaining membership program raised over $5.5 million in 1975, representing about 75 percent of the RNC's income, and in the first four months of 1976 it raised $3.9 million from over 128,000 donors.[61] The program continued to grow; by the end of 1976, it raised a record $11 million from over 250,000 donors.[62] Though RNC chair Bill Brock (1977–81) is often credited with launching the Republican Party's successful direct-mail program, his efforts clearly built upon the work of Ford's party-building team in 1975 and 1976.[63] Ford met with high rollers, too, to build up the Republican National Associates program for $1,000 donors and the Republican Eagles program for $10,000 donors. To lend his prestige to the programs, he invited these groups to the White House on several occasions.[64]

A far more significant amount of his time, however, was devoted to raising money directly for state party organizations. Ford believed that the state parties' debts "often inhibited good candidates from agreeing to run for office," and said that as a result, state parties were forced to worry more about their financial problems than "formulating a good campaign strategy." The ability to raise large sums of money, Ford said, was "the one thing that a President can do best for state parties."[65]

In early 1975, Ford's fund-raising efforts did not attract much attention, but by the fall, newspapers could not help but notice that Ford had single-handedly brought twenty state parties out of debt.[66] Records show that he raised at least $4.6 million in twenty-three events in as many states between February and November 1975.[67] At an RNC reception at the White House in September 1975, Ford explained that he wanted local party leaders to use their newfound financial strength to undertake "vigorous organizing" in their communities in order to "build a stronger Republican Party all across the country." He hoped that "every Republican state organization could enter 1976 with a balanced budget and some money in the bank."[68] Praising his tireless fundraising for the party, Smith argued that "President Ford has done more than any other single individual in 1975 to lift our spirits, to restore our sense of mission, and to get the Republican Party back on the road to victory."[69] By March 1976, Ford was able to brag that in his brief presidency he had traveled to twenty-three states to raise more than $6 million for the party. "This is the way we have to build," Ford said, "from the grass roots up."[70]

Ford's fund-raising efforts were clearly meant to help his party regain its competitive strength. But as I have noted, this did not mean that Ford did not also benefit personally from a stronger party organization: he was well aware that FECA would make his presidential campaign more dependent upon his party than ever before, and he also hoped to gain favor with state chairmen in advance of the battle for the nomination. His top political advisers, for example, noted that his fund-raising for state party organizations would "help raise needed funds for state organizations and enable the President to pick up political I.O.U.'s which can be cashed during the delegate selection process." Ford's fund-raising appearances were thus made on the basis of two criteria: "the state party's need for funds" and Ford's need for delegate support.[71] In this way, party building served Ford's multiple purposes simultaneously.

Integrating the Party into the Campaign

Every modern president, Democratic and Republican alike, established an independent campaign committee to run his reelection campaign, but only Republican presidents turned the campaign into a party-building affair. They integrated their formal party apparatus into their campaign, coordinated strategic activities with their party, and used the opportunity to make investments in their party's infrastructure. In contrast, Democratic presidents hoarded resources, knowledge, and human capital in their centralized campaign apparatus, diverted funds away from other Democratic candidates' campaigns, and squandered the opportunity to make improvements in their party's organizational capacities. By "running alone," they prevented their party from reaping the benefits of participation in the "main event" of American politics.[72] In consequence, their highly personalized campaign structures proved ephemeral.

To be sure, Ford was also motivated to work more closely with his party because of new FECA campaign finance regulations. But rather than design a campaign strategy that would use his party instrumentally and exploit its operational capacities without giving something back, Ford opted to make his party a full partner in his campaign, delegate critical tasks to the RNC leadership team, and make future-oriented investments in the party apparatus as a matter of course.[73] None of these actions were prompted by FECA regulations, and none of the FECA-era Democratic presidents followed suit. They were simply how Ford believed he could win the presidency in his own right while bringing a stronger, more competitive party with him into his first full term in the White House.

As early as November 1974, White House advisers began to discuss with Smith how best to coordinate campaign-related efforts between the RNC and the presidential campaign.[74] As far as Ford's staff was concerned, there was "no question that the RNC and its members and staff will serve a key function in President Ford's election effort." The only problem was that "the Republican Party comprises only 18% of the registered voters." This presented a potential source of friction, they wrote: "With the RNC trying to take care of their own constituency and the President seeking to attract the votes of Independents and Democrats, a natural conflict arises."[75]

To help ensure a smooth working relationship between the Ford campaign team and the RNC, the White House personnel office scheduled multiple "lunches with our RNC counterparts, face-to-face contact with the RNC workers themselves, and more frequent calls to the State Chairmen."[76] In early September 1975, Ford did some bridge-building of his own. He invited members of the RNC to the White House and emphasized his strong support for Register '75 and other ongoing preparatory efforts being undertaken by the RNC.[77]

In the fall of 1975 he also created a task force and charged it with scrutinizing the party's organizational capacities "from ground zero with no sacred cows" to determine how to coordinate campaign efforts with the party most effectively with the ultimate goal of transferring the bulk of his campaign operations to the RNC after the convention.[78] Ford also sought to move the convention date up a week so as to have a little extra time for "planning and reorganization to combine the PFC [President Ford Committee] with the RNC."[79]

In mid-December 1975, the task force concluded that the best way to integrate the PFC and the RNC was to coordinate strategic planning while delegating different operational responsibilities to each.[80] The PFC would have "primary responsibility and visibility in the critically important task of appealing to non-Republicans and non-Republican groups," and the RNC would "assume the responsibility for several critical programs (including voter identification and turn-out), as such programs cannot be deferred until August 20."[81] This pivotal decision to coordinate strategic operations and divide labor for major campaign tasks between the PFC and the RNC had important consequences for the organizational development of the Republican Party. Investments made in the party apparatus during the campaign facilitated later rounds of party building in the same areas.

One such investment involved the $3 million construction of a national telephone bank and database with 53 million telephone numbers, "identified by name, address and census tract," which was the "largest bloc of such valuable information ever assembled."[82] The RNC also set up call centers in every state, which ultimately made seven million calls to mobilize voters on Election Day.[83] Such investments were obviously made to help the campaign in 1976, but they also looked to support future efforts as well: like other party-building initiatives, the goal was to win now but also build a foundation for the future. The investments made in computer technologies, research capabilities, and human capital during 1975, for example, were expanded during the campaign season and closely monitored; strengths and weaknesses were identified, and improvements were noted for future campaigns.[84]

In the long run, these new organizational capacities remained with the party. In fact, the national convention adopted rules to institutionalize the mutually beneficial relationship established between Ford's presidential campaign committee and the RNC, especially in the area of campaign finance. It created a seven-member Select Committee on Presidential Campaign Affairs to "coordinate closely" with future nominees on their "full plan of financial expenditures" and to "review and monitor" their campaign spending.[85] By integrating the formal party apparatus into his campaign, Ford had thus laid the groundwork for similar efforts in the future.

The Politics of Addition, Not Subtraction

Fundamentally, presidential party building aims to expand the party's reach and add new voters to its electoral coalition. Organizational initiatives are designed to "fish" for new voters, prospect for new candidates, seek out "switchers" and "converts," probe for hidden sources of votes, and activate the party's "silent" majority. This inclusive thrust was evident in Eisenhower's efforts to reach out to former Citizens and moderate Democrats in the South and in Nixon's efforts to reach out to the groups he believed represented the New Majority. Using rhetorical themes like "the party of the open door," Republican presidents infused their nuts-and-bolts party-building efforts with meaning and purpose.

Party of the Open Door

As we have seen, minority-party presidents tend to latch onto rhetorical themes that stress inclusiveness and openness: Eisenhower's Modern Republicanism was designed with such purposes in mind, and his new initiatives at the RNC were described as the "open-door" policy. Nixon, too, repeated the exact same "party of the open door" theme in his speeches in 1971 and 1972, and Ford followed suit. In the fall of 1975, he announced:

> I think the door of the party should be wide open for those who want to join us and believe in our philosophy. I don't believe we should open that door just a crack for a limited few. We have to have

a wide spectrum of people who are believers in our philosophy and who want to join us in literally a crusade, and let's work for common victory.[86]

Stressing the "open door" theme was not altogether easy for Ford. Just as Eisenhower's Modern Republicanism exposed him to criticism from Goldwater and others from the right wing of the party, Ford's "open door" arguments ran into the same critique from the next generation of conservatives.

Conservatives tended to support Ronald Reagan in his bid for the nomination in 1976 and frequently floated the idea of starting a third party, partly to voice their discontent with the administration and partly to give Reagan his own political vehicle with which to make a bid for the presidency in 1976.[87] Ford directed his political team to monitor the conservatives' rumblings and consistently tried to keep them at bay.[88] In the fall of 1974, for example, he invited Reagan to the White House to discuss appointments and later in the month hosted conservative intellectual luminary Irving Kristol for a "wide-ranging, informal conversation."[89] In the middle of April 1975, he met with New York senator James Buckley, who had earlier warned Ford he might start a third party, and thanked him for being "one of those who urged working within the party framework. I agree with this posture and you can count on my cooperation with you," his talking points read.[90]

In March 1975, Ford and Smith hosted a Republican Leadership Conference in Washington, D.C., that was attended by over 2,000 party activists and elected officials. The stated purpose of the conference was to discuss "how the party can broaden its base and how it can hold its own officeholders accountable."[91] It held "breakout sessions" for smaller groups to discuss how to rebuild the party.[92]

From Ford's perspective, the conference was also an opportunity to announce his candidacy while demonstrating to state and local party leaders that he was "personally involved in the Party."[93] He emphasized his commitment to rebuilding the party in the wake of Watergate and explained that the "healing" he wished for the nation, he also wished for the Republican Party. He said: "It can be argued by some that because our national problems are so serious we should not be wasting time on the problems of our party—or any other party—yet it is precisely because of our national problems that it is essential to look to our party and its revitalization everywhere."[94] He also reemphasized the "open door" theme:

We must discard the attitude of exclusiveness that has kept the Republican Party's door closed too often . . . we must erect a tent that is big enough for all who care about this great country and believe in the Republican Party enough to work through it for common goals. This tent, as I see it, must also be kept open to the growing number of independent voters . . . these voters must be welcomed and won to our cause.[95]

Reagan, scheduled to speak the next morning, discounted Ford's centrist, big-tent approach to party building and echoed Barry Goldwater's sentiments from a decade earlier. He called for a "new second party," arguing that

> a political party cannot be all things to all people. . . . It cannot compromise its fundamental beliefs for political expediency, or simply to swell its numbers. It is not a social club or fraternity engaged in intramural contests to accumulate trophies on the mantel over the fireplace.[96]

The clash between Ford's and Reagan's concepts of the GOP dominated press accounts of the conference and served as a prelude to their fight for the party's presidential nomination the following year.

After the conference, over 90 of the 144 incumbent House Republicans and nearly 20 of the 38 Republican incumbent senators signed a statement supporting Ford's "concept of a 'broad-based' political party and rejecting the conservative ideological approach of Ronald Reagan and others."[97] They wrote: "We rededicate our efforts to truly making our party the party of the open door and the open mind. We welcome the challenge of reassessing and redefining our party's identity and goals."[98] At a reception for party activists later that month, Ford reiterated: "If we are going to broaden the base of the party—to make the politics of addition—instead of subtraction—work, we must commit ourselves again and again to accommodation, conciliation and cooperation—not to mention hard work."[99]

This inclusive rhetoric was a prelude to the organizational component of Ford's party-building program. Following the Leadership Conference speeches, attendees participated in short training sessions on "the fundamentals," including "identification, registration, and getting out the vote."[100] In subsequent months, training seminars were held around the country emphasizing campaign management, fund-raising, and media and communications. This flurry of human-capital building programs was followed in short order by Register '75.[101] The "politics of addition" was thus not only a rhetorical flourish; it was a description of these concerted organizational efforts to bring new voters into the Republican Party.

Creating and Nurturing New Party Organizations

Ford also sought to realize the "open door" concept with initiatives designed to reach out to nontraditional Republican voters. His interactions with various Republican subgroups illustrate his interest in building a new majority for the GOP that included a greater diversity of groups.

African Americans. Though African Americans aligned overwhelmingly with the Democratic Party after the 1960s, the GOP had its own National Black Republican Council (NBRC), a quasi-independent organization formally housed within the Republican Party umbrella. In Ford's first month in office, he met with representatives of the group to assure them that he wanted to "broaden the base of the GOP with blacks as an integral part of this effort." He told the group's leaders of his intention "to make the GOP truly the 'Party of the Open Door.'"[102]

The NBRC routinely consulted with state party chairmen and coordinated efforts to reach out to African Americans. The executive director of the NBRC said that Ford had created a "climate of acceptance" for African Americans who were considering joining the GOP through his "openness and obvious sincerity about welcoming new converts into the Party."[103] Ford also hired Stan Scott, a black Republican, to work in his administration as liaison with the black community; Scott planned a series of meetings with Ford, Smith, and representatives of the black community to discuss how the party could improve its outreach to African Americans.[104] Rather than run the initiative out of the White House and push the party to the sidelines, Ford brought his party into the liaison process and used RNC programs as a central part of the effort.

Ethnic groups. Under Nixon, the Republican Party began to make a concerted effort to reach out to ethnic groups and work with the National Republican Heritage Groups Council (NRHG), another auxiliary group within the party umbrella, as part of the New Majority initiative.[105] The advantage of the council, according to Ford's advisers, was that it provided a formal entrée for "Americans of ethnic origins" to "have a voice in the RNC."[106] When the NRHG held its fifth annual convention in Washington, D.C., in May 1975, Ford met with its representatives at the White House and encouraged them "to start laying the plans to recruit people, to better organize, to raise money, to go out and be missionaries in selling a philosophy that is good for our country, for all our people—young, old, those yet unborn."[107]

Hispanics. Ford's team also believed it could make inroads in the Hispanic community—after all, 70 percent of Hispanics were still unregistered in 1976.[108] Throughout 1975, it held discussions with the National Republican Hispanic Assembly, which also had "affiliate status" at the RNC, and met with the group in December "to give recognition and visibility to this newly organized group" and to encourage their ongoing registration and mobilization efforts.[109] At the national convention the following year, the National Hispanic Assembly was "formally recognized" and added to the Executive Committee of the RNC.[110]

Republican mayors. In September 1974, one of Ford's assistants told Smith that the idea of forming a Republican mayors organization, "perhaps along the lines of the Republican Governors Association," had been floated to her by the mayor of Bridgeport, Connecticut.[111] Ford met with a group of Republican mayors to discuss their problems and priorities and encouraged them to organize.[112] By June 1975, the group had taken preliminary steps to forming its own organization, called the Republican Mayors Association, and at the July meeting of the U.S. Conference of Mayors, the new Republican group made an "unprecedented show of power": by controlling "all the major votes in one of the most heavily Democratic lobbying organizations in America."[113] They supported Ford's policy initiatives, such as revenue sharing, and successfully hamstrung a proposal to increase urban aid at the expense of defense funding.[114] Thanks in large part to Ford's encouragement and support, the Republican Mayors were so well established by 1976 that they gained seats on the RNC Executive Committee.[115]

■

As we have seen, along each of six dimensions of party activity, Ford undertook a wide variety of constructive organization-building initiatives over the course of his brief tenure in the White House (see table 5.1). His efforts also illuminate some of the more distinctive characteristics of presidential party building as a general phenomenon: (1) inherited institutional structures, human capital, and strategic priorities shape the president's party-building efforts and are in turn shaped by them; (2) fund-raising is one of the most important ways presidents can help to build their party; (3) when minority-party presidents integrate their party organization into their campaigns, they allow it to benefit from participation in the "main event" of American politics; (4) presidential party building aims to expand the party coalition: it is fundamentally outward-reaching.

The Republican Party's minority status served as a strong motivation for Ford's party building. While Ford had little realistic hope of building a new majority that would stand as a durable testament to his presidency during his difficult and brief time in office, he did seek to give his party all the benefits the presidency had to offer. He put the full weight of the White House behind the party's programmatic planning efforts, fund-raising initiatives, candidate recruitment programs, human-capital development projects, voter registration drives, and campaign-service delivery programs.

In many of these areas, Ford and his party-building team built directly upon the organizational initiatives inherited from Nixon. Indeed, Nixon's efforts shaped Ford's menu of options and made certain choices more attractive than others. Likewise, Ford's own contributions to the cumulative organizational development of the Republican Party cannot be overlooked. In a personal interview with Eddie Mahe Jr. many years later, Ford's RNC executive director noted, "I will say categorically . . . in those two years, '75, '76, we put the Republican Party back on the map."[116]

Even after he lost the 1976 election, Ford continued to advocate for initiatives that would enhance the party's organizational capacities and expand its reach. He met with prominent Republican governors and members of Congress to discuss the future of the Republican Party and how it might continue to grow, even without the White House as a resource, in the next four years.[117] Concerned about the party's enduring minority status, Ford wanted to "see

Table 5.1 Ford's Party Building

Provide campaign services	Build human capital	Recruit candidates	Mobilize voters	Finance party operations	Support internal activities
Regional field director program (1974+)	Regional field director program (1974+)	Regional field director program (1974+)	Regional field director program (1974+)	RNC finance directors to states (1975+)	Regional field director program (1974+)
Investments in voter files (1974+)	Expand CMC (1975+)	Build state party infrastructures (1974+)	Support NRBC (1974+)	Direct-mail programs (1975+)	Build state party infrastructures (1974+)
Research and polling capabilities (1974+)	Register '75 (1975)	Ford's personal assistance (1975+)	Support NRHG (1975+)	High-roller programs (1975+)	Investments in voter files (1974+)
CMC sends graduates into campaigns (1974+)	Post–Republican Leadership Conference training sessions (1975)	Register '75 (1975)	Support NRHA (1975+)	Ford's fund-raising for state parties (1975+)	Support Republican Mayors Association (1974+)
Party building in southern states (1974+)			Register '75 (1975)		Party building in southern states (1974+)
Register '75 (1975)			PFC-RNC voter file integration (1976)		Register '75 (1975)
Phone banks and call centers (1976)					PFC-RNC voter file integration (1976)
					Republican Policy Committee (1977)

what could be done" to prepare the GOP for the "out party" period.[118] Again turning to the party's organization, Ford called for the creation of a Republican policy council, a thirty-five-member "shadow cabinet," which would offer policy alternatives to counter the initiatives of the Carter Administration.[119]

Smith's successor at the RNC, Bill Brock, took Ford's advice on the policy committee and continued to build upon each and every party-building initiative undertaken during Ford's presidency. For example, in a prominent move, Brock expanded the regional field director program launched under Ford and Smith in 1974 with his Regional Political Directors program in 1977.[120] He also sought to refine and improve the "remarkably strong data base" established "under the leadership of Mary Louise Smith" and supplement it with sophisticated demographic and attitudinal analysis at the state level." He also targeted the direct-mail programs developed under Ford for expansion.[121] Perhaps most importantly, Brock created a "Local Elections Campaign Division" to coordinate future campaign and organizing training seminars, and its centerpiece remained the Campaign Management College, created under Nixon and expanded under Ford.[122] Brock also institutionalized and expanded upon Smith's program to send RNC-funded finance directors into the states.

Without taking any credit away from the impressive work Brock did as chairman from 1977 to 1981, we should note that his efforts were not, in fact, "entrepreneurial," as some have suggested.[123] Rather, he contributed to the Republican Party's cumulative organizational development by building upon the work done by Ford and his team, moving those initiatives forward, and introducing new programs of his own. As the party changed hands from Eisenhower to Miller to Bliss to Nixon to Ford, each party leader and his team made his own contributions to the party's organizational growth. Because party building was the priority of presidents as well as "out-party" chairmen, the GOP was able to benefit from the unique resources and support of the White House, and its organizational party-building programs could continue to develop, virtually uninterrupted, over the course of many years. When Ronald Reagan assumed the presidency in 1981, the party organization was prepared to take major steps toward translating Reagan's popularity into a stronger, larger, and more competitive Republican Party.

6

Building the Republican Base | Ronald Reagan

The Reagan Revolution wasn't just fought in 1980 and it won't be concluded in 1984. We're talking about a major shift, making the Republican Party the majority party on all levels of government, and that requires strategic planning. Some of the changes you are seeing now will be contributing to our victory in 1984, but those and many others will continue to build into the next decade.

—RNC chairman Frank Fahrenkopf[1]

Reagan called his presidency a "New Beginning," and in many ways it was: through his rhetoric and policy initiatives, Reagan offered a clear ideological alternative to New Deal liberalism.[2] What's more, his two elections durably altered the electoral map: by the end of his eight years in office, the defining features of Kevin Phillips's "emerging Republican majority"—especially GOP gains in Sun Belt states—were coming to fruition.[3] Reagan won over 90 percent of the electoral votes in both of his elections, and in 1980 the GOP won control of the Senate for the first time since 1952 and kept it for six years. Perhaps even more important, the GOP made significant gains in party identification. From 1952 to 1980, the Democratic Party averaged an advantage of twenty-one percentage points over the Republican Party; by 1988, that margin was reduced to six points.[4]

Yet Reagan was much stronger than his party: at the district level, he ran ahead of more than two-thirds of his fellow Republican congressional candidates in both of his elections. House Republicans remained stuck in the minority throughout his presidency, and the GOP never rose above 41 percent of state legislative seats or won a majority of governorships. Thus, while the Republican Party was clearly on the rise, it still lagged behind the Democrats in state and local elections. Moreover, its weak "farm system" indicated that the GOP would likely remain at a decided competitive disadvantage unless further inroads were made. Reagan consequently faced the same fundamental challenge as his partisan predecessors: to build a durable new Republican majority that bore his imprint.

At the level of the Republican Party organization, Reagan's presidency represented less of a New Beginning than a continuation of familiar practices. Rather than sweep into office and introduce a wholly new party-building program, Reagan embraced the organizational arrangements he inherited, showered his party with presidential largess, and urged it to continue along its current trajectory of organizational development. While he and his team introduced a number of significant organizational innovations during his eight years in office, his party building was characterized more by continuity than change.

Indeed, the party organization Reagan inherited from his predecessors was a relatively robust apparatus with many ongoing party-building programs. After thirty years of persistent organizational development, it was poised to seize upon the opportunity afforded by a popular presidency like Reagan's to improve its competitive standing. The party boasted the latest in computer technology, updated voter lists, direct-mail systems, and campaign training programs. Even more important, it was home to a cadre of party professionals who were dedicated to party building. It was fully equipped with institutionalized processes for raising funds, providing campaign assistance, supporting state and local party activities, mobilizing voters, recruiting candidates, and reaching out to new groups. All this popular president had to do was signal his support for his party, and its gears would begin to turn.

For example, by refusing to engage in fund-raising for any entity other than the formal party apparatus, Reagan ensured that donors who wished to express support for his presidency would feed the Republican Party's coffers. And because Reagan embraced his party and elevated its public stature, new voters inspired by his presidency registered as Republicans; new activists joined their local Republican Party organizations to promote his agenda within their communities; and new candidates ran for office as Reagan Republicans. Through its many ongoing programs and activities, the party organization was able to transform the intensity of Reagan's support into activities that would further expand the party and strengthen its operations at all levels.

To observe the independent influence of the Republican Party organization is to hint at the second distinguishing characteristic of Reagan's party building: his detachment from the details. By all accounts, Reagan was consistently very supportive of party-building programs at the national, state, and local levels. He set priorities, established strategic commitments, and lent his personal assistance to the party's fund-raising efforts, candidate-recruitment efforts, voter mobilization drives, and infrastructure-building activities whenever his help was needed. But from what we can discern from available historical records, Reagan seems to have been less personally involved in directing party-building efforts than his three Republican predecessors.[5] This would seem to be consistent with his general "operating style," which has been described as heavy on delegation and "habitually indifferent to detail."[6] He articulated party-building goals but delegated most of the responsibilities for carrying them out to his loyal and competent political team at the RNC and the White House. And yet his approach reveals more than his operating style: it also reminds us that Reagan did not have to be as personally involved in party building as, say, Dwight Eisenhower. The party Reagan inherited had a momentum all of its own. Whereas Eisenhower had to take the initiative in getting party-building programs off the ground, Reagan could simply give his blessing and offer his support when needed.

	Party Building						Party Predation					
	C	H	R	V	F	I	C	H	R	V	F	I
Republicans Eisenhower	●	●	●	●	●	●						
Nixon	●	●	●	●	●	●	●			●		
Ford	●	●	●	●	●	●						
Reagan	●	●	●	●	●	●						
Bush	●	●	●		●	●						
Democrats Kennedy				●	●		●	●		●	●	●
Johnson							●	●		●	●	●
Carter							●	●	●	●	●	●
Clinton (1st term)							●	●	●	●	●	●
Clinton (2nd term)	●	●		●	●	●						

C=Provide campaign services, H=Build human capital, R=Recruit candidates, V=Mobilize voters, F=Finance party operations, I=Support internal activities

Figure 6.1. Reagan's Party Interactions

Nevertheless, Reagan did interact with his party organization frequently to support numerous party-building programs along each of the six dimensions of party activity (see figure 6.1). While examining these efforts, this chapter also elaborates upon four new characteristics of presidential party building as a more general phenomenon: (1) presidential party-building innovations are often refashioned organizational templates borrowed from extrapartisan networks; (2) because building a new majority is a long-term proposition, party-building strategies are often undertaken in the hope that incremental gains in the near term will produce larger gains in the future; (3) by running an integrated campaign, the president can help to swell the party's base of registered voters; (4) the president's personal influence can be a powerful party-building tool.

Borrowing Organizational Templates

Minority-party presidents are driven to innovate and experiment with new techniques. Whereas old approaches have become associated with the party's current problems, new techniques are perceived to be necessary to build a new majority. Party-building innovations, however, are rarely made from scratch: they usually involve the "recombination of old elements" or the "transposition" of existing organizational templates into new contexts.[7] As we have seen, Eisenhower drew freely upon his personal connections in the business community to develop new methods of party building. Reagan's team, similarly, found that the business community offered not only a key source of votes, contributions, and candidates, but also valuable organizational scripts that could be adopted and adapted to facilitate Republican party-building efforts.

Fund-raising Amway-style, 1981–1982

Upon assuming the presidency, Reagan selected Richard Richards from Utah as his new RNC chairman. Richards served as RNC political director under Nixon and was described as a "nuts and bolts and grass-roots politician."[8] "Winning elections is not an art; it is a science," Richards announced at his inauguration. Making "the GOP the nation's majority party before 1990," Richards said, required a continued emphasis on organizational innovation.[9] Along these lines, billionaire cofounder of Amway Corporation, Richard DeVos, was asked to assist Richards by serving as the new finance chairman of the Republican Party. His charge was to bring the key features of his Amway model to the Republican Party.[10]

The simple and wildly successful Amway business model encouraged individuals to tap their social networks to sell ordinary household products and to recruit ("sponsor") their friends and family to do the same.[11] New recruits owed a share of their earnings to their recruiter. This model made the top of the "pyramid" exponentially richer as the network expanded. DeVos and partner Jay Van Andel explained in their manual "Professional Sponsoring, Step by Step" in 1979:

> [There are] certain practical limits to how much total dollar volume you can produce by yourself, but when you sponsor others as distributors, who in turn sell products and sponsor other distributors, you can greatly expand the potential sales volume generated by your efforts. You grow by sharing with others the opportunity you have—and, in sharing, you add to what you already have.[12]

Person-to-person contact was the key to Amway's success, but Amway's network-building model depended on the sustained enthusiasm and commitment of each individual "distributor." Amway conventions, attended by thousands of people, were designed for these motivational purposes. DeVos was himself a celebrity; people traveled far and wide to hear him "extol the virtues of patriotism, free enterprise, and positive thinking." Inspirational books and motivational cassettes supplemented the conventions.[13]

Though DeVos only served as RNC finance chairman from January 1981 to August 1982, he fundamentally reconstructed the party's fund-raising apparatus and redoubled its commitment to nurturing small donors.[14] His main goal was to turn small donors into grassroots party activists on a mission for the Republican Party.[15] After the 1980 election, many Reagan voters supported the president but were not registered as Republicans and did not have a personal stake in the Republican Party. DeVos sought to capitalize on Reagan's popularity to build enthusiasm for, and commitment to, the Republican Party.

Now extolling the virtues of the Republican Party rather than Amway, DeVos launched a series of motivational conventions for small-donor "sustaining members." The conventions explained to attendees that they were the party's "shareholders" who had a "vested interest in the work of the RNC."[16] Prerecorded messages from Reagan were played to inspire the attendees, who were then encouraged to go "enlist the support" of their personal networks of friends, family, and neighbors. For example, at a Houston convention in February 1982, 8,000 RNC sustaining members saw a message from Reagan, heard Vice President Bush speak, enjoyed a performance by singing star Pat Boone, and responded to DeVos's request that each attendee write down the names of three friends and then "contact those friends and encourage them to join in the New Beginning."[17] RNC staffers then called attendees after the conference to ensure that they contacted their three friends. More than 4,000 new names were added to the rolls of Republican supporters after the Houston conference alone, and more than half of the attendees doubled their initial donation.[18]

DeVos also reorganized the party's major-donor apparatus into five hierarchical clubs. In descending order, the Republican Eagles, the President's Club, the Vice President's Club, the Cabinet Club, and the Ambassador's Club gave donors separate designations depending on how much money they contributed each year. The benefits of membership grew with each donor threshold— large donors received invitations to White House events and yacht rides with senior officials. Reagan's popularity, DeVos explained, presented a terrific "opportunity to bring increasing numbers of major contributors into our party."[19]

In November 1981, Richards commented that "we have put together the most sophisticated fund-raising apparatus of any political organization ever." After only ten months of concentrated network-building, the Amway model had helped the party raise $28.8 million from 1.5 million individuals, with a $29 average donation.[20] This success bred further successes: a significant portion of the funds raised were reinvested in the party's fund-raising apparatus. The new funds enabled the RNC to buy new high-speed presses and send 25 million direct-mail appeals to prospective new donors by the end of 1981, thereby bringing in even more revenue the following year. The RNC also used these funds to develop a new computer system that linked phone banks to donor contribution records, which enabled the party to begin to identify and analyze contact-donation patterns.[21]

Applying the Amway model to the Republican Party's finance operations was an unqualified success. Reagan's popularity, combined with new mechanisms for soliciting and collecting donations, helped the RNC raise upwards of $30 million in 1981 and more than $40 million in 1982 (with average donations of $25 and $26 in each respective year), each year shattering previous nonpresidential election year records.[22] Most importantly, this dramatic influx of cash allowed Reagan's party-building team to make new investments in every area of the party developed by Ford and then Brock: field operations, training seminars, new technologies, and coalition-expansion efforts. Let us review each briefly.

Field operations. The RNC Field Operations Division housed the Regional Political Directors (RPDs), the Regional Finance Directors (RFDs), and the Local

Program Field Representatives (LPFRs). These "liaisons to the states" were responsible for "keeping the RNC up-to-date on the feelings, needs and attitudes of the state and local parties, while offering valuable assistance in campaign methods and techniques . . . [and] solidifying the long-term goal of stronger party development."[23] First created under the direction of Eddie Mahe, Jr., during Nixon's presidency, these liaison teams were expanded under Ford and institutionalized with more clearly defined roles and responsibilities under Brock. By 1981 there were eight RPDs, four RFDs, and nine LPFRs. In preparation for the 1982 midterm elections, Reagan's team at the RNC expanded the field operation by 50 percent, adding four more RPDs, two more RFDs, and several additional LPFRs.[24]

Training. The RNC's Political Division was charged with "building the party and attaining real majority status by the end of the decade."[25] Its flagship program, the Campaign Management College, was expanded to forty-eight programs—double the number of sessions held each year under Ford—and eight specialized seminars were added to focus on themes such as outreach and "campaign talent maintenance."[26] After the 1980 elections, many of the campaign managers who had been trained in the 1970s were "hired away" to the White House, Cabinet departments, and federal agencies; the expanded training workshops were thus partially aimed at addressing the new "shortage" of campaign managers, finance directors, and press secretaries in the party.[27] From Reagan's inauguration to the 1982 midterm elections, the RNC trained over 2,000 new campaign staff and assisted state parties in running over seventy of their own training seminars and workshops for state candidates.[28]

New technologies. While sophisticated computer technology had been used at the RNC for several years to manage voter lists and financial donor lists, during Reagan's first two years the RNC expanded its computer hardware and installed new software programs for use in a variety of party-building programs. For example, field staffers were given "portable terminals" to enable direct communications with the RNC's "base computer," and a new List Development Program was launched to continually upgrade voter data.[29] The RNC leveraged these technologies in its new Redistricting Division, which had a $1 million budget, twenty-five staff, and a team of technical and legal experts to help state parties with their efforts.[30] In addition, the RNC purchased a new video satellite teleconference system to "beam" Reagan into GOP gatherings across the country, and expanded the party's polling operation. These investments benefited the White House as much as the RNC: polls, for example, gave the president critical information about public attitudes on a wide variety of issues.[31] At the same time, political research helped the RNC with its strategic planning: "If the political mood is favorable, then it's a good time for a registration drive," explained RNC deputy chairman Charles Bailey.[32]

Coalition expansion. The auxiliary organizations for African Americans, Hispanics, and "ethnic" groups that were nurtured and expanded under Ford were increasingly integrated into the RNC structure under Reagan. Each group was given additional financial resources and organizational assistance to "recruit more Republicans into the Party . . . identify outstanding ethnic and minority Republican candidates, help with their elections, give them campaign management assistance and encourage them to create their own constituencies."[33] Richards explained that the move was intended to help the party expand: "Before, we gave each little group so much money and subconsciously felt we had done our duty," he said. But "they didn't have access to the committee's total resources and didn't grow."[34]

The White House oversaw each of these party-building efforts at the RNC and treated national party leaders as members of Reagan's political team. Director of the White House Office of Political Affairs Ed Rollins was the key liaison to the party during the first two years. Rather than sideline the party or circumvent it, Rollins sought to leverage the capacities of the White House to support the projects undertaken at the RNC. Every Wednesday afternoon throughout 1982, for example, RNC deputy director (and day-to-day chief of operations) Richard N. Bond would meet with Rollins and the directors of the two congressional campaign committees to discuss organizational operations, campaign strategies, and financial planning. Rollins's goal was to understand the RNC's needs so that he could "bring the mission of the commander-in-chief of the party fully into focus."[35] According to Bond, Rollins would ask:

> How many fundraisers are you going to expect us to do here for you in Washington? What pieces of fundraising mail would you like us to sign? What commercials would you like us to tape in behalf of candidates? Who would you like to have us help recruit to run for Congress, to run for Senator, to run for Governor? And occasionally either Reagan or Bush would make calls urging so and so to run for Congress.[36]

Because Rollins was part of the White House senior staff, he was in a position to "provide early warnings about coming presidential decisions that may have an important impact on candidate strategies and choices of campaign issues."[37]

Despite the party's unprecedented financial gains in 1981–82, Republicans won only one Senate seat in 1982 and lost twenty-six House seats, seven governorships, 158 state legislative seats, and control of four state legislatures. While these losses were viewed as "far better than the party in control of the White House normally does during its first off-year election," they were clearly not a positive development for the GOP.[38] But rather than abandon his party organization in favor of a separate, independent, and highly personalized campaign structure during 1983–84, Reagan headed into his reelection campaign with a newfound determination to strengthen and expand his party.

This decision, of course, raises the question of why Reagan chose to continue along the party-building path once it became clear that his organizational-development efforts had not paid off. During the winter of 1982–83, Reagan's reelection in 1984 appeared to be anything but certain, future RNC chairman Frank Fahrenkopf said: "We can all sit back now and say everybody knew it was going to be a slam dunk—but we didn't know it was going to be a slam dunk."[39] Why, then, persevere with party building?

First and foremost, the above-mentioned efforts were never intended for the sole purpose of winning victories in the short run. A better showing in the midterm elections of 1982 would have been desirable, of course; but that was not the point of party building. The goal was to build a new majority, which was an inherently long-term proposition. Second, the condition of the party apparatus had grown sufficiently strong to warrant Reagan's confidence, even after disappointing midterm losses. Over the next two years, the party's organizational capacities were viewed by Reagan's team as an asset, not a detriment, to Reagan's goals, including reelection. But most importantly, unlike Nixon—but thanks in part to Nixon and his successors' earlier efforts—Reagan did not perceive a trade-off between his own reelection goals and his party-building goals. As we will see, he believed he could pursue his majority-building and reelection goals simultaneously.

Party Building as Incremental Change

As discussed in the last chapter, party building is a "politics of addition," not subtraction: it aims to expand the party coalition into a new majority. But building a new majority that is durable and secure takes time and concerted effort. Party-building initiatives are therefore often designed with the knowledge that large-scale political change only happens gradually and cumulatively: they aim to produce small gains in the present with the hope of achieving larger gains down the road.[40] This approach characterized the efforts of Reagan's team in 1983–84 to cut into the Democrats' majorities one percentage point at a time.

The Republican Strategic Triad

When Richards left his post after the 1982 midterm losses, Reagan decided to appoint a new party leadership team and elevate the importance of the RNC. "If I run again in 1984, I believe it is very important that the Republican National Committee play a major role," Reagan told congressional party leaders.[41] Adopting Nixon's approach from 1971–72, Reagan appointed a "general chairman" (close friend Senator Paul Laxalt) to serve as party spokesman and a new RNC chairman (Nevada state party chairman Frank Fahrenkopf) to run the organization. Laxalt, known as the president's "first friend," would put Reagan's stamp on the party, while Fahrenkopf would ensure that the RNC's party-building programs continued apace.

At a farewell reception for Richards, Reagan praised his outgoing chairman for his success in "raising money and providing expertise" to candidates and in "fortifying" Republican county and state organizations. The Republican

Party, Reagan predicted, would be prepared for the 1984 elections: "We'll do well because of what you might call the 'Republican Strategic Triad'—that's fundraising ability, nuts and bolts organization, and talented candidates."[42]

Reagan charged Fahrenkopf with designing and implementing organizational programs to realize this triad. Fahrenkopf's new grassroots party-building plan, published in a thirty-three-page document, emphasized all three elements while seeking to expand the party's reach, even into solidly Democratic areas. He later explained:

> A lot of times in the past, grassroots programs wouldn't spend much time on the strong Democratic counties, just focused on the base— well we did that, we went there—but also, if there was a county where normally the Democrat won 60–40, if we could cut it down to 55–45, that was our focus. We even went into Democratic strongholds, thinking we could pick off the margin of defeat.[43]

Making investments in these heavily Democratic areas might have seemed irrational in the context of the upcoming elections. Why not devote maximal resources to marginal races in 1983–84 rather than to areas unlikely to yield victories now, if ever? Fahrenkopf argued that Reagan's popularity offered a propitious opportunity to make a real push toward majority status:

> In the old days, people would say no, that's a losing district, we're not going to do anything there, we're not putting a dime in there. Well, we wouldn't put a dime in, maybe we'd put a nickel in, though. Because we were building. You've got to build, you've got to build.[44]

To cut into the Democrats' margins, Fahrenkopf focused on strengthening the county party organizations: "We actually went *through* the state party organization right down to the local organizations."[45] The rationale was twofold. First, increasing the Republican vote share at the district level, even if it did not produce House victories now, increased the likelihood that higher-quality congressional candidates could be convinced to run as Republicans in the future. Higher-quality candidates would attract more voters, and more voters would attract even higher-quality candidates; over time, this cycle would build a new Republican majority. Second, small gains in each county and district were additive across the entire state. A small percentage-point increase in each district might not be enough to win House elections, but when aggregated across the state, it could provide the margin of victory in the senatorial, gubernatorial, or presidential races.

Fahrenkopf directed the RNC's regional field directors and state party officials to evaluate the 3,707 county party organizations on a scale of one to ten based on whether they had "1) raised money for Republican candidates; 2) provided in-kind services to help candidates; 3) organized a get-out-the-vote program; 4) organized a voter registration program; and 5) developed a candidate recruitment and training program."[46] The counties that were found to be in the worst shape in each of the twenty-five to thirty states deemed critical to the 1984 elections (presidential swing states or states with a competitive Senate campaign) received the most financial and organizational assistance from the national committee.[47] Fahrenkopf invested in the county parties' "political efforts in every sector—from fundraising and management skills, to candidate and volunteer recruitment, to training seminars and policy meetings, to get-out-the-vote drives" and sent the RNC's expanded field staff to help local party leaders develop new programs.[48] Particular emphasis was placed on helping local parties develop their own fund-raising base; mirroring Mary Louise Smith's belief that a well-funded local organization would be better able to attract strong candidates and run effective campaigns, Fahrenkopf wrote: "Increasing economically self-sufficient county parties by 300 to 400, in the short run, will have a geometrically greater effect in winning races."[49]

The RNC also organized over fifty training sessions for state and local party leaders. Films, instructional materials, and skilled personnel from the "RNC bank of experts" were used at the seminars, and Reagan addressed several of the conferences in person, others through satellite television.[50] "The President was a firm supporter of going grassroots," Fahrenkopf said. "He was very, very supportive of what we were doing."[51] After hearing Reagan's inspirational message, attendees were taught "best practices" for electoral coalition-building, voter registration, campaign management, and fund-raising.

The RNC continued to act as the "nerve center" of operations. It extended its "institutional advertising" program and sent media experts to "coach grass-roots activists on breaking through to radio talk shows, television programs, regularly scheduled news conferences and other media events."[52] The computer equipment first purchased in 1975 under Ford was significantly upgraded and was now used extensively in a variety of party operations: integrated with the RNC's phone bank, the computer dialed on average 3,500 phone numbers a day for the purposes of fund-raising and voter mobilization.[53]

While Reagan clearly delegated a great deal of responsibility to his RNC chairman and political team, his personal involvement proved to be a tremendous asset. "The hardest job in the world would be chairman of the party without the White House," Fahrenkopf insisted.[54] Reagan made it a policy that he would only sign "fundraising and party building" letters for the RNC or the congressional campaign committees so as to maximize the impact of his signature and ensure that the party organization was the primary beneficiary of his prestige.[55] "If we needed money," Fahrenkopf said, "it was a marvelous thing. I'd go over and say I need a letter signed by the President," and after the White House tinkered with the wording, "the letter would drop in the mail Wednesday night, and the mail trucks would pull up in front of the RNC on Monday, Tuesday, Wednesday morning with those dirty old mailbags just full of letters with checks for $25, $35, $45. No better fundraiser than Ronald Reagan."[56]

In 1983, the RNC raised over $35 million, more than double what it raised in 1979, the last year before a presidential election year. Seventy-five percent of its contributions came from small donors, with an average donation of $25.

At the start of 1984, the RNC had a list of 1.7 million donors and 12 million "probable donors." With the nation's focus turning to the reelection campaign, the RNC ramped up its efforts and sent a whopping 35 million "prospect letters" to tap those who were enthusiastic about Reagan. Such an effort also offered a way to identify potential volunteers and measure the party's support in key areas.

In 1983, Rollins explained that whenever Reagan traveled, he met with state and local party leaders. "Reagan recognized very early on the importance of strong national and state party organizations," Rollins said.[57] White House records indicate that in the brief window between January and March 1984, Reagan participated in forty-nine photo ops, receptions, seminars, social events, meetings, or luncheons planned by the RNC.[58] Reagan also made a special point of visiting college campuses to stir up support for College Republicans groups. According to Fahrenkopf, Reagan was pleased to learn that more young people were registering as Republicans than at any time since the end of World War II, but was concerned that their turnout rate was still quite low.[59]

These party-building efforts in 1983 and 1984—investing in county party organizations, training state and local party leaders, expanding the party's network of activists and volunteers, and prospecting for new donors—were unabashedly long term in their focus. While Reagan's upcoming reelection campaign certainly provided the most compelling rationale for mobilizing activists, these initiatives aimed to improve the party's institutional capacities and make durable improvements to its operations. They looked to capitalize on Reagan's popularity to make incremental improvements in the hope of producing cumulative gains that would pay off later. These efforts were but a precursor of the most significant party-building initiative of Reagan's first term: using the presidential campaign to build the party's base of registered voters.

Building the Base

As discussed in the last chapter, close coordination with the Republican Party during Ford's presidential campaign in 1976 paid dividends for the development of the party's institutional infrastructure. New investments in phone banks, voter lists, computer technology, and research capabilities remained with the party after the election had passed. But running an integrated campaign can also yield other equally important majority-building benefits, such as a dramatically expanded pool of newly registered voters. By integrating the party organization into his campaign in 1984, this was precisely what Reagan sought to do for his party. Swelling the ranks of registered Republican voters ranked second only to securing Reagan's reelection as a campaign goal. Widespread enthusiasm for Reagan's presidency was to be turned into a wider, deeper, more durable base for the Republican Party that would remain long after the 1984 elections.

Three separate entities collaborated to expand the Republican Party's base of registered voters during the campaign. Each worked to mobilize slightly different cross-sections of voters: the RNC was charged with registering "likely" but unregistered Republican voters, the Reagan-Bush '84 campaign committee sought to convert registered Democrats ("Reagan Democrats") into registered Republicans, and extrapartisan evangelical groups targeted unregistered evangelical voters, primarily in the South. Each entity played an important role in making the President's reelection campaign redound to the benefit of the Republican Party. Let us consider the integrated RNC/Reagan-Bush '84 campaign first.

The Integrated Campaign: The RNC and Reagan-Bush '84

The RNC committed $4 million to voter registration in 1984 and aimed to register three million new Republicans across all fifty states in time for the election. It concentrated its registration drive in areas such as military installations and suburban "growth areas" that often attracted likely Reagan voters. What we now consider a routine element of campaigning—"microtargeting"—was first put to use in earnest during the 1984 presidential campaign. By 1983 the national committee had been adding and updating information in their centralized database for eight years; Fahrenkopf found that by adding new, unconventional data to existing lists, he could make his voter-targeting operations even more efficient and effective. For example, Fahrenkopf bought hunting and fishing license data from states and added it to the RNC's database, "and then every fisherman and hunter would get a letter from Ronald Reagan focusing on those things."[60] And in high-growth areas like suburban Denver, Fahrenkopf would merge and purge voter registration lists with drivers' license lists to identify those new residents who had yet to register. His operation would then target these new residents and seek out more information about their political preferences. If they were sympathetic to Reagan, they would be encouraged to register:

> We'd have a warehouse with fifty phones, and we'd start phoning those people, saying, "If the election were held today, would you vote for Ronald Reagan or Walter Mondale?" And if they said Walter Mondale, we'd say thank you, have a nice day. If they said Ronald Reagan—or George Bush four years later—we would say, "Well, we noticed you're not registered to vote. Are there other people in your household who are not registered to vote?" Usually you'd get one or two.

On Election Day, the RNC would work with county party organizations to ensure these newly registered Republicans were mobilized to vote. Where volunteers were in short supply, the RNC would hire telephone bank operators "to see that the job got done."[61]

In conjunction with Reagan-Bush '84, the RNC also planned a grassroots effort during the last two weeks of the campaign called "Victory Blitz '84" to mobilize volunteers. The program used the lure of competition and prizes to encourage local activists to design innovative get-out-the-vote drives. After the election, the programs were evaluated on how much news coverage they managed to generate, how many volunteers they recruited, and how successful their voter contact program was. "Outstanding Volunteers" were recognized and rewarded for their efforts with trips to Washington for the inauguration.[62]

Reagan helped to raise large sums of soft money for the Republican Party to aid in these efforts: throughout the spring of 1984, Reagan's White House political team met with the party leadership and the campaign committee leadership to coordinate direct mailings and plan receptions at the White House for major party donors.[63] Through these types of efforts, the Reagan-Bush '84 committee and the RNC cultivated a synergistic, cooperative relationship during the campaign.

The full integration of the party into the reelection campaign redounded to the long-term benefit of the party. A wealth of individual-level voter information was added to the RNC's computerized data-banks, newly recruited and trained activists and volunteers gained valuable experience, and new operating relationships were established between the RNC and state and local parties. All of these new organizational capacities could be drawn upon in future elections.[64]

Even more important, of course, was the addition of millions of newly registered Republicans. More Republican voters meant potentially more Republican victories—but it also meant that local party organizations would have an easier time recruiting candidates to run for office. This was particularly important in the South, where prospective candidates were often reluctant to run as Republicans because most voters were registered as Democrats. Being able to demonstrate growth in the number of registered Republican voters proved to be an invaluable recruitment tool.[65]

Whereas the RNC sought out unregistered "likely" Republican voters, the Reagan-Bush '84 committee sought to *reregister* blue-collar workers and other conservative Democrats who voted for Reagan in 1980 (so-called "Reagan Democrats") as registered Republicans, as well as to register those in the same demographic group who remained unregistered. Blue-collar workers made up more than 30 percent of the workforce in 1983; Reagan-Bush '84 aimed to turn this large group into a core Republican constituency.[66] Reagan-Bush '84 allocated the same amount of funding as the RNC ($4 million) to its voter registration drive and another $3 million for its get-out-the-vote operation on Election Day.[67] The campaign committee concentrated on the South and West and recruited "thousands of volunteer workers to register and turn out Republican voters."[68]

Throughout 1984, the reelection committee insisted that its goal was to use the campaign as a means of creating an enduring Republican majority. "Unlike previous presidential campaigns," a campaign committee announced, "Reagan-Bush '84 will leave a lasting legacy for the Republican Party. . . . The base built by Reagan-Bush '84 organizational efforts will do more than win a huge majority in 1984. It will help make the GOP a majority party in years to come."[69] By late October 1984, the campaign had registered more than one million Reagan supporters as new Republicans, bringing the total of new Republican voters registered by the RNC and Reagan-Bush '84 to four million. Lest one think the campaign was seeking to mobilize Democrats who would vote for Reagan but register as Democrats, the campaign noted that "in the 29 states that register by party, 98% of those registered by the Reagan-Bush '84 program did so as Republicans—a boost in our party's membership."[70] Even the campaign's Election Day voter mobilization program explicitly sought to provide gains for the entire party: its stated aim was to "ensure a Reagan-Bush *and* Republican victory."[71]

With new voter registration the centerpiece of the coordinated campaign effort, Reagan's popularity was explicitly leveraged to expand the Republican Party. Both the party and the president stood to benefit: the new Republican base strengthened the party's competitive standing, and from Reagan's standpoint, a stronger, larger party would be a central component of his historical legacy. New Republican voters would identify their partisanship with Reagan personally, even after he left the White House: Reagan would be remembered as the one who led his party out of the wilderness.

Evangelical Republicans

Administration and party strategists recognized that a particularly promising— but still untapped—source of Republican voters was traditionally nonpartisan, nonvoting evangelical Christians. With over 15 million unregistered with either party, evangelicals had yet to discover the benefits of collective action in the political arena.[72] Registering evangelicals as Republicans and mobilizing them to vote, however, was a delicate task—their traditional political passivity was to some extent "rooted in religious conviction."[73] But Reagan's campaign team believed that if these groups were mobilized, they could give "Republicans a way to reach white southerners in a systematic, well-funded way, with messages to which they were likely to be receptive."[74]

Some evangelical groups began to organize during the 1970s and early 1980s in the South; by developing a strategic relationship with them and helping them grow, the administration hoped to secure a new source of "organizational support to buttress the fairly weak [Republican] party organizations in the region."[75] Indeed, as one journalist commented, "In many parts of the South, the Republican Party is still in its childhood. . . . Party structures are less settled, and the G.O.P. leaders still think of themselves as electoral underdogs. Their tolerance for new sources of strength is high."[76] Reagan and his team therefore had good reasons to try to link their party-building programs with the efforts of emerging evangelical activists.

One of the most important evangelical groups to get involved in the campaign was the American Coalition for Traditional Values (ACTV, pronounced "active"), an umbrella organization for a number of smaller evangelical Christian groups. ACTV claimed to represent 45 million evangelical Christians and millions more who stood for "traditional moral values." In 1984, ACTV launched a concerted effort to provide its nationwide network of three hundred pastors with assistance in their local political organizing activities. Each pastor was encouraged to distribute "calls to action" and "educational materials" to all "Bible-believing pastors" in their cities and to encourage those pastors to "reproduce them and give them out at the church door."[77] These materials included user-friendly guides to issues such as abortion, religious freedom, and school prayer. In separate columns, the literature compared the Democratic platform's position to the Republican platform's position on each issue.

The chairman of ACTV, Tim LaHaye, explained that the targeted congregations were like new political precincts: "church-based precincts." He said: "We are launching an all-time first in the Bible-believing churches. All the pastors are going to be asked to divide their congregations into family groups of 15 and recruit telephone volunteers, so that on Election Day all 15 will be called and asked if they have been out to vote. They will be called right up until the polls close."[78] ACTV's "church-based precinct captains" were not officially working on behalf of the Republican Party, but after the election, LaHaye proudly reported to Reagan that ACTV expanded the rolls of registered Republican voters by approximately two million in 1984 and turned out between six and eight million on Election Day.[79] By registering churchgoers and teaching them about the stark differences between Democrats and Republicans, ACTV's technically nonpartisan activities were used for Republican party-building purposes. "If 80 percent of the people go out and vote for Ronald Reagan, we'll be happy," said ACTV financier and former RNC finance chairman Joe M. Rodgers.[80]

Reagan went to great lengths to encourage the Christian conservative groups' efforts. In April 1984, for example, the White House authorized a letter with Reagan's signature to be sent to anonymous "Christian leaders" along with the packet ACTV mailed to its pastor-activists. The letter read:[81]

> National polls show that more than 60% of Americans profess to have had a born-again experience in their religious lives, yet fewer than 50% of these same people exercise their God-given right to go to the polls and vote. To help reverse this apathy . . . [ACTV] is inviting you to make voter registration a top priority. . . . ACTV hopes to see 2–2½ million new eligible voters contacted and registered through the efforts of concerned religious leaders like yourself. I personally commend ACTV for undertaking this noble project. . . . As your President, I thank you for your faithful patriotism. Please continue working to get eligible men and women in your area registered to vote in November. And then do all you can to make sure they go to the polls when Election Day arrives.[82]

The RNC, doing its part, distributed a handbook for "churchgoing Christians" on how to become politically involved.[83]

To provide even further support, in early July Reagan held a reception for ACTV at the White House. He expressed his determination to "wage all-out war against the evil people who use drugs and pornography to prey on our families and loved ones." He offered his solidarity in their quest to bring back school prayer, eliminate abortion, and tackle other social problems.[84] In no uncertain terms, Reagan indicated that he supported their political mobilization efforts:

> I can't stress strongly enough that what you are doing is important, is necessary, and is right. And as long as I am president, you, and others who stand up for our Judeo-Christian values, will be welcome here because you belong here. Now, of course, if you could help register a few million voters, then maybe you could send a message of thunder from the grassroots that no one in Washington could ignore.[85]

LaHaye reported to chief of staff James Baker that the White House meeting was a "smashing success." He said Reagan's words inspired ACTV's "242 pastoral leaders" to return home and "continue voter registration right up until the October cut-off date." The "key," LaHaye said, "is our network to the 300 city chairmen that are activating the 350–500 pastors in each of their cities or regions."[86] The White House followed up: ACTV board member Reverend James Robison was asked to open the Republican National Convention, and Reagan met with the ACTV board again after the election to "solidify and rally their commitment to mobilize their followers over the next term."[87]

By the end of Reagan's presidency, it was clear that these evangelical activists had become an integral component of the Republican Party coalition and that they would offer a source of critical manpower for future Republican campaigns. By the mid-1990s and early 2000s, scholars noted that evangelical Christian conservatives had "spread out" and "dug in" by joining the ranks of state Republican parties and rising to positions of party leadership.[88]

Together, the RNC, the Reagan-Bush '84 committee, and evangelical groups registered millions of new Republican voters in 1984. The Committee for the Study of the American Electorate (CSAE) found that between 1980 and 1984, twelve million more voters were registered to vote, and of those who registered in 1983–84, 61 percent voted for Reagan. And perhaps more importantly for the party's long-term strength, 45 percent of these newly registered voters cast ballots for the Republican congressional candidate versus 39 percent for the Democratic candidate. A disproportionate number of these voters came from the South; 55 percent identified themselves as Republicans and 28 percent self-identified as "fundamentalist Protestants." The director of CSAE pronounced: "The age of Democratic dominance in the South is dead."[89]

In the 1984 election, Ronald Reagan won forty-nine states and 98 percent of the electoral votes; the GOP lost one seat in the Senate but held its small majority, gained sixteen House seats, took control of seven state legislative chambers, added 314 legislative seats, and gained one governorship. Reagan attracted 64 percent of young and first-time voters.[90] In the initial months after the election, national polls showed that the number of voters identifying with the Republican Party had reached "near parity" with the Democratic Party. By March, the Democratic Party had reclaimed its lead, but Reagan's pollster Richard Wirthlin commented that the GOP's increase in partisan identification in the electorate was the "single most important political development in the last decade." A *Washington Post* poll showed that the Democratic-Republican split of 59–31 percent in 1979 had shrunk to 52–42 percent in 1985.[91]

One of Reagan's first moves after being reelected was to ask Fahrenkopf to continue to serve as chairman. Reagan commended Fahrenkopf on "the grassroots organization which he has emphasized," and expressed his "agreement that the best way to build the Party is indeed from the Courthouse to the White House."[92] Fahrenkopf remained chairman until Reagan left office: his six-year tenure made him the longest-serving RNC chairman of the twentieth century. In Reagan's second term, Fahrenkopf sought to keep up the momentum from Reagan's landslide victory. He announced that the RNC would continue to focus on new voter registration, develop new programs to "entice Democrats into our ranks," and lay the groundwork for redistricting in 1991. Because of redistricting, the years ahead would be "the most decisive years in our struggle to build the party of choice into the majority party," he said.[93]

Party Building and Presidential Influence

A long tradition of scholarship has identified persuasion as the key to presidential power, and this is particularly true in the area of party building.[94] Indeed, one of the most important assets presidents bring to their party-building projects is their prestige and personal influence. Of course, party building may require less subtlety in interpersonal relations than other areas of presidential leadership, but the currency of presidential prestige is no less valuable here. A basic willingness on the part of the president to leverage the awesome stature of his office on behalf of his party is usually sufficient to achieve his party-building objectives. In the two main party-building initiatives of Reagan's second term—a campaign to convert "Reagan Democrats" into Republicans and an effort to recruit candidates and prepare for redistricting—Reagan used his personal prestige and influence to help make the Republican Party the majority party of the future.

Operation Open Door

In an uncanny—and unintentional—repetition of the now-familiar party-building slogan, Fahrenkopf announced in May 1985 a new program called Operation Open Door. This new initiative would spend $500,000 in four states (Louisiana, North Carolina, Florida, and Pennsylvania) to persuade 100,000 registered Democrats to convert to the Republican Party in one hundred days. Each of these states went for Reagan in 1980 and again in 1984, each appeared to be trending in the Republican direction, and each had an important Senate race in 1986.

Though Fahrenkopf was unaware that the phrase *open door* was used by all three of Reagan's partisan predecessors in their party-building initiatives, this striking coincidence serves as a reminder of the common thread that binds these four minority-party presidents together.[95] While Eisenhower, Nixon, Ford, and Reagan all undertook party-building activities in very different contexts and pursued very different proximate purposes, each president found himself saddled to a party that was stuck in the perpetual minority in terms of partisan identification in the electorate and number of public offices held across the nation. Each aimed to grow his party into the new majority by welcoming new voters, activists, and candidates into the party.

Despite Reagan's landslide reelection victory and signs of steady GOP gains in party identification, the GOP remained the minority party by most measures in 1985. In particular, it had yet to build a robust "farm team" at the state and local levels: Republicans held only 41 percent of state legislative seats and seventeen governorships. Operation Open Door was thus designed to exploit the "golden opportunity" of Reagan's landslide election victory to make an aggressive push forward: "The demographics are on our side," Fahrenkopf noted. "There are plenty of new Republicans to be found. We are the emerging majority."[96]

Yet Reagan's team believed that Reagan's current popularity provided only a brief window of opportunity in which to make significant gains for the party. Rollins said: "My assumption is that we will be making a serious mistake if we don't devote the next four or five months to the attempt."[97] Fahrenkopf explained that the decision to launch Operation Open Door was made immediately after the election: "We decided very quickly that what with all these Reagan Democrats, we wanted to make them Republicans. And so we were very aggressive and really spent a lot of time and effort at it."[98]

The effort was especially important for ongoing party-building efforts in the South. While the South was becoming an increasingly secure region of support for Republican presidential candidates, at the local level it remained largely Democratic.[99] In many southern states it was necessary to be registered as a Democrat to cast a meaningful vote for sheriff, county commissioner, or school board. "We were trying to build a Republican Party in those areas," Fahrenkopf explained:

> And you've got to get Republican voters to do it. . . . If we can develop a base of Republican voters who say, "I am a Republican," well, then, you can build a party. You can't build a party with people who are just voting Republican in just the presidential and then the senatorial races. To build a party, you've got to get Republicans.[100]

Using direct mail, door-to-door canvassing, telemarketing, and television advertising, Operation Open Door set out to redeploy those county party organizations that had performed effectively in the 1984 election campaign.

"All levels of the party must work in tandem," Fahrenkopf told party workers. "County organizers can lend a personal touch to Operation Open Door, already knowing many of the potential switchers on a first-name basis. The state parties have the operational know-how and resources to boost local programs. At the national level, I have already traveled to the target states and will continue working with them to coordinate party efforts."[101]

The influence of the president, however, was pivotal. Reagan brought publicity to the conversion campaign by holding a reception at the White House for Democratic officeholders who switched parties in June 1985.[102] Reagan, a proud party convert himself, drew upon his own experience to motivate the approximately one hundred new Republican converts in attendance. He said:

> Welcome to the Republican Party. Welcome to the party of the open door. . . . Many of you hold public office, and you were longtime Democrats, and you changed parties at considerable risk. It was an act of courage and an act of conscience. . . . You're not isolated cases. You're part of a great national change, a national movement that is sweeping the electorate.[103]

At an RNC meeting later that month, new converts had clearly become the pride of the party. RNC members "stomped feet and loosed tentative rebel yells" as party converts "marched onto the stage." Bo Callaway, Ford's campaign director from 1976, remarked: "I have been coming to these meetings for a long time, and. . . . I've never seen so much enthusiasm in the party."[104] By the 100-day mark, however, the RNC was forced to stretch the numbers to report that it had met its goal of 100,000 conversions. Only about 54,000 former Democrats had reregistered as Republicans; the RNC had to add 45,000 or so "pledges" to declare success. It did, however, announce that approximately 200 elected officials had switched parties.[105]

Fahrenkopf stressed that the first 100 days were merely "Phase One," or "the 'hook,'" meant "to provide more momentum for the Republican Party's next party-building operation, called the '1991 Plan.'"[106] The fall campaign would focus on laying the groundwork for redistricting through "candidate recruitment, re-electing Republican incumbents and finding ways to recognize Republicans in the 22 states that do not register by party."[107]

The 1991 Plan

In Fahrenkopf's view, Reagan's landslide reelection represented the "first step" toward a partisan realignment. But the GOP needed to make significant gains in House elections before that realignment could become a reality. The problem was structural: in the 1984 congressional races, Fahrenkopf pointed out, Republican candidates "received 50 percent of the nationwide vote but only won 42 percent of the seats" because most districts had been drawn by Democratic state legislatures in 1981 to favor Democratic candidates. By winning more state legislative seats and governors' mansions, Reagan's team hoped "to have Republicans drawing the lines" in 1991.[108]

The problem, as he saw it, was that the Republican Party was still suffering from Watergate's effect on the party. "It devastated us," he said. "We lost a generation of state legislators. We were almost at parity, and what happened was we were back 1,000 seats in the hole." The "people who would have normally been coming up through the ranks, we lost them," he explained. "So we had to rebuild the infrastructure at the state legislative level, so that we would be in the position, when reapportionment came in 1990, 1991, to be players."[109]

It was difficult, however, to recruit GOP candidates to run for state legislature, particularly in the South. The best resource the Republican Party had, Fahrenkopf said, was Reagan, who frequently sought to persuade prospective candidates to run. He would "pick up the phone and call them," to "put the hard push on them." Reagan would primarily call prospective gubernatorial or congressional candidates; for prospective state legislative candidates, Reagan's political team would invite them to the White House:

> If you get some guy who's thinking about running for the state senate, it's an important position, and he's invited to come to Washington, and he meets Ed Rollins or Lyn Nofziger, and he's taken to lunch in the White House mess, and he walks out of there with a pair of Ronald Reagan cufflinks and a pen, that's pretty big stuff.[110]

In his first term, Reagan focused his personal efforts on recruiting women, Hispanics, and other minority candidates to run for office as Republicans.[111] During the second term, he continued these efforts but shifted his emphasis to the Sunbelt region and those states that were most likely to gain congressional seats through reapportionment in 1991. Reagan's personal touch proved to be particularly valuable in those states where Republicans had little chance of winning a state legislative majority and where fielding a high-quality Republican gubernatorial candidate (who could veto "egregious gerrymanders" drawn by Democratic legislatures) became the primary goal. The RNC also worked to secure a sufficient number of state legislative seats to sustain those vetoes.[112]

In addition to recruiting strong candidates, the 1991 Plan emphasized further efforts to build the infrastructures of county party organizations. In preparation for the 1986 and 1988 elections, the RNC offered local parties assistance in seven areas: "volunteer activities, voter list development, ballot integrity, voter contact mailings, voter registration, absentee ballots and voter identification and turnout programs."[113] According to the RNC's communications director, the goal was to preserve the party-building work of the past and continually upgrade the organization's capacities: "What we're trying to do is not let it all come apart." In the short run, the RNC hoped to provide the Republican nominee in 1988 with "a meaningful vote-delivery system in the key electoral counties in each of the 50 states."[114] Looking ahead to 1991, the goal was to ensure the smooth functioning of the party's technology and information databases in 650 critical counties.[115] Though Republicans lost control of the Senate in 1986 and five seats in the House, they scored a net gain of eight new Republican governors. While the partisan balance in state legislatures remained essentially the same, the new governors gave reason for optimism.

As the 1988 elections approached, the RNC launched a Volunteer Incentive Program that once again leveraged Reagan's popularity to help recruit activists to work for the party. The purpose was to build an institutionalized, durable network of volunteers nationwide. Several hundred thousand potential activists received letters from Reagan asking for their "time and effort" for the presidential campaign in 1988, whoever the nominee might be. Those who accepted received newsletters featuring messages from Reagan, and those who provided "exemplary service" received "special recognition."[116]

Many of the party activists recruited during Reagan's presidency remained with the party and assumed positions of leadership in subsequent years. Several prominent figures from the George W. Bush administration, for example, got their start in Republican party-building programs during the 1980s: "Ari Fleisher . . . Ed Gillespie, most of those guys started down in the phone banks in the basement of the RNC when I was chairman," Fahrenkopf recalled. Persistent party building served to continually replenish the ranks of the Republican Party's activist base. Fahrenkopf explained:

> It's always been that we in the Republican Party have a cadre of people who have done presidential races and done national conventions, and who every four years are there. So we're not reinventing and retraining people. We've got people who have been involved in the process and know how it's done. And whoever our nominee is can push that button and they're there, and they've done it before.[117]

Indeed, one of the major assets Reagan bequeathed to his successor was an expanded cadre of party professionals. The party inherited by George H. W. Bush also benefited from a dramatic increase in registered Republicans, upgraded technologies, new voter lists, enhanced fund-raising systems, better-trained local party leaders, and an operational commitment to win more legislative and gubernatorial seats in advance of reapportionment.

■

As we have seen, along each of six dimensions of party activity, Reagan supported a wide variety of party-building initiatives (see table 6.1). Taken all together, these episodes illustrate four additional characteristics of presidential party building as a general phenomenon: (1) valuable organizational models for use in party building can be drawn from a party's extrapartisan networks; (2) party building is often undertaken with the hope that incremental gains in the present will produce larger gains in the future; (3) presidential campaigns offer a unique opportunity to expand the party's base of registered voters; (4) the president's prestige and personal influence can be leveraged on behalf of party building to great effect.

Table 6.1   Reagan's Party Building

Provide campaign services	Build human capital	Recruit candidates	Mobilize voters	Finance party operations	Support internal activities
Field operations (1981)	CMC expansion (1981)	Republican Strategic Triad (1983–1984)	Investments in county party organizations (1983+)	Amway model for sustaining members (1981+)	Investments in computer technology (1981)
Investments in county party organizations (1983+)	State and local party training (1983+)	Investments in county party organizations (1983+)	RNC voter registration drive (1984)	New direct-mail presses (1981+)	Field operations (1981+)
1991 Plan (1985+)	RNC voter registration drive (1984)	RNC voter registration drive (1984)	Victory Blitz '84 (1984)	High-roller clubs (1981+)	Redistricting division (1981)
	Victory Blitz '84 (1984)	Reagan phone calls (1985+)	Reagan-Bush '84 registration drive (1984)	Republican Strategic Triad (1983–1984)	Video teleconference system (1981)
	Volunteer Incentive Program (1988)	White House invitations (1985+)	Evangelical voter registration drive (1984)	Investments in county party organizations (1983+)	Polling services (1981)
			Operation Open Door (1985)	Reagan direct-mail signatures (1983+)	Bring auxiliary organizations into mainstream (1981)
					Republican Strategic Triad (1983–84)
					Investments in county party organizations (1983+)
					Investments in phone banks (1983+)
					Voter list expansion (1984+)
					1991 Plan (1985+)

Reagan sought to build a durable new majority for the Republican Party that would reflect and perpetuate his personal brand of politics. His team launched a variety of initiatives to capitalize on his popularity and graft it onto the party; the goal was to gain significant ground on the Democrats at the state and local level and in party identification in the electorate. In Reagan's final years, his political team looked ahead to the 1991 redistricting process and to the opportunity to level the playing field in House elections. By investing in the organizational capacities of state and local parties, Reagan's team sought to equip the GOP to influence the redistricting process, win control of the House of Representatives, and bring about a historic shift in the competitive balance between the parties in the 1990s.

Reagan's efforts to build his party at an organizational level were historically significant, but they were not entrepreneurial. The party Reagan inherited was already moving along a trajectory of organizational development. But just as Reagan's party-building efforts were shaped by the organizational capacities he inherited, his contributions shaped the party-building efforts of his successors. As we will see in the next chapter, the party organization he bequeathed to George Bush had an increasingly robust national infrastructure, enhanced links with local parties, new technologies, firmly established strategic commitments (such as the 1991 Plan), and an abundance of human capital.

7

Leveling the Playing Field | George H. W. Bush

*We've shed a lot of blood, sweat, tears to rebuild the Republican Party since
the early seventies. The best way to keep our party growing is to win more
elections in 1990, from the courthouse to the statehouse to Capitol Hill.*

—President George H. W. Bush[1]

When George H. W. Bush assumed the presidency in 1989, the Republican
Party had won five of the previous six presidential elections and enjoyed eight
years with a popular Republican in the White House. Yet the GOP still held
only 175 seats in the House, 45 seats in the Senate, a minority of governorships, and less than 40 percent of state legislative seats. Over the course of
Bush's four years in the White House, an average of only 38 percent of the
public identified with the Republican Party. Like all other minority-party
presidents, Bush ran ahead of the Republican congressional candidate in a
majority of House districts.[2] While Bush and his team believed the GOP to be
on the rise, they also recognized that it remained at a competitive disadvantage. With reapportionment and redistricting just around the corner in 1991,
Bush had a strong incentive to make a major push forward to "become the
majority party in America."[3]

Fortunately for Bush, the party organization he inherited from Reagan
offered almost all the tools he needed to pursue these ambitions. The RNC
was already making investments in organizational capacity in preparation for
redistricting battles in 1991, human capital and financial resources were abundant, grassroots party-building operations were in full swing, and strategic
coordination between the national and local parties was ongoing. The party
organization Bush inherited was, in short, easily built upon. At an RNC luncheon two days before Bush's inauguration, the president-elect announced
that he was aware of the party-building work done by Reagan and that he
intended to continue along the same path:

> I'm here to say I want to work with the party. I believe I know as well
> as any president-elect the importance of Party. We're not going to be
> able to do everything exactly the way every member of the National
> Committee thinks it should be done. . . . But there's a general thrust,
> and President Reagan set that tone . . . we're not coming in to correct
> the ills of the past, we're coming in to build on a proud record that
> has already been established. So, to do that building, we'll need your
> help. I am interested in this party and in the Republican National
> Committee. I'll work hard to merit your confidence.[4]

		Party Building						Party Predation					
		C	H	R	V	F	I	C	H	R	V	F	I
Republicans	Eisenhower	•	•	•	•	•	•						
	Nixon	•	•	•	•	•	•	•				•	
	Ford	•	•	•	•	•	•						
	Reagan	•	•	•	•	•	•						
	Bush	•	•	•		•	•						
Democrats	Kennedy				•	•		•	•		•	•	•
	Johnson							•	•		•	•	•
	Carter							•	•	•	•	•	•
	Clinton (1st term)							•	•		•	•	•
	Clinton (2nd term)	•	•		•	•	•						
C=Provide campaign services, H=Build human capital, R=Recruit candidates,													
V=Mobilize voters, F=Finance party operations, I=Support internal activities													

Figure 7.1. Bush's Party Interactions

Over the course of his four years in office, Bush lived up to this pledge of continuity. Indeed, in contrast to Eisenhower, Reagan, and Nixon, who assumed the White House after "out-party" periods, Bush had little need to realign the party's operations to be more responsive to the White House. Over the previous eight years, the Republican Party organization had been built to be highly responsive to presidential leadership while providing services to state and local parties. It stood ready to capitalize on another Republican presidency to make further organizational gains. Consequently, Bush's task was rather straightforward. He set out to push the GOP forward along its current trajectory of organizational development while making additional contributions of his own.

This chapter examines Bush's efforts to strengthen the GOP along five of the six dimensions of party activity (figure 7.1).[5] Along the way, it also elaborates upon three characteristics of presidential party building as a more general phenomenon: (1) the once-in-a-decade opportunity to redraw congressional districts is a powerful motivator of presidential party building; (2) presidential party building offers little by way of political protection for the president; (3) persistent investments in human capital tend to reinforce the party's operating norms.

Leveling the Playing Field

Nothing exemplifies the intimate relationship between majority building and party building better than the effort to prepare for redistricting. Reapportionment and the accompanying redistricting process offers a once-in-a-decade opportunity to level the playing field and redress perceived structural imbalances in the political landscape. Taking advantage of this opportunity, however, requires a rather complex organizational effort. In the first two years of

Bush's presidency, preparing for redistricting became the primary focus around which all other party-building efforts revolved.

In late 1988, Bush named Lee Atwater, his campaign manager, as the new chairman of the RNC. He made it clear that this arrangement would continue the strong, cooperative relationship between the RNC and the White House: "He will be my political eyes and ears," Bush said.[6] Only thirty-seven years old, Atwater was perhaps best known as a ruthless campaign tactician; he was also a self-described "nuts and bolts" organization man who helped to build the GOP in South Carolina.[7]

Their top priority, Bush said, would be to influence the redistricting process in 1991. If the GOP was to become the new majority party during the 1990s, it would have to redress what was perceived to be a structural disadvantage for the Republicans at the district level. "Today Democrats now have a redistricting advantage in states that compose about 90 percent of the seats in Congress," Bush explained.

> And that is why we Republicans must make solid gains at the state level. Critical gubernatorial and legislative races in the eight largest states alone will determine whether Republicans will be treated fairly in the drafting of 209 congressional districts. . . . A majority or even a large minority of Republicans in state legislatures can join with Republican Governors to sustain the veto of outrageous gerrymandering schemes, strengthening our numbers in the U.S. House.[8]

Bush argued that continuing to build "strong state parties" was critical to this task, as was aggressive candidate recruitment. These priorities represented "my strategies for victory," Bush said, but added they were not novel. Linking his party-building efforts to those of his predecessors, Bush acknowledged the long road traveled by Republicans since his tenure as RNC chairman under Nixon:

> We've shed a lot of blood, sweat, tears to rebuild the Republican Party since the early seventies. The best way to keep our party growing is to win more elections in 1990, from the courthouse to the statehouse to Capitol Hill.[9]

Echoing Bush, Atwater argued that the most important challenge facing the Republican Party was to make enough electoral gains at the state level in 1989 and 1990 to have an influence on the redistricting process in 1991. In 1989, Republicans only controlled eight state legislatures; Democrats clearly had the upper hand, holding more than 60 percent of all legislative seats and twenty-eight governorships. "There's no question about it, from a big picture standpoint, our number one goal must remain reapportionment," Atwater said. "We consistently get 48 percent of the vote in these national congressional elections, yet we're only sitting on 40 percent of the seats in the U.S. House," Atwater argued. "It's undemocratic, it's unfair, and it's unAmerican. And we've got to fight."[10] Thankfully, Atwater noted, his predecessor had made significant investments in the organizational capacities of the party through his 1991 Plan. His challenge as chairman, consequently, was to "follow Frank [Fahrenkopf]'s footsteps in terms of working on apportionment."[11]

Indeed, the transition from the Reagan-Fahrenkopf leadership team to the Bush-Atwater leadership team at the RNC did not disrupt the 1991 Plan. The RNC's traveling field force, its finance operations, and its candidate recruitment processes were scrutinized for how they might be improved or expanded, but they were not dismantled or replaced. Under Bush, the RNC set out to make additional investments in the same areas as it had under Reagan—in the party's infrastructure, its campaign services, and its party conversion programs—while designing innovative strategies to maximize Republican gains from redistricting. Let us consider each type of effort in turn.

Investing in Infrastructure

Under the Bush team at the RNC, the general thrust of the 1991 Plan remained the same, with only a slight shift in emphasis. Whereas Reagan's RNC had emphasized services to local parties, candidate recruitment drives, and activist enrollment programs, Bush's RNC emphasized investments in the party's computer technology, its field teams, and its legal resources.

Thanks to continual upgrades in the party's computer technology since the mid-1970s, vast stores of data on voting patterns and demographic information for every county in the country were already on hand at the RNC and easily manipulated. Once the new census data arrived, the RNC would be ready to merge the new data with its preexisting data and offer sophisticated analyses to help state and local party leaders redraw district lines in ways that favored Republican candidates.[12] The quality of the information used and the precision of the redistricting operation were expected to be critical factors in potential court battles, as well. Party leaders thus sought to compile evidence that newly drawn districts adhered to constitutional standards and were based on sound data. With upgraded computer technology and a new staff of "computer geniuses," the RNC aimed to be prepared "from the moment the legislators receive the census data to the likely day that the courts finally certify the redistricting plans."[13]

Thomas Hofeller, redistricting director at the NRCC, worked with the RNC to create a unified software system so that all formal party committees would work together more efficiently. "If the national party does not take the lead here and build this system, then we'll have Republicans all over the country going in 16 different directions, and the technical process of redistrict development is going to cost the GOP as a whole five to ten times more than it will if it's done together," he said.[14] Redistricting could be a touchy subject: asking an incumbent congressman to accept a plan that turned his 65 percent majority district into a 55 percent majority district in order to make a neighboring district more competitive was a sensitive issue. If the party developed a unified approach in advance with a "kind of cohesion," redistricting efforts might be more successful across the board.[15]

Atwater also invested in the party's legal resources. The RNC created legal handbooks for Republican lawyers at the state level, established a "legal clearing-house for redistrict information," and held training seminars on how to maximize redistricting gains for state party leaders.[16] A new organization staffed with Republican loyalists, called Lawyers for the Republic, was also created outside the party structure to accept large, tax-deductible contributions.[17] Atwater said this expanded legal team was prepared "to fight gerrymandering in the courts—if we must."[18]

Assistance in Running Campaigns

Investments in technology and legal resources would be useful to state legislators as they designed new districts in 1991, but to have a "strong impact," Republicans needed to win more governorships and legislative seats in 1990. "We've got the best attorneys; we've got the best technology. But let's face the facts," Atwater said. "The best way to gain power is through elected offices, and the elected offices I'm talking about are governorships and state legislative."[19] The first step was to expand the RNC's regional field teams and offer state party leaders assistance with designing campaign plans; Atwater also initiated a new program, called the Legislative Strike Force, which targeted "hot" races in pivotal redistricting states.[20]

Atwater also assembled an advisory panel composed of the party's "top political professionals" and charged it with developing a unified, national party campaign strategy. The advisory group was chaired by Charles R. Black, a former consulting partner of Atwater's, and included Ford's and Reagan's pollster and strategist Robert M. Teeter and Richard N. Bond, who served as deputy RNC chairman under Reagan. This "kitchen cabinet on redistrict" deliberated on how best to gain "at least a toehold" in key states prior to 1991, considering, for example, whether to devote more resources in a given state to the gubernatorial election or to state legislative races.[21] Atwater acknowledged that the push to prepare for redistricting was optimistic, but he also insisted that it was not tilting at windmills: "I know we aren't going to be the majority party by the end of this year," he said in January 1990. "But my goal is to help make us the majority party in Congress. The sooner the better."[22]

Candidate recruitment figured prominently in the effort, and here Bush lent a hand directly. Prospective candidates were brought to Washington to meet with Bush, Vice President Quayle, and other high-ranking Republicans. "Bush did it all the time," Bond explained. "You tell them we're going to put you on the receiving line for Air Force One, Air Force Two, meet and greet 'em, and we're going to let you ride in the limo."[23] Candidate recruitment was also done more efficiently: on a single day in October 1989, for example, sixty prospective state legislative candidates from eight states were brought to Washington and "told how important everyone at the top of the political ladder thinks it is to fill some of the lower rungs with able younger versions of themselves." Three more recruitment days were planned for legislators to come to Washington before the end of the year.[24] Atwater noted: "We're not waiting until the 1990 election cycle begins to recruit and train strong candidates and new Republican voters; we're doing it now."[25] Because of looming redistricting, the joint White House–RNC candidate recruitment programs were "less focused on interim victories than on possible long-term gains," journalist David Broder observed.[26]

In addition to helping to recruit candidates, Bush also personally lent a hand in raising money for the party. During 1989 alone, Bush signed eighteen mass mailings that raised over $3.2 million for state party-building efforts, party conversion efforts, and candidates' campaigns.[27] Between May and December of 1989, he also participated in twenty-two fund-raising photo ops, receptions, luncheons, or dinners that raised over $24.5 million for state parties, congressional campaign committees, the RGA, or candidates' campaigns.[28] He redoubled his efforts in 1990, and in June 1990 he "broke records" at the party's annual fund-raising dinner by raising $7 million in a single evening. The White House reported that in his first two years, Bush had helped to raise an unprecedented $94 million for the GOP.[29] The notable aspect of these efforts was that this money went directly to the party organization to fund its many activities; as we will see in Part II, Democrats, in contrast, diverted the vast majority of funds they raised to their own reelection campaigns and for other presidential purposes. Bush also dispatched Cabinet members to help raise funds for state parties and Republican candidates: Cabinet members traveled to 181 cities in forty-four states for a total of 393 visits between September 1989 and March 1990 alone.[30]

Records show that Bush also worked to strengthen the large-donor programs that were designed in the 1970s and 1980s to leverage the prestige of the presidency.[31] He was happy to help the party in any way that he could, Bush said, especially with "the governors' races, because they are key when you look at this concept of redistricting that we're going to have to grope with in the years ahead."[32]

Operation Switch

To supplement these efforts, Atwater launched a new party conversion effort in 1989 called Operation Switch. The timing was favorable for such a drive, Atwater said, since voters and elected officials had been "switching to our party in record numbers" in recent years: five million new voters had registered as Republicans in the last two years alone.[33] But whereas Fahrenkopf's Operation Open Door sought to convince individual voters to switch parties, Atwater now targeted elected officials. The operation produced fast results: by the fall of 1989, 154 former Democratic public officeholders had already converted to the GOP, almost all from the South. The two most prominent "switchers" were members of Congress, but Atwater argued that even more important were the state legislators, councilmen, judges and justices of the peace, sheriffs, and mayors who switched.[34] Those conversions not only created a "sense of movement to the Republican Party," but built a "cadre of elected officials" at the "local, courthouse level" in southern states "where incumbents are very hard to beat. It puts peer pressure on other politicians in those states. It says to them, 'You can be in a job like yours and be a Republican.' It also gives us on-the-ground candidate recruiters who have shown you can run for office as a Republican at every level."[35]

Bush offered his personal support for Operation Switch as well; like Reagan, he welcomed sixty-five fresh converts to the White House. Speaking to the switchers as well as to prospective party switchers, he offered ongoing assistance from the national party and the White House:

> Each of you here has made a courageous decision, sometimes a very tough political decision, to join us—taking considerable political risk in the process . . . when you made that bold choice to join us, we made a choice, too. We will support you; we will back you up in every way we can . . . when you're out there on the front lines for us, you won't be fighting alone. This party will stand with you shoulder to shoulder. . . . The party will become the majority party in America. We can do it—I want to help—we will do it because of the courage of you and thousands like you.[36]

Bush lived up to his promise, and as late as 1991 was receiving letters from recent converts who thanked him for spending his personal time with them. Governor Buddy Roemer of Louisiana, a prominent party convert in 1991, for example, wrote that Bush's personal efforts "epitomize the Republican Party's support for those of us who make the switch."[37]

To put these various programs into perspective, Atwater consistently explained that nuts-and-bolts party building served the larger purpose of building a new Republican majority. "We have a chance to become the *majority* party in this country," he reminded party activists.[38] The timing was propitious for an all-out push:

> With George Bush leading our party, I believe we are at last prepared to break out of 50 years of minority status. This is a vision that George Bush and I deeply share. We seek to broaden our party's base, to strengthen it at every level, and to be the party of all Americans, of every race, creed and color. And with George Bush as president, we have a unique opportunity to make that happen. As the national committee's new chairman, I have one overriding goal for our party—to achieve majority status by the year 2000.[39]

Collaborating with African Americans

To maximize the party's gains from reapportionment, the Republican Party made concerted efforts to coordinate redistricting efforts with groups of African American activists. By mid-1991, the Republican Party was sharing its software, legal and technical advice, and money to help carve up old district lines and create more majority-minority districts to increase the number of African American representatives both in Congress and in the state legislatures. While some focused on the potential pitfalls of such a strategy, those involved argued that the new districts would ultimately serve the interests of African Americans better than the alternative of remaining a diluted minority group in many different districts. From the Republican Party's standpoint, helping to create majority-minority districts promised direct benefits for the GOP. By grouping overwhelmingly Democratic voters into concentrated areas, more competitive seats would be created for Republicans. Republicans also believed that in cases where Republican gerrymanders might be challenged in court, if the party could show that it had drawn up new district lines in direct consultation with African American groups, they stood a better chance of winning legal cases.[40]

But because the unusual collaboration between Republicans and black activists drew so much media attention, it obscured other serious efforts undertaken during Bush's first two years to reach out to African Americans. Bush and Atwater believed that the GOP could attract economically successful African Americans to the Republican Party if they courted them effectively, even though black voters tended to give Republican presidential candidates only between 8 and 10 percent of their vote. Ronald Reagan had conspicuously avoided making appeals to African Americans; he was reluctant to sign an extension of the Voting Rights Act or support a federal holiday for Martin Luther King Jr's birthday. Bush, in contrast, wanted to make gains in the black community his signature contribution. Atwater explained:

> The fact of the matter is we are looking to the future. I am the new chairman of the Republican Party and George Bush is the new Republican president and we are making an unprecedented effort to reach out. . . . What I'm hoping is the people will realize that we are on the dawn of a new era. We are going out of our way to do something that has never been done before.[41]

Skeptics argued that Atwater's highly publicized outreach effort was designed either to force Democrats to spend their resources on shoring up the support of African Americans or to appease socially liberal suburban Republicans who were uncomfortable with Reagan's record on race.[42] Whatever the true motive, the outreach effort constituted a full-fledged party-building initiative.

By mid-1990, Bush's team at the RNC was implementing a comprehensive effort to recruit African Americans to run as Republicans for local and statewide offices. They offered prospective candidates direct financial assistance, support in developing independent fund-raising capacities, and strategic help in designing campaign plans. In addition, three regional training conferences were held in 1990 for black candidates, campaign managers, and volunteers "to teach black Republican activists the fine points of fund raising, media relations, and campaign strategy." They also encouraged new College Republican organizations to form at historically black colleges, and met with some success, boasting the establishment of five new chapters in a year.[43]

Atwater went to the annual meeting of the U.S. Conference of Mayors and announced the RNC's intention to "actively recruit blacks as mayoral candidates" and "support them financially." He called mayors a "potential farm team" for the Republican Party and said that he hoped to establish a "political beachhead" for the GOP in urban areas by winning mayoral races in 1989 and 1990.[44] Bush made a number of symbolic gestures to the African American community as well: he met with the NAACP director five times in his first eighteen months in office (Reagan only met with him once in eight years); spoke at the National Baptist Convention and the Southern Baptist Convention; met with Desmond Tutu; appointed several African Americans to high-profile positions in his administration; and made visits to predominantly African American neighborhoods.[45] While many questioned the sincerity of the effort—especially Atwater's role in it—a record number of African Americans ran for public office as Republicans in 1990.[46]

Party Building and Political Success

Minority-party presidents are drawn to party building because it appears to offer a promising way to build a new majority that bears their stamp; of course, they hope to extract some short-term political benefits for their administrations as well. But as we have seen, even the most operationally successful party-building program does not guarantee either a new majority or the accomplishment of the president's short-term goals. In fact, more often than not, these presidents fail to achieve their grand ambitions and find party building to be less politically beneficial than they had hoped. Yet their dissatisfaction with their competitive political environment continually motivates them to hazard the attempt.

In the previous four chapters, we observed that it was somewhat easier for Bush's predecessors to extract some short-term benefit from party building than it was to build a new Republican majority. In Bush's case, we observe the opposite: his party-building efforts helped to improve the Republican Party's competitive standing, but they generated extraordinarily little political support for his presidency.

Bush reached record highs in public approval during the Persian Gulf War (about 89 percent), but in the summer of 1991 he began to lose support; by the 1992 election, his approval ratings had dropped to about 30 percent. Within his own party, his support seemed to fall even more precipitously. There were many reasons for Bush's political collapse, not the least of which involved his "breach of faith" on tax policy and his "umbrella party" concept for the GOP.[47] Our objective, however, is not to pinpoint the cause of Bush's political problems but to observe that Bush's operationally successful party-building efforts during his first two years could do nothing to prevent the unraveling of his political support in his second two years. Bush made valuable contributions to the Republican Party's organizational development, but these contributions did little to resolve his own political troubles.

Early in his presidency, Bush enjoyed a generally amicable relationship with the conservative wing of his party. Chief of Staff John Sununu was considered a credible conservative, as was Lee Atwater. In their early staffing decisions, appointments, and other political actions, Sununu and Atwater managed to keep most conservatives mollified. Mixing metaphors, *Business Week* noted in the middle of 1989 that "the bones Bush has tossed to conservatives have been enough to keep activists in the tent, where the President needs them for battles to come."[48]

But in early 1990, fissures within the party began to appear. The first involved the abortion issue. Once a supporter of abortion rights, Bush adopted a pro-life position as Reagan's vice president and continued to support pro-life public policies as president. But in January 1990, Atwater announced in a highly publicized speech that he and the president viewed the GOP as an "umbrella party" that was "big enough to accommodate different views" on the issue. "That, my friends, is part of the growing pains of becoming a majority. And we are an umbrella party."[49] President Bush was "solidly opposed to abortion," he said, but there should be no "litmus test" for any Republican candidate "who believes in our overall philosophy and who supports this President and supports this party. . . . I would hope that Republicans support Republican candidates regardless of their position on abortion."[50]

Conservatives inside and outside the party, including the director of the National Conservative Political Action Committee, sent angry letters to the White House demanding that the president stand firmly against abortion rights. For the rest of his term, the debate raged on over whether abortion should be a party issue or a personal issue where individual candidates should follow their conscience, and whether the party ought to support a constitutional amendment to outlaw the procedure in its platform.[51] Neither Bush nor Atwater retracted the "umbrella party" concept for the GOP, but the Republican platform in 1992 did adopt ardently pro-life positions, including support for the constitutional amendment.

Though the abortion issue had begun to create fissures in January 1990, it was not until Bush's reversal of his "Read my lips, no new taxes" pledge in the summer of 1990 that influential party leaders began to publicly rebel against the administration.[52] An analyst at the conservative Heritage Foundation noted: "If there's one thing that can bind the conservative movement together, if it's not the threat of the Soviet Union, it would be George Bush reneging on the one campaign pledge that everyone remembers and that really distinguished conservatives from liberals."[53]

Meanwhile, Atwater was diagnosed with inoperable brain cancer and died in the spring of 1991. His absence was deeply felt within the administration. Bush not only lost a personal friend, but also his top political strategist and one of his strongest bridges to the conservative community. To shore up his support among right-wing Republicans, Bush asked social conservative leader William Bennett to replace Atwater at the RNC in December 1990. Heartened, *National Review* editors hoped that the move indicated the administration had acknowledged "its lack of direction" and was now planning to make "Bennett the compass."[54] But Bennett withdrew his name from consideration (for personal financial reasons, he said), which only compounded Bush's problems with social and economic conservatives.[55] In a last-ditch effort in early 1991 to find an acceptable RNC chairman, Bush named Clayton Yeutter, then secretary of agriculture, to the post.

Yeutter had previously served as the Midwest regional director of Nixon's CREEP and as a fund-raiser for Bush during his first presidential bid in 1980; he was generally considered a stalwart Republican who, if uninspiring, had broad support within the party.[56] "Not everyone has expressed happiness with the budget negotiations of last year," Yeutter said in his understated acceptance speech, "but that's no excuse for sitting on our haunches in 1991 and 1992."[57] Yeutter only served as RNC chairman until the end of 1991, but in his short tenure he oversaw implementation of the 1991 Plan.[58] Ensuring that redistricting was carried out effectively was the "highest priority item on the agenda," he told a gathering of Republicans:

> What happens this year will lay the groundwork or the foundation for what transpires next year on the national political scene. . . . Redistricting is going to alter [the] odds in a very substantial way in a whole lot of states . . . obviously, we're concentrating very heavily on those redistricting battles, both legislatively and in court, if need be, in an attempt to try to level the playing field.[59]

While most attention was devoted to redistricting during 1991, Yeutter also oversaw efforts to recruit strong candidates for 1992, continued to raise party funds, and began preparations for the Republican National Convention in 1992.[60] By the end of 1991 the redistricting process was complete and widely viewed as a success.[61]

But ongoing party-building at the RNC did little to quell the discontent of the conservative wing. One way that Bush tried to reach out to them was by lending his support to GOPAC, the political action committee chaired by Representative Newt Gingrich, who was still infuriated by Bush's "breach of faith" on tax policy.[62] Bush and Atwater had long viewed GOPAC's candidate recruitment efforts as a complement to their party-building efforts, and in early 1990 RNC funds had been used to sponsor GOPAC's nationally televised workshops. By educating party activists and potential candidates on policy substance and political technique, GOPAC workshops aimed to groom the Republican leaders of the future.[63]

In October 1991, Gingrich extended an invitation to Bush to speak at the GOPAC Charter Meeting in early November. GOPAC, Gingrich wrote, was a "major building block in our effort for a House Republican majority and for a successful second term for your presidency." Since 1986, GOPAC had contributed nearly $2 million "to candidates for state and local offices, while at the same time providing training seminars for literally thousands of Republican candidates and activists," Gingrich explained.[64] The new initiative to pick up seats in 1992, called "Change Congress *Now!*," targeted 170 House districts held by Democrats. GOPAC encouraged workshop participants to recruit strong candidates to challenge those 170 incumbents, identify 100 financial contributors in each congressional district who could raise $1,000 each (amassing $100,000 for each candidate), and mobilize at least 1,000 volunteers to work "on behalf of the entire Republican ticket." GOPAC planned to contribute an additional $1 million in direct support for challengers who faced incumbents in 1992.[65] Gingrich said that the 150 charter members of GOPAC—those who contributed at least $10,000 annually to the committee—would be inspired by the president's support for their efforts, and added that "you would do us a great honor, and me a great favor, if you would consider hosting the charter group at the White House" or speaking at its main reception. Bush agreed and spoke to the group on November 11, 1991.[66]

Bush's efforts to placate conservatives intensified during the 1992 primary season when his ultraconservative challenger for the nomination, Pat Buchanan, sought to exploit Bush's weaknesses with conservatives. In an effort to unify the party, Bush invited Buchanan to speak at the Republican National Convention.[67] Buchanan delivered his now-famous "culture war" speech where he described Democratic nominee Bill Clinton as a "pro-gay" supporter of "abortion on demand" who "figured out how to dodge the draft" and who now stood on the wrong side of a "religious war."[68] NBC news anchor Tom Brokaw opined that Buchanan "gave the impression that if you're not a white heterosexual Christian . . . you're not welcome in the Republican Party."[69] While giving Buchanan this opportunity may have been consistent with the party-building tradition of holding open party forums to build consensus—and while it may have helped to cement the allegiance of social conservatives to the Republican Party—its immediate effect was to contradict the inclusive rhetoric of the Bush campaign and make the convention themes seem "muddled" and "jumbled."[70]

Throughout the campaign, Bush found himself on the defensive and lacking strong support from within his party for his reelection bid. His experience thus offers us a portrait of a party builder who contributed to the development of his party's organizational capacities but whose efforts were no remedy for the particular political dilemmas he faced as president. Like Eisenhower, whose organizational innovations did little to quell a conservative revolt, and like Ford, whose party building failed to prevent a challenge from his party's right wing, Bush's efforts could not defend against the unraveling of his political support.

Human Capital and Party Operating Norms

Every Republican president from Eisenhower to Bush invested in the GOP's human capital. By sponsoring training schools, holding campaign management seminars, and continually promoting the leaders of past programs, they helped to develop a culture of party building among their party membership. Win or lose in the current election cycle, experienced party professionals remained committed to developing the party's organizational capacities and to building a Republican majority. Indeed, despite Bush's political collapse in 1992, his team of professional party builders continued to push the project forward.

The party Bush inherited in 1989 was already well endowed with "a cadre of political professionals and party activists all across America" who were trained, skilled, and experienced in campaign management.[71] To ensure that the GOP maintained its advantage on this front, Bush's RNC team awarded these professionals lucrative consulting contracts with the expectation that their expertise would be leveraged on behalf of upcoming campaigns and party-building initiatives. In 1990 alone, the RNC spent $3.1 million on political consultant retainer fees. The consultants included a familiar cast of characters: Eddie Mahe Jr., key party builder under Nixon and Ford; Richard Bond, former deputy RNC chairman under Reagan and future RNC chairman; longtime GOP pollster and Ford campaign strategist Robert M. Teeter; and future president of Fox News, Roger Ailes.[72]

As discussed, some of these consultants played a prominent role in making preparations for redistricting; they also became critical players in Bush's 1992 reelection campaign. The *National Journal* reported that Bush was following a well-established pattern in the Republican Party:

> Although the GOP's team of presidential footmen changes every four years to suit the tastes of the party's standard-bearer, operatives who have been tested in previous presidential races are routinely recruited into a nominee's general election organization with apparently little thought to whose side they were on in the primary season. When Republicans assess their chances for success in the fall, they always take comfort in their ability to reassemble a lineup of experienced players to guide their candidate to the White House.[73]

Mary Matalin, appointed chief political adviser and director of state and local campaign operations during the reelection campaign, was a case in point. Matalin had served as an aide to former deputy RNC chairman Rich Bond in 1982, director of the RNC's get-out-the-vote operation in 1988, chief of staff at the RNC to Atwater, and acting chair of the RNC while Atwater was in the hospital in 1990.[74] "The trick to presidential campaigns is experience," she said, "knowing how to pull things together from the big picture to the mechanics, how to marshal your resources."[75] Bush's campaign manager, Frederic V. Malek, also embodied this principle. Malek's first experience with party building was in the White House under Nixon. During the 1988 campaign, Malek was responsible for coordinating the day-to-day interactions between the Bush-Quayle campaign and the RNC; he then served as Atwater's deputy during the first year of Bush's presidency.[76] Now his task was again to make "sure that all the gears are meshing" between the two entities.[77] Robert Teeter, who saw "action in every GOP presidential contest since 1968" and whose strategic assistance helped guide the party-building work of Nixon, Ford, and Reagan, became campaign chairman.[78]

In January 1992, Bush replaced Yeutter at the RNC with Bond, who, in addition to serving as former deputy RNC chairman under Reagan and adviser to Lee Atwater during the first two years of Bush's term, was also a personal friend of Bush's. Bond was viewed as a "flame thrower" whose leadership was said to be "sorely needed to 'invigorate' the Republican apparatus."[79] Reportedly, Atwater requested from his deathbed that Bond be selected as his replacement. Bond was described as "the consummate tactician, the quintessential mechanic, the fitter of nuts and bolts. According to those who know him, he is energetic. He is loyal. He is can-do. He gives good follow-up." Bond was included as a member of the reelection campaign's so-called "A team."[80]

When Bond arrived at the RNC, the party was in a strong financial position and the party staff enjoyed a close working relationship with the White House. The first task Bush gave to Bond was to ensure that the state party operations were "firing on all eight cylinders."[81] As it turned out, bolstering the state parties' organizational capacities in preparation for the election campaign proved to be easy, Bond said. After many years of state- and county-level party building, "The professionalism [of state and local parties] had gone up vertically. There were shifts. There was a shift in organization, there was a shift in fund-raising, and there was a shift in communications."[82] Bond sent the RNC's field force to conduct a "needs assessment" or "inspection tour" in each of the campaign's targeted states to determine their preparedness: "How are the state parties doing? Are they ready for it? What's their budget for the year, what's their level of professionalism? What are their needs?" The RNC provided the technical, financial, and personnel assistance needed to bring each party unit up to speed.[83] While the primary goal of the Bush-Quayle reelection campaign was, of course, to win, Bond noted that "Bush cared about party building," too.[84]

Bond met weekly for lunch with the president and was given a seat at Cabinet and congressional leadership meetings. "I actually had a very minor speaking role at the end of every meeting to report what was going on in politics," Bond noted. Bush relied on Bond to "keep his finger on the pulse" of national politics and requested memos from Bond—"about once a week," the president requested by hand—to keep him apprised of key congressional and state-level campaigns and to receive updates on the financial picture at the RNC.[85] Bush was "always asking 'what's going on, what's going on,'" Bond recalled. For example, in an early March 1992 memo, Bush was pleased to hear that the RNC was on budget and that Bond was developing plans to expand the RNC's direct-mail "small donor lifeblood" program. He thanked Bond for the information, he wrote, because: "It keeps me in touch. Keep up the fine work."[86]

Training programs for party activists continued throughout 1992 through the "standard operating unit" at the RNC headquarters: "We've run thousands of campaign schools out of there," Bond recalled.[87] According to campaign manager Frederic Malek, the campaign committee and the RNC worked closely together and "coordinated on the message" as well as on the organizational challenges facing the campaign. Malek said "the ground game" was eventually moved "from the campaign to the RNC" so that the "campaign people" could focus on "positioning, message, and key endorsements," while the RNC would oversee state-level operations.[88] After years of party building, the RNC was perceived to be a sturdy, reliable, and vertically integrated organization.

Of course, designing a campaign that relied heavily upon the party's most experienced party professionals was no guarantee of success: in fact, the results of the 1992 election suggest that the "stickiness" of human capital may not always be such a valuable asset. Bush's campaign team in 1992 had many years of experience, but that experience did not translate into victory: Bush received the lowest share of the popular vote of any incumbent president since William Howard Taft in 1912. In the eyes of many GOP insiders, the campaign had only itself to blame: Ed Rollins called it "the worst campaign ever seen."[89] To be sure, there were enough recriminations to go around. But whatever caused Bush's defeat clearly did not derail the Republican party-building project.

When Bush left the White House, his party organization was in strong shape. Its physical assets—including its computer technologies, voter lists, and state party infrastructures—had received continual upgrades over the course of Bush's four years, and were expanded even further during the reelection campaign. The RNC's regional field program was expanded and strengthened by Bush's team, and Bond's successor at the RNC, Haley Barbour, found it to be a reliable program through which to implement further party-building initiatives in subsequent years. In 1993 the party was observed to be fully "service oriented" and prepared to offer ongoing support to state parties.[90]

What's more, the organizational culture of the party had been shaped by decades of persistent party building. Barbour described the RNC staff he inherited from Bond as "mature, experienced, and motivated." A sense of "mission" and "teamwork" was said to have permeated the organization. RNC division heads reported that their "seasoned and enthusiastic senior staff" adhered to a "team" concept, "not only among themselves but also in their dealings with the state parties, campaigns and other GOP groups." RNC leaders, in short, were described by Barbour as a "strong crew" that was well trained, committed to building a new majority, and capable of providing organizational "leadership and management ability themselves."[91] Thus, even though Bush suffered electoral defeat, his efforts helped to spread a shared commitment to party building throughout the Republican Party.

■

Along five of the six dimensions of party activity, Bush supported a variety of constructive organization-building initiatives (see table 7.1).[92] His efforts also illuminate some of the more distinctive characteristics of presidential party building as a general phenomenon: (1) the potential to make long-term

Table 7.1   Bush's Party Building

Provide campaign services	Build human capital	Recruit candidates	Mobilize voters	Finance party operations	Support internal activities
Expand regional field teams (1989)	RNC Campaign Management College (1989+)	Bush candidate recruitment (1989+)		Expand regional field teams (1989)	Investments in computer technology and data analysis (1989)
African American recruitment drive (1989+)	African American training (1990)	Operation Switch (1989+)		Cabinet travel (1989)	Investments in legal resources (1989)
Build state parties during campaign (1992)	Consultants at RNC (1989+)	African American recruitment (1989+)		African American training (1990)	Advisory panel "Kitchen Cabinet" (1989)
				Bush fund-raising (1989+)	
	Train campaign staff (1992)	GOPAC support (1989–91)		Yeutter fund-raising program (1991)	African American collaboration on redistricting (1989–91)
				GOPAC support (1989+)	1991 Plan (1989–91)
				Expand small-donor program (1992)	

electoral gains through the redistricting process encourages presidential party building; (2) presidential party building offers little by way of political protection for the president; (3) persistent investments in human capital can reinforce the party's strategic commitments and operating norms.

As we have seen, Bush's top party-building priority was to prepare for redistricting in 1991. Investments in the party's infrastructure and the RNC's flurry of candidate recruitment drives, outreach campaigns, fund-raising efforts, and campaign services for state and local parties were meant to put the Republican Party in an advantageous position as it headed into the redistricting battles of 1991. According to some, the party's modest gains in 1992 were, in fact, "rooted in redistricting successes."[93] Despite a lack of enthusiasm for Bush at the top of the ticket, Republicans picked up nine seats in the House, gained 148 state legislative seats, won control of two state legislatures, gained two points in party identification, and lost only one Senate seat and two governorships. It is difficult, if not impossible, to demonstrate a causal relationship between organizational activities and electoral success. But as political scientist Gary Jacobson has argued, the Republicans' dramatic fifty-four-seat gain in the House in 1994 was partially the result of the GOP's successful redistricting efforts in 1991. There is "no question that reapportionment and redistricting did contribute to their victory," he writes. "The effects of reapportionment were muted in 1992 because Bush was a drag on the whole Republican ticket, but the potential was evident in the party's gain of [nine] House seats that year despite losing the White House. In 1994, Republicans more than fulfilled that potential."[94] While many factors surely contributed to the GOP's electoral gains in the 1990s, the implementation of the 1991 Plan clearly put the Republican Party in a position, organizationally and technologically, to influence the redistricting process and begin to level the playing field.

Even clearer is that Bush's support for organizational development tied together the party-building programs of the past with those of the future. When Haley Barbour and Newt Gingrich set out to develop a coordinated, national congressional campaign in 1994, they were not starting from scratch at an organizational level.[95] Four years of coordinated party-building efforts had further vertically integrated the party apparatus and reinforced the commitment among party activists to build a new Republican majority. Over the next eight years, as the Republican Party won control of both houses of Congress and nearly reached parity with the Democrats in state-level elections, the party's organizational development continued uninterrupted, thanks in no small part to Bush's efforts to move the party-building project forward.

PART II The Democrats

8

Operation Support | John F. Kennedy

I think we could have shored up the party structure and probably have a greater impact at the state and local level than it has had over the years, if we had given some evidence that there was direct presidential interest and involvement and support of the chairman. But that wasn't forthcoming, and it was just ignored.

—Lawrence O'Brien, special assistant to Presidents Kennedy and Johnson[1]

When John F. Kennedy was elected president in 1960, the competitive standing of the Democratic Party was strong and secure. Though the party was regionally and ideologically divided, Democrats held 260 seats in the House and 64 seats in the Senate, controlled 61 percent of state legislative seats and two-thirds of governorships, and a solid majority in the electorate favored the Democratic Party. Kennedy, however, won only 49.7 percent of the popular vote, and his margin of victory over Richard Nixon was less than five percentage points in thirteen of the twenty states he won. Thus, while Kennedy's party represented the ostensible majority in American politics, he could not claim all of that support for himself. In fact, Kennedy trailed the Democratic congressional candidate in over 63 percent of all House districts.[2] Kennedy's political challenges—and the approach he took to his party—flowed from this peculiar political environment.

Whereas minority-party presidents seek to transfer their broader support onto their weaker party, majority-party presidents try to tap into the broader support of their party and use it for their own purposes. Their challenge is not to build a new majority for their party, but to put to productive use the majority they inherit. Consequently, they perceive no urgent need to make constructive, forward-looking investments in their party's organizational capacities. If party building occurs to them, it ranks extremely low on their list of priorities. They assume that their party's future will take care of itself; their focus is on maximizing the immediate benefit to their administrations. Whatever they seek—securing legislative accomplishments, generating popular support for their agenda, planning their reelection campaigns, and so on—the condition of their party apparatus is a peripheral concern at best. Usually, they are indifferent toward their party; often, they seek to exploit it; occasionally, their approach is antagonistic. Whichever approach they take in any given instance, by refusing to build their party, they effectively allow its organizational capacities to languish.

Because the condition of the Democratic Party organization was of little concern to Kennedy, there is no overarching, unifying theme to his party interactions. Along five of the six spheres of party activity, he undertook a

		Party Building						Party Predation					
		C	H	R	V	F	I	C	H	R	V	F	I
Republicans	Eisenhower	•	•	•	•	•	•						
	Nixon	•	•	•	•	•	•	•				•	
	Ford	•	•	•	•	•	•						
	Reagan	•	•	•	•	•	•						
	Bush	•	•	•		•	•						
Democrats	Kennedy					•	•	•	•		•	•	•
	Johnson							•	•		•	•	•
	Carter							•	•	•	•		•
	Clinton (1st term)							•	•	•	•		•
	Clinton (2nd term)	•	•		•	•	•						

C=Provide campaign services, H=Build human capital, R=Recruit candidates,
V=Mobilize voters, F=Finance party operations, I=Support internal activities

Figure 8.1. Kennedy's Party Interactions

hodgepodge of generally self-serving actions aimed at maximizing his benefit in the short term (see figure 8.1). In two instances, as we will discuss, his party interactions were constructive, albeit only briefly so. As his proximate concerns differed in each instance, he employed different tactics and strategies.

While examining Kennedy's interactions with the Democratic Party organization, this chapter also elaborates upon four characteristics of the approach majority-party presidents tend to take to their parties: (1) the priorities of majority-party presidents are often reflected in the types of activities they foist on their parties in lieu of organization-building projects; (2) majority-party presidents typically hoard their party's resources for their own political purposes; (3) majority-party presidents often prefer to work with responsive extrapartisan groups rather than with their party organization; (4) the president's indifference toward his party organization can thwart its organizational development.

The "Issue Approach" to Party Politics

When majority-party presidents do not neglect their party, they often seek to use it to help pursue their objectives. They enlist it in the service of their current political projects and exploit its existing capacities in order to achieve their immediate goals. With secure majorities, these presidents have no compelling reason to worry about the long-term effects of such an approach: they perceive no pressing need to invest in their party and strengthen its organizational capacities. They simply seek to use it to help solve their current problems.

I will discuss the consequences of these activities over the next few chapters. For the moment, it is worth noting that this bald instrumentalism often reveals itself in the *kinds* of activities in which these presidents engage their party. For example, with much of their attention focused on securing significant legislative accomplishments—on making the most of the governing majorities they inherit—majority-party presidents tend to turn their party into a public relations vehicle. They use it as a cheerleader to build support for their policy agendas. These support-generating activities usually supplant other party activities, including core electoral routines such as voter registration, campaign assistance, fund-raising, and candidate recruitment. By using their party without giving anything back, their political purposes come to permeate its activities.

No single initiative is more emblematic of this typical majority-party presidential approach than Kennedy's Operation Support. Dubbed the "issue approach to party politics," Operation Support offers a sharp contrast to the "organizational approach" practiced by Republican presidents. A publicity-generating program that sought to exploit existing party capacities without strengthening or developing them in any appreciable way, Operation Support was the most visible initiative run out of the DNC during Kennedy's first two years.

Operation Support

Unlike Republican programs such as Eisenhower's Operation Dixie, which aimed to build new party organizations in the South, or Reagan's Operation Open Door, which sought to convert Democrats into new Republicans, Operation Support was not geared toward enhancing the party's organizational capacities or extending its reach. As the name implies, Operation Support aimed to generate public support for Kennedy's legislative program; it was part and parcel of his "going public" strategy to influence members of Congress by "going over their heads to appeal to their constituents."[3] With conservative southerners in Congress giving Kennedy some of his greatest difficulties, this public relations program aimed to tackle one of his most pressing governing problems. Like his partisan successors Jimmy Carter and Bill Clinton, Kennedy found the heterogeneous Democratic majority in Congress to be anything but reliable and supportive of his programs: Operation Support was therefore one way to tame his unwieldy congressional party and put his ostensible majority governing coalition to work. Overseen by Theodore Sorensen in the White House, the initiative was run on a day-to-day basis by DNC vice chair Margaret Price.[4]

The main purpose of Operation Support was to enlist state and local Democratic Party organizations in a concerted effort to monitor bills as they moved through Congress and to pressure congressmen to vote with the president.[5] The operation encouraged a "shift of emphasis" away from routine party activities at the state and local levels. The "time is now," Price told state and local party leaders, to provide "specific assistance to President Kennedy and his programs."[6]

Notably absent from the Operation Support program were provisions for building stronger local organizational capacities. In contrast to Republican party-building initiatives, which aimed to leave behind a robust organizational foundation for a variety of party activities in the future, Operation Support assumed a basic level of competence on the part of local party workers and sought to exploit it: "*You know how to organize to do this job*," the Operation Support action kit insisted.[7] With the expectation that the party organization already had sufficient organizational capacity to carry out the initiative, the White House and DNC simply distributed "fact sheets" and talking points on Kennedy's specific policies—his health care plan for the elderly, his federal education assistance plan, his civil defense program, his job-training program, and his trade policies.[8]

Presumably, Operation Support could have encouraged local party activists to build new voter lists and identify new pockets of support within the electorate while they were out in the field generating enthusiasm. But expanding the party's ranks and building a strong foundation for future party operations was not the goal of the program: its purposes were more immediate and straightforward. It aimed to activate the natural Democratic majority to bring pressure to bear on Congress in *this* session, on behalf of certain policies that were being considered *now*.[9] Once the legislation was enacted, the operation was complete.

In contrast to the traditional organizational approach to party politics, Price explained that Operation Support sought to realize a new kind of approach—an "issue approach to party politics." The objective was to bring about responsible party government once and for all by ensuring that congressmen were aware of the party's grassroots support for the president. In this way, the "issue approach" would unify the party and bring about "eventual party victory."[10] The success of the Democratic Party would thus not be measured in terms of its organizational effectiveness, but rather in terms of its policy accomplishments. The concept of using the party to build consensus around a particular policy agenda was consistent with prevailing notions of the proper function of parties in the political system, but as a plan of action for the party, it was necessarily impermanent. It looked no further than the current legislative calendar. For all the virtues of the issue approach, it conspicuously lacked the kind of durability that accompanies a more organizational approach.

Though it was geared toward the short term, Operation Support was no mere adjunct program of the DNC: it constituted the centerpiece of the Democratic Party's operational strategy during 1961 and 1962. By the end of 1961, Operation Support had become the central focus of forty-four state parties.[11] At Kennedy's inaugural anniversary fund-raising dinner in January 1962, Price proudly announced that "your programs, Mr. President, are being talked about, explained, debated, supported in community after community across the nation."[12] Discussing the DNC's plans for the new session of Congress in 1962, DNC chairman John Bailey announced in January that "Operation Support will be intensified" and its efforts redoubled "in all 50 states" in order to secure "active backing" for the president's legislative program.[13]

Initially, the administration kept its role in Operation Support hidden from public view. Sorensen provided "guidance," "counsel," and information for the action kits, but remained behind the scenes.[14] But by May 1962 the program had become so central to the party's activities that the administration decided to give it a full public endorsement. Some of the most prominent administration officials—including Cabinet secretaries, undersecretaries, White House policy advisers, the vice president, and others—were sent to brief Operation Support leaders and give "reports on the programs and objectives of the Kennedy Administration." The president also met with Operation Support coordinators to encourage their efforts.[15]

Kennedy actively supported these party activities and lent the informational resources of the White House to them, but his efforts stopped there. In fact, his approach in this instance—neither hostile, indifferent, nor constructive, yet wholly exploitative—nicely illustrates the distinction between the Democratic and Republican approach. While Republican presidents also used their party to build public support for their legislative programs, they simultaneously equipped it to run more effective campaigns, recruit new candidates, develop self-sufficient fund-raising methods, build the party's human capital, and so on. To be sure, they wanted whatever support they could get from their party on behalf of their legislative initiatives in the short term, but they also wanted to build a new political majority that would stand as a durable testament to their presidency. For this reason, they did not use their party instrumentally without trying to strengthen its organizational capacities at the same time. The challenge facing Democratic presidents was different: with a ready-made majority, their task was to govern now, not build for later. Thus, initiatives like Operation Support sought to awaken the Democratic majority and put it to work on behalf of the president's immediate purposes without concern for the long-term effects on the party's organizational capacities.

Cram Courses for Incumbents

Kennedy consistently struggled to build and maintain support for his legislative program in Congress. The Democratic congressional majorities were large, heterogeneous, and ideologically diverse. To keep Democrats in line behind his proposals, Kennedy's team believed that a coordinated "information program" could be of some use. Because congressional Democrats would have to run "on the record made by this Administration" in 1962 and again in 1964, Sorensen wrote to the president, "We might say that it is in their interest to speak out" on behalf of the administration. It simply remained for Kennedy's team to provide incumbents with useful information.[16]

Under the Sorensen plan, every key department and agency of the federal government was to prepare materials summarizing the work being done in their agencies that might have a "political impact." This information would be received at the White House, "screened, edited, and then passed on to" Democratic officeholders "as well as being used in publications of the Democratic

Party." A well-designed information-dissemination program such as this would be the best way to "assist public officials in carrying forward the philosophies and programs of the Administration."[17] Some might have seen the plan as self-serving, but Sorensen explained this was not the case. "We must bear in mind," Sorensen noted, "that while it may appear that we are asking these elected office holders to do us a great service, we at the same time are providing them with the leg work, brain power and writing so that material will be readily available to them when they are called for engagements. To many officials this indeed is a windfall."[18]

In coordination with the DNC, the White House hosted a "series of information and education conferences for candidates" for these purposes beginning in May 1962 and continuing through the summer. The goal was to "provide candidates with a thorough briefing on legislation affecting national and international affairs."[19] Over 200 Democratic congressional candidates and their aides attended the first session, where they received "factual information on the state-of-the-nation" from members of the administration.[20] Called "cram courses for candidates," these conferences focused on how the administration approached the most salient political and policy issues of the day. These were not merely throwaway conferences: their importance was signaled by the keynote addresses given at the conferences in the July session by the president and vice president.[21]

Given that these were major undertakings—hundreds of candidates attended the cram courses—and given that the Kennedy team appears to have put considerable thought and preparation into the proceedings, it is curious that the only mention of organizational activity at the conferences was a reference to a campaign manual drawn up two years earlier by special assistant to the president Lawrence O'Brien in advance of the 1960 elections; it was said to be a good resource for candidates to draw upon in their campaigns.[22] No systematic attention was paid to teaching campaign management techniques, raising funds, recruiting candidates, overcoming get-out-the-vote obstacles, and managing other nuts-and-bolts campaign issues.[23] The point of the conferences was simply to disseminate information and build support for Kennedy's legislative agenda.

Kennedy helped many Democratic candidates in the 1962 midterm elections by giving stump speeches and making joint appearances, and his efforts were widely credited with producing better than expected results for the Democratic Party.[24] But stump speeches are not equivalent to party building: they offer little beyond the president's symbolic support. Rather than train and equip party leaders and activists with the tools, funds, and expertise needed to run effective campaigns both now and in the future, the Kennedy Administration was wholly focused on keeping fellow Democrats in line. Whereas Republican presidents tended to treat upcoming midterm elections and reelection campaigns as opportunities to invest in local party organizations and provide valuable knowledge and resources for use in future campaigns, Democrats conducted "information programs" while neglecting their party's organizational capacities. In consequence, little of enduring value was left for the party once the election campaigns were over. When we view these otherwise unremarkable programs in this light, they appear as incremental steps toward eroding the capacities of the Democratic Party organization.

Hoarding Financial Resources

As we have seen, every modern president demonstrated unparalleled capacities to raise money efficiently and productively. Our concern is not with the amount of money a president collects, however, but whether he uses his "star power" to improve the state of his party's finances. On this score, Kennedy clearly did not, and he does not stand alone in this category: each of his Democratic successors followed directly in his footsteps. Their typical approach was to divert funds away from local party units and general party treasuries toward a more centralized location where the president could exercise full discretion over how the monies were spent. This approach remained remarkably similar over the years: Democratic presidents raised enormous sums of money for their campaigns while leaving state and local party organizations to fend for themselves. Their objective was to amass the funds they would need to run successful reelection campaigns—and occasionally also to have a pile of cash on hand to distribute to members of Congress on whose support they depended.

Republican presidents had similar concerns and goals, of course, but rather than hoard their party's financial resources for their personal use, they sought to ensure the financial solvency of their national, state, and local parties. This difference in approach was not due to the Republican presidents' deeper pockets: Democrats were hardly short on cash and could have engaged in more profit-sharing with their party without sacrificing their own interests if they had chosen to do so. The main difference had to do with the two parties' different competitive positions. With far more incumbents than challengers standing for office, there was no pressing need for Democratic presidents to raise money for their state and local parties. Incumbents could be left to raise their own funds and run their own campaigns. Republican presidents, in contrast, felt a pressing need to recruit and train Republican candidates to challenge those Democratic incumbents; they had a strong incentive to help their party finance these electoral operations.

Early in 1961, there were signs that Kennedy might not be so indifferent toward his party's fund-raising capacities. The 1960 presidential campaign left the party about $4 million in debt, and as part of an effort to erase the debt, the DNC used Kennedy's signature and picture on behalf of a "sustaining membership" drive.[25] This use of the president's image for a constructive purpose is sufficient, for our purposes, to "count" as a party-building move (see figure 8.1 and table 8.2). However, soon after this mailing, it became clear that helping his party regain solvency was not a priority of Kennedy's. Bailey was always "hopeful that the President would get involved in fund-raising activity that would be helpful to discharge the debt," O'Brien recalled, but "that's a subject that the President chose to ignore. It would not be in the forefront of his mind. He had other things on his mind."[26]

Republican presidents, we have seen, consistently supported small-donor drives such as sustaining membership programs, often with great determination and purpose. Kennedy's participation, however, seems to have been perfunctory. As soon as it became apparent that he could raise large sums of money and keep it for his own purposes, his support for broad-based fundraising programs ceased. Without sufficient resources to reinvest in the system and prospect for new contributors, the sustaining membership program began to dry up. Herbert Alexander writes that Kennedy's turn to a "fat-cat" strategy "worked against serious efforts to achieve more democratic means of financing the Democratic Party. The Democratic National Sustaining Fund was permitted to languish, and the Dollars for Democrats program was ignored."[27]

Kennedy simply had more urgent concerns than erasing the DNC's debt or providing funds for party-building activities. His election in 1960 had been too close for comfort, and his sights were set on amassing a large war chest well in advance of the 1964 campaign. Consequently, Kennedy and his team decided to create a mechanism "where the money would not go to the party, but would go to the President directly for his political purposes."[28] In late 1961, Kennedy's chief aides Kenneth O'Donnell and Richard Maguire, along with well-connected New Yorker Arthur Krim, established the President's Club, an organization for $1,000-plus donors. In exchange for generous contributions, donors received special access to the president or his White House staff. Their names were not made public, and their donations were received in Krim's New York office, not at the DNC. As the club expanded to new cities and states, separate administrative units were established in those locations as well. Funds were set aside from the DNC's general treasuries, earmarked for the president's 1964 reelection campaign, and not made available to fund regular party operations.[29] Kennedy's memorable birthday parties—including the Madison Square Garden event where Marilyn Monroe famously sang "happy birthday" to JFK—were President's Club events.

The President's Club served as the centerpiece of Kennedy's effort to tightly control the party's funds and use them strategically for his own benefit. He used President's Club money, for example, to pay off New York City mayor Robert Wagner's campaign debt in 1962 as a reward for his assistance in weakening troublesome Tammany Hall politicians and as a down payment on the help Kennedy might need from Wagner if New York governor Nelson Rockefeller became the Republican nominee in 1964. According to Krim, the centralized fund-raising system was set up for the explicit purpose of end-running state Democratic Party organizations; rather than let state parties keep a significant portion of the money raised in their states, the funds were funneled into President's Club bank accounts controlled by the White House.[30] By circumventing the state parties' normal fund-raising processes, Kennedy intentionally undercut their organizational capacities and made them dependent upon the White House rather than the other way around.[31] "In several states," Herbert Alexander reported, "the regular party organization grumbled at the President's Club attracting away certain large contributors and focusing their attention on Washington."[32] Tellingly, the President's Club—Kennedy's most "predatory" move—was one of only two party initiatives that Lyndon Johnson continued and built upon after JFK's death.

The President's Club was not the only way Kennedy undercut the party's capacity to raise and distribute funds. In March 1963, his administration announced a new policy whereby state parties and Democratic candidates would be charged by the White House for the appearance of administration officials at campaign or party events. Heads of major agencies, Cabinet secretaries, and the vice president were included in the list of high-ranking officials who would only be available to help raise money at a cost to local party organizations. "Formulator of this new political policy is President Kennedy himself," a reporter noted.[33]

In a letter to administration officials, Maguire promulgated the new rules. Any and all speaking engagements would need to be cleared by Maguire in advance. At least 50 percent of the money raised would go directly to the DNC account where Kennedy's reelection war chest was kept—and it would remain up to Maguire to decide if the funds would "apply to a state's quota of contributions to the 1964 campaign fund." Kennedy hoped to amass $5 million in advance of what was expected to be the most expensive presidential election in American history.[34]

Kennedy's various fund-raising practices were instrumental to the point of being counterproductive for his party's long-term functionality. But while his practices were clearly self-serving, it is important to keep in mind that they were fundamentally shaped by the political environment in which Kennedy found himself. With large Democratic majorities at every level of government, Kennedy had no particular reason to be concerned about the availability of financial resources for other party members; the party was doing just fine on its own.

Nurturing Extrapartisan Organizations

With no incentive to build a new majority, majority-party presidents perceive no urgent reason to work with their party organization rather than alternative political vehicles when those extrapartisan groups are considered to be more responsive, efficient, or effective. Indeed, to the extent that such alternative vehicles are available and the party organization is viewed as somewhat cumbersome, majority-party presidents have every reason to adopt the strategy that promises the highest short-term political payoff.

Whereas Republican presidents labored to integrate their extrapartisan networks into their formal party apparatus and worked closely with their party organization even as they formed independent campaign committees, Democratic presidents did the opposite. They nurtured supportive extrapartisan networks and ran their reelection campaigns independently while leaving their party with little, if anything, to do. Their efforts were not necessarily meant to weaken the Democratic Party, per se, but they were not intended to strengthen it, either. Democratic presidents simply opted to pursue the course of action they perceived to be most efficient and effective.

Encouraging "Citizens for Kennedy" Groups

Kennedy arrived at the White House convinced that traditional party organizations were more trouble than they were worth. Throughout his career, end-running the party organization had proven to be a winning formula: his earliest campaigns in Massachusetts were designed to circumvent what he perceived to be a cumbersome state and local party organization, and he met with success in the 1960 primaries by building volunteer networks that bypassed state party organizations.[35] Yet even if Kennedy were not already predisposed to circumvent his party organization, its strong competitive standing would have provided little incentive for him to work closely with it. Neither Eisenhower nor Reagan had much use for traditional party organizations during their prepresidential careers either, but their majority-building ambitions motivated them to make the Republican Party organization a central component of their political projects. Kennedy, in contrast, had no reason not to seek out the most efficient and responsive vehicles for building political support for his presidency, irrespective of the long-term effects on his party organization.

Even before he was inaugurated, his team began laying the groundwork for an independent organizational network that would exist outside the Democratic Party and remain active throughout his presidency. His advisers noted that the president-elect had performed poorly in the western states in the recent election; his presidential campaign in those states had been a "crash program," they said, with "only the beginnings of organization." This presented something of a problem for the new president, because if the administration "carries out its civil rights platform, we may be faced with a bitter southern rebellion by 1964," the memo explained. "If an election were held tomorrow it would be within their power to take victory from us. In 1964 the western states, with fences mended, could make the difference between victory and defeat. Let's get moving on this—early!"[36]

But rather than strengthen the Democratic Party's state and county committees in the western states, Kennedy and his team purposefully aimed to circumvent them to build a more personalized and responsive apparatus. The plan called for Kennedy's political team to "visit and diagnose [the] situation in each state," keep in touch with the "thousands of key local Kennedy supporters who inevitably have been left off thank-you lists," issue an "inauguration newsletter," and establish new offices in the western states. Instead of working through the formal Democratic Party apparatus, the "western office staff men" were to "report directly to Larry O'Brien on political matters, and as otherwise directed on other matters." The idea was to have the new groups launch "grassroots programs to support the new administration's policies."[37]

The model for these programs would be the Citizens for Kennedy groups that helped to elect Kennedy in 1960.[38] Kennedy's advisers explained that it was important to nurture these independent groups carefully so as not to incite a rebellion in the formal party apparatus. But they were optimistic: "We have been in communication with a number of people who believe present Kennedy enthusiasm can be channeled productively without getting local machines upset over 'competitive' activity."[39]

Building personalized, extrapartisan organizations was an ongoing preoccupation of the Kennedy Administration. In February 1961, Kennedy's special assistant Frederick G. Dutton wrote to Sorensen to discuss the specific method by which the administration might encourage the growth of Citizens groups around the country.[40] The plan was evidently never carried out, but it is worth considering the stated reason for wanting such groups in the first place: the "real benefit" of an extrapartisan network, Dutton wrote, was to get constituents to send "letters and [put] other pressure on Congress in support of our legislation."[41] Again, the primary goal was not to expand the party's reach and find new sources of political support, but to tap existing support and use it to promote the president's policy purposes.

Performing traditional party functions from the White House rather than the DNC was a somewhat risky undertaking. "We must be sure that if a big public drive is launched," Dutton said, "it does not sputter and lend itself to press interpretations that the President lacks active community-level support. If the trumpet is sounded, we should be sure troops are ready to respond." A full-fledged Citizens for Kennedy movement would probably require "TV and press outlets, a theme, and even (for local motivation) badges like the PT boats, seminar materials, and other paraphernalia." They would need to hire an "outside national publicist" to help them develop a "detailed blue-print of the undertaking." A steering committee composed of "national figures" would then form the "organizational shell" of the extrapartisan group.[42]

Eisenhower, of course, also had broad support from Citizens groups. But he saw these extrapartisan groups very differently from Kennedy. For him, these groups were flattering but posed a threat—not a benefit—to his legacy. Insofar as their raison d'être was bound up in him as an individual, he viewed them as inherently temporary. Because he sought to build a durable new majority that would reflect and perpetuate his political purposes well into the future, Eisenhower sought to strengthen his party organization rather than nurture extrapartisan groups. With no such majority-building concerns, Kennedy was much more attracted to outside groups: after all, they could bring pressure to bear on the legislative process and help him pursue his policy ambitions. The long-term effect that these extrapartisan groups might have on his party organization did not factor as a significant concern.

An Independent Campaign

Kennedy also sought extrapartisan support for his reelection. Rather than develop a reelection plan in coordination with his party organization, Kennedy and his team worked to construct an independent campaign apparatus that bypassed existing party structures. Reluctant to give the national and state parties a prominent role, Kennedy's loyal team of advisers hoarded knowledge and information in a campaign superstructure and diverted financial and operational resources into its centralized apparatus.

As early as April 1963, Kennedy's "personal political organization" could be found preparing for the reelection campaign in New York State. Kennedy's brother-in-law, Stephen E. Smith, worked to undermine Rockefeller while taking pains to "bypass all the factional rivalries and personal disputes that have caused divisions within the New York state Democratic organization."[43] Smith also began to develop highly personalized arrangements for Kennedy's reelection campaign in Ohio, Pennsylvania, and Michigan, all key electoral battlegrounds with Republican governors who were viewed as potential Republican challengers in 1964.[44]

Smith, along with the rest of the so-called Irish Mafia—O'Donnell, O'Brien, Maguire, Robert Kennedy, and others—was determined to bypass problematic party leaders where necessary in order to shore up Kennedy's political weaknesses.[45] For example, in Ohio, Smith created an informal council of Democratic county chairmen favorable to the administration to whom he planned to turn for assistance in the coming year; William Coleman, the state party chairman, was to be "respectfully, courteously, and definitely bypassed."[46] Smith was not concerned with the condition of the Democratic Party organization in these key areas; his goal was to develop a responsive, if temporary, support structure that would follow through on Kennedy's particular campaign plan. Summing up the effort, journalist Tom Wicker noted that despite having office space reserved for him at the DNC, Smith's "commitment is notably to the President and the head of the family," not to the Democratic Party.[47]

As Kennedy looked toward 1964, the emerging "New South" came to be seen as a potential source of strength. "There is little doubt that the South will have as spectacular an economic growth as the West has just witnessed," Kennedy's pollster, Louis Harris, wrote to him in September 1963. "A new South is in the making right now, but is hidden mostly from view over the surface manifestations of segregation and the pratings about states rights and super-conservatism."[48] Kennedy's southern strategy, Harris suggested, should be less organizationally minded than policy-centered. Kennedy should carefully hone his rhetoric to link his New Frontier policy program to issues regarding the rapid industrial development occurring in urban areas of the South.[49] To the extent that Kennedy listened to Harris's strategic advice—and we know he did frequently—his reelection campaign was shaping up to be a largely rhetorical campaign that emphasized policy innovations appealing to the "New South" over strengthened organizational capacities in that region.[50]

In sum, two key Kennedy objectives—securing legislative accomplishments and winning reelection—were pursued through extrapartisan means. By building partylike networks to generate support for his legislative program and reelection campaign, Kennedy purposefully pushed the formal Democratic Party apparatus to the sidelines and evidenced little concern for its organizational capacities. He had other more pressing business to attend to than party building. O'Brien recalled:

> If [Kennedy and Johnson] gave a thought to the national committee, it wasn't in the sense that, "The national committee can be awfully helpful, effective in promoting my program, in off-year elections, and the upcoming national election." The role of the national committee in the election context wasn't really focused on. I don't remember any meaningful discussions with the Presidents in that area. As things unfolded, you became totally absorbed in your role as president, commander in chief.

Thwarting Party Building

Presidents are formidable actors whose party interactions can either facilitate or thwart their party's organizational development. They can strengthen their party's organizational capacities and move the party-building programs they inherited forward, as every Republican president did, or they can avoid taking constructive action altogether. In either case, their choices have important consequences for their party's trajectory of organizational development. In the following episodes of Kennedy's party interactions, the blunting force of presidential indifference is on full display.

Voter Registration

During his first month in office, Kennedy sent a memo to DNC chairman John Bailey asking what the DNC was doing in the area of opposition research, what it was doing to assist local party organizations, and "what plans are we now making to have a massive registration drive in 1962 and 1964."[51] As I will discuss below, Kennedy ultimately did not lend his support to either of the first two items, and the party's support services consequently went nowhere. But in the third area—voter registration—Kennedy offered his initial support, which produced a constructive organizational change at the DNC. But because his support for the program soon waned, so too did the party's new organizational capacity.

According to Matthew Reese, the member of Kennedy's inner circle who was sent to the DNC to oversee the party's voter registration efforts, JFK believed in the importance of registration: "The President almost had a fetish about voter registration. He felt it was the way to win elections, and he directed the Chairman to emphasize always voter registration."[52] Indeed, Reese recalled, Kennedy had "won because of the voter registration drive that happened prior to the general election in 1960," and he understood the benefits he could reap in 1964 from a major effort.[53] Kennedy offered Reese his personal encouragement for his efforts at the DNC.[54]

Unfortunately for the development of the party's voter registration capacities, however, Kennedy's attention soon shifted elsewhere. He soon came to understand that with a majority of the electorate identifying as Democrats, nonpartisan efforts could be even more efficient and beneficial for his purposes.

Kennedy knew that if all those eligible to vote registered and voted according to their stated party preferences, then all else equal, Democrats would win every time. As Bailey wrote, "Available data indicates that the great majority of unregistered voters would vote for Democratic candidates if they did vote. With current registration totals far below 1960, it is of critical importance to increase voter registration *to the greatest possible extent* to assure a Democratic victory at the polls in 1964."[55] This calculation, of course, can only be made by majority-party presidents. As we saw in chapter 6, Reagan and his team believed that broad, sweeping voter registration programs would be detrimental to their purposes. Because it was the minority party in terms of party identification in the electorate, the GOP had to develop new strategies—like microtargeting—to produce more Republican votes without accidentally turning out more Democrats. The last thing minority-party presidents want to do is to register and mobilize all voters who are eligible to vote. But a broad and comprehensive program to activate the maximum number of voters is precisely what majority-party presidents want. In order to turn out the party's "natural" majority in the electorate, however, there is no need to rely strictly upon the party organization.

Consequently, Kennedy's early interest in the DNC's voter registration efforts soon came to represent only one small piece of a much larger nonpartisan effort to swell the ranks of registered voters nationwide. Throughout 1962 and 1963, Kennedy supported a flurry of nonpartisan voter registration initiatives, including the nonpartisan National Voters Registration Committee,[56] National Voter Registration Month in September 1962,[57] and the President's Commission on Registration and Voting Participation in March 1963;[58] he also lent his support to the AFL-CIO's political unit COPE, the American Heritage Foundation, the League of Women Voters, and other independent groups also seeking to register voters.[59]

Kennedy's support for these various registration initiatives served multiple purposes: in addition to pursuing his reelection interests in 1964, they helped him steer a middle course on the question of civil rights for African Americans. Rather than push for a comprehensive civil rights act, Kennedy could promote voter registration and promise "to give blacks the power to secure their rights" while minimizing the "electoral costs of any further Democratic defections among southern whites."[60]

Upon inspection, his early foray into party building on this front—which does, indeed, "count" as a party-building action—seems to have been a mere flirtation, a passing consideration at the outset of his term. At the DNC, Reese admitted, "I didn't get as much [support] as I wanted" from the White House.[61] This was typical, O'Brien explained: while Kennedy loyalists like Reese were sent to the DNC to oversee party operations, "the reality was there was little attention from the Oval Office and from the immediate staff."[62] Though a new division was created, Reese was only given two staff. His division also lacked the kind of institutional capacities it needed to fulfill its mandate—the dilapidated physical infrastructure of the DNC stymied his efforts. For example, Reese was not even able to make legible photocopies; he complained of having to run across the street to use someone else's Xerox machine to make routine copies.[63] Thanks to Kennedy's efforts to hoard the party's resources in the President's Club, the DNC lacked the budget to fully fund the registration initiative.

By the summer of 1963, authority over voter registration was handed over to brother-in-law Smith. Reese continued to work out of the DNC's voter registration division, but the scope of his mission had diminished considerably. As the campaign approached, his main task was to head up a "Special Negro Project" to register African Americans in a handful of big cities. By the end of 1963, the main accomplishment of the DNC's voter registration division was that it reached agreement on "a coordinated campaign with AFL-CIO on the national, state, and local levels."[64] The campaign team fully intended to outsource voter registration activities during the 1964 campaign to organized labor, as was the custom.[65]

In sum, despite his early indication that he would support the DNC's effort to undertake a massive voter registration drive, Kennedy did not take steps to provide the DNC with the budget, resources, or organizational capacity it needed to become a major player in the 1964 election campaign; consequently, the party effort was pushed to the margins of the campaign. As we will see in the next chapter, Lyndon Johnson found the division to be a waste of resources and swiftly terminated it.

DNC Reorganization

While Kennedy offered early support for Reese's efforts at the DNC, there is no evidence that he ever lent his support to, or was even interested in, two bona fide party-building plans developed by DNC chairman John Bailey. Though Kennedy had initially asked Bailey to keep him apprised of the DNC's research operations and efforts to support local party organizations, his subsequent moves evidenced a compete lack of interest.

Yet these episodes illustrate two important lessons. First, there was nothing about the Democratic Party's inherent characteristics or its external partner network per se that prevented Kennedy from undertaking party building. Bailey certainly believed it possible to undertake large-scope party-building initiatives and even took steps to implement them, despite not receiving the support of the president. The second lesson follows from the first: without presidential support, even elaborate party-building plans like Bailey's are likely to go nowhere.

In June 1961, Bailey sought to enlist national committee members in a strategic planning effort to determine what programs the party should pursue in the coming years. Described as a "national drive to consolidate and build the strength of the Democratic Party," Bailey's plan created ten subcommittees to "deal with the problems and opportunities" in the areas of elections, organization, finance, nationalities, young voters, senior citizens, women, support groups, registration and voting, and communications.[66] Members of the national committee were to be divided into these ten groups, regional meetings would be held, and the groups would report their findings in the fall. The initiative never got under way, however, presumably on account of insufficient funds.[67]

In December, Bailey tried again. This time, he dropped the idea of regional meetings and instead had the subcommittees agree to meet in advance of the annual DNC meeting in January 1962 in order to make more efficient use of national committee members' time. Clearly enthusiastic about the undertaking, Bailey described it as "the first planned program I know of in either party to make full use of the experience and know-how of the members of the National Committee."[68] Yet without the president's support, the initiative remained only an idea: a comprehensive program to reorganize and revitalize the national party was never launched. The DNC's attention turned back to Operation Support before the month was through.[69]

Operation Know-How

Bailey was not satisfied with the singular focus on Operation Support, however. In February 1962, he launched a new initiative called Operation Know-How to teach state and local party organizations how to perform get-out-the-vote operations and other campaign techniques for the upcoming midterm elections.[70] The program had all the characteristics of a full-bodied party-building initiative and was nearly identical, in its aims, to the initiatives launched under Republican presidents. The main difference was that Kennedy refused to lend his support to Operation Know-How. Indeed, the total lack of support Bailey received from the White House stands in stark contrast to the experiences of Republican "in-party" chairmen who consistently received the public relations, administrative, and financial support of the White House for their party-building activities.

Before the first Operation Know-How conference in February 1962, deputy DNC chairman Charles D. Roche sent a request to the White House for "the President and Mrs. Kennedy to help us on two projects." First was a request for Kennedy to film a brief, one- to two-minute announcement for the program. Bailey wanted to play a clip of the president at the start of each Operation Know-How meeting to inspire the participants.[71] The second request was for Jacqueline Kennedy to film "spots aimed at women and particularly the Spanish-speaking element." Roche wrote that "we consider both of these requests extremely important."[72]

The president and Mrs. Kennedy, however, never filmed the spots. In fact, Kennedy never mentioned Operation Know-How in any of his public statements, no White House releases made any mention of the initiative, and there is no archival evidence to suggest that his staff even discussed it behind the scenes. In his lengthy oral history, Bailey did not even mention the initiative as part of his record of accomplishments as chairman. Whereas administration officials gave highly publicized presentations for Operation Support conferences, no such efforts were made on behalf of Operation Know-How. Operation Know-How conferences were headlined by the top staff at the DNC, but not a single White House or executive branch official participated.[73] Without the support of the White House, Bailey's conferences soon dissolved into Operation Support–like pep rally forums where Bailey would bash Republicans and champion the administration's causes.[74]

If Kennedy gave any thought whatsoever to Operation Know-How, it would seem that he found Bailey's independent party-building program to be less than satisfactory. The last of three Operation Know-How conferences was held on June 12, 1962; only six days later, Bailey was replaced in his role as coordinator of the party's midterm election campaign. Kennedy's close confidant H. W. "Bill" Brawley resigned his post as deputy postmaster general to "take a temporary assignment as Executive Assistant to the Chairman at the DNC," with the responsibility of coordinating all election-year activities.[75] We cannot know for certain, but it seems that Kennedy was not pleased with Bailey's rogue party-building initiative.

While Kennedy certainly could have chosen to support Operation Know-How, bring it greater visibility, and send his best organizers—such as O'Brien, O'Donnell, and Stephen Smith—to help teach local Democratic activists campaign tactics, he refused to do so. Instead, Kennedy showed his thanks for Bailey's freelance effort by replacing him in his election-coordination role. O'Brien explained that although Bailey had a good relationship with the White House, "going back to the first day we walked in with Jack Kennedy, with John Bailey at the DNC, we were not supportive of the DNC."[76] He recalled:

> During the Kennedy period, very frankly, we probably lost sight of the existence of the national committee. It was a vehicle solely for us when negatives came along, appointments particularly, to put the burden on the national committee . . . there was little or no direction or guidance from the White House. There was no meaningful public support of the committee on the part of the President. And the same in the Johnson era . . . to be supportive of it so that it is performing meaningful tasks just didn't take place.[77]

Table 8.1   Kennedy's Party Predation

Provide campaign services	Build human capital	Recruit candidates	Mobilize voters	Finance party operations	Support internal activities
Support for Citizens groups (1961+)	Support for Citizens groups (1961+)		Operation Support (1961+)	President's Club (1961+)	Operation Support (1961+)
Operation Support (1961+)	Ignore Bailey's Operation Know-How (1962)		Support for Citizens groups (1961+)	Speaker fees (1963)	Information program (1962+)
Cram courses (1962)			DNC voter registration (1962+)		Ignore Bailey's DNC reorganization (1961–62)
Ignore Bailey's Operation Know-How (1962)			Ignore Bailey's Operation Know-How (1962)		Ignore Bailey's Operation Know-How (1962)
Independent reelection campaign (1963)			Independent reelection campaign (1963)		

Note: All instances indicate the absence of party building; that is, they confirm the conventional wisdom about the president-party relationship. Whether, in any given instance, the president undercuts his party, exploits it, or neglects it, the effect is to undermine the party's organizational capacities along these six dimensions of party activity.

Table 8.2   Kennedy's Party Building

Provide campaign services	Build human capital	Recruit candidates	Mobilize voters	Finance party operations	Support internal activities
			DNC voter registration support (1961)	Sustaining member direct-mail drive (1961)	

Nevertheless, it is clear that the main obstacle to party building during Kennedy's presidency was not the party's heterogeneous interests or its strong partner networks: it was Kennedy's lack of interest in his party organization. Bailey, for his part, did not perceive the Democratic Party's coalitional and organizational characteristics to be a deterrent to party building. The reason Kennedy did not support Bailey's plans, it seems, was simply that he was concerned with other things: as a majority-party president, he perceived no pressing need to strengthen his party's organizational capacities. But his indifference was not without effect: by refusing to support his party's organizational development and by highly personalizing its remaining activities, Kennedy left his party dependent upon the White House and without any organizational momentum of its own. His untimely death left his party without a sense of direction and with little for his successor to build on.

■

The Kennedy presidency offers something of a "hard case" for our competitive standing explanation. Kennedy was elected by the slimmest of margins and was determined to expand his share of the vote in 1964. For his reelection purposes alone, the party organization would seem to have offered a useful resource. But there is no a priori reason for any president to turn to his party rather than work with alternative political vehicles perceived to be more responsive. So long as his party was doing fine on its own, Kennedy could design a political strategy that suited his own purposes without concern for his party's long-term organizational capacities. Aside from his early flirtation with a DNC voter registration drive and a single mailer, Kennedy did precisely that; party building did not appear on his radar screen.

Kennedy had no overarching designs for his party: his actions varied in each instance. His presidency therefore reveals several different faces of the "party predator." In any given instance, whether Kennedy did something to undercut his party, something to exploit it, or nothing at all, the effect was to weaken its organizational capacities along five of the six dimensions of party activity (see table 8.1). In two areas, his party interactions were constructive, but only briefly so, and in both cases, he allowed the party's programs to languish (see table 8.2). Taken together, these episodes illustrate four characteristics of the typical approach majority-party presidents take to their parties: (1) the priorities of majority-party presidents are often reflected in the types of activities they foist on their parties in lieu of organization-building projects; (2) majority-party presidents typically hoard the party's financial resources for their own political purposes; (3) whereas minority-party presidents are drawn to their party organization, majority-party presidents are drawn to extrapartisan groups; (4) the president's indifference to his party organization can hinder its development.

The state of national mourning following Kennedy's assassination swelled the Democrats' already large majorities; when Lyndon Johnson assumed the presidency, he discovered an unusual opportunity to put these majorities to work on behalf of his ambitious legislative agenda. Based on his appraisal of his competitive political environment, Johnson found no particular reason to engage in party building. What's more, the party he inherited from Kennedy offered little incentive to begin building from scratch: it was filled with "Kennedy men," unresponsive to his leadership, and lacking in significant independent organizational capacities. Johnson vowed to continue in his predecessor's footsteps, and in one way he did: he continued to eschew party building.

9

The President's Club | Lyndon B. Johnson

*It was just a matter of lack of focus on the party organization full time. . . .
I didn't detect any particular difference in approach and attitude towards
the national committee with either [Kennedy or Johnson]. There was the
same sort of neglect, not purposely, but due to overriding circumstances.*

—Lawrence O'Brien[1]

Throughout Lyndon Johnson's five years in the White House, Democrats
enjoyed dominant majorities in the House and Senate, at the state level, and
among self-identified partisans in the electorate. In 1964, when Johnson received the highest share of the popular vote in the history of American two-
party politics, the Democratic Party secured 68 percent of the seats in both
the House and the Senate and reached 61 percent of party identification in
the electorate. Even after suffering major across-the-board losses in 1966, the
Democrats' majorities remained strong and secure.

Under these conditions, Johnson had the luxury of looking beyond his
party to the "overarching political consensus" that seemed to have emerged.[2]
He aspired to interpret this consensus and translate it into effective government action. When biographers note LBJ's desire to "out-Roosevelt Roosevelt,"
they mean he wanted to surpass FDR in his ability to address the needs of
Americans through the instruments of government.[3] With the strongest governing majority since Roosevelt, Johnson had that chance.

Under these favorable conditions, Johnson had little reason to be concerned about his party's organizational capacities: he saw no urgent need to
enhance its electoral operations or expand its reach. With his party firmly in
the majority, Johnson's actions were guided by his short-term interests: if a
particular party program was deemed useful to him in the moment at hand,
he used it. If it was not deemed useful, he either converted it into something
useful or eliminated it. Taken all together, Johnson's party interactions either
exploited or undercut the party's capacity to perform five of the six party activities examined here (see figure 9.1). Because Johnson's wholly instrumental and occasionally antagonistic approach to his party did not involve any
simultaneous investments in its organizational capacities, his actions had a
uniformly detrimental effect: by 1968, the party organization he passed along
to Hubert Humphrey was described as "disorganized and in financial chaos."[4]

In the existing literature, Johnson's interactions with his party organization are usually described in colorful language: he "slashed" the DNC payroll
"to the bone," led a "ruthless attack" on its programs, and "savaged" its organizational apparatus.[5] He was "uncommonly niggardly" toward the party, and
when he was not "gutting" it of its vitality, he set out to "humiliate" its chairman

		Party Building						Party Predation					
		C	H	R	V	F	I	C	H	R	V	F	I
Republicans	Eisenhower	•	•	•	•	•	•						
	Nixon	•	•	•	•	•	•	•			•		
	Ford	•	•	•	•	•	•						
	Reagan	•	•	•	•	•	•						
	Bush	•	•	•		•	•						
Democrats	Kennedy				•	•		•	•		•	•	•
	Johnson							•	•		•	•	•
	Carter							•	•	•	•	•	•
	Clinton (1st term)							•	•	•	•	•	•
	Clinton (2nd term)	•	•		•	•	•						

C=Provide campaign services, H=Build human capital, R=Recruit candidates,
V=Mobilize voters, F=Finance party operations, I=Support internal activities

Figure 9.1. Johnson's Party Interactions

and "purge" its staff.[6] As it turns out, this vivid imagery hardly overstates the case: Johnson was no party builder. But in the standard frame, his party interactions tend to be viewed as illustrations of his deeper "psychic structure," as evidence of his "paranoia," his need for "power and control," or his "demands for submission" by those around him.[7]

To be sure, his "paranoiac"[8] tendencies were on full display when he fired DNC staff he thought loyal to Robert Kennedy.[9] His "fears of illegitimacy" might be seen in his instrumental use of the DNC to ingratiate himself with fellow party members in Congress.[10] As a "Texas wheeler dealer who played fast and loose with the rules," Johnson may have been more inclined to engage in dubious fund-raising practices that promised him full control over party funds.[11] And Johnson's lifelong determination to cultivate a favorable public image might be observed in his decision to use the party's remaining resources to generate publicity for his administration.[12]

But Johnson's approach to his party characterized the efforts of every other majority-party president in the modern period as well, irrespective of their "psychic structures." Thus, this chapter brackets Johnson's peculiarities and idiosyncrasies and considers what his case illustrates about "party predation" as a more general phenomenon. Four lessons emerge: (1) every president must negotiate with the organizational arrangements he inherits: majority-party presidents tend either to eliminate programs that seem to offer little immediate benefit to their administrations, or to convert them to serve their personal purposes; (2) with many more incumbents than challengers, majority-party presidents focus on building their support among officeholders rather than recruiting new candidates or providing enhanced campaign services; (3) the challenge facing majority-party presidents is not to build a new majority but to sustain the support of their large and oftentimes ideologically divided party; (4) party building in the Democratic Party was not perceived to be too difficult or too costly: Democratic presidents simply did not perceive any pressing need to undertake the effort.

Conversion or Elimination of Inherited Party Programs

Majority-party presidents approach their party organization very differently from minority-party presidents: they perceive it differently, they seek different things from it, and they do different things to it. As we have seen, Republican presidents consistently viewed the party organization they inherited from their predecessors as a foundation for further party building. Because each round of organizational investments left an increasingly robust party apparatus for the next incumbent to use and build upon, Republican presidents found it in their interest to make additional investments that reinforced the basic organizational trajectory of their party.

Democratic presidents, in contrast, viewed the organization they inherited as either an obstacle to overcome or as an instrument to exploit for their short-term gain. What programs they did not need they eliminated, and what they deemed useful they converted to serve their immediate purposes. Consequently, they left their successors to negotiate with an organizational structure that was highly personalized and not designed to transfer from one leader to the next.

In Johnson's transitionless transition to the presidency, this process of institutional negotiation is on prominent display. Johnson did not have the luxury of a three-month transition from his election to his inauguration to select a new party leadership team and design a new program of his own: whatever he did, he would have to contend with the arrangements Kennedy had left behind. Unfortunately for Johnson, Kennedy left behind a party organization that was jerry-rigged to maximize the benefit to his administration in the short term: the President's Club was designed to tap Kennedy's biggest supporters, Operation Support was designed to reinforce the cult of personality around JFK, the reelection campaign was designed to play to Kennedy's particular electoral strengths and compensate for his particular weaknesses, and the DNC's voter mobilization program was designed to fit within Kennedy's larger campaign strategy. Johnson had to negotiate with all four of these programs in some way. Tellingly, the only party activities that he kept and converted to serve his purposes were the two that were purposefully designed by his predecessor to exploit the party for the president's benefit. The other two, which could have been turned to more constructive party-building purposes, were eliminated.

Converting the President's Club

As I discussed in the previous chapter, the President's Club was the mechanism through which Kennedy funneled political donations away from his party and into separate bank accounts where funds remained under his direct, personal control. After Kennedy's assassination in November 1963, President's Club director Arthur Krim cautiously approached senior Johnson aides Bill Moyers and Walter Jenkins to see what LBJ wanted to do with the blossoming fund-raising operation, which boasted over 2,000 members.[13] Krim believed that club donations were not likely to subside in the wake of Kennedy's death; in fact, because of Johnson's strong ties to the business community, he thought the club "could probably raise more support for President Johnson than for President Kennedy."[14]

But Krim wanted the new president to be fully briefed on the club's secretive fund-raising methods and have a chance to assent to its continuation or terminate it as he wished: for all Krim knew, Johnson might prefer to work through formal DNC fund-raising processes so as to benefit the entire party. But Johnson immediately indicated his support for the continuation of the club concept:

> I might say, I was pushing through an open door because as far as he was concerned that's the way he wanted it, because the money would flow in a way where if the President wanted to help the party or to help senators or congressmen, it would be coming from him and not from the party.[15]

Johnson told Krim he wanted to maintain the President's Club's momentum and make the transition as smooth as possible: he promised to make his "top group" available for meetings with large donors for a "give and take" on political issues, as Kennedy had done.[16] Membership in the President's Club "didn't get you a favor with the government," Krim explained, "but it got you an awful lot of fun for yourself and a feeling of being close to the charisma of power . . . an occasional invitation to a state dinner . . . an appointment to a commission overseeing Annapolis or the fisheries . . . missions abroad," and so on.[17]

The press described the rewards of being a President's Club member as gaining "a direct relationship with President Johnson." The 2,500 members who joined the club prior to the Democratic National Convention in Atlantic City in 1964, for example, reportedly "wined and dined there with the President, and lounged with party notables in an exclusive hospitality room."[18] The effort literally paid off, and by the fall of 1964, the President's Club had become Johnson's primary fund-raising vehicle (see figure 9.2).

After the 1964 election, Johnson continued to raise large sums of money for the President's Club. His well-known penchant for dinner and dancing parties certainly did not keep him away from the club's many dinners, theater parties, and ballroom affairs. In mid-1965, Johnson's enthusiasm was revealed in his scribbled response to a calendar of proposed President's Club events: "I'll do all the above. . . . Let's go all out."[19] The following year Johnson continued to emphasize the importance of the club, handwriting: "Get busy quick—get all our best people working *fast*."[20]

Though Johnson did not initiate any new party-building activities over the course of his five years in office, he did use President's Club funds to pay

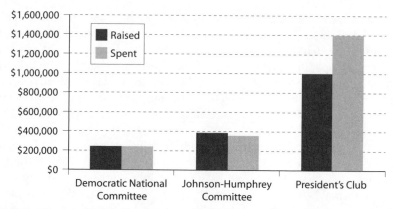

Figure 9.2. Campaign Fund-raising, September 1, 1964 October 19, 1964

down the DNC's post-1964 election debt, which had reached over $4 million by the end of 1965. His interest in debt reduction served his personal interests: if he did nothing to pay down the debt, then routine DNC operations would compound the deficit, and eventually "some part of the funds raised in 1968 for the presidential campaign would have to be used to pay old debts," Johnson's chief of staff Marvin Watson told him.[21] So long as Johnson intended to seek reelection in 1968, the debt would go from being the party's problem to Johnson's problem. In his memoirs, Watson explained that Johnson purposefully paid down the debt in lieu of undertaking more constructive party activities: "The fact that the President honored his duty to repay past debts of the Committee did not prevent him from taking a hard look at the Committee's future . . . at the President's direction, I began a process of radically cutting the Committee's staff and budget."[22]

By the end of 1967, Johnson had completely erased the DNC's debt. But at the same time that Johnson was undertaking this seemingly constructive action on behalf of his party, Watson was making good progress on "materially diminishing the organization": expenditures were cut, staff was laid off, and programs were eliminated.[23] Even the party's "Sustaining Membership" program, which some party leaders hoped would be a source of steady revenue, was curtailed.[24] Responsibility for coordinating the grassroots "Dollars for Democrats" drive was passed off onto the Women's Division, and Johnson refused to lend his support for the initiative when asked.[25]

Meanwhile, Johnson used the bulk of the President's Club funds to promote his immediate interests. For example, leading up to the 1964 election, the club donated $25,000 to organizational pro Jesse Unruh, then California Assembly Speaker, to ensure his support during the presidential campaign.[26] Funds also went to support affiliated groups deemed useful to Johnson's campaign: for example, two $25,000 President's Club gifts were made to the All Americans Council and to the Senior Citizens for Johnson-Humphrey committee, both extrapartisan groups supporting Johnson's election.[27] As I will discuss further below, Johnson's trademark practice of giving direct financial assistance to candidates and ensuring that he received proper credit for the support was another common use of President's Club funds.[28] And when Eugene McCarthy mounted a formidable challenge to Johnson in the 1968 New Hampshire primary, Johnson directed that President's Club funds be given to the governor of New Hampshire to "take care of supporting the write-in vote." Krim was "authorized [by Johnson] to give [the governor] certain President's Club money for support, which I did."[29] Of course, the "big money" of the President's Club could only help so much: McCarthy's impressive second-place showing in New Hampshire catapulted his candidacy into the national spotlight, encouraged Robert Kennedy to announce his own bid for the nomination, and may have factored into Johnson's decision to drop out of the race.

The premise of the President's Club was to provide secrecy for large donors—especially for Republicans and independents from the business community who wanted their donations to remain anonymous. If money were channeled through state committees and into separate President's Club accounts rather than through the National Committee, the names of donors and the amount donated would remain secret, Watson discovered: "Pres. Club raise thru state committees—will not have to report."[30] Using such tactics, the club continued to grow, and by the end of 1966 it claimed over 4,000 members and was generating $3 to $4 million per year.

This impressive effort was not without consequence for the party organization: perhaps even more important than its deleterious effect on the DNC was its effect on local parties. A state senator from New York, for example, argued in late 1966 that the President's Club had "weakened the state party through its fund-raising activities." None of the money it raised in New York "has been returned to the state organization since the 1964 Presidential campaign," he said. In addition to hurting the state party's operations "by siphoning away contributions . . . the club also has sapped party strength at the grassroots level and hindered the normal development of young potential candidates and party leaders," since young prospective Democratic candidates "found it difficult to get financial help from those already contributing substantially to the party nationally."[31] Biographer Doris Kearns Goodwin concluded that "Johnson's principal fund-raising device, the President's Club, diverted money and contributions from party organizations at all levels, concentrating control over party funds in the President's hands, and thus further contributing to the disintegration of the local party."[32] Indeed, it is difficult to imagine a more "predatory" action than this fund-raising operation, which served the personal needs of the president at the direct expense of the party.

Converting Operation Support

In the summer of 1965, Watson asked the president which of three party activities he wanted to support in the coming months: the first was a meeting with Operation Support coordinators, the second was a President's Club event, and the third was a meeting of state and county Democratic chairmen from the sixty largest cities. Of the three activities, Johnson enthusiastically supported the first two and backed out of the third.[33] Watson sent the president's regrets to the scores of snubbed Democratic chairmen.[34] With little reason to spend his time building ties with local party chairmen, he opted instead to support only those programs that could be used to further his immediate purposes.

Operation Support was precisely this kind of program. Its mission remained the same as it was under Kennedy: to provide "complete information on all key issues by means of information kits, pamphlets, and other materials" to those who wanted to help promote "the President's record of achievement and plans for future progress."[35] While Operation Support had been created to promote and capitalize on Kennedy's "cult of personality," Johnson jumped at the chance to convert it into a vehicle to support his presidency instead.

As discussed in the previous chapter, the program was perhaps most notable for what it did not do—it did not build local party organizations. It was an educational program that explicitly emphasized an "issue approach" over an organizational approach to party politics; where necessary, it even supplanted state and local party operations. As the program was being refitted to support the Johnson Administration, some party professionals suggested that Operation Support be expanded and used as a grassroots vehicle to undertake more constructive organizational activities at the state and local level.[36] But Johnson opted to keep the program in its present form. The only change he allowed was a name change: it now became "Operation Support for the Great Society."[37]

In a signal of his support for the program, Johnson made a rare party-related appearance when he attended Operation Support's first national conference in the fall of 1965.[38] Given the countless party invitations Johnson declined, it is revealing that he chose to accept the one whose sole purpose was to promote his policy agenda without strengthening the party organization. The program continued to operate throughout Johnson's presidency.

While Johnson did not support any constructive party activities, he did not ignore his party, either. In fact, Johnson micromanaged many party minutiae. Records indicate that he had a hand in deciding such small questions as which lawyer to hire at the DNC, whether to have one or two DNC meetings in 1966, what speeches John Bailey should give, whether to move the headquarters to the Watergate building, and even how the tables should be arranged and whether there should be dancing at a DNC meeting in March 1967.[39] Johnson did not personally supervise all national party activities, of course: Watson was given primary responsibility for DNC oversight, and between 1963 and 1966, Johnson gradually sent a team of loyalists to the DNC to replace most of the "Kennedy men" he inherited. Longtime aide Clifton Carter, close friend Krim, and John Criswell constituted the de facto team of directors at the DNC. John Bailey, still formally in the role of DNC chairman, became a figurehead who spent most of his time in his home state of Connecticut.[40] With each loyalist taking responsibility for overseeing different areas of party activity, Johnson's team reliably carried out his wishes that the DNC either be employed in the service of the president's direct interests or else subdued.

Eliminating Voter Registration

The voter registration division of the DNC, directed by Kennedy loyalist Matthew Reese, remained in operation through the 1964 election. Journalists reported that the effort was "phenomenally successful" and that the DNC had brought about "a significant increase in the percentage of Democratic Party voters, particularly in traditionally Democratic areas."[41] This positive view of the program, however, was not shared by Johnson's team. The idea that the DNC program was successful, Criswell wrote, was "primarily one of conversation, that . . . has somehow caught the imagination of an awful lot of people who do not know the facts."[42] Rather than view Reese's program as worthy of the president's support, Johnson viewed it as a lot of hype: he believed that his landslide victory in 1964 owed little to the DNC's efforts.[43]

During the 1964 campaign, Reese received little support from the White House.[44] He complained that the White House was willing to cultivate the support of organized labor, but "no corresponding effort was made to recognize the State Chairman and other Party leadership" whose support was needed to implement the registration drive. "This situation was very noticeable," Reese cautioned, and "we need to guard against this happening again."[45] But Johnson viewed the DNC voter registration program as a waste of resources. Like Kennedy, he thought it more effective to "investigate possible restrictions on registration and voting" and to reform "voting laws and voting practices" to "produce increased voting interest by all the people" instead.[46] In addition to pleasing civil rights advocates, a universal voter registration strategy was rational so long as unregistered voters leaned Democratic, a belief shared by both the Johnson and Kennedy teams.[47]

Reese called for a renewed focus on voter registration after the election in 1964. For the coming year, he proposed that Johnson hold regional voter registration seminars, build stronger alliances with organized labor, and enhance coordination between the DNC and the President's Commission on Registration and Voter Participation.[48] But Johnson did not heed Reese's advice. In February 1965 Watson indicated that the White House would not allow any additional staff to be hired at the DNC in the area of voter registration, and argued that "adequate organizations are presently working" to increase voter registration.[49] In the spring of 1965, Reese was pushed out of the DNC, and by the end of the year, plans were formulated to "take advantage of non-partisan organizations" to promote voter registration drives in the future.[50] In August 1966, with the voter registration division at the DNC effectively eliminated, Johnson directed that its remaining $600,000 budget be put in escrow so that the interest earned over the subsequent two years would give Johnson an additional $70,000 for "voter registration on a non-partisan basis" during the 1968 campaign.[51]

As the 1968 election approached, members of Johnson's team reaffirmed their view that building the capacity to undertake a voter registration drive from within the formal party apparatus was a losing proposition. In those areas where Democratic voter registration had lagged in the past, it had not been a problem the party organization could have solved, Criswell wrote. "We could not have sent enough money to haul a significant number of new voters," as the primary problem was "very stringent registration laws which exist in most of our states."[52] Rather than invest in the party organization, then, it was preferable to "strongly join in support of American Heritage" so that "they could carry the ball," Criswell wrote.[53]

As for voter mobilization around the election, Johnson's team anticipated the need for an unprecedented number of activists and volunteers in 1968; but building the human capital of the Democratic Party through training programs and other activist recruitment efforts was never discussed. Early discussions assumed that Johnson would rely primarily on organized labor—especially the AFL-CIO's political arm, COPE (Committee on Political Education)—to perform essential voter mobilization needs. Because COPE had always helped Democratic campaigns in the past, there was no perceived need to build parallel capacities in the DNC.[54] But by refusing to strengthen the party's "in-house" organizational capacity to register and mobilize voters, Johnson increased the Democratic Party's dependency upon organized labor. Unfortunately for Johnson, labor leaders were uneasy with his administration and resentful of his assumption that COPE would pick up the party's slack; they offered his prospective candidacy only lukewarm support. Lacking a robust party organization or even the reliable support of organized labor, Johnson thus entered 1968 without a firm organizational foundation on which to base a potential reelection campaign. If he wanted to run, he had not made it easy on himself.[55]

Supplanting Kennedy's Campaign Apparatus

How a president approaches his party organization is determined largely by the party's competitive standing, but it is also shaped by the condition of the organization he inherits. Without up-and-running party-building programs on which to build, presidents are not likely to start from scratch: unless, that is, they have a strong electoral motivation to do so, as we saw with Eisenhower and will observe with Clinton. In Johnson's case, the party apparatus he inherited from Kennedy in the fall of 1963 had little to offer by way of organizational capacity. Because it did not inspire his confidence, and because he had no reason to do otherwise, Johnson opted to circumvent it rather than integrate it into his 1964 campaign. By 1968, his repeated efforts to sideline his party left him in the same position he was in four years earlier: with little to build on and little reason to begin party building anew.

The stories of the 1964 and 1968 presidential elections, like most presidential elections in modern American history, are well known; Johnson's rout of conservative Republican Barry Goldwater in 1964 is one of the more memorable contests, and his unexpected withdrawal from the race on March 31, 1968 amid social unrest and political turmoil over the Vietnam War is widely remembered as a pivotal time in American history. What is less well known, however, is how Johnson interacted with his party and its various organizational components in the time leading up to the elections, why he acted the way he did, and whether his actions had any lasting effect on his party's organizational development.

In late 1963, the Kennedy campaign structure was largely an ad hoc arrangement of personal alliances that papered over or bypassed local party problems. In contrast to Republican presidential campaigns, which tended to seize the opportunity of the campaign to make long-term investments in party organization, Kennedy's inchoate campaign focused on finding temporary solutions to long-term party problems—solutions that hinged on gentlemen's agreements, personal loyalties, and shared purposes.[56] Upon assuming the presidency, Johnson found himself the presumptive nominee of a disorganized party that was preparing to reelect John Kennedy to the exclusion of virtually everything else.

With little time to spare before the 1964 election, Johnson bypassed Kennedy's thoroughly personalized campaign structure and began to layer a new superstructure of loyal state and regional coordinators atop existing state party organizations. He linked his national campaign to local candidates' campaigns and circumvented state party organizations. Temporary and ad hoc like Kennedy's campaign, Johnson's campaign was equally unconcerned with the party's capacities to run campaigns in the long run; he was not interested in building something that might last beyond the moment at hand.

Not only had Kennedy left little for Johnson to build on in the party organization, but his highly personalized approach had left the DNC in the hands of stalwart Kennedy supporters. In the fall of 1963 the DNC was still being run on a day-to-day basis by treasurer Richard Maguire and Kenneth O'Donnell, both key members of Kennedy's close-knit team. As preparations for the 1964 election got under way, Johnson assumed that these "Kennedy men" were orchestrating a behind-the-scenes effort to nominate Robert Kennedy for the vice presidency at the Democratic National Convention in Atlantic City in August 1964. "He didn't trust Dick Maguire," Arthur Krim remembered, and "had the same feeling there . . . about Kenny O'Donnell and [Sorensen's deputy Myer] Feldman, and that is that they were just living out the days but not really loyal to him."[57]

To maintain the appearance of continuity after Kennedy's assassination, Johnson asked the holdover staff to remain in their roles, but insisted that they report to his new campaign leadership team. Carter became "Chief Coordinator," Watson was put in charge of the national convention, trusted ally James Rowe became coordinator of auxiliary "special" organizations, and Moyers was put in charge of publicity.[58] O'Brien, whom Johnson did not initially trust but whose talent he respected, was charged with coordinating the overall organization of the campaign.[59]

Johnson applied the same technique as Kennedy and handpicked "state campaign coordinators" to supervise the delegate selection processes in several key states.[60] Carter then divided the country into seven geographical regions and named coordinators for each region. While a regionally structured campaign organization may have ensured greater loyalty and responsiveness to Johnson's campaign needs, it was far removed from the nuts and bolts of a field organization: "It was clear that you weren't going to pursue this to the grassroots," O'Brien recalled.[61] The campaign had no networks of volunteer door-knockers, no precinct chairmen, and no mechanism for implementing get-out-the-vote operations on Election Day.

This lack of organizational capacity did not escape Johnson, who wanted to win by a large margin, bigger than any president before him. To generate a "100 per cent vote," Johnson knew he needed a high turnout.[62] Because the conventional wisdom was that the more competitive the race the higher the turnout would be, the widespread assumption that Johnson would win decisively concerned the president immensely. Johnson thus directed O'Brien to go into the field to investigate the linkages between Carter's regional organization and existing campaigns for Democratic candidates at local levels. Their best chance of turning out voters, Johnson believed, was by leveraging other Democratic candidates' independent campaign organizations. However, grassroots activity was most critical to House campaigns—as gubernatorial and senate campaigns were statewide in scope—yet fewer than a hundred House seats were considered competitive, which meant that there were relatively few campaign organizations with which Johnson could partner.

But rather than seize the opportunity to strengthen local Democratic Party organizations and enhance their operational capacities, Johnson bypassed his party organization and told O'Brien to develop ties with affiliated nonpartisan groups: "key people in the urban areas, the local level, the activists, the labor leaders, the women's groups."[63] Johnson was "extremely anxious" and demanded daily reports on the state of the campaign.[64] The information O'Brien collected revealed that there was "little concern regarding the presidential campaign, it was a walk-through. Consequently there was a lack of registration activity, nuts and bolts activity to ensure maximizing get-out-the-vote, all of that."[65] Rudimentary organizational activities were either not being done or were in disarray. Simple procedural and administrative roadblocks, for example, had prevented the release and distribution of printed materials from warehouses around the country; O'Brien had to spend his time streamlining these processes and getting the material in the hands of campaign activists. All the while, no effort was made to integrate state or local party organizations into the campaign.[66]

According to O'Brien, the organizational side of the Johnson campaign effort in 1964 was too ad hoc and temporary to be effective, even in the moment at hand—it was "a far cry from an in-depth organizational drive in which you would normally be engaged. That would have extended over a period of months and would have been very intensive, conducted in depth. This was more surface activity." O'Brien said that he was the only member of the president's team designated with an organizational focus: "I was the only one involved, really. So that was the extent of the campaign."[67] O'Brien admitted that his main task was not to redress the party's deficient organizational capacity across the country, but simply to make "the president feel more comfortable about things."[68]

Johnson's campaign also involved an effort to support nonpartisan citizens groups.[69] Johnson believed that supportive organizations that were not formally affiliated with the Democratic Party could help to steal moderate Republican votes away from the conservative Goldwater. Rowe, who coordinated the extrapartisan groups, later called the Citizens' Committee "really a Republican thing, which was [Johnson's] own idea." Because many moderate Republicans were uneasy with Goldwater, "we had to create a home for them," Rowe said. These were "the Eisenhower partisans," as they called them: "the lawyers and bankers and doctors and so forth . . . the renegades leading the Republicans' votes from Goldwater for Johnson."[70] But rather than make an effort to integrate them into the Democratic Party as Eisenhower had done with the Citizens groups in 1956, Johnson and Rowe kept the effort entirely separate from the Democratic Party. Rowe was "very careful . . . to put Republicans in charge of all this" and maintain its nonpartisan status.[71]

Johnson's makeshift campaign in 1964 therefore consisted of an independent Johnson-Humphrey regional campaign structure, which developed strategy; Citizens' Committees, which primarily provided funding; organized labor, which provided most of the grassroots work; incumbents' campaigns, which supplemented those efforts in targeted areas; and the President's Club, which was the primary fund-raising vehicle. All the traditional roles of the formal party apparatus—voter mobilization, interstate campaign coordination, fundraising, even the distribution of pamphlets and literature—were being performed by this temporary, ad hoc campaign structure while the party sat on the sidelines. This arrangement suited Johnson's needs and ultimately proved to be sufficient, but there was no reason to keep its organizational form intact after the election was over; the ad hoc campaign promptly disbanded.[72]

Over the next several years, Johnson gave little indication whether he would run again in 1968. But in the fall of 1967, he asked O'Brien to draw up plans for what a potential Johnson campaign organization might look like.[73] In a detailed "White Paper," O'Brien surveyed Johnson's many organizational challenges and proposed that he quickly form an independent campaign organization to operate separately from the party.[74] As for the Democratic Party's role, O'Brien was frank:

> Nationally, the Democratic Party faces serious organizational problems. Many of the state organizations are flabby and wedded to techniques which are conventional and outmoded . . . the Democratic National Committee is not staffed or equipped to conduct a

successful Presidential election. The Democratic Party, to a greater or lesser extent, has lost contact with the voters.[75]

A series of heated discussions ensued between O'Brien and Rowe on the nature of the campaign and the role the party should play. Rowe argued that the DNC should play a central role and not be "further downgraded" by the campaign; his main complaint with O'Brien's White Paper was that it "does not put enough emphasis on revitalization of the Democratic National Committee to enable it to do the routine jobs it should do."[76] Johnson "carefully considered Rowe's suggestions," Watson later wrote, "but his lack of faith in the Committee remained unchanged through March 31, 1968, when he withdrew."[77]

Throughout the fall and winter of 1967–68, Johnson refused to make his plans clear, and O'Brien complained that his campaign plan had been left "sitting around with the President since September."[78] The only party activity undertaken during that period involved a series of regional party conferences designed by Criswell as a "taking-the-party-to-the folks" initiative to generate "good coverage over specific geographic areas" and to provide a "natural forum for speakers to attack the opposition who will be at their loudest during this time."[79] Called "Victory '68" conferences, Bailey explained that they aimed to get "a true reading on how the people feel."[80] Rather than train local party activists and develop concrete operational plans in conjunction with local organizations, the conferences were simply designed to gauge Johnson's support within the party.[81] Johnson also had Watson call every state party chairman to determine how "strongly" they would be for the president in 1968.[82]

By early February 1968, Criswell and Watson went ahead and began to develop a presidential campaign structure that systematically bypassed the formal party apparatus. They rented offices, hired staff, and set up equipment for a "Citizens for Johnson-Humphrey" organization in downtown Washington, D.C. The organization planned to rely on a network of field operatives who would report directly to the Citizens group.[83] Though they tried to establish a flexible campaign structure that could accommodate Johnson's presumed late entry into the race, as of mid-March they had little to show for their efforts.[84] Whatever motivated Johnson to bow out of the race on March 31, the effect of his earlier party predation had altered the organizational landscape of Democratic Party politics. The party apparatus he bequeathed to Vice President Hubert Humphrey proved to be an added burden on Humphrey's late-breaking campaign.[85]

The Incumbency Advantage

One obvious but extremely consequential difference between majority- and minority-party presidents is the number of incumbents within each party. Minority-party presidents, with fewer incumbents, are much more focused on finding, recruiting, training, funding, and assisting candidates to challenge the majority party's incumbents for their seats. Majority-party presidents, in contrast, are rarely concerned with the business of recruiting and supporting candidates: their emphasis is on placating incumbents and building support for their legislative agendas. In Johnson's case, extraordinarily large majorities in Congress meant that the president had many more incumbents to tend to; recruiting challengers was never on his radar screen. Johnson's priority was to keep his fellow elected Democrats in line, and he consequently used all resources at his disposal to do so.

Direct Assistance

One of the central purposes of the President's Club was to enable Johnson to collect favors from elected officials whose support he would need for his legislative agenda. Repeating a tactic he had used successfully as a congressman and senator in the 1940s and 1950s, Johnson sought to circumvent normal party channels and hand cash directly to Democratic candidates.[86] Rather than use President's Club money to help fund organizational activities in his party, Johnson used it to build loyalty among congressmen.

According to O'Brien, it was he who made the recommendation that Johnson give "immediate cash assistance to congressional candidates" because "if the money comes from you, these candidates unquestionably will feel some obligation to you for your help." The idea was to set aside a pile of money and begin "pumping this cash directly into selected congressional campaigns. The money could be delivered to the candidates in your name."[87] Johnson liked the idea and directed Krim and Watson to implement it. Once Krim had raised several hundred thousand dollars, he would deliver the cash to Marvin Watson in the White House, "where it was locked in my office safe," Watson explained. "Once the cash was available, word was sent to every Democratic congressional candidate for reelection that I would like to meet with him."[88] Watson began every meeting with prepared remarks about "how much the President appreciated their work," and how LBJ wanted to see them reelected. Then he would deliver an envelope of cash to the incumbent: $2,000 if the candidate had an opponent, $1,000 if he was unopposed.[89]

Although some congressmen refused to take the money, most took it eagerly. "Because the money was delivered to them in the White House," Watson said, "it was a symbolic demonstration of the President's appreciation and gratitude." Johnson and his team were aware of the "sensitivity" of the clearly dubious process, and according to Watson, they "went to considerable lengths to retain total secrecy" of their actions.[90] The purpose of providing direct assistance was clear: Johnson was not building a new majority for the Democratic Party, he was building support for his legislative program.

Congressional Support Program

During Johnson's first three years in the White House, he used the slimmed-down DNC to implement the same sort of "information program" that Sorensen had orchestrated under Kennedy. The effort commenced with a

Democratic Congressional Candidates' Conference for all Democratic incumbents in Congress in 1964. To avoid interfering in nomination contests, "non-incumbent candidates" were prohibited from attending. Incumbents met with Johnson at the White House and heard speeches from Cabinet members.[91] The goal was not to provide campaign services to the incumbents, but to inform them about the administration's policy program and create a unified party message in advance of the elections.

After the elections, Johnson directed the DNC to provide ongoing "News and Information Services" from its headquarters "ONLY for Senators and Members of Congress."[92] Talking points, speech material, radio and TV scripts, and a valuable teletype service were made available to incumbents through the DNC. Based on reports Watson sent to the president throughout 1965, it is clear that the congressional support program was the primary activity undertaken by the DNC staff.[93] In early February 1966, for example, Watson reported that out of the DNC's budget of $720,000, "in excess of $500,000 is being spent for Congressional Support Program," with no mention of campaign training, voter mobilization techniques, fund-raising assistance, or the like.[94] The program was purely meant to build goodwill among Johnson's fellow congressional partisans and to disseminate information about policy accomplishments.

During 1966, as divisions over Johnson's Vietnam War policies deepened within the Democratic Party, Carter noted that Johnson's support in Congress was beginning to slip: "You could detect some of them were beginning to show a little independence."[95] Johnson was concerned and began to seek methods of keeping members of his party in line. "We were constantly trying to provide statements and information to the Congress for utilization in the Congressional Record or elsewhere," O'Brien recalled. "The President became more concerned as time went on, even in 1966, when he would learn about party leaders or members of Congress questioning the policy. He would try to blunt that, urge people to speak to those members, urge them to avoid anything negative and hang in there."[96] In September 1966, Johnson reemphasized the importance of the DNC's information dissemination program for keeping members in line. He authorized his staff to put together a set of major speeches in pamphlet form "with an index" and had the DNC distribute it to congressional candidates.[97]

Johnson's efforts did little to prevent major Democratic losses in the 1966 midterm elections, which many perceived as a public repudiation of his unpopular policies: Democrats lost forty-seven seats in the House, four seats in the Senate, 762 state legislative seats, and eight governorships. Democrats still maintained strong majorities in Congress and at the state level, but Johnson's "issue approach" clearly had not helped.

Asserting Control over Party Proceedings

The predominant "party predator" model of president-party relations is de-rived, in part, from observations of presidential behavior around the four-year tradition of the national party convention. In this area of routine president-party interaction, one can readily observe Republicans as well as Democrats treating their party as an instrument for their personal reelection purposes. Presidents from both parties have worked to control convention proceedings by installing their loyal deputies in key coordination roles and by shaping proce-dural rules and agenda schedules to be most advantageous to their purposes.

But while Republicans were no different from Democrats on this score, they consistently used party forums as occasions to demonstrate their com-mitment to party building. They opened the floor for their opponents to speak and promoted themes to advertise their "open door" party-building efforts. In contrast, with deep and durable majorities, Democratic presidents perceived no need to be so generous. Their challenge was not to expand their party and broaden its appeal, but rather to sustain their support within their large, of-tentimes ideologically divided majority party. Consequently, they sought to assert their control over party proceedings and foreclose opportunities for intra-party challengers to rise up and question their leadership. While these moves do not "count" as party predation, they help to illustrate the main concerns driving the Democrats in their interactions with their party organization.

Johnson's biggest political task, as he saw it, was to make his large, di-verse, and vocal majority party fall in line behind his leadership: he sought to sustain support for his policy initiatives, preempt alternatives from emerging, and maintain the appearance of consensus. His efforts to tightly control the 1964 and 1968 Democratic National Convention proceedings were, in this way, symptomatic of his general approach to party organization.

In 1964, Johnson went to great lengths to ensure that Robert F. Kennedy would not be selected by the 1964 convention as his vice presidential candi-date. At the convention in Atlantic City, Johnson had Watson coordinate the schedule of events to prevent an emotional surge in favor of Kennedy from occurring. A movie tribute to the fallen JFK was rescheduled so that it would play only after Johnson and Humphrey had delivered nomination and ac-ceptance speeches, and RFK was slotted to speak on the final night, once all important convention business was complete.[98]

Johnson also frequently tested the loyalty of fellow partisans by asking if they would support his choice for the vice presidency, whomever it might be. He asked Carter to be sure that New Jersey would "be for Mr. Pat Brown for Vice President, if I wanted him? . . . What about New York?" he pressed.[99] LBJ had no intention of selecting California governor Pat Brown as his vice presi-dent, but he wanted to ensure that he would have full discretion over his choice of running mate. He directed Cliff Carter to try to "persuade several Demo-cratic state chairmen to adopt resolutions for their delegates stating that LBJ shall have the free choice of selecting his running mate as Vice President."[100]

Johnson's determination to maintain control over the convention proceedings was perhaps best illustrated by his handling of the tense standoff
over the legitimacy of Mississippi's delegation to the convention. The Mississippi Freedom Democratic Party (MFDP) offered its slate of delegates as an
alternative to the "regular" delegation, arguing that the state party organization had discriminated against African Americans in their delegate selection
process. The conflict posed a dilemma for Johnson, not simply because he
had to choose between supporting civil rights activists or conservative southern Democrats. Johnson feared that the conflict might create an opening for
Robert Kennedy to exploit, Watson explained:

> All that Johnson wanted was a smooth, issue-free convention. All
> that Kennedy wanted was the opposite. Thus, Johnson believed that
> if a compromise could be reached that prevented the issue from reach-
> ing the floor of the convention, the emotional opportunity sought by
> Kennedy would be denied him.[101]

Johnson hammered out a compromise: two delegates from the MFDP would
be seated as delegates at large and the "regular" Mississippi delegation would
have to take a loyalty oath to support the nominee. These steps, pleasing none,
kept Johnson in control of the convention and subdued the Kennedy threat.

Of course, Republican presidents also faced challenges to their authority
from within their party: Eisenhower was publicly rebuked by Senator Barry
Goldwater; Ford was challenged by then-governor Ronald Reagan; Bush was
challenged by Pat Buchanan. But these minority-party presidents adopted
wholly different responses: while Democrats like Johnson (and later Carter)
sought to eliminate opportunities for their challengers to voice their alternatives, Republican presidents opened party forums and invited their opponents
to engage in a public dialogue about what the party stood for. Identifying
their party with the imagery of an "open door" or an "umbrella party," they
used these forums to illustrate and promote their larger goal of building a
new majority for their party. It is ironic, of course, that Republican presidents
consistently sought to demonstrate that the GOP was the party of the "open
door" by welcoming to the stage Republicans who championed a narrower,
more doctrinaire conservatism. Nevertheless, in their effort to broaden the
party's appeal, Republican presidents insisted on adopting an inclusive approach to party proceedings. Democrats, with no such majority-building
designs, reacted to internal challenges by tightening rules, enforcing loyalty,
and limiting debate.

Four years later, Johnson again intervened aggressively to control the
national party convention. While not an official candidate himself in 1968, he
was anxious to ensure that the party platform did not repudiate his handling
of the Vietnam War. House majority leader Carl Albert of Oklahoma was
Johnson's handpicked chairman of the 1968 convention; in an oral history taken
later, Albert revealed that while Johnson was neither a candidate for president
nor even physically present in Chicago, he "was in control of the convention

up to the time Humphrey was nominated . . . he had his way with the platform. He had his way with the agenda. He selected the temporary and permanent officers of the convention, and everything was run by the National
Committee through him."[102]

When peace advocates sought to push through an alternative statement
on how to end the war (stop bombing before negotiating peace), Johnson
"insisted that the Democratic platform and the Democratic convention should
endorse his stand," Albert recalled. "He wanted all the candidates . . . to know
that they weren't going to put any weak Vietnamese plank in there in that
platform. If they did—I'm not going to tell you what he said."[103] Criswell, Watson, and Krim worked behind the scenes to monitor action on the floor, and
Representative Hale Boggs of Louisiana, who was close to the president, served
as the head of the platform committee and reported back to Johnson regularly.[104] Johnson's approach in this instance was neither constructive nor particularly destructive for his party's organizational capacity—yet it was aimed
at closing what would otherwise have been a more open organizational forum
in order to reduce the likelihood that opposition could emerge to undermine
his policy legacy.

Thus, while containing the "Bobby problem" and subduing the "peaceniks"
were the proximate reasons for Johnson's insistence upon rigid convention
proceedings, there is also a more general explanation for this typical Democratic behavior: in contrast to their Republican counterparts, Democratic presidents simply perceived no need to open the floor to demonstrate their party's
broad appeal. There was nothing to be gained from such an approach.

Rejecting Party-Building Plans

While Democratic presidents certainly experienced many frustrations in
dealing with the diversity of groups that composed their large and heterogeneous majority party, they did not eschew party building because it was perceived to be too difficult or because the Democratic Party was too divided,
too heterogeneous, or too resistant to change. In fact, every Democratic president had party-building plans presented to him by party professionals who
understood the potential difficulties as well as the potential benefits of creating organizational change in the party, and these party professionals believed
that party building was eminently possible. And yet every Democratic president until Bill Clinton in his second term rejected or ignored those plans.
With deep and durable majorities, investments in the party's organizational
capacities were simply perceived to be a waste of resources.

Following the midterm losses in 1966, for example, Johnson received a
flurry of advice about how to redress the Democrats' growing organizational
weaknesses. Various party professionals and White House staff drew up party-
building plans and implored the president to support them. In each case, he
refused. Let us review these suggestions and Johnson's responses briefly.

In November 1966, Johnson's press secretary and longtime aide George Reedy encouraged Johnson to make many changes over the next two years, and "rebuild the Democratic National Committee." The reason was that "there is virtually no liaison between the National Committee and the State organizations. This has had the effect of breaking down morale among the Democratic forces in the field and they lack the buoyancy and the élan that are essential to political victory." Johnson thanked Reedy for his suggestions on other issues, but ignored his advice on party building.[105] A few weeks later, Johnson confidant Louis Martin similarly suggested that Johnson put "regional men from the DNC working in the four main geographical areas of the country" to help state and county party leaders with "sparking registration drives," with "the search for classy and vigorous candidates who might run for local, state, and congressional posts in 1968," with public relations, and with "organizing fund raising activities."[106] A few days later this "regional field-man program for the DNC" was again proposed and strongly endorsed by Vice President Hubert Humphrey in a meeting with Bailey, Criswell, and a few others.[107] Criswell, representing the president, explained that "this is a suggestion I have often heard but have not been an advocate of this idea."[108]

Yet even Criswell eventually came around to the idea that the Democratic Party was in need of some presidential nurturing and support. In part this was because he had become frustrated with local party leaders, members of Congress, and members of the media who consistently criticized Johnson's neglect of the party organization. He wrote: "We are not going to satisfy critics by using the arguments of what we have done, in my judgment, but rather in coming with some program of what we plan to do for the Party in '67."[109] Criswell proposed a multifaceted plan to invest in the party's organizational capacities and activate new party programs.[110]

Johnson agreed to only one item on Criswell's action list: to host the state party chairmen at the White House. Once in 1967 and again in 1968, the state chairmen came to the White House for a day of briefings so that the administration could "at least show an interest in them" before they were called upon to help in Johnson's potential 1968 campaign, Criswell wrote.[111] The meetings were so well received by the local party leaders that Criswell pondered whether the administration might have benefited from developing a closer relationship with local party leaders all along: "We might sometimes not give full weight to the impressiveness of the White House, and the frosting of The President," he wrote.[112] But the next time Criswell sought to leverage the "frosting" of the president to boost morale among state chairmen, Johnson refused.[113]

Generating support for Johnson among the state chairmen was a far cry from making investments in the party's organizational capacity. Republican presidents, as we have seen, not only invited state chairmen to the White House, but also provided them with training, financial resources, and institutional support. Johnson simply sought to ensure their loyalty. Criswell was directed to keep in touch with them and make sure they continued to support Johnson throughout 1967.[114]

Another rejected party-building plan was proposed by Robert Kintner, Johnson's special assistant. Kintner worried that Democrats were losing their base in metropolitan areas and noted that it was "axiomatic that strong political bases must be built in the urban-suburban centers before 1968 . . . this can only be done through manpower and money, and ultimately with attractive candidates." He also reported to Johnson that "good loyal Democrats are talking about the need to rebuild the Democratic national, state, and local organizations through the Democratic National Committee."[115] Johnson spoke to Kintner a few days later, but did not bring up the issue of party building.[116]

Johnson preferred Sherman Markman's proposal. Markman suggested that Johnson designate a White House staff member who would travel to different states to have "in depth conversations with the various Democratic State Chairmen, National Committee people and, where appropriate, Governors." The White House representative would "(1) find out their problems, (2) obtain their suggestions on matters of mutual interest, and (3) explain the Presidential perspective." Such an effort would demonstrate the president's "deep interest in their problems and viewpoints," foster "rapport between the White House and the state parties," and provide the president with "eyes and ears" inside the party. This idea appealed to Johnson: he noted that the plan "may be good. I think [former Florida governor Farris] Bryant ought to do that."[117] Johnson may not have wanted to invest in his party apparatus, but he did want to quiet factional infighting and avoid embarrassments. Markman's plan promised just the thing: a symbolic overture to anxious party leaders that did nothing to resolve the party's organizational problems. Johnson followed through, and in characteristic fashion, asked Bryant, Humphrey, and O'Brien to undertake the same conciliatory tours around the nation at the same time, leading to some "crossed wires."[118]

At a Democratic conference in January 1967, western party chairmen and national committeemen passed a series of resolutions calling on Johnson to support training "seminars dealing with everyday practical political matters . . . financial programs stressing state and local cooperation," more initiatives to reach out to young Democrats, "regional conferences . . . to provide added leadership needed by the National Committee," and an emphasis on early "candidate development."[119] The party-building resolutions, however, received more attention from the media than from the White House. Watson assured Johnson that party-building proposals were simply the party leaders' way of getting "some things off their mind in resolution form," but the important thing was that "it was unanimous that all those attending the Western Conference were 100% for the President."[120] Johnson was paying attention, but his focus was on how to stabilize his fluctuating support among party elites.

Johnson also received frequent party-building proposals from Margaret Price, the organizationally adept, widely respected vice chair of the DNC. Price was a determined and convincing party leader, but Johnson employed dilatory tactics to avoid having to lend her his support. Despite her persistent attempts to get him to participate in various Democratic Women's activities,

Table 9.1 Johnson's Party Predation

Provide campaign services	Build human capital	Recruit candidates	Mobilize voters	Finance party operations	Support internal activities
1964 campaign structure (1964)	Reject multiple party-building plans (1966+)		1964 campaign structure (1964)	President's Club (1963+)	Materially diminish DNC (1964+)
Citizens groups (1964)	Victory '68 Conferences (1968)		Operation Support (1965+)	DNC budget cuts (1964+)	Operation Support (1965+)
Democratic Congressional Candidates' Conference (1964)			Eliminate DNC voter registration division (1965)	Downgrade sustaining membership program (1966)	Congressional support program (1964–66)
Operation Support (1965+)			Outsource voter registration operations (1966+)	Direct cash assistance to candidates (1966)	Reject multiple party-building plans (1966+)
Reject multiple party-building plans (1966+)			Reject multiple party-building plans (1966+)		
1968 campaign structure (1968)			1968 campaign structure (1968)		

Note: All instances indicate the absence of party building; that is, they confirm the conventional wisdom about the president-party relationship. Whether, in any given instance, the president undercuts his party, exploits it, or neglects it, the effect is to undermine the party's organizational capacities along these six dimensions of party activity.

for example, Johnson often refused to see her, and his staff refused to return her calls.[121] Johnson was similarly unresponsive when Price made multiple pleas for "a more direct and personal statement by the President" in support of the flagging "Dollars for Democrats Drive."[122] And her creative suggestion that the White House host the entire party leadership—"state, House, and Senate members"—for a one-day seminar was gently put on hold.[123] When Price enthusiastically presented a plan and budget for Mrs. Johnson and Mrs. Humphrey to tape a fifteen-minute television spot to "appeal to the woman voter to go to the polls and vote," Johnson's only response was: "Where is the money coming from?"[124]

In each of these instances, party-building plans were laid out and party professionals volunteered to spearhead the efforts. But in each case, Johnson refused. It is tempting, of course, to attribute Johnson's refusal to engage in party building to the Democratic Party's internal characteristics: its heterogeneous constituency, its ideological diversity, or its commitment to procedural democracy. Indeed, it is even tempting to attribute Johnson's behavior to personal factors, such as his paranoia, his decision not to seek reelection in 1968, his background in party politics, or his distraction with more pressing administrative issues. But when we consider his rejection of these various party-building plans alongside Kennedy's rejection of John Bailey's Operation

Know-How, Carter's rejection of Kenneth Curtis's party-building program (discussed in the next chapter), and Clinton's rejection of Donald Fowler's suggestions (chapter 11), the main obstacle to party building in these administrations begins to take shape: the Democratic Party did not stand in the way of presidential party building, Democratic presidents did. Based on their perception of their competitive political environment, they simply did not perceive it to be in their interest to undertake the effort.

■

Johnson's party interactions offer a somewhat more extreme illustration of the "party predator" than that observed in the Kennedy case. Whereas Kennedy exploited his party and undercut its capacities in several instances, he just as frequently ignored it. One could argue that the Democratic Party would have been better off, in the long run, had Johnson ignored his party more and interacted with it less: along five of the six dimensions of party activity, Johnson either undercut, exploited, or supplanted his party's organizational capacities; he also frequently neglected his party and refused to undertake a more constructive approach (see table 9.1).

These episodes illustrate four characteristics of the typical approach majority-party presidents take to their party: (1) majority-party presidents tend either to eliminate the party programs they inherit or to convert them to serve their personal purposes; (2) with many more incumbents than challengers, majority-party presidents tend to focus on placating those incumbents, not recruiting new candidates; (3) the challenge facing majority-party presidents is not to build a new majority, but to sustain the support of their large and oftentimes ideologically divided majority party; (4) party building in the Democratic Party was not too difficult or too costly: Democratic presidents simply did not perceive any pressing reason to undertake the effort.

As we shall see in the next chapter, Johnson's party interactions had enduring consequences for the Democratic Party's organizational development. Forced to run a national campaign in 1968 without a robust party organization or a strong fund-raising operation, Humphrey had to take the DNC deep into debt; this debt became a major hindrance during the "out-party" years from 1969 to 1977 and remained a problem throughout Jimmy Carter's time in the White House. Johnson's indifference toward his party's organizational capacities, his intentional efforts to undercut its operations, and his exploitation of its remaining programs thus helped put his party on a trajectory that was markedly different from the path taken by the GOP in the modern period.

10

Alternative Priorities | Jimmy Carter

I didn't take on as a major project the change in the Democratic structure that I think now was needed. I think in retrospect it was needed. . . . My relationship with the Democratic Party was not particularly good and I could have done more had I made it a higher priority. It was not a burning commitment or interest of mine, and I think in the long run it was costly.

—President Jimmy Carter[1]

When Jimmy Carter narrowly defeated Gerald Ford in the 1976 election, the Democratic Party held onto its strong majorities at all levels of government. With 292 House seats, sixty-one Senate seats, 68 percent of state legislative seats, thirty-eight governorships, and 52 percent party identification in the electorate, the Democratic Party was the undisputed majority party in American politics. Under these conditions, Carter perceived no need to build a new majority; he viewed his primary task as translating his party's existing majorities into effective government action.

During the eight years between Johnson's presidency and Carter's inauguration, "out-party" chairmen had done little to revitalize the enervated organization LBJ left behind. A prohibitive debt from the 1968 election ($9 million) hampered new party-building initiatives, and a series of efforts to hammer out policy and procedural agreements among liberals, moderates, conservatives, and affiliated interest groups consumed the attention of party leaders. By 1977, the party had fallen well behind the Republican Party in direct mail, campaign services, and infrastructure development.[2] Carter's political team observed during the transition period that "at the present time, the DNC office has little staff and only a few ongoing programs. (State parties are in even worse shape!)"[3]

With its "can-do" attitude, Carter's ambitious team drew up plans to make new investments in the party's infrastructure and improve its voter contact capabilities.[4] But once Carter assumed office, the new president found no particular reason to treat his party's dilapidated organization as a problem requiring his urgent attention, and he did not follow up on his team's early plans. As is characteristic of majority-party presidents, he emphasized certain types of priorities over others: policy leadership over party leadership, "message" over organization, placating incumbents over recruiting challengers, suppressing dissent over opening party forums. With no urgent need to strengthen his party's organizational foundations or expand its reach, Carter became skeptical of its usefulness, dismissive of its organizational problems, and burdened by its traditions. Consequently, he sought either to subdue his party, circumvent it, or exploit it.

Carter had many reasons to eschew party building: some were specific to him as an individual, and others he shared with all majority-party presidents. Among the individual-level factors: he was a "party outsider" who felt that he owed little to the party establishment for his nomination and election;[5] he hailed from a weak one-party state and was thus not adept at party organizational matters;[6] and his policy positions put him at odds with many Democratic constituencies.[7] If we consider Carter's presidency in isolation from all other presidencies, each of these factors might seem to explain his lack of interest in party building.

But when the backgrounds of other modern presidents are taken into account, these individual-level explanations appear much less satisfactory. After all, Eisenhower, too, was a party outsider who owed little to his party for his nomination or election; neither Eisenhower nor Reagan had a strong background in organizational party politics; and Eisenhower, Ford, and Bush all took policy positions that were out of step with many of their party's most powerful constituencies. Yet because all four of these Republican presidents sought to build a new majority for their party, they all engaged in party building. With deep and durable Democratic majorities at every level of government, Carter did not share the same party-building impulse. His individual-level factors therefore only reinforced his competitive incentive to subordinate his party to more urgent priorities.

As we will see, along six spheres of party activity, Carter either undercut his party organization, purposefully exploited it for his short-term benefit, or neglected its organizational capacities (see figure 10.1). While examining these episodes of president-party interaction, this chapter also elaborates upon four characteristics of the typical approach majority-party presidents take to their parties: (1) with more urgent priorities, majority-party presidents often express indifference toward their parties; (2) when majority-party presidents

		Party Building						Party Predation					
		C	H	R	V	F	I	C	H	R	V	F	I
Republicans	Eisenhower	•	•	•	•	•	•						
	Nixon	•	•	•	•	•	•	•				•	
	Ford	•	•	•	•		•						
	Reagan	•	•	•	•	•	•						
	Bush	•	•	•		•	•						
Democrats	Kennedy					•	•	•	•		•	•	•
	Johnson							•	•		•	•	•
	Carter							•	•	•	•	•	•
	Clinton (1st term)							•	•	•	•	•	•
	Clinton (2nd term)	•	•			•	•	•					

C=Provide campaign services, H=Build human capital, R=Recruit candidates,
V=Mobilize voters, F=Finance party operations, I=Support internal activities

Figure 10.1. Carter's Party Interactions

exploit their party organizations, they work with them cooperatively but do not simultaneously invest in their organizational capacities; (3) the persistent refusal of Democratic presidents to engage in party building perpetuated a cycle of "negative feedback" in the Democratic Party; (4) majority-party presidents tend to devote considerable amounts of time and energy to controlling and manipulating their party's rules and procedures.

The Alternative Priorities of Majority-Party Presidents

Like all majority-party presidents, Carter did not seek to construct a new majority around his ideological commitments, nor was his goal to build a new party or reshape the political landscape. His primary objective was to achieve policy success and "repair the mechanical defects" of government.[8] This was no small task: it drew Carter into intensive and extended engagement with the peculiarities of the governing process. In an oral history, Carter recalled:

> I spent hour after hour after hour studying the structure of the federal government in preparation of the budgets . . . because I felt that this was one of the managerial weapons or tools that I had to exert my influence in a definitive way. . . . If something was important to me, like the energy legislation, which was comprised of thousands of meticulous details, I took the time to learn them. When . . . House and Senate conferees would be called into the Cabinet room to resolve a particular detail that meant the passage or failure of the entire bill, I wanted to understand what I was talking about as well as the chairman of a Senate subcommittee. And I did. I devoted the time to it.[9]

Carter's determination to master the details of administration was half of his leadership challenge: the other half involved mastering the finer arts of legislative leadership in the context of an unusually large and unwieldy Democratic majority in Congress.

Carter complained of having to "woo" members "on an individual basis" and exercise hands-on leadership through every step of the legislative process: "It was a constant, never-ending, complicated, and fragmented process to get all the legislation to pass through" Congress, he said.[10] Hamilton Jordan, Carter's top political adviser and chief of staff, recalled: "There we were with a solid Democratic majority in both houses, and our fights were always with the Democrats."[11]

Carter exhibited no personal animosity toward his party and did not set out to do it harm. But because his priorities pointed him in a different direction, he never took the time to rebuild his party organization. In his first year, Carter's DNC chairman drew up a comprehensive party-building plan and implored the president to help raise the funds needed to implement it. But with more urgent business to attend to, Carter repeatedly ignored his chairman as well as the rest of the party membership. As party leaders began to clamor for more presidential action, Carter increasingly came to view his party as a burden and a distraction rather than as a useful and important resource worthy of his attention.

Unheeded Party-Building Plans

Carter gave his first DNC chairman, former governor Kenneth Curtis of Maine, the impression that he would receive the full support of the White House. In his inaugural speech, Curtis announced that the new president had promised him "very direct access to the White House" and had conveyed the importance of having "a strong and active Democratic Party."[12] Consequently, Curtis said, he had begun to draw up detailed party-building plans that were "unprecedented for a party in power." New DNC programs would enhance voter registration activities, reorganize the national committee, "set up a regional desk system at headquarters here for closer liaison with the states," and emphasize closer voter contact.[13] The party was still deep in debt from 1968, Curtis said, but with "a President in the White House," it could finally be paid off.[14] Curtis's speech pleased DNC members and state chairmen, who eagerly awaited Carter's help. Yet in an early sign of what was to come, Carter chose not to attend the first party meeting, despite the urgings of his staff that he go.[15] His attention was already shifting elsewhere.

Within two months, Curtis submitted his detailed plan to the White House. He defined "the goal" as "helping to strengthen the Democratic Party in the national, state, and local levels throughout the nation." With a few structural investments, the DNC could be built into a powerful service organization, he wrote, able to "assist party organizations at all levels in their efforts to broaden the base of their support."[16]

Critical to the success of future party endeavors would be new investments in technology and research capabilities. "Presently, no system of permanent record keeping, ongoing data collection and post-election analysis exists within the DNC," Curtis noted. A program called Target '76, run out of the DNC the previous year, was the DNC's "first attempt to assist candidates and parties with voter registration and GOTV [get-out-the-vote] targeting information"—but it "was a one-time effort." No efforts had ever been made to invest in durable forms of information technology in the Democratic Party. Building a new "data bank" would enable the DNC to readily access "basic statistical information needed for party funding, voter registration, and GOTV programs," he wrote. The DNC could then draw on its data bank for multiple purposes: to assist candidates' campaigns, to help state parties manage reapportionment in 1981, and to recruit new volunteers and activists.[17]

With a few additional investments in the coming months, the party could establish a new Campaign Services Division "to aid Democratic candidates, to train campaign workers, and to expand and strengthen state and local parties," Curtis wrote. While the DNC would not likely be able to provide "direct financial assistance" to candidates in the 1977 and 1978 elections, the party could offer "technical skills," research, and administrative support. If the DNC began early to "build organizations and strengthen the party," it would be well equipped to help in future campaigns, including Carter's 1980 reelection campaign, Curtis noted.

Additional proposals included strengthening the DNC's relationship with congressional campaign committees, supporting the Democratic mayors' and governors' groups, revitalizing the DNC Women's Division, expanding the Field Operations Division, and charging it with integrating the "Carter base" into the regular party apparatus. The "bounds of these programs are limitless," Curtis wrote, but "they are costly."[18]

The fact of the matter, Curtis wrote, was that the DNC's financial situation "paints a rather bleak picture." The committee was still carrying at least $4 million in debt; debt repayment and basic operating expenses would cost $3 million over the next four months alone. "Obviously, our success depends on Administration cooperation," as the program was "totally dependent on financial support," Curtis argued. If Carter and his top staff were willing to engage in a series of fund-raisers on behalf of the party in the spring and summer of 1977, the DNC could quickly become the active, flexible campaign-service organization that Curtis envisioned.[19]

But Curtis's reports were ignored by the White House. In his first year in office, Carter participated in only two DNC fund-raisers, one in June and one in October, and he refused urgent requests to lend his signature to a small-donor direct-mail initiative at the DNC.[20] Indeed, there is no record that Carter's team even discussed Curtis's party-building plans.

Carter's lack of interest in Curtis's proposal was but one example of the indifference he showed to the Democratic Party during his first year. He also ignored the rising discontent among the party's active membership. Local party leaders felt neglected by the president, and by April 1977 they began to actively seek more involvement in patronage and policy matters. "An 'us/ them' mentality has now developed in the party," presidential assistant Mark Siegel warned Carter.[21] The DNC Executive Committee even took the unusual step of passing a formal resolution to get the White House's attention.[22] But only Siegel seemed interested in conciliating the unhappy party leaders; his suggestions that Carter work to strengthen his relationship with state party chairmen were not echoed by other members of the senior staff.[23]

Still trying to get the president's attention, Curtis submitted a second and more concise draft of his proposal to Carter in May.[24] He reiterated his earlier request for the president's fund-raising support, and in executive-summary fashion, stressed the benefits that would accrue to Carter's 1980 reelection campaign. But Curtis still received no response from the White House. In a last-ditch attempt to generate funding for his program, Curtis resorted to asking DNC members and state party chairmen for donations.[25]

By the end of the year, Curtis had had enough of being ignored by the White House and decided to resign. Announcing his departure, he called the chairmanship a "lousy job." He had reportedly become "dispirited by the problems of trying to breathe new life" into the party. While Curtis did not explicitly blame Carter for being unwilling to help with fund-raising, he did complain that the lingering debt prevented him from supporting candidates or "instituting innovative computer and television operations." It would take "several years of hard work" to bring the party back up to speed, Curtis said, and "I'd like to do something else with my life." He added wryly: "Did you ever try to meet a payroll every two weeks for a bankrupt organization?"[26]

One member of Carter's staff, speaking to a reporter on the condition of anonymity, acknowledged that Curtis's resignation might have had something to do with "the 'indifference' of the President toward party affairs and the preoccupation of his chief political adviser, Hamilton Jordan, with other matters."[27] In a confidential memo to Carter, Jordan revealed that Carter's team simply did not view the president's relationship with the party as a two-way street: he argued that helping the party improve its structures and operations was not something the White House should be concerned with. Unless the president could count on the party's support in pursuing his political goals, the party was useless, or worse: "A DNC operation that requires a lot of time and supervision from here is more of a problem than a help. . . . *In short, the DNC has become an additional political burden for us instead of a resource,*" Jordan wrote.[28]

Curtis's resignation led to much media scrutiny and accusations that Carter did not care about his party. In an attempt to quell the public relations fallout, Carter appeared before the DNC in January 1978 and admitted, with his characteristic candor, that his party had ranked low on his list of priorities during his first year in office. He had been consumed by the demands of governing, he said, and had been forced to devote all of his time learning the ropes of being president. He promised to give his party more attention in the coming years:

> I came to Washington for the first time just about a year ago. And we had a massive program to propose, campaign commitments to honor, a Congress for me to learn about, and a quizzical American public about a newcomer to national politics whom they really didn't know. I had to do hundreds of hours of personal study about the history and present circumstances concerning the Middle East, Africa, Latin America, Panama, SALT, comprehensive test bans, domestic programs. And I have to admit to you that in many instances, I put those responsibilities ahead of my responsibilities to the Democratic National Committee. I don't think you've had the support that was needed from the White House. But I don't have to restudy those issues. I've become fairly well educated, and now I can keep up with changing circumstances. This year, there will be a much closer allegiance and alliance from the White House toward the Democratic National Committee.[29]

The audience of DNC members was receptive to his explanation and gave him three standing ovations.[30]

While Carter did not ultimately live up to his pledge, it is worth taking seriously his "mea culpa." Here was a president who evidenced no hostility toward his party organization: he simply did not consider party building to be worth his time. He had more urgent priorities than restoring his party's organizational vitality: "It was not a burning commitment or interest of mine," he later admitted. "And I think in the long run it was costly."[31]

Party Exploitation

In the previous two chapters, we have seen that majority-party presidents often interact with their parties, work with them, and call upon them to undertake significant political activities; yet these efforts are not considered constructive, party-building efforts. The reason is that in these instances, the president does not make any effort to strengthen the party organization or enhance its organizational capacities. The efforts are purely exploitative: they draw upon existing party capacities and supplant normal party activities without giving anything back. They are wholly instrumental actions, aimed at maximizing the president's immediate benefit without concern for the long-term effects on the party's organizational capacities. Operation Support and the various DNC "information programs" conducted under Kennedy and Johnson are prime examples of party exploitation.

One can discern a difference between party exploitation and the two other types of approaches we have observed in the previous chapters, neglect and antagonism. Party neglect is nicely illustrated by Carter's indifference toward Curtis's party-building plans and Kennedy's refusal to support John Bailey's party-building efforts. Party antagonism, as we have seen with the President's Club and Johnson's elimination of the DNC's voter registration, intentionally undercuts or removes the party's operational wherewithal.

These approaches are all variations on the same theme: each is a response to the president's perception of his competitive political environment and each reflects the limited appeal of party building in this context. Each also produces similar effects: whether the president *undercuts* his party, *exploits* it for short-term gain, or simply *ignores* it, he does not contribute to its organizational development. Indeed, as we have seen, party building is a collective endeavor that takes time, resources, and persistent attention: if the president is not contributing to his party's organizational development, he is effectively setting it back.

Whereas Carter's party interactions during 1977 are best characterized as party neglect, his main points of contact with the party organization during his second year are best characterized as party exploitation. He interacted with his party quite frequently and used it to promote his political purposes without making any simultaneous investments in its organizational capacities.

Later we will discuss how Carter's actions contributed to a cycle of negative feedback in the Democratic Party. But first, let us examine two particularly good illustrations of party exploitation.

A Public Relations Offensive

Curtis's departure prompted Carter and Jordan to reevaluate the administration's relationship with the party. In "rethinking the role of the DNC," Jordan wrote, "we should lower our expectations of what the DNC can do for us." Rather than ask the DNC to repair its existing problems or expand its activities, we should "ask them instead to do fewer things better."[32] Carter's choice to lead this leaner, pared-down DNC was deputy agriculture secretary John C. White. With little background in managing party organizations, White's main qualification for the job was his unwavering loyalty to Carter.[33]

White began his chairmanship by streamlining party operations—firing thirty of the eighty staff he inherited from Curtis and cutting payroll by a third—and designing a program to exploit the DNC's existing capacities on Carter's behalf. In a confidential memo to Carter, White argued that nearly all of Carter's political problems flowed from "the failure to convey [the administration's] message . . . at every appropriate opportunity." This hurt the president's relations "with Congress and our constituents." The problem was most serious within the Democratic Party coalition itself: almost all of the major traditional constituencies in the Democratic Party were reluctant to support the administration, he wrote. "Little needs to be said about our difficulties with the Jewish community, with Labor, with the Congress, within the Democratic Regular Party, or with the 'West.'"[34]

The "remedy" White proposed was to use the DNC to launch a "public relations offensive" to "constantly remind" these groups of the administration's accomplishments. Such an information-dissemination campaign would help to bring at least the semblance of unity to the large and heterogeneous Democratic majority. In an uncanny replication of Kennedy's "information program" and Johnson's Congressional Support Program, Carter's team sought to use the DNC as a central clearinghouse to provide Democratic candidates with the information and talking points they would need to help sell the administration's program as the 1978 midterm elections approached.[35] White explained to DNC members that "the most useful service that the DNC can perform at this moment in time is to supply Democrats with chapter and verse on the accomplishments of the Democratic partnership—represented by the Administration and the Congress."[36]

White was responding to the president's needs, not the party's. It was not the party's message that caused the greatest discontent among the activist base: it was the condition of the organization. At the same time that White was launching a "public relations offensive," state party leaders were becoming increasingly anxious about the rise of formidable Republican Party organizations in their states. Western state party chairmen, for example, repeatedly asked for "more money from the party and responsiveness from the White House to stop it."[37] But Carter's DNC did not waver from its determination to "systematically spread the message of the Administration," even if that meant perpetuating the party's financial liabilities, campaign deficiencies, and weak state party operations.[38] If anything, White's approach became more heavy-handed as time wore on: at DNC meetings in 1979, for example, he gave a "series of harsh lectures to party leaders," urging them to "close ranks around the president."[39] With no help forthcoming from Carter or the DNC, state leaders began to launch new party-building programs on their own initiative. In the summer of 1978 they began to build new fund-raising capacities and field operations "that are politically independent from the White House."[40]

Curtis's 1977 proposals for strengthening the party's organizational capacities were now long since forgotten. Despite periodic calls from highly regarded DNC staffers like political director John Rendon to make investments in education and training programs, opposition research, new technologies, field staffs, new fund-raising units, and new voter registration efforts—to replicate the much-publicized party-building programs being undertaken at the RNC—Carter and White refused to initiate such programs.[41]

Breakfast Briefings with State Party Leaders

In another illustration of how presidents can interact with their party without investing in it or strengthening its organizational capacities in any way, Carter and his staff began to host regular breakfasts with small groups of state chairmen at the White House in May 1978 and continued the practice periodically through 1980. Without doubt, these breakfast meetings represented the most systematic, ongoing interaction between the White House and the state parties during Carter's presidency. By most accounts, they were successful in mollifying many state party chairmen and repairing some of the bruised egos from 1977. But lest one confuse these breakfasts with constructive presidential efforts to build state parties, White House memos reveal that the breakfasts were no more than symbolic affairs meant to cultivate the president's support among local party leaders. The parallel between these breakfast briefings and Johnson's short-lived efforts to bring state chairmen to the White House and expose them to the "frosting" of the presidency to maintain their loyalty in 1967–68 is striking—and revealing of their shared incentives and purposes.

Rather than offer training, financial resources, or strategic assistance with party building, the White House used the breakfast briefings to generate support for Carter's policy initiatives and to placate disgruntled chairmen before their discontent reached the newspapers. Each of the gatherings included a "brief greeting and photo" where Carter would "thank for their interest and involvement in policies of the Administration; urge them to speak out on programs to Congress and at home."[42] The purpose was straightforward: "To give them some insight into Administration policies and legislative initiatives."[43] Carter and his team told state party leaders that "sometimes we will be calling to notify them of major legislative initiatives; at other times we will call on them for their opinions on certain considered initiatives; at other times we will be asking for their help."[44] Conspicuously absent were offers of White House support in building local parties.

By the end of the summer, the breakfast briefings were expanded to include "Carter Network" volunteers, state legislators, mayors, and other elected local officials. As time wore on, discussions turned from policy to politics as Carter's staff began to line up commitments of support for 1980. One southern Democrat who attended a White House breakfast said: "Jimmy is stroking us now because he knows he is going to need us in 1980." Other attendees reported that "a new presidential message, at least by implication, is coming through loud and clear. Get behind Mr. Carter for 1980."[45]

When Republican presidents interacted with their state parties, they tended to offer assistance in building durable infrastructures and institutional capacities. By sponsoring training programs, offering technological assistance, helping with fund-raising, and providing a variety of other programs, they helped the GOP build new structures and activities at all levels of the party. In comparison with those explicitly constructive president-party interactions, Carter's otherwise generally friendly interactions with state party leaders appear crudely instrumental and short range in focus. Carter certainly had a choice about how he would interact with his party's local leaders, but rather than combine an instrumental approach with a constructive one, his approach was purely instrumental and exploitative. He sought the state chairmen's help with his political problems rather than offer his help with theirs.

While majority-party presidents interact with their party in a variety of ways, activities like these—which *use* the party structure without giving anything back—may be the most common. They are not hostile, nor are they neglectful; they fit somewhere in between. Whatever the intent, these efforts stand out for what they do not do: they do not simultaneously invest in the party organization. As the next section explores, these decidedly nonconstructive acts have real political consequences.

A Cycle of Negative Feedback

The persistent refusal of Democratic presidents to build new party structures or sponsor new party-building activities perpetuated a cycle of "negative feedback" in the Democratic Party. By keeping the party's operational capacities inchoate, Democratic presidents left their successors with little to build on and few resources with which to begin building from scratch. This dynamic was self-reinforcing in that each round of organizational neglect or exploitation made it increasingly likely that future presidents and party leaders would direct their attention to nonorganizational priorities, which, in turn, would sap the time and resources that might otherwise have been devoted to making organizational repairs. Short of a dramatic reversal in their party's competitive position, each new Democratic president found it in his interest to follow in his predecessors' footsteps. While this dynamic is observed over the course of many years, it can also be seen within a single presidency. Carter's earlier refusals to engage in party building clearly shaped his menu of options later in his term.

Political Liaison in the White House

During a reevaluation of Carter's political troubles in late 1977, Jordan argued that the discontents of "traditional or institutional Democratic constituencies —labor, teachers, farmers, Jews, minorities, party activists, liberals, etc.," few of whom had supported Carter enthusiastically in 1976, were causing the new administration its greatest difficulties. The problem was not Carter's policy positions, "because in my judgment they are correct and defensible," Jordan wrote, but they "stem rather from inadequate procedures, communications and courtesies" and "a sense of remoteness and at times unresponsiveness they have in their dealings with us. Among many politicians there is a sense of exclusivity in the White House; they feel they are not particularly needed or wanted."[46] This sense of estrangement from the administration presented a real problem, he wrote, because Carter would need their help in 1980.[47]

Time was short: "We have only the first six or eight months of 1978 to consolidate our relations with these groups," Jordan noted. But because the DNC was viewed as cumbersome, Jordan proposed building a public liaison team inside the White House that would become "the focal point, under your direction, for all White House political activities and contact."[48] Such a move would allow Carter's team to focus exclusively on redressing his political liabilities. Carter agreed with Jordan's suggestion, and in early 1978 he appointed longtime Democratic Party activist and deputy undersecretary of commerce Anne Wexler and Tim Kraft, his appointments secretary and political adviser, to serve as his chief liaisons.[49] Their responsibilities primarily involved nurturing constituency groups and developing strategy for Carter's reelection campaign.

Establishing a political team inside the White House was not an exclusively Democratic presidential practice, of course: Nixon and Ford had similar arrangements, and Reagan institutionalized the concept with the White House Office of Political Affairs. But whereas Republican presidents used their White House political teams to coordinate and support their various party-building initiatives, Carter used his political team to circumvent his party and supplant its traditional functions.

Support-Our-President

In another example of Carter's decision to turn away from his party rather than make new investments in it, his political team launched a concerted effort to keep the nonpartisan networks of Carter volunteers from the 1976 campaign active and prepared to support the administration. In December 1977, the administration initiated contact with the approximately 150,000 activists by sending each a Christmas card (while charging the DNC for the postage). The goal was to create a new organization, loosely called "Support-our-President," outside of formal Democratic Party channels. The grassroots Carter supporters were asked for small donations—ten dollars every six months—to fund the new organization, which would operate mainly through a "phone network or 'tree' designed to alert the volunteers."[50]

The new Support-our-President organization was essentially an extrapartisan replica of Kennedy and Johnson's Operation Support. It encouraged Carter supporters to send mail to congressmen in support of the president's program, generate letters to the editor, "provide well-informed, articulate supporters of the President's policies to participate in panel discussions . . . debates and radio call-in programs," "provide a ready-made organization for the 1980 primaries and general election," and so on.[51] The White House reportedly saw the extrapartisan group as the primary mechanism for generating "political support and field work rather than the formal structure of the DNC."[52] The Christmas card mailing was followed up with a reception in Atlanta for approximately 1,000 volunteers on the anniversary of Carter's first inaugural address; Carter personally delivered the keynote speech.[53] This reactivation of the 1976 Carter Network was said to "drive state chairs crazy."[54]

Because Carter did not take decisive action to break the pattern of organizational neglect in the Democratic Party, he contributed to its perpetuation. By building a more responsive political agency inside his White House, activating nonpartisan volunteers, and continually ignoring proposals to strengthen his party organization, Carter reinforced his party's organizational deficiencies.

A Dearth of Campaign Services

As the midterm elections of 1978 approached, Carter's earlier actions (and nonactions) began to negatively affect Democratic candidates across the board. By cutting a third of the DNC staff in order to do "fewer things better," White left the DNC without the administrative support it needed to carry out even the most basic coordinative tasks. Carter's staff complained in the summer of 1978 that working with the DNC to prepare for the midterm campaigns had become an enormous challenge. The "major drawback" to dealing with the DNC, Carter's assistants wrote, "has been simply a shortage of staff to carry on the effort on the scale needed."[55] The DNC was slow and cumbersome, but even more problematic was its lack of capacity to provide campaign assistance, financial support, or even the most elementary elections data to Democratic candidates.

Rather than provide data to candidates, the DNC asked candidates to compile data on voters in their localities and send it to the DNC's centralized system to be merged with the DNC's demographic and census data, and reformatted.[56] Candidates were then charged for accessing the repackaged voter data they had provided: 50 percent of the cost was demanded upfront, and candidates were responsible for paying shipping charges, service charges, and even "sundry expenses incurred in maintaining the DNC Data Bank."[57] Putting the financial burden on the candidates was no mistake; records show that the program was meant to generate revenue for the DNC: "As the data bank program develops, it should be possible for the DNC to realize a profit," DNC consultants wrote.[58] Ann Lewis, who later became DNC political director, remarked that not only the data bank, but all of the campaign services offered by the DNC imposed a financial burden on candidates. Polls produced by the DNC, for example, were also made available to candidates, but only at a steep cost; in many cases, the output was never even delivered.[59]

These exploitative "services" for candidates stand in stark contrast to the voter data and political research made available to Republican candidates under Gerald Ford. As discussed in chapter 5, by making significant investments in the RNC's technology and human capital, Ford's RNC team was able to offer data and research at a deep discount to candidates. By creating an incentive for candidate participation, they built momentum for coordinated party activities in the future. Carter's lack of interest in building momentum for organizational development in the Democratic Party, in contrast, reverberated throughout the party and affected even its most basic capacity to offer campaign services to candidates.

The justification for the Democrats' inadequate campaign services was provided in a revealing memo from Jordan to Carter. There was no urgent need to be concerned about the party's organizational capacities, Jordan wrote, because "incumbents don't want or need technical help from the party. . . . So if we're planning to do much in this area it's bound to be largely wasted. That's not true, however, with non-incumbent candidates. They do want and need this kind of assistance."[60] But because most Democratic candidates standing for office in 1978 were incumbents, not challengers, Carter's team simply did not believe that the party's provision of "technical help" should be a priority.

Carter enthusiastically campaigned for many of his fellow Democrats in 1978, and his efforts on the stump were nothing short of impressive.[61] But while presidential endorsements may help individual candidates' campaigns in the moment at hand, it does not leave behind anything more durable. Indeed, presidential efforts on behalf of congressional candidates should not be confused with party-building efforts to enhance the party's organizational capacity to compete in the electoral arena. Carter's personal campaign assistance might have helped build his support among members of Congress, but it only served to distract from the party's organizational deficiencies.

Democrats suffered only mild losses in 1978, and the party maintained its strong electoral position during Carter's final two years.[62] Yet at the organizational level, the party was in no better condition after 1978 than before. As preparations for Carter's 1980 reelection campaign started to take shape, Carter and his team began to experience for themselves the consequences of the president's earlier neglect of the party.

Organizational Deficiencies

As the 1980 elections approached, Carter's staff argued that the White House should look to the DNC for one thing primarily: soft money. Recent amendments to the Federal Elections Campaign Act (FECA) and FEC rule changes, they noted, were likely to "have a significant impact on the outcome of the general election." They determined that the DNC should make as its "most important program" the "General Election expenditure program."[63] Political parties were now legally allowed to spend unlimited amounts of money on campaigns (for such activities as voter mobilization, education, and registration activities). This created a strong incentive for presidential candidates to work closely with their parties on fund-raising and campaign expenditures. The Carter team was enthusiastic about what these new changes meant: "The campaign may simply send over bills to be paid by the National Committee on behalf of the campaign for media, headquarters expenses, campaign paraphernalia, etc.," wrote Elaine Kamarck, director of special projects for the Carter campaign.[64]

But unfortunately for Carter, his earlier neglect of his party's financial problems had now come back to haunt him. The party organization, it turned out, did not have the capacity to raise as much money as Carter needed. With no significant direct-mail program to solicit donations, a precarious dependency upon "fat cat" donors, and a drawn-out battle for the nomination between Carter and Senator Edward "Ted" Kennedy that attracted most Democratic dollars, Carter's campaign staff wrote in March 1980 that 40 percent of the DNC's budget for the campaign had "yet to be solicited and collected." Raising this money was seen as a "massive task" that was "perhaps impossible" given the current weak state of the DNC's operations: "Whatever program is put together to raise these funds probably should have started already," the campaign memo stated. The long "lead time" required for fund-raising events and the lack of personnel to coordinate such an operation meant that the prospects for full utilization of party structures were bleak: "There must be a massive increase in staff at the DNC to properly conduct this size program," aides warned.[65]

Carter began a focused fund-raising drive in the late summer and early fall to raise soft money for his campaign, "to counter what Democrats contend could be a $20 million advantage the Republicans have in this new area of cooperative campaigning." But by late July 1980, the Republican advantage remained steep. The GOP had established finance committees in all fifty states, while the Democratic Party was disorganized in most states and lacked any presence whatsoever in at least fifteen.[66] Carter's earlier indifference toward party building at the national, state, and local levels now stood in the way of his ability to benefit personally from the new campaign finance system.

Equally problematic was the lack of experience and expertise among Democratic Party leaders and activists at the state and local levels of the party. Although state parties could raise and spend unlimited sums of money on Carter's behalf under the new campaign finance regime, most state party chairmen were viewed as either "incompetent" or unreliable.[67] Scrambling to make up for lost time, the White House hosted a workshop for all fifty state chairs and executive directors to explain "the implications of the new FEC law" in June 1980. But unlike Republican Party workshops, which were regularly used to build the party's stores of human capital, Carter's workshop was designed for the sole purpose of informing state chairmen about new legal requirements.[68] Increasing awareness of the new campaign finance laws, however, did little to compensate for the local party operatives' lack of campaign expertise.

At the same time that Carter was playing catch-up on the organizational front, RNC chairman Bill Brock was in the process of building upon Ford's efforts to recruit, train, and put freshly minted campaign workers to work in campaigns across the country. While the Republican Party was described as "polishing the working parts of this new national quasimachine, turning out 160 graduates this year from its 'college' for high-level campaign managers," the Democrats had not yet even entered the "dawning era" of national party building, the *New York Times* reported. While Carter held his one-day FECA-training workshop for state chairmen, the GOP was running 100 workshops throughout the summer of 1980 "to prepare this year's crop of candidates throughout the country."[69]

Though Democratic presidents did not view their lack of party's human capital or campaign service capacities to be terribly important, their own re-election prospects still depended on their ability to ensure that sympathetic voters would be registered and mobilized to vote on Election Day. But whereas Republican presidents tended to strengthen their party organization's capacity to perform voter registration and mobilization, Democratic presidents looked to their "party partners," especially organized labor, to perform the same tasks, while supporting legislation to ease registration procedures and maximize turnout across the board. Carter, too, vigorously supported legislative reforms, such as a proposal to allow registration on Election Day.[70]

While administration officials and DNC leaders often spoke of voter registration as an important activity, few resources were dedicated to developing this most critical organizational capacity "in-house" during Carter's presidency.[71] Indeed, records show that the DNC intended to coordinate its 1980 registration activities "with outside organizations conducting drives among Democratic constituencies to attempt to allocate voter registration resources to projects which complement one another."[72] But the party's dependence on outside groups such as organized labor ultimately became a political problem for Carter, as he recalled: "The labor unions, their support of me was tentative at best, and reluctant. They were looking for someone else to support. [Senator Edward] Kennedy was the repository of their support."[73]

In sum, Carter's earlier indifference toward his party's campaign services, financial systems, human capital, and voter mobilization operations became conspicuously evident around the 1978 midterm elections and the 1980 presidential campaign. By refusing to take steps to address his party's organizational problems, he reinforced the cycle of negative feedback in the Democratic Party.

Manipulating Party Rules and Procedures

Party conventions, conferences, and other proceedings are often tension-filled affairs in both parties. How a president chooses to approach these party forums—as an opportunity to welcome a diversity of viewpoints or as a potential embarrassment requiring the suppression of dissent—reveals much about how he perceives his political environment. Carter perceived no need to use these forums to convey his interest in attracting new constituencies or expanding the party's reach. While preparing for the major party forums of his presidency, Carter and his team worked hard to limit discussion and quiet dissent by manipulating rules, altering procedures, and asserting control over the agenda.

Like Johnson, Carter always expected that a more liberal Democrat would challenge him for the nomination in 1980 and worried that the party's vocal liberal constituencies would embarrass his administration by repudiating his more controversial policies. Tightly controlling the rules and procedures for party forums, therefore, was one way to reduce the likelihood that a challenger would emerge from within the party to exploit his tenuous support from rank-and-file Democrats. Carter perceived no pressing need to build new organizational capacities in his party or promote an image of his party as one that was "opening its doors." Thus, he and his team spent enormous amounts of time and energy trying to control party proceedings and reduce their political impact.

Midterm Conference of 1978

In a practice begun in 1974 and discontinued after 1982, the Democratic Party met during midterm years to discuss party policy and hammer out a consensus around pressing issues. A legacy of the procedural reforms initiated between 1968 and 1972, the Midterm Conference served the interests of the Democratic Party's heterogeneous coalition who demanded a regular voice in the party's councils.[74] The 1978 conference was considered by most observers to be an important event for Carter: it "could be a celebration of party success and a wholesale endorsement of the Carter Administration," the *New York Times* predicted, "or, alternatively, a forum where diverse critics of the president could win attention."[75] A "wide-open, free-wheeling forum for Carter critics within the party could be damaging as Carter's forces crank up for the 1980 presidential election," the *Washington Post* agreed.[76]

While Carter may have eschewed party-building plans and ignored his party's activist base, the sheer volume of White House documents detailing Carter's team's efforts to control the 1978 Midterm Conference reminds us that Carter was not prevented from party-building by a lack of time or White House resources: he simply chose to devote his energies to other things. In this case, he chose to devote his energies to subduing his party. As early as May 1977, the White House was already on high alert: "Politically, we must pay special attention to the 1978 Mid-Term Conference," Jordan and Siegel reminded Carter. "It can very easily be used by certain elements in this Party to embarrass the President and the Administration." The "ultimate goal," they wrote, was for the conference to be "small, manageable, understated, and not embarrassing to the Administration."[77]

The first order of business was to limit the number of delegates permitted to attend. Initially Carter wanted a "small conference, perhaps no more than 400 delegates." That number was "probably too low," Jordan suggested gently, adding, "I think that 600 is the lowest we can go."[78] After much back and forth, Carter accepted that the number of delegates would have to be much larger than he had originally hoped in order to accommodate the many elected officials, DNC members, and representatives of the many interest groups, caucuses, and subdivisions of the Democratic Party. By mid-1977 Carter had "ok'd" the "1500 range" for the conference but insisted: "We must hold down cost."[79] With Siegel's careful "prodding," the DNC Executive Committee approved a formula to send 1,626 delegates to the conference. While this was four times larger than Carter had initially desired, it was 20 percent smaller than the 1974 conference.[80]

Throughout 1978, administration officials worked with loyalists at the DNC to physically disperse those who might oppose the administration at the conference. Seating, they decided, should be drawn randomly. Those who were "friends" of the administration would be tapped to serve as floor whips and stationed at each "row, column, area," and in each issue workshop. An elaborate system of whip reporting and coordination was designed to hold all the pieces in place once the conference got under way. A "field system" of four field directors would "float" on the floor and be available in case of any emergencies. From July through November, Carter's staff labored to identify, train, and assign the whips.[81]

Carter forces also sought to shape the rules of the conference. For example, each miniworkshop that would meet to discuss particular issues would be allowed to submit written reports, but those reports would not be taken to the conference floor for a vote unless they had signatures from 20 percent of the delegates: that is, of all the delegates, not just those present. To pass, the resolutions required the support of a majority of all delegates; David Broder noted that "the odds are very heavy against there being 817 votes for any of four mildly dissenting resolutions that will be brought up for debate."[82] The panels should "produce enough sparks to be interesting—but not set off fireworks!" an internal White House memo noted.[83]

Despite a well-orchestrated, tightly controlled proceeding, dissent was impossible to stifle completely. Kennedy gave a "rousing" speech, and those who opposed the reduced social welfare spending and increased defense appropriations in Carter's budget "just barely" lost their motions. "There was loud and angry protest against administration policies in every workshop," but "it was a formless, scattershot criticism, held firmly in check by adminis- tration forces."[84] One liberal delegate laughed that "they've over-reacted to us . . . this is overkill. We went at them with a pea gun and they rolled out the cannons."[85]

Winograd Commission

In a similar episode of intensive White House effort to manipulate party rules for Carter's personal political benefit, Carter and his team sought to shape the proposal being drafted by a commission charged with revising the delegate selection rules governing presidential primary contests. The Commission on Presidential Nomination and Party Structure, or Winograd Commission, named for its well-respected chairman, Morley Winograd of Michigan, then chairman of the Association of State Democratic Chairs, set out to make sev- eral recommendations to improve primary procedures, including changing the percentage of the popular vote a candidate would need to win delegates in a given state. In 1976, when Carter emerged from obscurity to win the nomi- nation by capitalizing on new primary selection procedures, no uniform prac- tice was in place for awarding candidates delegates. Now the incumbent, Carter wanted to establish a higher threshold to reduce the likelihood that a challenger could garner enough delegates to influence the convention and nomination in 1980. Carter wanted to raise the threshold to 25 percent of the vote.

Doing so would "not only reduce the number of delegates won by trailing candidates but would also increase the value of coming in first," one reporter noted. Siegel argued that the change in procedures was a "mechanism to build consensus."[86] But the change was clearly designed to benefit Carter's political purposes. Jordan described to Carter in great detail how "in a field with two or more challengers, the 25% proposal would have a substantial effect in your favor."[87] But when it became clear that a 25 percent floor faced significant opposition from party reformers, Carter asked, "How about a mandatory 20%?"[88] Carter's 20 percent compromise was relayed to his liaisons to the Winograd Commission, who told Jordan that they would "posture for 30 and 25%" at the commission, even though 20 percent was their goal.[89]

After multiple meetings of the Winograd Commission and many confi- dential debates at the White House, the commission's final report recommended a "sliding door" system.[90] Those primaries held in the first four weeks of the twelve-week nomination cycle would require 15 percent, the second third of the contests would require 20 percent, and the final third would require 25 percent of the vote to qualify for delegates.[91] The proposal satisfied Carter, but the Winograd report still had to be voted on by the full DNC. Jordan led an intensive lobbying campaign to ensure the outcome that the White House desired.[92] Thanks to Carter's team's unrelenting efforts, the rules changes were passed essentially as Carter and his team wanted.[93]

At the end of the day, Ted Kennedy's strong primary challenge in 1980 made the threshold question a moot point. But the struggle to control party proceedings continued. While Carter managed to win enough delegates to lock up the nomination by early June, the administration became concerned that the national convention in August could be used by Kennedy and his supporters to embarrass the president.[94] For an upcoming meeting between Carter and White, Jordan reminded the president to be adamant in his insistence that White dedicate the bulk of his time and energy between April and August to controlling the convention proceedings, at whatever the cost to other party activities:

> Let him know that you are expecting him to focus primarily on the convention. It is very important that we have a very good convention. This is particularly important, as the possibility of a Kennedy challenge at the convention is likely. You should let John know that you want him to focus most of his time and efforts on the convention.[95]

Maintaining control over party proceedings proved to be a difficult task: the defeated Kennedy was said to have "won the party's heart and soul" at the convention with his stirring speech and successful efforts to insert more liberal planks into the party platform.[96] Like Johnson, who also tried to control his convention proceedings and found that total control was elusive, Carter discovered the reality that his party had become neither an instrument of his control nor a reliable organizational basis for support in his own campaign.

However presidents choose to interact with their party, their choices implicate them in its development. Those who build their parties tend to foster organizational conditions in which future party leaders will find it more attractive to follow in their footsteps; those who ignore, exploit, or undercut their party's organizational capacities tend to encourage their successors to do the same. Presidents can be either a force of positive or negative feedback in their party's organizational development, but in either case, their choices shape their party's organizational trajectory.

The presidency of Jimmy Carter offers a third variation on the theme observed in the Kennedy and Johnson presidencies. In several instances Carter exploited his party, but in most instances he simply ignored it. With more pressing alternative priorities, Carter simply did not devote time to party building (see table 10.1). After the fact, he admitted as much: "I didn't take on as a major project the change in the Democratic structure that I think now was needed. I think in retrospect it was needed."[97]

Table 10.1   Carter's Party Predation

Provide campaign services	Build human capital	Recruit candidates	Mobilize voters	Finance party operations	Support internal activities
Ignore Curtis's party-building program (1977)	"Support-our-President" (1977+)	Ignore Curtis's party-building program (1977)	Ignore Curtis's party-building program (1977)	Let direct-mail and financial systems languish (1977+)	Ignore Curtis's party-building program (1977)
"Support-our-President" (1977+)	Ignore Curtis's party-building program (1977)	Ignore Rendon's party-building suggestions (1978–1979)	"Support-our-President" (1977+)	Ignore Curtis's party-building program (1977)	Public relations offensive (1978+)
Little technical help to candidates (1978+)	Breakfasts with state chairmen (1978+)		Public relations offensive (1978+)	Ignore western state party chairmen requests (1978)	White to focus on Democratic National Convention (1980)
Public relations offensive (1978+)	Ignore Rendon's party-building suggestions (1978–1979)		Voter registration outsourcing and legislation (1978+)	Ignore Rendon's party-building suggestions (1978–1979)	Ignore western state party chairmen requests (1978)
Ignore western state party chairmen requests (1978)	State chairmen FECA training (1980)		Ignore Rendon's party-building suggestions (1978–79)		Ignore Rendon's party-building suggestions (1978–79)
Ignore Rendon's party-building suggestions (1978–79)					

Note: All instances indicate the absence of party building; that is, they confirm the conventional wisdom about the president-party relationship. Whether, in any given instance, the president undercuts his party, exploits it, or neglects it, the effect is to undermine the party's organizational capacities along these six dimensions of party activity.

Carter's presidency also illustrates four characteristics of the typical approach majority-party presidents take to their party: (1) with more urgent priorities, majority-party presidents often express indifference toward their parties; (2) majority-party presidents also frequently *use* their parties without simultaneously investing in their organizational capacities: this is party exploitation; (3) in either case, by consistently refusing to engage in party building, Democratic presidents perpetuated a cycle of "negative feedback" in their party organization; (4) majority-party presidents tend to devote considerable amounts of time and energy to controlling and manipulating their party's rules and procedures.

While he addressed the characteristic challenges faced by majority-party presidents in his own way, Carter sits quite comfortably next to Kennedy and Johnson. Eschewing party building, all three of these presidents not only set their party's organizational development back, but they made it more costly for future party leaders to launch new programs. Despite intermittent efforts to relieve the party of its debt, for example, Carter was constantly distracted by more urgent concerns: consequently, the party carried its 1968 debt forward into 1981. Indeed, Carter's failure to strengthen his party's fund-raising capacities is striking when viewed in light of the Republican Party's simultaneous fund-raising efforts: 1.2 million people contributed to the GOP in 1980 alone. Carter, in contrast, left behind a prospective donor list of only 27,500 names at the DNC.[98] Operating costs for the DNC's direct-mail program were draining approximately $200,000 to $300,000 per month in 1979 and had to be reduced; by 1980, donations solicited through direct mail only accounted for around 20 percent of the DNC's income. In contrast, the Republicans raised 73 percent of their income from small donations solicited through direct mail.[99]

The party apparatus Carter bequeathed to new DNC chairman Charles Manatt in 1981 was described as "beaten, broke and virtually bedridden."[100] Manatt, who, like all out-party chairmen, faced a strong electoral incentive to engage in party building, found himself "essentially starting from scratch."[101] By insisting that new funds raised should be reinvested into the party's fund-raising systems, he managed to expand the Democrats' donor base to over 300,000 active contributors. And mimicking the GOP, Manatt launched a training program for state party leaders to learn "advanced campaign techniques, stressing the pooling of resources and information at the various political levels."[102] While Manatt tried desperately to turn the Democratic ship around and met with some success, he was forced to make difficult trade-offs—such as the party's in-house voter registration capacities—in order to invest in its fund-raising capacities. Thanks in no small part to Carter, Manatt found the start-up costs of party building during the ensuing "out-party" period quite high.

11

Culmination and Reversal | Bill Clinton

*Clinton was a believer in political oratory and not organization—he thought
that having him and Al Gore out there on television and doing and saying
things was what really made the difference, and not organization.*

—Former DNC chairman Donald Fowler[1]

When Bill Clinton took office in 1993, Democrats held almost 60 percent of
House seats, fifty-seven Senate seats, 59 percent of state legislative seats, thirty
governorships, and a twelve-point advantage over the Republicans in party
identification. The competitive standing of the Democratic Party appeared,
by these measures, to be only marginally weaker than it had been under Carter:
its majorities seemed strong and secure. Under these conditions, Clinton had
no reason to act any differently from his majority-party predecessors. Indeed,
available evidence suggests that he did not. Like Kennedy, Johnson, and Carter
before him, Clinton did not seek to build a new majority; his challenge was to
convince the existing Democratic majority of the virtues of his "New Democrat" approach to governing.[2] The condition of his party organization was
decidedly peripheral to his main purposes. Consequently, he either ignored it
or exploited it for his short-term political benefit.

But as Clinton's competitive political environment changed, so too did
his approach to his party. During his first four years, Clinton took the party-
predator approach to new heights. But once it became clear that his party's
loss of majority status in 1994 represented something more than a temporary
aberration, he began to change his behavior. His party interactions became
increasingly constructive and forward-looking. By 1999, Clinton had successfully dug his party out of the deep financial hole he had helped to put it in
during his first term, and in a dramatic reversal of the long-standing Democratic pattern of party predation, he began to make targeted investments in
party organization. Along the six spheres of party activity, we therefore observe Clinton undertaking both constructive and exploitative actions, albeit
at different times (see figure 11.1).[3]

Clinton's reversal of the traditional Democratic pattern thus offers important insights into the party-building impulse and the challenges presidents
face as they chart a new path for their party organization. This chapter examines Clinton's party interactions while elaborating four lessons about party
predation and party building: (1) majority-party presidents routinely pass up
opportunities to turn their exploitative party interactions into something more
constructive; (2) the president's response to changes in his competitive political environment turn more on his perception of that environment than on
anything else; (3) there are significant start-up costs associated with launching

		Party Building						Party Predation					
		C	H	R	V	F	I	C	H	R	V	F	I
Republicans	Eisenhower	•	•	•	•	•	•						
	Nixon	•	•	•	•	•	•	•				•	
	Ford	•	•	•	•	•	•						
	Reagan	•	•	•	•	•	•						
	Bush	•	•	•		•	•						
Democrats	Kennedy				•		•	•	•		•	•	•
	Johnson							•	•		•	•	•
	Carter							•	•	•	•	•	•
	Clinton (1st term)							•	•	•	•	•	•
	Clinton (2nd term)	•	•		•	•	•						

C=Provide campaign services, H=Build human capital, R=Recruit candidates,
V=Mobilize voters, F=Finance party operations, I=Support internal activities

Figure 11.1. Clinton's Party Interactions

new party-building programs from scratch; (4) party building is a collective, cumulative process that takes time, resources, and persistent attention.

Missed Party-Building Opportunities

Every modern president, Democratic and Republican alike, enlisted his party organization in the pursuit of his short-term goals. But as we have seen, Republican presidents also made investments in their party organization as a matter of course. They did not let opportunities to strengthen its foundations or make incremental improvements in its operations pass them by; even as they *used* their party instrumentally, they sought to leave behind something more durable. Democratic presidents also called their party into action in pursuit of their short-term goals. But in so doing, they tended to supplant core party activities and overwhelm routine operations. As soon as their need for the party's services had passed, they dismantled its operations and allowed whatever the organization had gained to be lost. They let experienced personnel drift and operational mandates expire. With seemingly deep and durable majorities, they simply perceived no pressing need to build for the future: they had little reason to believe that their exploitation of the party apparatus in the short run would make much of a difference in the long run. In Clinton's first term, he played to type.

National Health Care Campaign

In the spring of 1993, the White House directed the DNC to lend almost thirty staff and provide $100,000 in "seed money" to establish a "nonprofit, nonpartisan foundation" outside the formal Democratic Party structure that would lobby for Clinton's health care reform proposal. The new entity would seek to raise $37 million from corporations, labor unions, and rich donors in order to fund an extensive public relations and lobbying campaign. The Clinton team preferred to use the "nominally independent" entity rather than the DNC so that donations would be exempt from campaign finance disclosure laws.[4] But before the extrapartisan operation got under way, it was met with opposition from potential donors and partners, skepticism from "health care veterans" in Congress, and a negative reaction from the press. "The judgment was made that even if it was a bipartisan effort nobody ever would have believed it," said Kent Markus, DNC chief of staff. The operation was shut down and its twenty-seven staff members were sent back to the DNC.[5]

While it might have seemed that bringing the operation inside the DNC would be a boon to the party organization—by bringing in new funds and creating a training ground for party professionals—the opposite proved to be true. Rather than turn the experience into a party-building affair, Clinton's health care campaign swamped normal operations at the DNC and supplanted electoral activities in many state and local party organizations. Rather than prepare for the 1994 midterm elections by registering voters, enlisting volunteers, recruiting candidates, raising money, and drawing up campaign plans, state party organizations were told to focus their efforts on selling the president's agenda. State party chairmen and their executive directors in more than twenty states carried out the day-to-day public relations activities of the initiative, and at the DNC, "all 150 employees contribute[d] to the effort." DNC chairman David Wilhelm, who had served as Clinton's campaign manager in 1992, admitted that "health care is our No. 1 priority. It is what we are spending the vast majority of our time and resources on."[6]

Former Ohio governor Richard Celeste, hired as a "traveling spokesman" for the initiative, roamed the country to build support. According to Celeste, wherever he went, party leaders "grumble[d] that they [felt] overwhelmed by the dual demands of the upcoming 1994 elections and a major policy initiative." There was a clear trade-off, Celeste observed, between policy promotion and building the party's electoral capacities. Celeste acknowledged that "it's a little different task than what the Democratic Party is used to . . . some may think of this as a distraction" from routine party activities like fund-raising and candidate promotion.[7] Nevertheless, the White House argued that the president's policy success would redound to the benefit of the entire party.[8]

But not all Democrats agreed that Clinton's success on health care reform would be sufficient for them to win in 1994. One Democratic consultant, for example, argued that "Bill Clinton is not necessarily the Democratic Party." He said: "They are spending a huge amount of time on the health care campaign when we have some very tough elections coming up next year."[9] A former Democratic Party executive director added: "If they're trying to push health care reform instead of building voter files, they're down the wrong road in my opinion."[10] But while party insiders clamored for more organizational assistance, Clinton remained focused exclusively on his policy campaign.

The initiative, dubbed the DNC's National Health Care Campaign (NHCC), was intended to mirror Clinton's 1992 campaign "war room." It would be fast, flexible, and effective. But the DNC was unaccustomed to such a role, and start-up costs proved to be high. The DNC's field coordinators, for example, were inexperienced; unlike the RNC's field team, which had been coordinating party activities on a regional basis since the early 1970s, the new DNC team was starting from scratch. The young staff, drawn largely from Clinton's 1992 campaign, did not have "the stature and connections to have credibility" with established party leaders in the states. Wilhelm acknowledged that this was a problem: "I think that is an area we need to strengthen . . . we need to have some of those people who enjoy some of those relationships."[11]

While the DNC sought to make adjustments, organized groups opposed to Clinton's reform proposal launched a devastating television advertisement blitz. The DNC's $3 million budget was "dwarfed by the opposition's bank accounts" and its rapid-response counterattack proved to be less rapid than it had intended.[12] As the DNC scrambled to respond, it became even less focused on the party's "traditional mission of building and financing the party's national political apparatus."[13] It was becoming increasingly clear that the party did not have the capacity to fully implement the public relations campaign without trading off its campaign support activities: in a symbolic illustration of this trade-off, the DNC conference room—traditionally reserved for "grip and grin" sessions for prospective candidates to network with prospective PAC directors and receive campaign contributions—was turned into a communications center to "stir up grass-roots support for President Clinton's legislative agenda."[14]

Because the health care campaign was overwhelming even some of the party's most basic electoral functions, congressional Democrats seeking reelection became increasingly worried as 1993 wore on. "It's a lobbying operation to get the President's agenda through," one House Democrat said, "but we also need a first-rate political operation up and running. We've got to turn our attention to reelecting Democrats."[15] This was a particularly pressing concern because a "rift" had developed between Clinton and organized labor over the president's support of NAFTA, and some party strategists anticipated that the party would need to play a more prominent role than usual in mobilizing voters in 1994.[16] To assuage these concerns, Clinton directed the DNC to transfer $2 million to the Democratic Congressional Campaign Committee to help with the fall campaigns.[17] But throwing money at incumbents' reelection campaigns was a far cry from helping the DNC to provide campaign services.

Even though the organizational components of the NHCC were not designed to be durable features of an ongoing party operation, a DNC field force was already on the ground in most states as the 1994 elections approached, and a grassroots network of concerned activists and volunteers was already working to sell health care. If Clinton had decided in early 1994 to turn the health care campaign into a constructive party-building program to enhance his party's capacity to run campaigns, attract new candidates and activists, raise money, register and mobilize voters, and provide institutional support to state and local parties, it certainly seemed that the NHCC would have given him a head start; he had something to build on if he so decided.

But when an "independent coalition" of consumer groups, labor unions, senior citizen groups, and proreform groups working on behalf of Clinton's health care initiative was shown to be outperforming the DNC, Clinton's political team decided to shut down the party operation. They gutted the DNC's programs, fired its field staff, and slashed its budget; remaining party resources were diverted to a "fourth-quarter [television] advertising blitz."[18] Whatever the party might have gained from its involvement in the health care campaign was abandoned as the 1994 elections loomed. Markus, who helped coordinate the effort, remarked that "there was not a sufficient appreciation (by the White House) of the type of resource the DNC was and could be for them."[19]

After dismantling the health-care campaign and stripping the national organization of its resources, Clinton asked former Democratic Congressional Campaign Committee (DCCC) chairman Tony Coelho to assume the honorary position of "chief strategist" for the DNC and coordinate all political activities for the midterm election campaigns. In an apparent response to Clinton's latest effort to undercut the party organization, Wilhelm announced his resignation—almost two months before Election Day.[20]

By the end of Clinton's first two years, the DNC had been thoroughly exploited: the White House had run roughshod over its staff, resources, and operational commitments. Though Clinton campaigned for candidates as the 1994 elections approached, he took no concrete steps to strengthen his party's organizational foundations. In an uncanny replication of Kennedy and Johnson's Operation Support and Carter's "public relations offensive," the NHCC diverted resources from the party's core electoral operations and supplanted existing routines with activities that were narrowly tailored to build public support for the president's policy initiatives in the short term. While the health care campaign created the image of a DNC hard at work, it did not build anything to last beyond the moment at hand.

Warnings of a potentially large Democratic defeat did not come until late in the fall: Clinton had no idea that the 1994 midterm elections would hand Republicans majority control of both houses of Congress, a majority of statehouses, and a majority of governorships for the first time in forty years. With seemingly permanent Democratic majorities during his first two years, the president's attention was focused on the legislative process and his volatile poll numbers, not on his party's organizational capacities.[21] While the Democrats' devastating midterm losses in 1994 cannot be attributed solely to Clinton's neglect and exploitation of his party organization during his first two years, it is clear that the party was not as equipped as it could have been to help support Democratic campaigns.

The Importance of Perception

In any given instance, the president's approach to his party organization will turn more on his subjective appraisal of his party's competitive standing than on anything else. He will consider his party's current standing, as well as its expected future standing, and adopt a strategy that seems most appropriate. Because presidents do not always perceive their party's competitive standing to be as weak as election returns might suggest, party building does not always follow automatically from downward shifts in the party's numerical strength. Clinton, for example, did not view the Democrats' dramatic losses in 1994 as a durable shift in his party's competitive standing; consequently, the midterm elections did not precipitate a major change in his approach to his party organization. Clinton was not alone: Democratic leaders from across the party also perceived their losses as little more than a temporary setback.

Had the Democrats' majorities not been so deep and so durable for so long, Clinton and other party leaders might have responded to the debacle of 1994 by calling for a thorough reexamination of the party's electoral operations and for the development of a new approach. But their faith in their old, tried-and-true electoral strategies was not shaken so easily. Despite the party's historic defeat, Clinton and other party leaders acted as if the Democratic Party were still the majority party, only temporarily dislocated. Rather than commence a broad-scale effort to rebuild the Democratic Party organization and invest in its operational capacities, they looked to tweak their message, hone their communications strategy, and try again.

In Clinton's view, the problem was that he had failed to communicate his policy agenda clearly or counter incoming House Speaker Newt Gingrich's arguments effectively. He wrote in his memoirs that "we probably would not have lost either the House or the Senate" if he had made different policy choices on taxes, assault weapons, deficit reduction, welfare reform, and of course, health care. His biggest misstep, Clinton believed, was that he had not "forced the Democrats to adopt an effective national counter-message" to the Republicans' Contract with America.[22] But Clinton also believed his party's misfortunes were temporary: "Time was on my side," he wrote.[23] Republicans were sure to overreach and voters would soon return home to the Democratic Party. First Lady Hillary Rodham Clinton wrote that in the aftermath of the election losses, "Bill counseled patience."[24]

Other party leaders agreed that the Democrats' losses were temporary and relatively easily remedied. According to Wilhelm's successor at the DNC, Donald Fowler:

> I think the psychology clearly was that this is an aberration and it was going to pass off pretty soon. That was particularly true in the House. I remember that some of those guys in the House who were the ranking members of those committees: their committee members would call them Mr. Chairman in anticipation of "The Restoration."[25]

The same sentiment was echoed at the state level of the party. After the elections, the Association of State Democratic Chairs met to discuss what went wrong and to make plans for moving forward. At the meeting, the prevailing sentiment was that the Democrats' newfound minority status was likely to be brief. Reversing the Republicans' recent successes, Democratic leaders declared, "can be achieved in the next two years."[26] The only question was how to do a better job conveying the party's ideas to the public. They argued that regaining the majority would depend on Clinton's ability to "return to his basic economic message of 1992 and stick to it."[27]

This same nonorganizational response could be heard from all corners of the party. Leaders of the centrist Democratic Leadership Council (DLC), for example, wrote that the election returns were the result of "fickle" independent voters who had briefly taken refuge in the Republican Party. But they were certain to remain a "swing bloc" in the future. To get back to Democratic dominance, the DLC suggested that Clinton offer the American people a new bundle of policies that reflected "the New Democrat formula of progressive ideas, mainstream values, and innovative, nonbureaucratic ways of governing."[28] In other words, the Democrats' problem was not organizational, it was ideological and policy-related, and it could be fixed with a different emphasis in priorities. The solution was to home in on more attractive ideas—"it's what we say, it's the message," said DLC founder Al From.[29]

Consequently, during the two years leading up to the 1996 elections, Clinton adopted his now-famous strategy of "triangulation," to "create a third position, not just in between the old positions of the two parties but above them as well," as Clinton's private consultant Dick Morris suggested.[30] Clinton followed Morris's advice and waged an "aerial war" of speaking directly to the people over the television airwaves rather than a "ground war" of rebuilding his party's infrastructure and equipping it to mobilize the troops and turn out the voters.[31]

Indeed, Clinton did nothing to address obvious signs of his party's organizational disrepair at the state and county level. After the 1994 elections, many state parties found themselves deep in debt and unable to raise the funds needed to rebuild their operations, recruit new candidates, and prepare for the campaigns of 1996. The Democratic Party of New York, for example, "existed in little more than a name, with only a telephone and a desk in some borrowed space," and was about $400,000 in debt. The Pennsylvania party was in debt approximately $200,000, and Illinois owed at least $175,000. In Texas, the party was still in debt from the mid-1980s and had at least $700,000 to repay. New Jersey, for its part, was reportedly living "month to month." In none of these rich electoral vote states was there a Democratic governor to help the state committee get out of debt; twenty-eight states also found themselves with brand-new state chairmen.[32] The state parties looked to Clinton for help. But perceiving the Democratic minorities to be only temporary, Clinton evidently felt no reason to devote resources to making repairs in his party organization.

Clinton asked South Carolina Democratic Party leader Donald Fowler to replace Wilhelm as DNC chairman.[33] Fowler was a widely respected former state chairman who was capable of directing a comprehensive party-building program if Clinton had directed him to do so. Fowler later admitted that he had hoped Clinton would give him an opportunity to repair the party's organizational deficiencies:

> I knew of the experience of Ray Bliss and what he did and what his successors Frank Fahrenkopf and others had done in the Republican Party. And so because of these experiences, I really did have a pretty clear notion of what I wanted to do in party building. I thought it was a great time to do it because we had the presidency, and also because the party was in such wrack and ruin after the 1994 elections.[34]

But instead of encouraging a party-building program at the DNC, Clinton directed Fowler to help him implement a scheme to funnel "soft money" through state party committees to pay for the Clinton campaign's television advertisements.[35] "In the two years leading up to the presidential [campaign]," Clinton White House political director Craig Smith recalled, "state parties essentially became vehicles or additional arms of the presidential campaign."[36] Through an elaborate process of soft-money fund-raising, fund transfers to state party committees, and closely monitored expenditures on television advertisements, Clinton interacted with his party organization frequently, but in a wholly instrumental fashion.

In a series of well-researched articles published during this period, James Barnes at the *National Journal* uncovered numerous instances of financial transfers from the DNC to state parties for the exact dollar amount that was then immediately spent by the state party treasuries to pay for television ads produced by the Democratic media consulting firm Squier, Knapp & Ochs— the very firm contracted for Clinton's reelection campaign.[37] Rather than pump money into state parties for legally defined "party-building" purposes such as voter registration, get out the vote, and voter education, as Gerald Ford and Ronald Reagan had done, Clinton's team was careful to ensure that state parties were only given the precise amount needed to pay for campaign advertisements.

Understandably, securing Clinton's reelection was the primary concern of the campaign as well as many Democratic Party leaders, who assumed that Clinton's success would redound to the benefit of the entire party. But according to Fowler, it was not a zero-sum game: "My only argument was there were a lot of other things we could have done because we had the financial capacity to help state parties . . . to do the voter files, to have field people, to have better media relations"—but such efforts simply were not made.[38]

Although he did not have the support of the White House, Fowler took it upon himself to host a one-time training session for party operatives in 1995. "We had to borrow and steal to do it," he said, because the White House was "really very dubious about that." The president was still "way behind in the polls," Fowler said, "and training people to go to Missouri—are you kidding me? But I was finally just enough of an S.O.B. that we did it."[39] In fact, the White House was resistant to any party activity not directly related to the president's reelection campaign: "Most of the conversation was 'Why are you doing that?' and 'Why are you wasting our money?'"[40]

The urgency with which the Clinton team funneled soft money into state parties for television advertisements in 1995–96 encouraged the kind of fundraising illegalities that were later revealed, including the DNC's acceptance of large donations from noncitizens and corporations seeking regulatory relief. In the rush to raise soft money, due diligence was not paid and proper oversight fell by the wayside. While Fowler absorbed the blame, the DNC's inadequate procedures were later traced back to the frenzied health care reform campaign in 1993 and 1994. The DNC's single-minded focus on promoting Clinton's legislative proposal had resulted in the termination of an administrative program that systematically screened large donors—a misstep that ultimately proved to be extremely costly.[41]

Taken all together, Clinton's interactions with his party in his first term represented the culmination of the Democratic pattern of party exploitation. Despite interacting frequently with state parties, Clinton intentionally ignored their organizational needs and supplanted their normal operating routines in order to benefit his reelection campaign. Although Clinton increased almost fourfold the party's use of soft money to fund "issue ads" that were legally categorized as "party-building" activities, this term was a mere legal technicality: none of that money was used to build state Democratic Party organizations.[42]

Clinton's victory in 1996 seemed to vindicate his strategy, but it also served notice that the party's newfound minority status was not going to be as easy to reverse as party leaders might have initially thought. Clinton's coattails were virtually nonexistent: Democrats gained only two seats in the House, lost three seats in the Senate, and lost a net of fifty-three state legislative seats, while Republicans maintained a nearly two-to-one advantage over the Democrats in governorships. While the Republican Party had yet to achieve political dominance of the sort the Democrats once enjoyed, the 1996 election results made it clear that 1994 was no mere aberration.

The Costs of Switching Paths

As his second term began in 1997, Clinton faced an altered set of incentives and constraints. The urgency of his reelection campaign was finally behind him, but he continued to face a hostile Republican-dominated Congress that was determined to deny him major policy accomplishments. Though he had resolved to press his policy agenda forward, Clinton was also willing to compromise with congressional Republicans when necessary in order to make progress on his unusually long and detailed list of objectives. Yet the policy route could hardly have been satisfying for a president with such grand ambitions.

Under the circumstances, Clinton had an incentive to seek out new opportunities to fashion a place in history on his own terms.

Foreign policy was one area where he could make his mark with minimal congressional interference, and by using the unilateral powers of the presidency, he could bring about important administrative changes in government —Clinton pursued both tacks vigorously. But in addition to these more familiar strategies, Clinton also adopted a more constructive approach to his party. This strategy made perfect sense under the circumstances: to the extent that Clinton could lift his party back onto its feet and convince his fellow partisans of the value of his New Democrat approach, he could fortify a durable organizational vehicle with which to perpetuate his personal brand of politics after he left the White House.

At the DNC meeting in January 1997, Clinton finally signaled an interest in rebuilding his party organization. He charged Steve Grossman, his new DNC chairman, with implementing the core party-building tasks of "mobilizing our state parties, of recruiting good, new candidates, of getting people to show up when you have these meetings back home, and of making people proud to be Democrats and of making people believe that they ought to send a small check to the Democratic Party on a regular basis."[43] Echoing the president's sentiments, Vice President Al Gore told a meeting of the Association of State Democratic Chairs that he and the president wanted to rebuild the party organization: "The only way we'll be successful is if we win the ground war," he said. "President Clinton and I will help you at the local and state level in any way we can."[44] Following up on Clinton's and Gore's apparent newfound interest in party building, the DNC political team drew up a full-fledged plan to invest in new technologies, build state party infrastructures, and run new training programs.[45]

But while a decline in the party's competitive standing creates new incentives for presidential party building, translating those incentives into durable change at an organizational level is hardly an automatic process. Invariably, there are financial start-up costs that must be paid, logistical obstacles that must be overcome, and everyday twists and turns of politics that must be navigated. Creating change in the party organization, in short, requires time and painstaking effort.

Indeed, Clinton and his team finally discovered the will to begin party building, but the imprudent practices of the past now made launching new party-building programs more difficult than either the president or Grossman had anticipated. Years of organizational neglect and exploitation had left few ongoing organizational initiatives to build on, and Clinton's campaign strategy in 1995–96 had left the party deep in debt and facing a constant stream of legal bills relating to the Republican-led congressional investigation into alleged campaign finance abuses in 1996. While Clinton and his team seemed genuinely committed, at long last, to making investments in the party organization, these financial liabilities proved to be prohibitive.

Fund-raising, in particular, was extremely difficult in this environment. Many longtime Democratic donors were reluctant to contribute for fear of being associated with the party's legal troubles. "The problem was, we were asking donors to give money to the party, and they knew that their money was going to pay legal fees and debt," Grossman explained. New party-building plans, consequently, had to be placed on the back burner.[46] Craig Smith confirmed that the White House had wanted to make investments in party organization, but the party's financial liabilities proved to be prohibitive:

> There was not a lot of emphasis in that '97–'98 cycle on state party building because the emphasis was almost exclusively on survival. Can we keep the doors open? Can we pay the bills? And have enough money left to help in the elections? There was no time to invest. There was no ability to invest. It was all about just keeping the doors open.[47]

Whether motivated by selfless concern for his fellow partisans or by the desire not to be remembered as the president who sacrificed his party at the altar of his personal interests, Clinton decided to take it upon himself to replenish his party's coffers. Despite the high probability that he would be branded a hypocrite, he set off on an extraordinarily ambitious campaign to raise large sums of soft money to help his party get back on its feet even as he called for campaign finance reforms to curtail the use of soft money.[48]

Whereas the typical Democratic approach since Kennedy was to hoard the proceeds from lucrative fund-raisers in presidential rainy-day funds, Clinton directed that 85 percent of the funds go toward helping Democratic candidates with their campaigns in 1998 and 15 percent go toward DNC debt relief. This new formula reflected an entirely new set of priorities for a Democratic president that for the first time in over forty years included giving a lift to the party organization.[49] The illusion that the 1994 losses were only temporary had now worn off, and Clinton was moving toward a party-building posture, albeit slowly because of the constraints imposed by his environment.

By the end of 1997, Clinton had made significant gains in reducing the party's debt, but still had a ways to go. The costs of changing the party's organizational trajectory were proving to be extremely high. In January 1998, however, the Monica Lewinsky scandal broke, and the ensuing political battles and Clinton's impeachment proved to be a windfall for the party. While the Lewinsky scandal may have hurt the party in other ways, it was considered "money in the bank" at the DNC.[50] Democrats showed their support for Clinton by donating large sums of money, and by July 1998, the DNC had reduced its debt to $3.24 million and had $3.66 million in cash on hand. It raised approximately $24 million during the first six months of 1998 alone.[51]

But facing impeachment and possible removal from office, Clinton became increasingly concerned with maintaining the support of those congressional Democrats on whose support his presidency would depend. Thus, despite coming tantalizingly close to party-building readiness at the DNC, he shifted course again. Clinton directed the DNC to go $3 million further into debt to help fund the two congressional campaign committees.[52] Throughout the fall of 1998, Clinton focused almost exclusively on raising money for congressional campaigns.[53]

While Clinton's efforts may have helped congressional Democrats gain several seats in the midterm elections, his actions temporarily put the DNC deeper into debt and prevented it from undertaking new organization-building programs. Grossman continually emphasized the importance of making long-term investments in party organization, but with Clinton's presidency on the line, the DNC's party-building plans were put on hold.[54] Grossman admitted that "we weren't able to deliver on our fondest hopes and dreams and aspirations [for investing in state parties] because so much of the money went to pay off debt and to pay legal fees." He continued "to preach this gospel about organizing . . . even though it was tremendously frustrating that I couldn't implement it."[55]

Nevertheless, in many ways the events of 1997–98 built the momentum that was needed for the next two years. Clinton's prodigious fund-raising and Grossman's rhetorical emphasis on party building helped to pay the start-up costs—financial and psychological—associated with reversing the Democrats' organizational trajectory. As 1999 began, the party was nearly out of debt, Clinton's impeachment trial was over, and the path had been cleared for the first Democratic presidential party-building program in modern American history.

The Party-Building Impulse and the Piecemeal Process of Organizational Change

In 1993, in reference to the administration's new fiscal policies, Clinton famously quipped: "We're Eisenhower Republicans here."[56] This statement would have been equally appropriate in reference to the party-building program Clinton launched in 1999. Like Eisenhower, Clinton sought to make new investments in his party organization after years of neglect, and like Eisenhower, Clinton found that creating organizational change was a slow, incremental process. Indeed, just as Eisenhower's investments in his party organization laid the groundwork for further gains in the 1960s, the Clinton experience, too, reminds us that the rebuilding process is characterized by gradual, not sudden, change. Party building is a collective, cumulative process that takes time, resources, and persistent attention. Parties, after all, are political institutions with their own complex structures, processes, and routines; like most political institutions, they are somewhat resistant to change. Thus, as it was with Eisenhower's efforts in the 1950s, Clinton's efforts during 1999–2000 did not fully reverse the Democratic Party's organizational trajectory in one fell swoop. They did, however, offer a down payment on future rounds of party building after Clinton left the White House.

America 2000

As 1999 began, Clinton must have known that his expansive policy agenda—including the "sixty initiatives to meet an ambitious set of goals" laid out in his final State of the Union address—could not possibly be accomplished during the brief time he had remaining in office.[57] He thus had an incentive to build something durable—some sort of vehicle to carry his personal brand of politics forward after he left office. Whether this vehicle was to be a Gore victory in 2000, a seat in the Senate for Hillary Clinton, or more "New Democrats" in Congress, one thing was clear: Democrats had to start winning more elections. And if more elections were to be won, the party's organizational machinery had to be repaired. Whatever else Clinton might have desired, the condition of his party had finally become an urgent concern.

When Steve Grossman stepped down for personal reasons at the end of 1998, Clinton replaced him with Joe Andrew, state party chairman from Indiana, best known for his innovative and effective party building in his home state.[58] Clinton hired Andrew to replicate his efforts in Indiana "on a national scale."[59] But when Andrew arrived at the DNC in December 1998, the White House was mired in impeachment politics. Andrew sought to lend a hand and began to lobby members of Congress on behalf of the president. "The Administration was very cautious about individually lobbying members of Congress," Andrew explained, but "the party was not." His dedication to helping Clinton weather the crisis helped him build a strong working relationship with the White House—a relationship that proved critical to the DNC's ability "to do things that had not been done before."[60]

On February 12, 1999, Clinton was acquitted by the Senate. His job approval remained high, but the Democratic Party remained stuck in the minority in Congress and at the state level. Combined with the perceived political fallout from impeachment, many Democrats were left feeling anxious that they would be at a competitive disadvantage for quite some time. "There was a tremendous malaise in the party," Andrew recalled. "The impeachment process got people worried that there was just no chance we could win."[61] Such sentiments represented a historic reversal in the outlook of Democratic Party leaders and activists. No matter how organized (or disorganized) Democrats might have been around election time, the assumption had always been that the party would remain in the majority. With such expectations, there was never an obvious incentive for the Democrats' diverse, heterogeneous coalition to work together in concert: elected officials, the national committee, state parties, organized labor, civil rights groups, and special interest groups were free to go their separate ways with minimal institutionalized coordination or long-term strategic planning.

The Democrats' traditional free-for-all approach was hardly irrational: it was, after all, a proven formula for success. Without the driving incentive to build a *new* majority—without the pressing need to win more offices, expand the party's reach, and hone its electoral operations—presidents, party leaders, and activists could focus on short-term concerns without regard for the party's long-term organizational condition. Incumbents could be left to run their own campaigns, electoral operations could be outsourced to the Democrats' reliable network of "partners," and the party's resources could be devoted to promoting internal democracy and developing more attractive policy ideas and rhetorical frames.

But with newfound uncertainty about the party's future competitiveness, the condition of the party organization now became a primary concern, something that had to be addressed before other goals and ambitions could be achieved. This party-building incentive was felt deeply across the Democratic Party: as 1999 began, the heterogeneous Democratic coalition finally began to come together to develop a cooperative organizational plan. According to Andrew, this had nothing to do with his, or even Clinton's, efforts to bring people together: it was simply a result of the changed electoral context.

> We didn't have all these guys around a table—for example organized labor—to do something for years. Literally, it wasn't because of me, I did nothing. I just invited them all to come to talk. They did it because of the fact that they were so concerned that we weren't going to win! There was no secret sauce here. People were willing to work harder together. People were willing to come together and talk and coordinate the way they had not been, because—what choice did they have?[62]

Inside the DNC, Clinton's team backed up this new party-wide commitment to coordination and strategic planning with a comprehensive party-building program called America 2000, which aimed to make unprecedented investments in the party's national and state organizational capacities.[63] The objective was to equip the party organization to win more elections up and down the line, both now and in the future: "From dogcatcher to the United States Presidency . . . not just in 1999 and 2000, but in 2009 and 2010."[64] Perhaps the most pressing task serving both short- and long-term goals was to "win control of legislatures in key states and put a Democratic stamp on redistricting."[65] Backed by the fund-raising star-power of President Clinton and the strategic and administrative support of the White House political team, the DNC began in the spring of 1999 to make investments in the party's human capital, in its campaign services, and in its technology. Let us take up each in turn.

To build the party's human capital, the DNC launched campaign management training seminars and activist-enrollment efforts; in all, twelve national campaign training programs were successfully completed in 1999–2000, and over one million volunteers were enlisted by the party to help in the 2000 election.[66] These initiatives were designed not only to level the playing field during redistricting in 2001 and to help win back control of Congress, but also to cultivate a "new generation of Democrats."[67] Andrew also initiated a National Executive Director Program to fund executive directors in targeted states "to help rejuvenate state party organizations . . . recruit and retain political professionals" and allow the state parties to dedicate more resources to campaigns.[68]

To enhance the party's campaign service capacities, the DNC expanded its field program and charged it with building new networks of "officeholders, donors, surrogates, members of organized labor, and activists" to coordinate voter registration, donor identification, and voter mobilization activities.[69] "There had always been field programs," Andrew explained, "but they had been delegated out to labor. And so my whole game-plan on day one was, I want to bring this in-house. Labor is going to sit around the table, but I want the table to be inside the DNC, to maintain . . . control over the process as well."[70] The DNC also launched a new "campaign store" for candidates to purchase campaign products at a discount.[71]

But it was investments in new computer technologies that constituted the centerpiece of America 2000. With Clinton's help, the DNC raised and spent more than $1 million to upgrade and standardize the voter file software and hardware used by state parties, create a new website for the party, and build new communication links between state and national party committees. The expanded field team systematically analyzed state party infrastructures, tailored technological investments to fit each state's needs, and offered technical support for the new systems.[72] The new investments in technology were warmly welcomed by state party chairs, one of whom exclaimed: "Joe Andrew has been a shot of adrenaline."[73]

Building a national voter file was another essential ingredient of the party-building program. As I discussed in the previous chapter, a centralized voter file was something that Carter's party chairman Ken Curtis had wanted to build in the late 1970s, but without the support of the White House, it went nowhere. In contrast, Andrew had the full support—in fact, the personal urging—of President Clinton: "Bill Clinton really wanted this done. It was one of the things that he personally pushed for," Andrew noted. "He understood and got convinced that having a national voter file was a very important part of the party."[74] But assembling a national voter file was the most difficult component of the party-building plan. Most state parties had their own voter files, and the quality and format of the data varied widely from state to state. Many state parties were also reluctant to share their data, as they were "the crown jewels, the key asset that they have."[75] First steps were taken to work out data-sharing agreements and construct a new database at the DNC, but the project was only in its early stages when the Clinton team departed in early 2001.

While the America 2000 program delivered only partial organization-building successes, it represented a dramatic change in the party's organizational philosophy. Whereas the "old" mantra at the DNC was "right races, right places"—meaning targeting the party's resources to competitive races—the new mantra was "the right mechanics," Andrew said.[76] This philosophical shift is exactly what we would expect from a party that once enjoyed a comfortable majority of elective offices and now found itself in the minority. As the majority party, resources would be allocated to close races in order to maintain that majority ("right races, right places"). In the minority, the party would be forced to develop its organizational capacities across the board in order to win more elections wherever possible ("right mechanics"). Andrew's goal was to equip every Democratic candidate with the tools and resources he or she would need to run an effective campaign. "A national political organization is not about prioritizing races," he said, "but rather prioritizing services it'll offer, empowering people no matter where they are to be able to win."[77]

Clinton's late-breaking party building was also particularly noteworthy for its explicit focus on innovation. Previous Democratic administrations acted in a decidedly noninnovative manner toward their party: they eliminated activities that did not directly benefit the president's immediate political purposes, exploited the party for short-term gain, and put its national organization in a kind of "caretaker status." In contrast, Andrew announced that the Democratic Party would need to become the party of innovation and expansion; with a rhetorical flourish reminiscent of the Republicans' "open door" and "umbrella party" themes, he said: "We must be adventurers who conjure new ideas, embrace new people, welcome new cultures, and deploy new technologies. We Democrats must always be the party of what's next."[78]

Funding these ambitious programs was costly, and clearly required the president's active sponsorship and support. "If you're going to spend a million dollars on a national training program, that means you've got to raise basically about two, because we're paying off the debt, we're paying for the infrastructure of the DNC, and then we've got a million dollars going out of the door," Andrew explained. Bill Clinton's assistance was therefore essential throughout 1999–2000: "He did a Herculean effort to raise the money . . . he was amazing." In the first six months of the off-year 1999, for example, Clinton delivered the keynote address at no fewer than nineteen DNC fund-raisers; Andrew announced that the party raised more than $21 million and completely liquidated its debt.[79] The political team at the White House also lent the DNC its considerable support. Deputy chief of staff Steve Ricchetti and political director Minyon Moore, in particular, were instrumental in helping Andrew coordinate logistical arrangements and develop strategy.

As the 2000 election approached, the DNC began to develop a new model for a coordinated campaign with the Gore team: "To actually coordinate with state parties so that you can share resources, share information: rising tide lifts all boats."[80] Using the DNC's new technology and the Gore campaign's resources and manpower, the coordinated campaign worked closely with state parties on voter registration and turnout throughout 2000. This kind of nurturing of state party operations during a presidential campaign represented another important shift away from past practices. No longer was the party a mere instrument for temporary gain; now it was a resource for building a new Democratic majority. The coordinated campaign claimed to have turned out the largest number of Democratic voters in history and "put an historic number of volunteers out in the street."[81] Despite the disputed election outcome and Gore's ultimate defeat, Andrew announced an organizational victory: "For all those who thought the parties were dead, or parties were irrelevant, what you've seen is a rebirth of Democratic state parties, Democratic local parties and the Democratic National Committee, that clearly, I think, has put us in a great position in order to be able to go forward."[82]

Though Clinton's team managed to get a number of significant initiatives off the ground during 1999 and 2000, rebuilding the Democratic Party organization required more than a handful of targeted investments over the course of two years. Much work remained. These early party-building efforts did, however, plant the seeds of the party's future organizational development; for the first time in over forty years, the Democratic Party was moving along a different organizational trajectory.

Unfinished Business: Piecemeal Change since Clinton

For the first time in the modern era of Democratic Party politics, a change in party leadership did not mean starting from scratch. In 2001, incoming DNC chairman Terry McAuliffe inherited an organizational foundation he could build on. Indeed, two of McAuliffe's four main goals for his chairmanship involved completing the unfinished business left by Clinton's team: building a new "state-of-the-art" headquarters and constructing the national voter file. A blueprint sketch of the new headquarters was printed on the back of the America 2000 document, but it had yet to be contracted by the time Clinton left office; the voter file, as noted, was in its very early stages of development. McAuliffe's third goal was to "strengthen state parties," and his fourth goal—or set of goals—was financial: to provide direct assistance to candidates, to create email and direct-mail lists that could be used to expand the party's donor base, and to make the party financially "self-sufficient" in the years ahead.[83]

With his uncanny knack for raising enormous amounts of soft money quickly, McAuliffe managed to erase the DNC's post-2000 election legal debts and raise the $20 million needed for the new DNC headquarters before the McCain-Feingold ban on soft money went into effect in November 2002. In the spring of 2004, the new DNC headquarters was built and ready to use; it came fully equipped with modern facilities, the latest in computer technology, and even a television studio. McAuliffe's fund-raising efforts were another unqualified success by the time he left the DNC chairmanship in 2005: the DNC's email and donor lists grew exponentially, and there were sufficient funds to provide direct assistance to Democratic candidates and spend $348 million in conjunction with the Kerry campaign in 2004, shattering all previous records.[84]

But McAuliffe's two other goals—building a national voter file and strengthening state parties—remained woefully incomplete by the end of his term. The national voter file, in particular, proved to be more challenging than McAuliffe had anticipated. Few states agreed to share their data, despite McAuliffe's assurances that the DNC would keep their voter lists continually updated. For those that did participate, the DNC claimed to have "corrected more than 27 million addresses and phone numbers": but by the end of 2004, the voter file was not even close to being operational.[85]

The difficulties McAuliffe experienced in constructing the voter file—perhaps the most important tool of modern party politics—illustrate how hard it is to orchestrate significant change in a large, complex organization like the Democratic Party. To create a single, unified national voter file, state party chairs had be convinced of its benefits, the software had to be made compatible across different party units, the data had to be integrated, and the output had to be functional and user friendly for activists and volunteers at the local level. According to one party activist, the system McAuliffe invested in had no "front end, no user interface." It "didn't do what a field organizer needs it to do. . . . You weren't going to get walk lists or other tools out of it. It doesn't do bupkus."[86]

Creating durable organizational change takes time, abundant resources, and the sustained collective motivation of many actors working in concert. Not only was the voter file incomplete when McAuliffe left the DNC, but his investments in state parties had barely scratched the surface of their organizational problems. He offered state parties $10 million to help gear up for redistricting in 2001 and another $65 million to help with the 2004 elections, but their organizations were in "sorry shape" when Howard Dean took over the national chairmanship in 2005.[87] A DNC assessment of state party structures and operations revealed widespread deficiencies that required a significant investment of time and resources to repair. Most state parties needed some combination of financial resources, additional staff, legal assistance, technological upgrades, help with media relations, and campaign support.[88]

Under McAuliffe, the voter file was stymied by logistical difficulties, and the failure to build state parties was a missed opportunity. But it is important to observe that McAuliffe's tenure was also filled with unexpected twists and turns that set back his party-building projects. First, there was McCain-Feingold Campaign Finance Reform Act, which undercut McAuliffe's primary area of expertise (raising soft money). Then there were the terrorist attacks of September 11, 2001, which temporarily shut down party-building efforts at the DNC: "I was like a caged rat," McAuliffe writes. "I couldn't travel. I couldn't make political calls. I couldn't make money calls. I couldn't do anything."[89] Third, while the new headquarters was being built, the DNC had to move into a temporary location for almost a year and a half, with all the disruption such a move invariably entails. Finally there was the Kerry campaign, which kept the DNC largely on the sidelines and refused to use the opportunity of the national campaign to make further investments in the party's organizational capacities.

To be sure, Democrats had come a long way from 1994. The mentality of most party leaders seemed to have changed, the party's lingering debt was finally erased, and critical investments were made in the party's physical infrastructure, technological capacities, and human capital. Yet none of this had translated into electoral success. By the end of 2004, after yet another round of heartbreaking losses at the national and local levels, the Democratic Party seemed likely to remain in the minority for the foreseeable future. Party leaders began to search for new solutions. Some consulted with cognitive linguistic experts and sought out new metaphors to use in speeches;[90] some designed new policy proposals;[91] some launched a progressive talk radio station;[92] and others, like new DNC chairman, Howard Dean, redoubled their commitment to invest in the party's organizational capacities.

The more we learn about Dean's chairmanship, the more his contributions appear to mark a significant step forward in the party's organizational development. His accomplishments were many. First, between 2005 and 2008, he and his team finally managed to build a functional national voter file. By investing $8 million in the program and running several pilot projects to test its effectiveness in grassroots campaigns, the new system, called VoteBuilder, was ready for the 2008 elections.[93] When used in conjunction with a new "Neighborhood Volunteer" online tool (dubbed "Neighbor-to-Neighbor" during the 2008 presidential campaign, reminiscent of Eisenhower's lower-tech program of the same name), the voter file aimed to help grassroots canvassers organize in their communities, retrieve information on individual voters from the centralized system, and feed newly collected information back into it.[94]

Dean's team also ran multiple training programs for campaign professionals, volunteers, and state party operatives in an effort to cultivate the "foot soldiers" of future campaigns. The DNC introduced several new innovations as well, including a customizable online organizing tool, appropriately called "PartyBuilder," and new mechanisms for generating a steady stream of contributions. Last but not least, Dean's much-vaunted fifty-state strategy, the centerpiece of his party-building program, funded at least four coordinators in every state to help rebuild state party operations. The sustained effort to support state party organizations generated rave reviews from state leaders and local activists.[95]

Yet Dean, too, encountered serious challenges to his party-building programs. His challenges were not financial like Clinton's or technological like McAuliffe's: they were primarily personal, and partly strategic. Dean's ambitious efforts were greeted with hostility from party "insiders" who strongly disagreed with his allocation of resources to "red" states—places that seemed to offer little chance of helping Democrats win back congressional majorities in 2006.[96] In a widely reported conflict, Representative Rahm Emanuel, chair of the Democratic Congressional Campaign Committee, forcefully argued that the DNC should transfer $10 million to help marginal races in 2006 instead.[97] Dean held firm, but ultimately did allocate an additional $2.6 million into field operations while continuing to fully fund the fifty-state strategy.[98] The dispute indicated that many in the party establishment either disagreed with, or did not understand, the notion that organizational party building is inherently a gradual process of piecemeal change. To them, the future was now, and Dean's highly publicized commitment to a long-term strategy for the party was quixotic, at best. Paul Begala, former adviser to Bill Clinton, said:

> [Dean] has raised $74 million and spent $64 million. He says it's a long-term strategy. But what he has spent it on, apparently, is just hiring a bunch of staff people to wander around Utah and Mississippi and pick their nose. That's not how you build a party. You win elections. That's how you build a party.[99]

Begala later apologized,[100] but even after the Democrats won back control of Congress in 2006, another Clinton consultant, James Carville, mocked Dean's leadership as "Rumsfeldian in its incompetence" and called for his ouster.[101]

Once it became clear that the state chairmen stood firmly behind Dean, the debate over his fifty-state strategy quieted for a time; and when Barack Obama turned eight formerly "red" states "blue" in the 2008 election, many commentators argued that Dean deserved some of the credit.[102] How much credit Dean deserved for the Democrats' electoral successes in the 2006–9 period may always be a subject for debate. But by the end of his four years as chairman, it was clear that Dean made important contributions to the Democratic Party's organizational development. By finally constructing the national voter file, making significant investments in the party's state and local infrastructure, developing new fund-raising capacities, creating new online organizing tools, and recruiting and training new activists, Dean left Barack Obama and his new DNC team a much more robust organizational foundation on which to continue building if they so chose.

In sum, change in the Democratic Party organization between 1999 and 2008 was incremental, and the gains were cumulative: each new round of investments built on prior rounds to enhance the party's organizational capacities. Each successive party leader found himself better positioned to complete the unfinished business of the past and push the party-building project forward. As Dean prepared to step down in late 2008, the Democratic party-building project seemed to have generated a momentum all of its own.

■

There is still much we do not know about the Clinton presidency; the eventual release of White House documents will undoubtedly shed new light on many of the episodes discussed here and reveal new pieces of the puzzle. But as the previous pages have aimed to show, we know enough at present to glean some important new insights about presidential party building and party predation as more general phenomena. Clinton's health care campaign at the DNC during his first two years, for example, illustrates that (1) while majority-party presidents often encounter opportunities to turn their exploitative party interactions into something more constructive, they perceive no pressing reason to do so. Clinton's continued indifference toward his party organization during 1995–96 serves as an equally strong reminder of the importance of presidential perception. For even as his party fell from forty years of majority

Table 11.1 Clinton's Party Predation

Provide campaign services	Build human capital	Recruit candidates	Mobilize voters	Finance party operations	Support internal activities
NHCC (1993–94)	NHCC (1993–94)	NHCC (1993–94)	NHCC (1993–94)	NHCC (1993–94)	NHCC (1993–94)
1996 reelection campaign (1995–96)	1996 reelection campaign (1995–96)		1996 reelection campaign (1995–96)	1996 reelection campaign (1995–96)	
				DNC into debt for 1998 campaigns (1998)	

Note: All instances indicate the absence of party building; that is, they confirm the conventional wisdom about the president-party relationship. Whether, in any given instance, the president undercuts his party, exploits it, or neglects it, the effect is to undermine the party's organizational capacities along these six dimensions of party activity.

Table 11.2 Clinton's Party Building

Provide campaign services	Build human capital	Recruit candidates	Mobilize voters	Finance party operations	Support internal activities
Expanded field program (1999–2000)	Campaign management training (1999–2000)		Expanded field program (1999–2000)	Fund-raising for America 2000 (1999–2000)	Investments in computer technology (1999–2000)
DNC Campaign Store (1999–2000)	Activist enrollment (1999–2000)		Coordinated Campaign (2000)		Provide tech support for state parties (1999–2000)
Coordinated Campaign (2000)	National Executive Director Program (1999)				Voter file first steps (1999–2000)
					White House strategic support for America 2000 (1999–2000)

status in Congress and lost its dominance at the state level, Clinton continued to play the part of the majority-party president (see table 11.1). Because he viewed his party's losses in 1994 as temporary, he perceived no pressing need to make investments in his party organization; rather, his attention was focused exclusively on securing his own reelection, and his party interactions continued to be wholly exploitative. This "lag" reveals that (2) the president's response to changes in his competitive political environment turns more on his perception of that environment than on anything else.

In his second term, Clinton's approach toward his party became much more constructive. But his earlier exploitation of his party organization had produced major financial liabilities with which he now had to contend: the start-up costs associated with changing paths consequently proved to be too high during 1997 and 1998 to get new party-building initiatives off the ground. This period of Clinton's presidency illustrates that (3) there are significant start-up costs associated with launching new party-building programs from scratch.

As 1999 began, however, the numerous obstacles standing in the way of Clinton's ability to launch party-building programs in the previous two years— a massive debt, endless legal fees, impeachment, and the midterm elections— no longer stood in his way. Clinton and his team were finally able to make targeted investments in the party's human capital, in its campaign services, in its technology, and in its strategic operations (see table 11.2). But as our brief review of the activities at the DNC from 2001 to 2008 illustrates, (4) party building is a process of piecemeal change that takes time, resources, and persistent attention. Even as each new round of party building set out to complete the unfinished business of prior rounds, new tasks were invariably left for the future. Party building, as we have seen, is truly a cumulative process of incremental change.

12

Conclusion | Presidents, Parties, and the Political System

In the previous chapters, we have seen that every Republican president since Eisenhower worked to strengthen his party organization, while every Democratic president since Kennedy—until Clinton in his second term—neglected, exploited, or undercut his party's organizational capacities. The best explanation for this variation in presidential behavior, I have argued, is that each president was responding to different challenges derived from his competitive political environment. With their party stuck in the perpetual minority, Republican presidents had a strong incentive to adopt a constructive approach toward their party organization; with deep and durable majorities, Democratic presidents perceived no pressing need to make forward-looking investments in their party organization.

Examining president-party interactions along six different dimensions of party activity, we have asked: Was the president's approach constructive—meant to enhance the party's organizational capacities—or nonconstructive? Did he invest in his party's capacities to provide campaign services, develop human capital, recruit candidates, mobilize voters, finance party operations, or support internal activities? In some of these activities? In none of them?

Along each of these dimensions, the Republican approach was consistently constructive. For example, when Republican presidents invested in new voter data and expanded their party's field teams, they helped to strengthen their party's capacities to provide *campaign services* to candidates. When they supported training programs and encouraged their party to expand its activist base, they helped to build their party's *human capital*. When they leveraged the prestige of the White House to woo prospective candidates and equipped their state and local parties to do the same, they enhanced their party's capacities to *recruit candidates*. When they integrated their party organization into their reelection campaigns, sponsored voter registration drives, and initiated outreach programs to attract new groups of voters, they strengthened their party's capacity to *mobilize voters*. By signing direct-mail solicitations, fund-raising for state parties, and tapping their personal donor networks on behalf of their party, they helped to *finance party operations*. By investing in their party's infrastructure and technology, and by creating new coordination mechanisms at the RNC, they enhanced their party's capacity to *support internal activities*.

Democratic presidents, in contrast, often undercut those same capacities. By eliminating or outsourcing voter outreach programs, for example, they undercut their party's capacity to *mobilize voters*; by diverting financial resources away from the party and hoarding them for personal use, they reduced their party's capacity to *finance party operations*; by pushing their party to the sidelines rather than integrating it into their reelection campaigns, they weakened its capacity to *provide campaign services.* Of course, their approach was not always so hostile or antagonistic: they often pursued their immediate purposes and exploited their party's existing capacities without giving much thought (if any at all) to the long-term effects of their actions. For example, by insisting that their party make the promotion of their legislative initiatives their top priority, they supplanted routine operations and undermined multiple areas of party functionality simultaneously. The long-term condition of their party simply did not factor as an urgent concern. Most of the time, however, Democratic presidents simply expressed indifference toward their party organization, eschewed opportunities to strengthen its capacities along each of these fronts, and turned their attention to higher-priority items. Yet whether they purposefully undercut their party, exploited it, or neglected it, their refusal to engage in party building effectively set its organizational development back.

Competitive Standing and the Alternatives

Across the many varied observations of president-party interactions presented in the preceding chapters, we find valuable clues, or indicators, of the competitive standing theory presented in chapter 2. First and foremost are the internal memos and strategic plans drawn up by Republican presidents and their teams discussing how their party-building innovations might help the party escape its perpetual "minority status." Improving their party's disadvantaged competitive position was a constant preoccupation of these presidents and their political teams. Democratic presidents, in contrast, turned their attention to other matters: the condition of their party apparatus was a decidedly second-order concern.

But more subtle clues can be identified as well. For example, because Republican presidents sought to help their fellow partisans win more elections, they poured resources into recruiting candidates, developing campaign management training programs, and providing new types of institutional support to state and local parties. Democrats tended to devote their energies to building goodwill among incumbent congressmen instead. This was a symptom of their party's majority status in Congress; with far more incumbents than challengers, Democratic presidents had no particular reason to be concerned with recruiting, training, or assisting new candidates. With a modicum of financial support, incumbents could be left to run their own reelection campaigns.

Or consider the difference between Republican and Democratic get-out-the-vote operations. Republicans employed "microtargeting" techniques long before the Democrats; but this was not because Democrats were unaware of marketing concepts—it was because Republicans and Democrats faced different competitive challenges. Microtargeting was necessary if Republican candidates were to turn out sympathetic voters in heavily Democratic areas without awakening the underlying Democratic majority. Democrats, in contrast, promoted legal reforms and broad-based nonpartisan get-out-the-vote campaigns to turn out the "natural" Democratic majority. These are but a few examples; close inspection of the data yields many observable implications of the competitive standing theory.

Other plausible explanatory factors—such as "inherent differences" or "party partners" discussed in chapter 2—do not offer nearly as much leverage: they help to frame the story, but they do not explain why a given president would choose to engage in party building. Several other "usual suspect" explanations can be put to rest as well. First, the hypothesis that every president acts differently on account of his unique personality, skill, and style does not hold up against the strong partisan pattern we observe in presidential behavior: men who could not have been more different from one another acted in strikingly similar ways when faced with the same sorts of competitive pressures. Second, the expectation that different historical breakpoints (such as the campaign finance reforms of the 1970s) will yield different president-party relationships is not wrong—we do see changes in how presidents act over time—but these breakpoints do not map onto the pattern of presidential party building. Third, the notion that party building is simply a second-term or "lame duck" phenomenon—something that presidents do when they begin to think about their legacy—can be refuted with reference to the party-building activities undertaken during each Republican president's first term. Likewise, the notion that presidential party building is driven primarily by reelection concerns can be equally well refuted with reference to the second-term party building undertaken by Eisenhower, Nixon, Reagan, and Clinton.

The competitive standing theory holds up quite well against these and other alternative explanations, yet it is not, by itself, sufficient to explain how each president chose to interact with his party. As we have seen, every president also had to negotiate with the institutional arrangements he inherited. Repeated rounds of party building in the GOP created the conditions in which successive Republican presidents found it in their interest to continue investing in the same party capacities. Inheriting up and running party-building programs and increasingly robust organizational capacities, Republican presidents were encouraged to reinvest in the same structures and operations rather than dismantle and replace them with new ones. On the Democratic side, the persistent refusal of Democratic presidents to engage in party building kept their party's organizational capacities inchoate and its resources scarce. Absent a strong electoral motivation to build a new majority, there was little reason for Democratic presidents to seek out organizational solutions—rather than policy solutions, public-relations solutions, rhetorical solutions, et cetera —to address the immediate political problems they faced. The condition of the party organization each president inherited thus directly influenced how he interacted with it.

This is not to say that inherited institutional conditions trump competitive standing as an explanation for presidential behavior. As observed in the Eisenhower and Clinton cases, so long as they are sufficiently motivated, presidents can overcome the start-up costs associated with launching new party-building programs from scratch. It remains to be seen, however, whether the "downstream" effects of persistent party building can prompt continued party building even in the absence of a strong competitive impulse to build a new majority. Barack Obama, who has yet to take office at the time of this writing, may offer the best test of the "downstream" effects of party building. The party he has inherited from Howard Dean appears to be more organizationally robust than at any time in modern history, and the Democratic Party's competitive standing in 2009 looks, once again, to be quite strong. If he continues to invest in the Democratic Party organization, his behavior may be prompted more by his calculation of the marginal cost and high upside potential of making additional organizational improvements than by a strong majority-building impulse. Of course, how Obama will perceive his competitive environment and how, precisely, the organizational capacities he inherits will shape his calculations remains to be seen.

Evaluating the Presidents

By bringing new evidence to bear, the previous chapters have subjected some of our most familiar presidents to some rather unfamiliar tests and raised new questions about how we evaluate them and understand their historical and political significance. It is only natural that we should want to weigh the evidence. How do these new findings stack up against everything we already know? How should we weigh Nixon's New Majority party-building project against his 1972 campaign or his publicly stated ambivalence toward the GOP? How does Eisenhower's ambitious party building reconcile with his bipartisan approach to legislative politics? How do Ford's important contributions at the level of party organization square with his ineffectiveness in other political realms?

One aim of this book is to make the case for bringing greater clarity to the discussion. When we debate each president's relationship to his party, it is important to be clear about which definition of "the party" we are using; it is equally important to specify which presidential actions "count" in our analysis. To avoid comparing apples to oranges, we must separate the president's feelings of partisanship, for example, from his interactions with his party organization; as we have seen, they are not the same thing. Likewise, campaigning for fellow partisans is altogether different from investing in the party's infrastructure; building policy coalitions is altogether different from building the party's human capital; and so on. These are different activities undertaken for different purposes with different effects, and they should be treated as such.[1] Of course, the scholarly enterprise benefits from diversity, and it is not necessary for every participant in a discussion to agree on which presidential actions and which definitions of "party" are best. It is necessary, however, to indicate clearly at the outset which definitions we are using.

But definitional clarity is not an end unto itself. We still want to know how to evaluate our presidents, all things considered. Can we rest content with the classification of Nixon as a "party builder?" Or Kennedy as a "party predator?" What, then, was Clinton? Despite the attraction of such pithy labels, these analytic categories are not, in fact, meant to pigeonhole each president into one "type" or another. As we have seen, some presidents are more consistent in their party interactions than others, and some fit more comfortably next to their partisan brethren than others. There are no archetypes: all are variations on a theme. The categories, in other words, are tools, not conclusions; they are not meant to end the discussion, but to open new lines of inquiry.

Indeed, as the previous chapters have aimed to demonstrate, categorization is necessary if we are to unpack the president-party relationship, identify important over-time patterns, and examine the causes and consequences of the variation we observe. These broader considerations, after all, bear directly on our ability to develop a full and accurate portrait of each president and his place in history. Our aim is not only to appraise each president's behavior, but also to evaluate his *political significance*—that is, to appreciate his impact on such things as his party, its historical trajectory, and the changing shape of the president-party relationship.

For example, whatever Eisenhower's intensity of partisanship or Nixon's concern for his fellow Republicans, both presidents made important contributions to the Republican Party's organizational development. And however John F. Kennedy or Jimmy Carter viewed the heterogeneous Democratic Party coalition he inherited, his neglect of its structures and operations had important repercussions for the party and its capabilities in the electoral sphere. We have also seen that all modern presidents contributed to the evolving character, internal operating culture, and political identity of their party: irrespective of their feelings of partisanship or actions along other fronts, by consistently adopting a constructive approach to their party organization, Republican presidents reinforced an organizational culture within the GOP that was committed to party building and responsive to presidential leadership. Likewise, however Democratic presidents personally viewed their party, by repeatedly subordinating organizational concerns and elevating alternative priorities, their actions reinforced their party's traditional operating norms. The relationship each president established with his party, in other words, made multiple and material contributions to the development of party politics in America. If we are to appraise individual incumbents, these sorts of contributions must be built into our standards of evaluation.

But once we begin to rethink how we evaluate our presidents, we are forced to reckon with even broader questions about the place of the presidency in the American political system as a whole. As we have seen, by constantly tinkering with their party's organizational machinery in the pursuit of their grand ambitions, presidents from both parties influenced how our politics are contested and our electoral battles are waged. By making their parties more or less capable of mobilizing voters, recruiting candidates, running campaigns, and so on, their actions became constitutive of the American polity itself. Thus, while the findings presented here challenge some of the received wisdom about individual presidents, in their most precise signification, they speak to long-standing concerns about how our political system operates, and perhaps, how it ought to operate. In conclusion, let us take up these considerations in greater depth.

Old Formulas and New Considerations

In the predominant narrative, the troubled relationship between presidents and their parties is depicted as an irony of American political development that has had deleterious consequences for the political system. The president's constitutional imperative to exert his independence is said to have chafed against expectations of collective party responsibility; this has been especially true in the twentieth century, as the demand for bold presidential leadership has intensified. In consequence, the modern president-party relationship is seen to have contributed to the decline of critical party functions: in their quest for power and control, modern presidents have run roughshod over whatever stands in their way, even the very parties from which they came.[2] Indeed, if the perennial presidential struggle is depicted as the "man against the system," then either the man, the system, or both will surely lose.

But what if our assumptions are mistaken? What if the president-party relationship takes different forms under different circumstances, and the approach presidents take to their parties is shaped more by contextual factors than by structural defects, more by political circumstances than by presidential pathologies? If presidential party "predators" are simply responding to incentives derived from their political environment, and that political environment is variable and subject to change, then not only have our empirical referents been largely mistaken, but our normative arguments have been deeply misguided.

For example, well-meaning reformers—from Woodrow Wilson to E. E. Schattschneider to James MacGregor Burns to David Broder—have called for a "more responsible two-party system" where the president would rise to the occasion and become "the unifying force in our complex system, the leader both of his party and of the nation."[3] They have envisioned unified majority-party government where the relationship between the president and his party would be mutually advantageous. The famous 1950 American Political Science Association report on responsible parties, for example, imagined that "with greater party responsibility, the president's position as party leader would correspond in strength to the greater strength of his party."[4] Reconstructed as responsible agents of democratic governance, these unified majority parties would serve both a policy-accountability function and a democratic-integrative function in the political system. They would provide clear policy choices, governing accountability, and democratic "mechanisms by which the party organizations can absorb the benefits of wider political participation."[5]

But if majority-party presidents are, in fact, the presidents who are most likely to exploit their party for personal gain and strip it of its wherewithal to function as an agent of democratic integration in the political system, then responsible-party reformers have unwittingly been pushing in the wrong direction. They have been calling for precisely those conditions under which presidents have the *weakest* incentive to act constructively toward their parties. As we have seen, presidents operating under these conditions tend to leave their parties in worse shape than they found them, *less* able to perform the democratic-integrative function they are supposed to perform. While majority-party presidents may be more likely to work with their parties to "bring forth programs to which they commit themselves," they do so at the expense of their party's capacity to integrate and mobilize citizens into the political process.[6] Unified majority-party government might be more conducive to "responsible" government, but it would seem to pose serious democratic trade-offs that reformers have not considered.

Ironically, we have seen that under conditions of divided government, though responsible party governance may be less likely, the integrative capacities of the parties are more likely to be strengthened by the president.[7] Minority-party presidents are driven by their party's disadvantaged competitive standing to enhance its capacities to mobilize voters, recruit candidates, contest elections, and welcome citizens into the political process. The less conditions seem to facilitate responsible government, the more they seem to facilitate organizationally robust integrative parties, and vice versa. In other words, it appears that it may not be possible for American parties to be "responsible" and "integrative" at the same time.

But before we advocate one form of party over the other, it is worth considering the trade-offs: from the look of the current GOP, the more integrative party that results from persistent presidential party building also seems to be highly responsive to presidential control; its processes appear more hierarchical than democratic. While this party might have stronger capacities to integrate citizens into politics, it might have lost some of its earlier capacities to hold presidents to account and handed them a new, formidable resource for the exercise of presidential power.[8] If the factors we have identified continue to motivate future presidents to commit themselves to party building, we may be witness in coming years to the development of two truly "new" kinds of parties that have stronger capacities to mobilize voters and enlist their active support in campaigns while allowing—even encouraging—the president's individual purposes to dominate our politics.

While it is tempting to end this book with an urgent call for future presidents to strengthen their party's democratic functions even as they pursue greater party responsiveness, such a plea would belie the core findings presented here. Indeed, while we should recognize these trade-offs so that we may better understand the events unfolding before us, we must also acknowledge that even as reformers over the last century labored to encourage presidents and parties always to work in harmony, electoral dynamics created a politics all their own. There is no reason to think that every Democratic president of the latter half of the twentieth century maliciously intended to trade off his party's integrative capacities in exchange for something barely approximating responsible party governance; nor is there reason to think that their Republican counterparts intended to shirk their roles as responsible agents of democratic governance in exchange for enhanced microtargeting capacities at the RNC. But in both cases, the structure of the competitive political environment motivated certain behaviors over others. Indeed, the competitive impulse did not yield to different personalities, much less to normative concerns. These patterns appear to reflect systemic dynamics that, short of constitutional overhaul, we will not escape anytime soon.

Afterword | George W. Bush and Beyond

From the 1950s until the 1990s, presidents had no trouble identifying which party represented the "majority party" in American politics. Democrats led in party identification in the electorate by a comfortable margin and controlled both houses of Congress, most state houses, and most governors' mansions for nearly the entire time. Despite losing more presidential elections than they won, the Democrats' advantage at the local, state, and congressional levels was strong and stable. As I have discussed, this durable competitive imbalance was of real consequence: it directly shaped how presidents from both parties pursued their ambitions.

The 1994 elections destabilized this competitive political environment, and from 1995 to 2007 the Republican Party controlled both houses of Congress (save a brief stint of Democratic control of the Senate in the 107th Congress, produced not by an election but by a party "switcher").[1] Republicans reached parity or better in state-level elections, and while the Democratic Party maintained its edge in party identification, the Republican Party narrowed the gap considerably (see figure 2.1).

George W. Bush's presidency thus offers a nice test of the argument presented in chapter 2 that it is not the party's numerical standing which prompts party building, but the president's *perception* of its overall competitive standing: its standing today as well as its expected standing tomorrow. The Republican Party achieved considerable electoral success during his presidency, and yet Bush continued party building. According to some, he was as aggressive in his party leadership as any of his predecessors, if not more so.[2] The explanation for his persistent party building, then, would appear to be that the Republican Party's competitive standing was *not strong enough* to satisfy his ambitions. Bush hoped to establish a durable Republican majority, and was not content to gain a temporary edge on the Democrats. With Bush still in office at the time of this writing, it is too soon to develop a full picture of his strategic considerations and party-building actions. Nevertheless, available evidence strongly suggests that Bush followed closely in his Republican predecessors' footsteps.

George W. Bush's Party Building

Bush assumed the presidency in 2001 with no background experience in organizational party politics. Yet he immediately dedicated himself and his new team to building "a long-lasting GOP majority in the country that could reverse the course set 70 years ago by President Franklin D. Roosevelt."[3] Quite notably, this ambitious plan was encouraged by top political advisor Karl Rove and other members of Bush's team who got their start in Republican party-building programs in the 1970s.[4] Previous efforts to build the party's human capital and develop a sense of "mission" within the party had clearly carried forward, and were now well represented in Bush's political team.

Building the Organization and Expanding Its Reach

Bush was not starting from scratch. The party organization he inherited had over $15 million in cash on hand, a voter list with 165 million names, an email list with one million addresses, and a donor list that had expanded by over 400,000 new names in the previous cycle alone.[5] It ran a routine campaign management training school out of the RNC, boasted state-of-the-art technology, and had a large pool of human capital on which Bush could draw. Consequently, Bush's first RNC chairman, Governor Jim Gilmore of Virginia, was able to build directly upon the direct-mail system, voter lists, and donor lists he inherited. Gilmore explained that Bush wanted him to use the RNC's organizational apparatus to expand the party's reach:

> To see the party broaden its base, and to bring additional people in
> . . . he's made it clear that this is the goal that he wishes the party to
> achieve, to bring more people in from the Hispanic community, the
> African-American community, all regions of the United States of
> America, and to make this party broader even than it is now.[6]

In 2001 Gilmore launched a new RNC division to reach out to "groups that we have not had the support of in the past and that we want the support of in the future," including blacks, Hispanics, Catholics, Asians, Jews, and middle-class women.[7]

By the end of Bush's first year, the RNC had launched several of these initiatives and raised a record $73 million.[8] When Gilmore left his post at the end of 2001, Bush replaced him with close friend and former governor of Montana Marc Racicot, who "knows how to build grassroots organizations," Bush explained. "He's going to reach out to members of the labor unions and the minorities, just like Jim Gilmore did."[9] Throughout his first term, Bush continued to stress the themes of grassroots organizing and party expansion: he reminded a gathering of the RNC in mid-2002, for example, that he knew "full well how important it is to have people who are willing to man the phones and to stuff the envelopes, to carry the signs, to stand on the street corners, to do all the work necessary."[10]

Ed Gillespie, Bush's third RNC chairman, argued that their aggressive voter outreach efforts were strategic, not quixotic. The Bush team might not be able to convert entire segments of Democratic voters into new Republican voters, but if they could cut into the margins of key Democratic constituency groups—such as African Americans—it might make a big difference in the long run. In this spirit, Gillespie worked to attract the "natural coalition of active military and veterans, entrepreneurs and religious conservatives in the

African-American electorate" to the GOP because incremental gains in the present "could result in Republican candidates doubling or even tripling our 10 percent average over the next decade," he wrote. What's more, Gillespie believed Bush's seven-point gain in the black vote in 2004 was pivotal in states like Ohio, where the RNC made a special effort to attract African American voters.[11]

Internalizing the Mechanics of the 2004 Campaign

In his reelection campaign in 2004, Bush followed in the footsteps of his predecessors and fully incorporated his party organization into the campaign. Described by journalist Matt Bai as the "multilevel marketing of the president," the Bush-Cheney reelection committee worked in close cooperation with the RNC, state, and local party committees to vertically integrate campaign operations. Whereas Ronald Reagan's team adopted the Amway model in 1981–82 for fund-raising purposes, the Bush campaign now adopted it for the grassroots component of his campaign. Local networks of volunteers gathered information on voters in Republican high-growth areas and passed the valuable data "through the up-line" to the campaign headquarters. As Election Day approached, the campaign would "flip a switch, and the suction will change direction; information will now move primarily from headquarters down to the volunteers. Canvassers in each county will await the message of the day from the campaign, and then, like suburban Paul Reveres, they'll be off to get the word out, by foot or by phone."[12] Together, the presidential campaign and the party organization claimed to have registered 3.4 million new Republicans in 2004, while over 1.4 million volunteers made a reported "102,000 calls into talk radio shows, 411,989 letters to the editor, 9.1 million volunteer door knocks and a total of 27.2 million volunteer phone calls."[13] The goal, of course, was to reelect George W. Bush. But these newly registered Republican voters, new networks of Republican volunteers and activists, new communication technologies, new voter files, and new coordinative capacities remained with the party after the election.

Indeed, in 2005, Bush appointed his campaign manager, Ken Mehlman, to be the new RNC chairman and charged him with making permanent these new organizational capacities by "internalizing the mechanics of the program" in the formal party apparatus. Special off-year elections, Mehlman said, offered opportunities to "test new and improved targeting and tactics" and to ensure that "grassroots activists remained energized in the political process." Similarly, a new round of investments and an expanded staff at the RNC were meant to help the party to "build on past success and grow the party."[14] Mehlman added seven new regional grassroots directors, set up an "eCampaign" team, expanded the party's communications and polling divisions, and sought to keep its grassroots volunteer networks active during off-years.

While enhancing the party's organizational capacities, Bush and his team continued to emphasize their commitment to "bringing people into the party who have never been in politics."[15] Mehlman announced at the start of Bush's second term: "GOP must continue to stand for Grow Our Party."[16] The RNC institutionalized new programs to recruit black GOP candidates and improve the party's appeal to African American voters.[17] It also created an "outreach series" to build ties to Jews and Hispanics and new "advisory committees" to incorporate the views of Latino and black community leaders into the party's higher councils.[18]

In preparation for the 2006 midterm elections, the RNC again served as the centralized location for party-wide strategic planning and operations. All of the party's turnout efforts, for example, were routed through the RNC, which also ran special candidate-training programs to recruit minority candidates and train their staffs. The RNC also launched its much-vaunted "72-hour program," now four years old, to leverage the national party's technology and the local parties' volunteer networks to make electoral activities more efficient.[19] Using technology to customize the individual messages received by each voter, the party's microtargeting operation identified "would-be GOP voters and their top issues early in the cycle" and fed that information into the central database to help party leaders "flood them with pro-Republican messages through e-mail, regular mail and local volunteers" and turn them out on Election Day.[20]

Despite suffering major losses on Election Day in 2006, Bush's team repeated the familiar rhetoric of organizational party building: Mehlman called the GOP's losses a "brief interruption in a generational effort to build a center-right majority."[21] The RNC performed intensive "post-election reviews" of its microtargeting operations and examined the record of "every person it contacted . . . how many times they were reached, which issues were discussed and whether they voted."[22] Measuring the effectiveness of state and local parties, the RNC recognized those who met or exceeded their goals and developed plans to address deficiencies. During the final two years of Bush's presidency, the RNC continued to develop its organizational capacities: it grew its donor lists, email lists, and volunteer networks to new heights; held multiple regional meetings; launched a surrogate-training initiative within its speakers' bureau; upgraded its "Voter Vault" and other voter files; added new online tools; and expanded its fund-raising operations.[23]

Though the Republican Party's numerical strength in Congress and in state-level offices ebbed and flowed over the course of Bush's two terms—reaching its strongest competitive standing since before the New Deal in 2002–6 and then reverting back to minority status in his final two years—Bush's commitment to strengthening the Republican Party's infrastructure and expanding its electoral coalition remained unchanged.[24] Even as his former rival, Senator John McCain, secured the GOP's presidential nomination and repudiated many of his policies, Bush continued to lend his support to his party's organizational efforts.[25] Despite his dismal approval ratings, Bush made 84 fund-raising appearances and raised $146 million for the Republican Party, its committees, and its candidates in the 2008 election cycle.[26]

Notwithstanding many twists and turns along the way, the objective consistently repeated by Bush's team throughout his two terms was "to create a durable Republican majority."[27] Like his Republican predecessors, Bush failed to achieve his grand ambitions: yet at the organizational level, he left his successors with a more robust party apparatus—what Karl Rove has called "a superior tool"—with which to run campaigns, expand the party's reach, and continue its organizational development.[28] As the party prepared to become the "out-party" once more, each of the contenders for the RNC chairmanship emphasized the need to broaden the party's appeal and make continued investments in its technological infrastructure and campaign services.[29]

Party Building in the Democratic Party

While Bush was working to build his party and establish a durable Republican majority, similar efforts were proceeding apace on the other side of the aisle. As discussed in chapter 11, DNC chairmen from 2001 to 2008 followed up on Clinton's late-breaking party-building efforts with incremental investments in their party's organizational capacities. It is worth noting that Democratic Party leaders did not adopt the Republican party-building model wholesale: this was not a case of outright mimicry or organizational isomorphism.[30] Rather, they designed party-building programs that fit their party's unique constituencies, distinctive operating norms, and preexisting organizational structures. For example, the investments Howard Dean made as part of his fifty-state strategy—tailored to meet each state party's distinctive needs—demonstrated that party building is not a one-size-fits-all proposition.

When Barack Obama won the Democratic nomination in the summer of 2008, he inherited a party that was active in more states and that reached more deeply into local communities than at any time in recent memory. The DNC boasted a fully functional national voter file, over 200 trained field operatives in all fifty states, grassroots training programs in each state, new cutting-edge technologies, user-friendly canvassing tools for volunteers, and multiple online campaign resources.[31] Obama's team moved quickly to "fully integrate DNC operations with the Obama campaign" and consolidate the various "political, field, and constituency operations . . . into one operation."[32] The campaign launched a fifty-state voter registration drive to test and refine the organizational apparatus while leveraging Obama's popularity to swell the number of registered Democrats. The drive appeared to be successful, especially in formerly "red" states like North Carolina, where 800,000 new voters were registered by the end of 2008 (and where Obama went on to score a narrow victory in November).[33] The Obama campaign was not oblivious to the long-term benefits such efforts could have for the party: even as it sought to win in 2008, the campaign announced its intention to build for the future as well. It pledged to extend its "massive volunteer and technological resources into states which won't necessarily produce electoral votes" in 2008 in order to help down-ticket Democratic candidates and lay the groundwork for re-districting in 2011.[34]

While the DNC's earlier party-building efforts may have "laid the ground-work" for Obama's successful campaign, organization cannot, by itself, win an election.[35] Without the unusual enthusiasm surrounding Obama's candidacy and the many other factors that combined to produce his victory in November 2008, we might be telling a very different story about the role of the party organization in the campaign. Even Howard Dean was reluctant to take credit for Obama's victory: "I thought we needed a long-term business plan, and we needed to stick to it," Dean says. "Little did I know we were going to have this incredibly charismatic candidate who would do it all in four years. I have to say it happened a lot faster than I thought it would."[36] The question, going forward, was whether Obama would continue to emphasize party building once he reached the White House. Dean, for his part, sounded confident: "He totally gets this party-building stuff," he said.[37]

As Obama prepared to take office and this book went into production, there were a number of indications that he might, indeed, become the first fully committed Democratic party-building president in modern American history. First were Obama's public statements on the matter. During the campaign, he pledged to continue funding the fifty-state strategy at full capacity if elected president.[38] Though his pledge was made during the heat of the primary contest, he reiterated his commitment during the transition to the White House, promising "not only to build on Howard [Dean]'s record of achievement, but to remake the Democratic Party to meet the challenges of the 21st century."[39] The moment was ripe to continue party building, he argued:

> It would be a mistake to take our success in the campaign as a sign that our work is somehow complete. At a time when the challenges we face in this country are so vast, we cannot afford to abandon the movement we've built. We have to strengthen it. We must build a movement for change that can endure beyond a single election, and that will require redoubling our efforts to reach out to Americans throughout our fifty states—North and South, East and West. It will require finding candidates for elective office whose policies and plans are rooted not in ideology, but in what works. And it will require . . . relying on small donations from ordinary Americans. We're in a strong position to rebuild a Democratic Party committed to these principles because of the outstanding work of its current chairman, Howard Dean.[40]

Obama's rhetoric was backed up with assurances that his vast network of supporters—3 million donors, 10 million email addresses, millions of volunteers, and tens of thousands of neighborhood coordinators—would be folded into the DNC rather than kept as an independent entity, a move that seemed to contrast sharply with Jimmy Carter's efforts to maintain and nurture his "Carter Network" outside party channels.[41] Indeed, his aggressive effort to pay off the DNC's campaign debt, launched only eight days after his election, was another sign that Obama wanted to prepare his party for the challenges that lay ahead.[42] Obama's early political appointments hinted at an interest in party building as well: Patrick Gaspard (director of White House Office of Political Affairs), Tim Kaine (DNC chair), and Jennifer O'Malley Dillon (DNC executive director) were organization-minded leaders who had successfully reached out to new groups and expanded the party's reach into new geographic areas in the past.[43] Obama's late-breaking appointment of O'Malley Dillon's husband, Patrick Dillon, as deputy director of political affairs was perhaps the clearest indication yet of the new president's desire to establish a close working relationship between the White House and the DNC.[44] Obama's DNC, one commentator noted, was shaping up to look like "Howard Dean's fifty-state strategy on steroids."[45]

Yet whether Obama will follow through on his party-building commitments once he reaches the White House is still uncertain at the time of this writing. Some of the plans leaked during the transition—especially proposals to use the DNC primarily as a vehicle to promote the president's legislative agenda—smacked of the Operation Support–like activities sponsored by Obama's Democratic predecessors.[46] What's more, the 200 staffers funded through the fifty-state strategy were laid off after the election, and though there were indications that Obama's team would continue funding operations at the state and local levels, many feared that the national party leadership would centralize control over those operations and reshape them to serve the president's interests without regard for local concerns.[47] Of course, as we have seen, presidents can be instrumental and constructive at the same time: they can *use* the party and *build* it simultaneously. Thus, at issue is not whether Obama structures his party's activities to redound to his own benefit—every president does that—but whether his top-down approach will be accompanied by serious efforts to strengthen his party's organizational capacities and prepare it for the electoral battles and redistricting challenges that lie ahead.

Prognostication is a treacherous business, and all the usual caveats apply. Yet it is worth asking how our two explanatory factors—"competitive standing" and "inherited institutional conditions"—appear likely to play out in the early years of Obama's presidency. First, consider the party's competitive standing. When Obama assumes the presidency, Democrats will claim fifty-nine senators, 257 members of the House, an advantage of nine percentage points over the Republicans in terms of party identification, and 55 percent of all state legislative seats.[48] Numerically, therefore, the electoral standing of Obama's Democratic Party will be quite strong.[49] As we have seen, strong majorities motivated earlier Democratic presidents to exploit their party's strength in the short term rather than to build it for the long term. On this reckoning, one might expect Obama to do the same.

But it is not entirely clear that Obama's competitive environment is all that similar to his predecessors'. When Kennedy, Johnson, Carter, and Clinton took stock of their party's competitive standing—when they looked backward as well as forward—they saw deep and durable majorities stretching back many years and no reason to anticipate major losses in the foreseeable future. Obama, in contrast, is likely to recall the widespread sense of failure and desperation felt by Democrats only four years earlier, when Republicans enjoyed across-the-board victories and when, as Howard Dean jokes, "it was not a fun time to be a Democrat."[50] Likewise, the dire economic and foreign policy challenges facing the incoming administration may encourage Obama to question the permanence of his party's newfound majorities: if he and his colleagues do not produce tangible change quickly, their electoral fortunes could easily be reversed. Whether Obama will make these sorts of retrospective and prospective calculations is, of course, an open question. But it is at least plausible that he will see things along these lines and view his party's competitive standing not as an excuse for complacency, but as an opportunity to consolidate the Democrats' recent gains and build the "new majority" about which he frequently speaks.[51]

Yet even if the Democratic Party's competitive standing does not provide an incentive for Obama to undertake party building, perhaps its organizational strength will. Not only has the party made multiple improvements to its infrastructure and operations in recent years, but its human capital—its activist base—is, by all accounts, more engaged, enthusiastic, and experienced than at any point in recent history. If Obama does not emphasize party building on his own volition, the party membership may exert pressure from below. Whatever the fate of the fifty-state strategy, party activists will undoubtedly demand further investments in new technologies, state party infrastructures, training programs, and campaign services for candidates. It is hard to imagine that Obama would resist their demands: with the start-up costs already paid by his predecessors, additional investments appear to be relatively cheap and quite valuable for his own purposes in 2012 and beyond. In sum, Obama would seem to have both electoral and institutional incentives to continue party building.

Taking all these developments together, it appears that we may have entered an altogether new period of American politics—one wherein *both* parties will remain intently focused on party building. In this era of competitive uncertainty, both parties have incentives to make investments in their organizational capacities as they probe for opportunities to establish a durable competitive advantage. Indeed, "competitive standing" and "inherited institutional conditions" appear to have dovetailed: future Democratic and Republican presidents will inherit increasingly robust party organizations, which will only reinforce their motivation to build a new majority. In short, we may be in store for even more presidential party building in the years ahead.

Appendix | Methods and Sources

Histories of the modern presidents abound: the literature on each incumbent is impressively large and always growing. The case studies in this book make no attempt to re-create comprehensive histories of each incumbent; that task is best left to those more capable than I. My objective is much narrower. Taking advantage of the vast collections of primary source documents stored in presidential libraries and other special collections, I aim to construct a record of all known president-party interactions in the modern period and explain the significance of such instances for the presidency, the parties, and American political development. The value of such an effort turns, in large part, on the defensibility and transparency of the decision rules and methods used; this appendix aims to explicate these moves.

The primary-source documentary record on these presidents is vast, but it is also fairly well organized and accessible. Though I inspected many times this number of documents while undertaking research for this book, I collected over 10,000 letters, memos, documents, and reports; perused hundreds of oral histories; listened to hours of presidential recordings; consulted thousands of historical newspaper articles; researched many secondary sources; and conducted many personal interviews. Somewhat surprisingly, this investigation yielded a rather manageable number of president-party interactions, and I have included nearly the whole dataset in this book.[1]

By "president-party interaction," I mean any instance in which the president seeks to effect a change in the status quo of his party organization and its operations. Sometimes this is a single action (for example, a single directive from the president to his party chairman) and other times it is a series of actions, which are treated as a single episode.[2]

One of the shortcomings of the existing literature is that it tends to treat as significant only those presidential efforts that successfully accomplished the objectives set forth by the president. This is partly due to the predominance of the "man against the system" perspective discussed in chapter 1. But presidential actions that failed or were incomplete are just as important for our purposes; to understand how each president approached his party's organization, we must include all types of party interactions without concern for the effects. Eisenhower, for example, failed to transform his party into a "Modern Republican" party, yet his party-building efforts were not without important consequences for the Republican Party's organizational development, as discussed in chapter 3.[3]

Having identified these episodes of president-party interaction, I assessed each for whether it was constructive or nonconstructive. A *constructive* presidential action is an effort purposefully designed to enhance the party's organizational capacities along any of the six dimensions of party activity.[4] A *nonconstructive* action is either indifferent, exploitative, or meant to undercut the party's organizational capacities along those same dimensions. Any evidence of a constructive action is classified as party "building," and any evidence of a nonconstructive action is classified as party "predation"—that is, as confirmation of the conventional wisdom about the president-party relationship.[5] If the episode cannot be clearly identified as party "building," it is classified as nonconstructive. Neutral or ambiguous party interactions are omitted, but these are rare and almost always plainly trivial. This classification effort is not as tricky as it might sound; with very few exceptions, party-building actions are self-evidently constructive in their aims and can be easily identified as such.

A "presidential action" is undertaken by the president himself, by a presidential assistant who has the authority to act routinely on the president's behalf, or by some other agent who can be shown to have received the president's explicit authorization to act on his behalf. If it cannot be established that the action under consideration is undertaken with the president's personal approval, it does not count as a presidential action.[6]

The "party" means the formal party apparatus—the national, state, county, and local party committees, as well as party activists and volunteers working for the party proper—that is, the formal party organization's structures, activities, and personnel. One reason for defining party in this way is for comparability purposes. Less strict definitions of party—even those used productively elsewhere—make cross-party and over-time comparisons rather problematic. Bill Clinton's interactions with the Democratic Party's diverse coalition of quasi-affiliated interest groups and organizations in the 1990s, for example, cannot be compared on equal terms with Eisenhower's interactions with the Republican Party's partner coalition in the 1950s—but their interactions with their national committees are much more commensurate.

Of course, even the formal party organization cannot be treated as a static or constant variable across more than fifty years: both parties have changed their structures, processes, and operations over the decades. Yet the power relationship between presidents and their party chairmen and the norms of behavior that characterize their dealings have been more constant since the 1950s than in earlier years.

This, more than anything, is why the study begins with Eisenhower. Every president since Eisenhower has exercised nearly absolute authority over the activities of his handpicked party chairmen and the goings-on at the national committee. Indeed, the fact that the national committee has merely ratified the president's choice for chairman in a pro forma election since around midcentury is emblematic of the modern president-party relationship.[7] Eisenhower was also the first president to forbid the national chairman or any other committee member to simultaneously hold a federal office, an important move that subordinated the party to the presidency even further. The further back in history we move, however, the less this power relationship holds: party chairmen, as well as the entire party structure, were much more independent from the president and less subject to his control. What's more, the national committees began to operate continuously and maintain a permanent staff and headquarters only by the late 1940s and early 1950s. Patterns of institutional development stabilized in the 1950s, and "by the 1960s, the basic organizational functions and duties of the Democratic and Republican national committees, chairmen, and headquarters were fairly well defined and stabilized."[8] While not a perfect control, restricting the investigation to the period from Eisenhower to the present reduces the likelihood that the differences we observe in president-party relations can be attributed to variations in the permanence, institutionalization, and responsiveness of the party apparatus.

While this periodization aids in making comparisons across presidencies, variations in the source data for each administration make matters somewhat more complicated. The most important question, on this score, is whether Democratic presidents were undertaking party building but the record of their efforts does not exist, is hidden from view, or I missed it in my investigation. (Missing evidence of Republican presidential party building would not significantly alter the main findings.) It is impossible to be certain, but there are three reasons to be confident that differences in the source data for each president do not lead to biased findings.

First, constructive party-building efforts are anything but private and secretive; they almost always involve some element of publicity. Holding a campaign management training program, running a voter registration drive, or creating a new party division, for example, is a highly public act, though it may not be so salient as to always capture the attention of the media or the public. (Most often, the coordinators of such programs strive to bring more publicity to their endeavors, not less.) Second, unlike persuasion or bargaining, which tend to go unrecorded and are often lost to history, presidential efforts to change the party organization always require some amount of planning, forecasting, and strategizing within the White House or at the national committee—processes that invariably require meetings and information exchanges. There is good reason to believe that some sort of paper trail would exist if such efforts were made; indeed, I found no evidence that Republican presidents or their party leaders sought to conceal their efforts. Most often, the paper trail is easily traceable. Third, the publications of the two parties—such as press releases and detailed reports announcing new party activities and developments—are roughly equivalent and commensurate over time, and the records are plentiful. Massive collections of DNC and RNC publications can be found in the presidential libraries and other locations. It is usually quite clear what the Democratic Party was doing in lieu of party building.

The greater difficulty is that the availability of White House documents classified as "political" diminishes with each successive presidency beginning with Reagan. There are many reasons for this, mostly pertaining to the Presidential Records Act of 1978 and subsequent executive orders.[9] While we await the release of the "political" documents from more recent administrations, I have sought to fill in the gaps by conducting personal interviews with administration officials and party leaders; a few also generously shared their personal paper collections with me. For these more recent cases, I have also relied more on newspapers, memoirs, published interviews, and other helpful secondary sources in order to make cross-case comparisons as rigorous as possible.

This brings us back to the importance of using a clear definition of "party." With the source data varying somewhat in each case and over time, it becomes quite difficult to compare one president to the next on equal footing if we treat each president's approach to his party as a single unit of analysis (the $N = 1$ problem). To get more variation and analytical leverage, we must be more specific. Searching for president-party interactions along the six discrete dimensions of party activity discussed in chapter 1 effectively divides presidential actions into more equivalent units and arranges them along more narrowly tailored dimensions of "party." This expands our number of observations many times over and allows for more reliable comparisons across time and space.

The six dimensions involve the party's capacity to (1) provide campaign services, (2) develop human capital, (3) recruit candidates, (4) mobilize voters, (5) finance party operations, and (6) support internal activities. Where, one might ask, do these categories come from? In the existing literature, there is no single definition of "party," or even "party organization," for that matter. Thus, these categories represent my best attempt to cull the six major areas of party organizational activity that scholars have tended to focus on in studies of American political parties in the postwar period.[10] While they do not follow any particular convention, they should not seem unusual; and while there is some overlap across the six dimensions, they should be sufficiently distinct to allow relatively independent comparisons along each.

To be sure, those who prefer to use different definitions, different decision rules, and different sources will discover new findings of interest that have escaped attention here. Such is the beauty (and burden) of historical research: recovering the past—and making sense of what we find—is always a work in progress. To the extent that the transparency of one's methods facilitates further research along the same lines or invites the formation of alternatives, the whole endeavor becomes all the more worthwhile.

Abbreviations |

DDEL	Dwight D. Eisenhower Library, Abilene, Kans.
GBL	George Bush Library, College Station, Tex.
GFL	Gerald Ford Library, Ann Arbor, Mich.
HDP	Harry Dent Papers, Clemson University Library, Clemson, S.C.
HSTL	Harry S. Truman Library, Independence, Mo.
JCL	Jimmy Carter Library, Atlanta, Ga.
JFKL	John F. Kennedy Library, Boston, Mass.
KOF	*President John F. Kennedy Office Files, 1961–1963*, ed. Paul Kesaris and Robert E. Lester, microform (Frederick, Md.: University Publications of America, 1989)
LBJL	Lyndon Baines Johnson Library, Austin, Tex.
MAP	Papers of Hugh Meade Alcorn, Jr., Rauner Special Collections Library, Dartmouth College, Hanover, N.H.
MLS	Mary Louise Smith Papers, Iowa Women's Archives, Iowa City, Iowa
MPP	Margaret Price Papers, Bentley Historical Library, University of Michigan
NLCP	Nixon Library, College Park, Maryland
NLYL	Nixon Presidential Returned Materials Collection: White Hose Special Files: Contested Materials, Richard Nixon Presidential Library and Museum, National Archives at Yorba Linda, Calif.
PNWH	*Papers of the Nixon White House, 1969–1974*, ed. Paul L. Kesaris, microfiche (Frederick, Md.: University Publications of America, 1987–92)
PRP	*Papers of the Republican Party, Part I: Meetings of the Rnc, 1911–1980, Series A: 1911–1960, 51 Microfilm Reels,* Paul L. Kesaris, ed., (Frederick, Md: University Publications of America, 1987, 1986).
PPP	Public Papers of the Presidents. Online at http://www.presidency.ucsb.edu.
RRL	Ronald Reagan Library, Simi Valley, Calif.
RMP	Rogers C. B. Morton Papers, University of Kentucky Special Collections, Lexington, Ky.
TMP	Thruston Morton Collection, University of Kentucky Special Collections, Lexington, Ky.

Notes |

1 | Introduction

1 See, for example, Matt Bai, "The Multilevel Marketing of the President," *New York Times Magazine*, April 25, 2004; Adam Nagourney, "Lost Horizons," *New York Times*, September 24, 2006.

2 "Special Elections Confirm the Importance of Grassroots Turnout Efforts," RNC Press Release, May 23, 2005.

3 "RNC Chairman Ken Mehlman Addresses the Republican Governors Association," RNC Press Release, November 30, 2006. See also "RNC Chairman Mike Duncan Addresses RNC Members at Winter Meeting," RNC Press Release, January 19, 2007.

4 "Remarks by the President after a Meeting with the General Leaders of the Republican National Committee," White House Press Release, November 14, 2006.

5 Chris Cillizza, "Martinez Will Reach Out to Latino Voters, Party Donors," *Washington Post*, November 14, 2006; "Republican National Committee: Chairman Duncan Announces Additions to Committee Political Team," Targeted News Service, February 27, 2007; Joshua Green, "The Rove Presidency," *The Atlantic*, September 2007; "GOP Chairman Dismisses High Democratic Turnout," *White House Bulletin*, January 23, 2008; Benjamin Wallace-Wells, "A Case of the Blues," *New York Times*, March 30, 2008; Karl Rove, "A Way Out of the Wilderness," *Newsweek*, November 15, 2008; Tom Bevan and John McIntyre, "Interview with President George W. Bush: Part One," *Realclearpolitics.com*, December 16, 2008.

6 Jodi Enda, "Howard's Beginning," *American Prospect*, August 2005, 20.

7 Ari Berman, "Where's the Plan, Democrats?" *The Nation*, July 17, 2006; Dana Fisher, *Activism, Inc.* (Stanford, Calif.: Stanford University Press, 2006).

8 Dana Fisher, "The Activism Industry," *American Prospect*, September 14, 2006.

9 Matt Bai, "The Inside Agitator," *New York Times*, October 1, 2006; Elaine C. Kamarck, "Assessing Howard Dean's Fifty State Strategy and the 2006 Midterm Elections," *The Forum* 4, no. 3 (2006); Daniel Galvin, "How to Grow a Democratic Majority," *New York Times*, June 3, 2006; Ari Berman, "The Prophet," *The Nation*, December 17, 2008.

10 Bai, "The Inside Agitator"; Kamarck, "Dean's Fifty State Strategy."

11 Jacob S. Hacker and Paul Pierson, *Off Center: The Republican Revolution and the Erosion of American Democracy* (New Haven: Yale University Press, 2005); Thomas B. Edsall, *Building Red America: The New Conservative Coalition and the Drive for Permanent Power* (New York: Basic Books, 2006); Tom Hamburger and Peter Wallsten, *One Party Country: The Republican Plan for Dominance in the 21st Century* (Hoboken: Wiley, 2006); Bill Bradley, "A Party Inverted," *New York Times*, March 30, 2005; Jerome Armstrong and Markos Moulitsas Zuniga, *Crashing the Gate* (White River Junction, Vt.: Chelsea Green, 2006); George Lakoff, *Don't Think of an Elephant!* (White River Junction, Vt.: Chelsea Green, 2004); Geoffrey Nunberg, *Talking Right* (New York: Public Affairs, 2006).

12 Classic works examining the efforts of "out parties" to regain political competitiveness in two-party systems include Maurice Duverger, *Political Parties,*

Their Organization and Activity in the Modern State (London: Wiley, 1954); Anthony Downs, *An Economic Theory of Democracy* (New York: Harper, 1957); E. E. Schattschneider, *The Semisovereign People: A Realist's View of Democracy in America* (New York: Holt, Rinehart and Winston, 1960); William H. Riker, *The Theory of Political Coalitions* (New Haven: Yale University Press, 1962); Robert A. Dahl, ed., *Political Oppositions in Western Democracies* (New Haven: Yale University Press, 1966). Notable contemporary works include Philip A. Klinkner, *The Losing Parties: Out-Party National Committees, 1956–1993* (New Haven: Yale University Press, 1994); Martin Shefter, *Political Parties and the State* (Princeton: Princeton University Press, 1994); Clyde P. Weed, *The Nemesis of Reform* (New York: Columbia University Press, 1994); Kenneth Finegold and Elaine K. Swift, "What Works? Competitive Strategies of Major Parties Out of Power," *British Journal of Political Science* 31, no. 1 (2001).

13 Clinton Rossiter, *The American Presidency* (New York: Harcourt, Brace, 1956), 53; James MacGregor Burns, *Leadership* (New York: Harper and Row, 1978), 328; and Richard M. Pious, *The American Presidency* (New York: Basic Books, 1979), 126.

14 David Broder, *The Party's Over* (New York: Harper and Row, 1971, 1972), xxiii; Klinkner, *The Losing Parties*, 2.

15 Cited in Robert Harmel, "President-Party Relations in the Modern Era: Past, Problems, and Prognosis," in *Presidents and Their Parties: Leadership or Neglect?* ed. Robert Harmel (New York: Praeger, 1984), 249; Thomas E. Cronin, "The Presidency and the Parties," in *Party Renewal in America*, ed. Gerald M. Pomper (New York: Praeger, 1980), 176; Harold F. Bass, "The President and the National Party Organization," in Harmel, *Presidents and Their Parties*, 251.

16 Hugh Heclo, "The Changing Presidential Office," in *Understanding the Presidency*, ed. James P. Pfiffner and Roger H. Davidson (New York: Pearson Longman, 2007), 264.

17 James MacGregor Burns, *Running Alone: Presidential Leadership from JFK to Bush II: Why It Has Failed and How We Can Fix It* (New York: Basic Books, 2006), 5.

18 Heclo, "The Changing Presidential Office," 5. Heclo writes: "Whatever the vagaries of personality, every contemporary president has been under pressure to move in the same direction."

19 Samuel Kernell, *Going Public* (Washington, D.C.: Congressional Quarterly Press, 1997); Theodore Lowi, *The Personal President* (Ithaca, N.Y.: Cornell University Press, 1985), 65; Lester G. Seligman, "The Presidential Office and the President as Party Leader (with a Postscript on the Kennedy-Nixon Era)," in *Parties and Elections in an Anti-party Age*, ed. Jeff Fishel (Bloomington: Indiana University Press, 1978), 300. According to Jeffrey Tulis, "There is a very real sense in which plebiscitary leadership—that is, the ideas that this term signifies—caused party decay." Jeffrey Tulis, *The Rhetorical Presidency* (Princeton: Princeton University Press, 1987), 15.

20 Pious, *The American Presidency*, 126.

21 Sidney M. Milkis, *The President and the Parties* (New York: Oxford University Press, 1993), 11.

22 See the appendix for more on methods and sources.

23 Except, perhaps, for the unusual attempt by John Tyler to form the "Democratic-Republican Party," alternatively called the "Tyler Party," after being formally expelled by the Whig Party. See Daniel Galvin and Colleen Shogan, "Presidential

Politicization and Centralization across the Modern-Traditional Divide," *Polity* 36, no. 3 (2004).

24 See Noble E. Cunningham, *The Jeffersonian Republicans in Power: Party Operations, 1801–1809* (Chapel Hill: University of North Carolina Press, 1963).

25 Notable studies of presidential coalition-building include Scott C. James, *Presidents, Parties, and the State* (New York: Cambridge University Press, 2000); Benjamin Ginsberg and Martin Shefter, "The Presidency and the Organization of Interests," in *The Presidency and the Political System*, 2nd ed., ed. Michael Nelson (Washington, D.C.: Congressional Quarterly Press, 1988); Paul Frymer and John David Skrentny, "Coalition-Building and the Politics of Electoral Capture during the Nixon Administration: African Americans, Labor, Latinos," *Studies in American Political Development* 12, no. 1 (1998); Lester G. Seligman and Cary R. Covington, *The Coalitional Presidency* (Chicago: Dorsey Press, 1989); David Plotke, *Building a Democratic Political Order: Reshaping American Liberalism in the 1930s and 1940s* (New York: Cambridge University Press, 1996).

26 See, for example, Broder, *The Party's Over*; Sidney M. Milkis and Jesse H. Rhodes, "George W. Bush, the Republican Party, and the 'New' American Party System," *Perspectives on Politics* 5, no. 3 (2007); Richard M. Skinner, "George W. Bush and the Partisan Presidency," forthcoming, *Political Studies Quarterly* (2009).

27 Frank J. Sorauf, "Political Parties and Political Analysis," in *The American Party Systems: Stages of Political Development*, ed. William Nisbet Chambers and Walter Dean Burnham (New York: Oxford University Press, 1975), 38. For another excellent argument in favor of using party organization as the analytical starting point, see Joseph A. Schlesinger, *Political Parties and the Winning of Office* (Ann Arbor: University of Michigan Press, 1991).

28 While the president-party relationship is usually assumed to be an important feature of American politics, most party scholarship either implicitly or explicitly pushes this relationship to the periphery of the analysis. Take, for example, the literature on party formation. In John Aldrich's influential *Why Parties? The Origin and Transformation of Political Parties in America* (Chicago: University of Chicago Press, 1995), presidents are presumed to face the same basic incentives and constraints as legislators, other officeholders, and "benefit seekers"; they do not stand out as significant engines of party change in their own right. Similarly, the new study by Marty Cohen, David Karol, Hans Noel, and John Zaller entitled *The Party Decides: Presidential Nominations before and after Reform* (Chicago: University of Chicago Press, 2008) expands the operational definition of party to include "traditional interest groups, issue advocacy groups, and ideological activists ... in long-term alignment with parties," but here too the emphasis is on how "party leaders, aligned groups, and political activists" shape important party activities like presidential nominations—the incumbent president is conspicuously absent from questions of party change and development. See Marty Cohen, David Karol, Hans Noel, and John Zaller, "Political Parties in Rough Weather," *The Forum* 5, no. 4 (2008): 2.

29 Klinkner, *The Losing Parties*, 191–96; "The Many Sides of Haley Barbour," *Campaigns and Elections*, August 1, 1996.

30 Klinkner, *The Losing Parties*, 171–75, 181–91.

31 See, for example, Cohen et al., "Political Parties in Rough Weather"; Fisher, *Activism, Inc.*; Edsall, *Building Red America*.

32 Note that the impressive capacities of presidents to direct party change reflect institutional developments in the presidency and in the parties over time, as well as changed norms and expectations about how the two should interact. See Daniel P. Klinghard, "Grover Cleveland, William McKinley, and the Emergence of the President as Party Leader," *Presidential Studies Quarterly* 35, no. 4 (2005); Milkis, *The President and the Parties*; Stephen Skowronek, *The Politics Presidents Make* (Cambridge: Harvard University Press, 1997); James W. Ceaser, *Presidential Selection* (Princeton: Princeton University Press, 1979); Lowi, *The Personal President*; and James W. Davis, *The President as Party Leader* (New York: Greenwood Press, 1992).

33 Klinkner, *The Losing Parties*.

34 For excellent discussions of the functionalist paradigm, see John Coleman, "Responsible, Functional, or Both? American Political Parties and the A.P.S.A. Report after Fifty Years," in *The State of the Parties: The Changing Role of Contemporary American Parties*, 4th ed., ed. John C. Green and Rick Farmer (Lanham, Md.: Rowman and Littlefield, 2003); Howard A. Scarrow, "The Function of Political Parties: A Critique of the Literature and Approach," *Journal of Politics* 29, no. 4 (1967); Anthony King, "Political Parties in Western Democracies: Some Skeptical Reflections," *Polity* 2, no. 2 (1969); Theodore Lowi, "Party, Policy, and Constitution in America," in Chambers and Burnham, *The American Party Systems*; Theodore Lowi, "Toward Functionalism in Political Science: The Case of Innovation in Party Systems," *American Political Science Review* 57, no. 3 (1963).

35 Sorauf, "Political Parties," 38.

36 See, for example, James A. Davis and David L. Nixon, "The President's Party," *Presidential Studies Quarterly* 24, no. 2 (1994); also Seligman, "Presidential Office."

37 Stephen Skowronek, "Leadership by Definition: First Term Reflections on George W. Bush's Political Stance," *Perspectives on Politics* 3, no. 4 (2005): 828–29; Milkis and Rhodes, "George W. Bush."

38 With a few important exceptions: Skowronek, *The Politics Presidents Make*; Martin Shefter, "Party, Bureaucracy, and Political Change in the United States," in *Political Parties: Development and Decay*, ed. Louis Maisel and Joseph Cooper (Beverly Hills, Calif.: Sage, 1978); and Mark Landy and Sidney M. Milkis, *Presidential Greatness* (Lawrence: University Press of Kansas, 2000).

39 Henry Jones Ford, *The Rise and Growth of American Politics* (New York: Macmillan, 1898) and Woodrow Wilson, *Constitutional Government in the United States* (1908; New York: Columbia University Press, 1961), probably best exemplify the Progressives' perspective; Arthur M. Schlesinger Jr., *The Imperial Presidency* (Boston: Houghton Mifflin, 1973) and Lowi, *The Personal President* exemplify the more recent critique. See Stephen Skowronek, "Presidency and American Political Development: A Third Look," *Presidential Studies Quarterly* 32, no. 4 (2002) and Sidney M. Milkis, *Political Parties and Constitutional Government* (Baltimore: Johns Hopkins University Press, 1999).

40 George C. Edwards III, "Campaigning Is Not Governing: Bill Clinton's Rhetorical Presidency," in *The Clinton Legacy*, ed. Colin Campbell and Bert A. Rockman (New York: Chatham House, 2000), 34. This argument is more fully developed in George C. Edwards III, *At the Margins: Presidential Leadership of Congress* (New Haven: Yale University Press, 1989).

41 Richard Neustadt, *Presidential Power* (1960; New York: Wiley, 1990); Erwin C. Hargrove, *Presidential Leadership: Personality and Style* (New York: Macmillan,

1966); James David Barber, *The Presidential Character* (Englewood Cliffs, N.J.: Prentice-Hall, 1977); Fred I. Greenstein, *The Presidential Difference: Leadership Style from F.D.R. to George W. Bush* (Princeton: Princeton University Press, 2004).

42 Neustadt, *Presidential Power*; Edwards, *At the Margins*; George C. Edwards III, *On Deaf Ears: The Limits of the Bully Pulpit* (New Haven: Yale University Press, 2003); George C. Edwards III, *The Public Presidency: The Pursuit of Popular Support* (New York: St. Martin's Press, 1983); George C. Edwards III, *Presidential Influence in Congress* (San Francisco: W. H. Freeman, 1980).

43 Terry Moe, "Presidents, Institutions, and Theory," in *Researching the Presidency*, ed. George C. Edwards III, John H. Kessel, and Bert A. Rockman (Pittsburgh: University of Pittsburgh Press, 1993), 367. Also see Terry Moe, "The Politicized Presidency," in *The New Direction in American Politics*, ed. John E. Chubb and Paul E. Peterson (Washington, D.C.: Brookings Institution, 1985).

44 Nevertheless, I would point out that some of the best work on the presidency in recent years takes this approach, including William G. Howell, *Power without Persuasion: The Politics of Direct Presidential Action* (Princeton: Princeton University Press, 2003); Andrew Rudalevige, *Managing the President's Program: Presidential Leadership and Legislative Policy Formulation* (Princeton: Princeton University Press, 2002); Charles M. Cameron, *Veto Bargaining* (New York: Cambridge University Press, 2000).

45 Ginsberg and Shefter, "Presidency and Organization of Interests." Along these lines, see also Frymer and Skrentny, "Coalition-Building."

46 Milkis, *The President and the Parties*.

47 Skowronek, *The Politics Presidents Make*, 4, 9.

48 See also, for example, Adam D. Sheingate, "Political Entrepreneurship, Institutional Change, and American Political Development," *Studies in American Political Development* 17, no. 2 (2003); Keith E. Whittington and Daniel P. Carpenter, "Executive Power in American Institutional Development," *Perspectives on Politics* 1, no. 3 (2003); and James, *Presidents, Parties, and the State*.

49 As we will see, Richard Nixon is a case in point. He eschewed partisan rhetoric throughout most of his first term, and even spoke critically of his party in public. Relying on his public statements would provide us with a picture of Nixon as hostile toward his party; we might assume this hostility characterized all of his party interactions—but this would not be accurate. These statements did characterize some of his actions, but as I discuss in chapter 4, when we consult primary sources from the Nixon archives, it becomes clear that he also initiated a series of party-building programs to expand and develop the party's organization's reach. Nixon's envisioned "New Majority" was to be realized through a revitalized party apparatus. Were it not for Watergate, he might have succeeded. Nevertheless, by recycling conventional wisdom and relying only on secondary sources, previous scholarship has missed out on this aspect of Nixon's party relations.

50 See, for example, Daniel Carpenter, *The Forging of Bureaucratic Autonomy* (Princeton: Princeton University Press, 2001); Steven M. Teles, *The Rise of the Conservative Legal Movement: The Battle for Control of the Law* (Princeton: Princeton University Press, 2008); Richard Franklin Bensel, *The American Ballot Box in the Mid-nineteenth Century* (New York: Cambridge University Press, 2004); Kathleen Thelen, *How Institutions Evolve: The Political Economy of Skills in Germany, Britain, the United States, and Japan* (New York: Cambridge University Press, 2004).

51 These assumptions have been productively used for decades, particularly in comparative analyses and in studies of congressional elections. See, for example, Downs, *Economic Theory of Democracy*; Aldrich, *Why Parties?*; Gary W. Cox, *Making Votes Count: Strategic Coordination in the World's Electoral Systems* (New York: Cambridge University Press, 1997); V. O. Key, *Politics, Parties, and Pressure Groups*, 5th ed. (New York: Crowell, 1964); also see the "textbook" literature on parties, for example, Frank J. Sorauf, *Party Politics in America*, 4th ed. (Boston: Little, Brown, 1980); Marjorie Randon Hershey and Paul Allen Beck, *Party Politics in America*, 10th ed. (New York: Longman, 2003).

52 On party systems, see for example, Richard P. McCormick, *The Second American Party System: Party Formation in the Jacksonian Era* (Chapel Hill: University of North Carolina Press, 1966); Walter Dean Burnham, "Party Systems and the Political Process," in Chambers and Burnham, *The American Party Systems*. On organizational isomorphism, see Paul J. DiMaggio and Walter W. Powell, "The Iron Cage Revisited: Institutional Isomorphism and Collective Rationality in Organizational Fields," *American Sociological Review* 48, no. 2 (1983).

53 This is the conventional view, and the one most prominently advanced by Neustadt, *Presidential Power*; Hargrove, *Presidential Leadership*; Barber, *The Presidential Character*; Greenstein, *The Presidential Difference*.

54 Kernell, *Going Public*.

55 Ceaser, *Presidential Selection*; Alexander Heard and Michael Nelson, *Presidential Selection* (Durham, N.C.: Duke University Press, 1987).

56 Specifically, the McGovern-Fraser reforms of 1972 and the Federal Election Campaign Act (FECA) Amendments of 1974 and 1979.

57 Theodore Lowi suggests that this tendency began with Eisenhower, culminated with Nixon's CREEP organization, and was "validated by imitation by both parties after 1972." Lowi, *The Personal President*, 79.

58 Where concrete evidence exists of either constructive or nonconstructive presidential behavior, it is classified as party building or party predation, respectively. Decision rules and other methodological issues are elaborated in the appendix.

2 | A Theory of Presidential Party Building

1 For example, when George H. W. Bush took office in 1989, Republican presidents had occupied the White House for sixteen out of the previous twenty years: yet he and his team still viewed the Republican Party as the minority party. His chief political advisor declared: "With George Bush leading our party ... we are at last prepared to break out of 50 years of minority status ... we seek to broaden our party's base, to strengthen it at every level, and to be the party of all." The "one overriding goal for our party [is] to achieve majority status by the year 2000" (Lee Atwater, "A Grand New Beginning," *First Monday* [Republican National Committee], Winter 1989, 2). Likewise, until the 1994 elections, the Clinton team viewed their party as the entrenched majority, albeit an increasingly vulnerable one: "After forty years of dominating Congress, our party had become a complacent feudal kingdom no longer bound by fervent belief or fear of the king. ... Our majority was more a tactical alliance of autonomous factions than a political movement based on shared values and a coherent governing philosophy." George Stephanopoulos, *All Too Human: A Political Education* (Boston: Little, Brown, 1999), 289.

2 While the structure of the American political system makes the terms "majority party" and "minority party" deceptive and even counterproductive in most instances, these terms have proven to be quite useful in reference to actors' *perceptions* of competitive imbalances between the parties and the effects these perceptions have on political behavior. From Anthony Downs' model of competitive two-party politics to Scott James' "party system perspective" on the different incentives and behaviors adhering to different political contexts, the terms have given us theoretical leverage on questions of great political significance. In this spirit, I am less concerned with which party is, in fact, the "majority" or "minority" party than with how each party's competitive standing is perceived by the president and how he behaves in consequence (further discussion below). Anthony Downs, *An Economic Theory of Democracy* (New York: Harper, 1957); Scott C. James, *Presidents, Parties, and the State* (New York: Cambridge University Press, 2000).

3 Federalist 72, in *The Federalist*, Modern Library College Edition (New York: Random House. 1937).

4 David R. Mayhew, *Divided We Govern: Party Control, Lawmaking, and Investigations, 1946–1990* (New Haven: Yale University Press, 1991); Cameron, *Veto Bargaining*, 176. Also see Richard Steven Conley, *The Presidency, Congress, and Divided Government: A Postwar Assessment* (College Station: Texas A & M University Press, 2003).

5 Stephen P. Nicholson, Gary M. Segura, and Nathan D. Woods, "Presidential Approval and the Mixed Blessing of Divided Government," *Journal of Politics* 64, no. 3 (2002): 717. Howell, *Power without Persuasion*, chap. 4, p. 85. Also see David E. Lewis, *Presidents and the Politics of Agency Design: Political Insulation in the United States Government Bureaucracy, 1946–1997* (Stanford, Calif.: Stanford University Press, 2003).

6 Indeed, Hamilton's point was that energy in the executive is dependent upon the president's expectations regarding the durability of his initiatives. A president would not pursue "extensive and arduous enterprises for the public benefit" if he "foresaw that he must quit the scene before he could accomplish the work, and must commit that, together with his own reputation, to hands which might be unequal or unfriendly to the task." *The Federalist*, No. 72.

7 "Remarks to New Members of the Republican Party," June 26, 1989, *PPP.* Also see "Lee Atwater," *First Monday*, Winter 1989, 4–6.

8 Andrew Kohut and Carroll Doherty, "Permanent Republican Majority? Think Again," *Washington Post*, August 19, 2007; Anne E. Kornblut and Michael D. Shear, "'Architect' Envisioned GOP Supremacy," *Washington Post*, August 14, 2007.

9 John Aldrich suggests that the political parties have persisted over time, perhaps against the odds, because "their existence creates incentives for their use." "It is to parties that politicians often turn, because of their durability as institutionalized solutions, because of the need to orchestrate large and diverse groups of people to form winning majorities, and because often more can be won through parties." Aldrich, *Why Parties?* 24, 26.

10 "Memorandum for John Mitchell from the President," June 6, 1972, H. R. Haldeman: HRH 1972 Memoranda from the President, Box 8, NLYL.

11 Kenneth A. Shepsle, "Losers in Politics (and How They Sometimes Become Winners): William Riker's Heresthetic," *Perspectives on Politics* 1, no. 2 (2003): 310.

12 This is characteristic of what Adam Sheingate in "Political Entrepreneurship" describes as political entrepreneurship in institutional settings.

13 Neustadt, *Presidential Power*, 4.

14 Nicholas Lemann, "The Controller," *New Yorker*, May 12, 2003; Edward Gillespie, *Winning Right: Campaign Politics and Conservative Policies* (New York: Threshold Editions, 2006); Green, "The Rove Presidency."

15 A similar argument is found in Aldrich, *Why Parties?* 24.

16 On the efforts of Democratic party chairmen during "out-party" periods, see Klinkner, *The Losing Parties*.

17 Douglas W. Jaenicke, "The Jacksonian Integration of Parties into the Constitutional System," *Political Science Quarterly* 101, no. 1 (1986); Jo Freeman, "The Political Culture of the Democratic and Republican Parties," *Political Science Quarterly* 101, no. 3 (1986); Lawrence Frederick Kohl, *The Politics of Individualism: Parties and the American Character in the Jacksonian Era* (New York: Oxford University Press, 1989); John Gerring, *Party Ideologies in America, 1828–1996* (New York: Cambridge University Press, 1998); Cornelius P. Cotter, James L. Gibson, John F. Bibby, and Robert Huckshorn, *Party Organizations in American Politics* (New York: Praeger, 1984); David R. Mayhew, *Placing Parties in American Politics: Organization, Electoral Settings, and Government Activity in the Twentieth Century* (Princeton: Princeton University Press, 1986), 324–32; Klinkner, *The Losing Parties*; Hugh A. Bone, *Party Committees and National Politics* (Seattle: University of Washington Press, 1958); David Nexon, "Asymmetry in the Political System: Occasional Activists in the Republican and Democratic Parties, 1956–1964," *American Political Science Review* 65, no. 3 (1971); Christopher Bruzios, "Democratic and Republican Party Activists and Followers: Interparty and Intraparty Differences," *Polity* 22, no. 4 (1990); Jonathan Bernstein, Rebecca E. Bromley, and Krystle T. Meyer, "Republicans and Golf, Democrats and Outkast: Or, Party Political Culture from the Top Down," *The Forum*, 4, no. 3 (2006).

18 William G. Mayer, *The Divided Democrats: Ideological Unity, Party Reform, and Presidential Elections* (Boulder, Colo.: Westview Press, 1996); William G. Mayer, *In Pursuit of the White House 2000: How We Choose Our Presidential Nominees* (New York: Chatham House, 2000); D. Jason Berggren, "Two Parties, Two Types of Nominees, Two Paths to Winning a Presidential Nomination, 1972–2004," *Presidential Studies Quarterly* 37, no. 2 (2007).

19 For an explanation and critique of these models, see Charles E. Walcott and Karen M. Hult, "White House Structure and Decision Making: Elaborating the Standard Model," *Presidential Studies Quarterly* 35, no. 2 (2005); Karen M. Hult and Charles E. Walcott, *Empowering the White House: Governance under Nixon, Ford, and Carter* (Lawrence: University Press of Kansas, 2004); Charles E. Walcott and Karen M. Hult, *Governing the White House: From Hoover through LBJ* (Lawrence: University Press of Kansas, 1995).

20 See, for example, the comparison in Barbara Sinclair, "Transformational Leader or Faithful Agent? Principal-Agent Theory and House Majority Party Leadership," *Legislative Studies Quarterly* 24, no. 3 (1999).

21 Gerring, *Party Ideologies in America*; Nexon, "Asymmetry in Political System"; Bruzios, "Democratic and Republican Party Activists."

22 A case could be made that presidential candidates found it advantageous to run as party "outsiders" well before 1972: JFK and Eisenhower made precisely that case in 1960 and 1952, respectively.

23 A most-likely case is "a case that is strongly expected to conform to the prediction of a particular theory. If the case does not meet this expectation, there is a basis for revising or rejecting the theory." Henry E. Brady and David Collier, *Rethinking Social Inquiry: Diverse Tools, Shared Standards* (Lanham, Md.: Rowman and Littlefield, 2004), 297.

24 Klinkner, *The Losing Parties*, on Strauss: 125–29; on Manatt: 171–75; on Kirk and Brown: 181–91.

25 Ibid. Klinkner shows that these organizational efforts were usually stymied by a lack of resources and were generally subordinated to alternative priorities; nevertheless, the inherent characteristics of the Democratic Party clearly did not deter these chairmen from undertaking the effort.

26 Jaenicke, "Jacksonian Integration"; Michael Wallace, "Changing Concepts of Party in the United States: New York, 1815–1828," *American Historical Review* 74, no. 2 (1968); Kohl, *Politics of Individualism.*

27 Milkis, in particular, demonstrates that FDR sought to remake the Democratic Party into a more national, programmatic party that would carry forward the ideological purposes of the New Deal. While FDR's vision would ultimately require the subordination of party to the presidency, Milkis writes, his party-building project involved the creation of new DNC divisions dedicated to reaching out to blacks, women, and labor; the development of new fundraising methods and sources; the strategic use of patronage to foster compliance among local party leaders; and an effort to "make use of the [1936] campaign and his great personal popularity in order to strengthen the party" (69). Savage adds to this list FDR's cultivation of machine bosses and Young Democratic Clubs. Both authors suggest that Roosevelt's party-building efforts were primarily concentrated in his first term and were geared toward expanding and solidifying his party's new majorities. This would seem to be consistent with our expectations under the "competitive standing" framework. Sidney M. Milkis, *The President and the Parties* (New York: Oxford University Press, 1993), esp. 62–74, quote on 74; Sean J. Savage, *Roosevelt, the Party Leader, 1932–1945* (Lexington, Ky.: University Press of Kentucky, 1991), esp. 17–102.

28 Cited in Sean Savage, "FDR's Party Leadership: Origins and Legacy," in *FDR and the Modern Presidency: Leadership and Legacy*, ed. Mark J. Rozell and William D. Pederson (Westport, Conn.: Praeger, 1997).

29 John M. Redding, *Inside the Democratic Party* (Indianapolis: Bobbs-Merrill, 1958), esp. 29–60, 86–87; Sean J. Savage, *Truman and the Democratic Party* (Lexington: University Press of Kentucky, 1997), chap. 3.

30 Ralph Morris Goldman, *The National Party Chairmen and Committees: Factionalism at the Top* (Armonk, N.Y.: M.E. Sharpe, 1990), 371, 383, 387. Also see Donald J. Lisio, *Hoover, Blacks, & Lily-Whites: A Study of Southern Strategies*, The Fred W. Morrison Series in Southern Studies (Chapel Hill: University of North Carolina Press, 1985), 159–165. Lisio notes that if Hoover wanted to be successful with his agenda, "obviously the practical politics of party building had to be taken seriously. Unfortunately Hoover had little or no sympathy for politics or politicians. He insisted that parties were built on principles by principled men who put public service and community welfare above sordid partisanship.... Hoover's high standards for public service and the imperatives of local southern politics strained or destroyed party unity" (160–61). On the more general Republican approach to the South, V.O. Key writes: "The national organization has been no more concerned than the patronage-minded state leader in building up the party in

the South. It encourages the state leaders to devote their energies to raising funds to be spent in doubtful states. It does not treat the South as a foreign mission which, of necessity, must be subsidized if converts are to be made. Instead it milks the missionaries to help maintain the mother church." No party building is undertaken "even when the Republican candidate has a fighting chance to win or when the Republican organization could gain strength by sustained effort over a period of years. The Republican national committee is so parsimonious that it does not always provide southern organizations with as much literature as they could use during a presidential campaign." V.O. Key, *Southern Politics in State and Nation* (Knoxville: The University of Tennessee Press, 1996, 1949), 296. Also see Vincent P. de Santis, "Republican Efforts to 'Crack' the Democratic South," *The Review of Politics* 14, 2: 244-264.

31 As we will see later, the difference between the parties' financial conditions has been as much a consequence as a cause of the Republicans' persistent investments and reinvestments in their party's fund-raising capacities.

32 Bai, "The Inside Agitator"; and see chapter 11.

33 See, for example, Key, *Politics, Parties, and Pressure Groups*.

34 Mayhew, *Placing Parties*, 325.

35 Ibid.; Raymond E. Wolfinger, "Why Political Machines Have Not Withered Away and Other Revisionist Thoughts," *Journal of Politics* 34, no. 2 (1972); also J. David Greenstone, *Labor in American Politics* (New York: Knopf, 1969).

36 For example, see James Q. Wilson, *The Amateur Democrat: Club Politics in Three Cities* (Chicago: University of Chicago Press, 1962); Bruce Miroff, *The Liberals' Moment: The McGovern Insurgency and the Identity Crisis of the Democratic Party* (Lawrence: University Press of Kansas, 2007); Fisher, *Activism, Inc.*

37 Robin Kolodny, *Pursuing Majorities: Congressional Campaign Committees in American Politics* (Norman: University of Oklahoma Press, 1998).

38 Key, *Southern Politics*, 387.

39 Byron E. Shafer, "Partisan Elites, 1946–1996," in *Partisan Approaches to Postwar American Politics*, ed. Byron E. Shafer (New York: Chatham House, 1998), 89.

40 Ibid., 114–27.

41 See, for example, Taylor E. Dark, *The Unions and the Democrats: An Enduring Alliance* (Ithaca, N.Y.: ILR Press, 1999), chap. 5.

42 Mayhew, *Placing Parties*; David Lublin, *The Republican South: Democratization and Partisan Change* (Princeton: Princeton University Press, 2004); Michael Goldfield, *The Decline of Organized Labor in the United States* (Chicago: University of Chicago Press, 1987).

43 What's more, while organized labor was a powerful force on behalf of the Democratic Party in many states, especially in the Northeast and Midwest, it was significantly less so in more rural southern and western states (Key, *Southern Politics*, 100, 480, 673–74). Yet Democratic presidents did not undertake party building in areas where organized labor was not a strong presence, either.

44 David J. Sousa, "Organized Labor in the Electorate, 1960–1988," *Political Research Quarterly* 46, no. 4 (1993); Mayhew, *Placing Parties*, 227.

45 Dan Gilgoff, *The Jesus Machine: How James Dobson, Focus on the Family, and Evangelical America Are Winning the Culture War* (New York: St. Martin's Press, 2007), 63; Laurie Goodstein, "For a Trusty Voting Bloc, a Faith Shaken," *New York Times*, October 7, 2007.

46 Ibid., 188.

47 On "legitimation" explanations for institutional reproduction, see James Mahoney, "Path Dependence in Historical Sociology," *Theory and Society* 29, no. 4 (2000): 523–24.

48 Milkis, *The President and the Parties*; David Plotke, *Building a Democratic Political Order: Reshaping American Liberalism in the 1930s and 1940s* (New York: Cambridge University Press, 1996).

3 | Building a Modern Republican Party: Dwight D. Eisenhower

1 "President to Giniger," November 24, 1956, Modern Republicanism, Box 21, Whitman Name Series, DDEL.

2 Eisenhower seemed to help down-ballot Republican candidates at the state level as well, where the GOP took control of more state legislatures and governorships than at any time in the previous decade (though Democrats regained their edge in 1954).

3 See, for example, "Campaign Plan" 1952, 1952—Campaign and Election, Box 10, Robert Humphreys Papers, DDEL; "Hall to the President," November 10, 1953, RNC (1)–(5), Box 30, Whitman File, DDEL.

4 See, in particular, Goldman, *National Party Chairmen*, 499–507.

5 With the exception of Cornelius P. Cotter, "Eisenhower as Party Leader," *Political Science Quarterly* 98, no. 2 (1983).The most impressive revisionist scholarship on Eisenhower's leadership includes Stephen E. Ambrose, *Eisenhower*, vol. 2: *The President* (New York: Simon and Schuster, 1983); also Fred I. Greenstein, *The Hidden-Hand Presidency: Eisenhower as Leader* (New York: Basic Books, 1982); Robert Griffith, "Dwight D. Eisenhower and the Corporate Commonwealth," *American Historical Review* 87, no. 1 (1982); and Chester J. Pach and Elmo Richardson, *The Presidency of Dwight D. Eisenhower*, rev. ed. (Lawrence: University Press of Kansas, 1991).

6 Ralph Ketcham, *Presidents above Party* (Chapel Hill: University of North Carolina Press, 1987), 231, 234. Similarly, Eisenhower is classified as a "nonpartisan" president in Ralph M. Goldman, "The American President as Party Leader: A Synoptic History," in Harmel, *Presidents and Their Parties*, 21.

7 John F. Bibby and Robert J. Huckshorn, "The Republican Party in American Politics," in Fishel, *Parties and Elections*, 55; James L. Sundquist, *Dynamics of the Party System* (Washington, D.C.: Brookings Institution, 1983), 287.

8 Klinkner, *The Losing Parties*, 42.

9 Lowi, *The Personal President*, 74; for precisely the same sentiment, see Broder, *The Party's Over*, 7.

10 Pious, *The American Presidency*, 124.

11 Walter Lippmann, "Today and Tomorrow," *Washington Post*, November 6, 1952.

12 John A. Andrew, *The Other Side of the Sixties: Young Americans for Freedom and the Rise of Conservative Politics* (New Brunswick, N.J.: Rutgers University Press, 1997); Nicol C. Rae, *The Decline and Fall of the Liberal Republicans: From 1952 to the Present* (New York: Oxford University Press, 1989); David W. Reinhard, *The Republican Right since 1945* (Lexington: University Press of Kentucky, 1983).

13 David Hackett Fischer, *Historians' Fallacies: Toward a Logic of Historical Thought* (New York: Harper Torchbooks, 1970), chap. 6.

14 Jeff Broadwater, "President Eisenhower and the Historians: Is the General in Retreat?" *Canadian Review of American Studies* 22, no. 1 (1991).

15 Lewis L. Gould, *Grand Old Party: A History of the Republicans* (New York: Random House, 2003), 334.

16 Even among those who have reexamined Eisenhower's leadership most thoroughly, the constructive relationship Eisenhower established with his party organization has remained hidden because it has not been the primary object of investigation. Fred Greenstein's seminal work on Eisenhower's political style, for example, acknowledges Eisenhower's interest in strengthening the Republican Party organization, but gives this finding only the briefest of attention. It notes that Eisenhower had an interest in "building a stable Republican majority" and that he sought to bring "young, attractive leaders into the party—leaders who would modernize the party's organizational procedures as well as its policy stance" (52), but does not elaborate. And in a footnote, Greenstein acknowledges that one of Eisenhower's comments recorded in James Hagerty's diary "indicates deeper Eisenhower penetration in party affairs than is generally assumed" (*The Hidden-Hand Presidency*. 269 n. 148). An earlier article on the same subject elaborates only a little more: Greenstein notes that Eisenhower undertook "efforts to broaden, unify, strengthen, and modify the Republican Party" but "avoided publicizing the extent of his participation in party leadership." But the nature, extent, and implications of Eisenhower's efforts are not explored any further. Fred I. Greenstein, "Eisenhower as an Activist President: A Look at New Evidence," *Political Science Quarterly* 94, no. 4 (1979–80): 579. Cotter's study, "Eisenhower as Party Leader," is the sole exception.

17 "President to Phillips," June 5, 1953, *The Papers of Dwight David Eisenhower*, ed. Alfred D. Chandler Jr., 21 vols. (Baltimore: Johns Hopkins University Press, 1970–2001), 14:275–76. (Henceforth, *Eisenhower Papers*.)

18 "President to Hall," November 7, 1953, Hall, Leonard, Box 17, Whitman File, DDEL.

19 Ibid.

20 "President to Humphrey, et. al.," November 23, 1953, RNC, Box 30, Whitman File, DDEL.

21 See "President to Robinson," November 19, 1953, *Eisenhower Papers*, 14:680.

22 Ibid.

23 "President to Humphrey, et. al.," November 23, 1953, RNC, Box 30, Whitman File, DDEL.

24 See, for example, "To Diary," March 5, 1954, in *Eisenhower Papers*, 15:933 n. 8, 998 n. 4.

25 "Executive Session," 1955-RNC–Campaign School, Box 13, Humphreys Papers, DDEL.

26 "Humphrey to Adams," May 18, 1955, RNC April–June '55, Box 466, White House Central Files (WHCF) General File, DDEL.

27 "Republican National Committee's Campaign School program," September 7–10, 1955, Box 13, 1955-RNC–Campaign School, Humphreys Papers, DDEL.

28 Allen Drury, "G.O.P. Leaders Set Out to Win Friends in '56," *New York Times*, September 11, 1955.

29 "Executive Session," 1955-RNC–Campaign School, Box 13, Humphreys Papers, DDEL.

30 "Hall to the President," September 15, 1955, Hall, Leonard, Box 17, Whitman File, DDEL.

31 Russell Baker, "President Warns His Party to Shun One-Man Outlook," *New York Times*, September 11, 1955.

32 Ibid.; also see 1955-RNC–Campaign School, Box 13, Humphreys Papers, DDEL.

33 Ibid.

34 "President to Giniger," November 24, 1956, Modern Republicanism, Box 21, Whitman Name Series, DDEL; see also "Alcorn to Herman," September 3, 1957, Folder 5, Box 5, MAP; "Hall to Cushing," September 6, 1955, Campaign 1954–7, Box 6, RNC Office of the Chairman Records, DDEL.

35 "RNC's Campaign School," June 18–20, 1958, 1958-RNC–Campaign School, Box 13, Humphreys Papers, DDEL.

36 Press Release, June 1, 1958, Folder 33, Box 3, MAP.

37 "How to Overcome a Democrat Majority," June 18–20, 1958, 1958-RNC–Campaign School, Box 13, Humphreys Papers, DDEL.

38 Lester Tanzer, "GOPers Go to School to Learn New Tricks in an Ancient Trade," *Wall Street Journal*, January 20, 1958.

39 RNC Executive Session Transcript, December 11, 1959, Folder 5, Box 36, TMP.

40 Press Release, Folder 6, Box 41, TMP.

41 "Finance Committee Notes," 2, 1958, Folder 17, Box 2, MAP.

42 "President to Dart," November 1, 1958, in *Eisenhower Papers*, 19:1181; also see Ann Whitman Memorandums, October 6, 1958 and November 2, 1958, on Eisenhower's meetings with financiers in Chicago and New York.

43 See, for example, Wayne Phillips, "T.V. Parties Friday to Aid G.O.P. Fund," *New York Times*, January 15, 1956; W. H. Lawrence, "Party Campaign Funds Climbing to a New High," *New York Times*, January 29, 1956. Also see "Republicans Plan $100-a-Seat Fete," *New York Times*, November 16, 1955; and "100 Dinners on Jan. 20 Will Salute Eisenhower," *New York Times*, September 19, 1955.

44 See, for example, "G.O.P. Dinners Pushed," *New York Times*, November 27, 1957; "President Opens G.O.P. Vote Drive in Talk Tonight," *New York Times*, January 20, 1958; "Bay State's Four-Way GOP Handshake," *Christian Science Monitor*, January 21, 1958; "80 G.O.P. Dinners Set Wednesday," *New York Times*, January 24, 1960.

45 "From Meade Alcorn," July 19, 1957, Folder 74, Box 2, MAP.

46 "United Republican Neighbor-to-Neighbor Campaign," July 19, 1957, Folder 74, Box 2, MAP.

47 Ibid.

48 Press Release, September 5, 1957, Folder 18, Box 4, MAP.

49 "To Fellow Republican from the President," July 1957, United Republican Neighbor-to-Neighbor Campaign, Box 718, WHCF Official File, DDEL.

50 "Kirlin to Alcorn," Report, December 13, 1958, Folder 46, Box 5, MAP.

51 Stephen E. Ambrose, *Nixon: The Education of a Politician, 1913-1962* (New York: Simon and Schuster, 1987), 334–35.

52 Pach and Richardson, *Presidency of Eisenhower*, 70.

53 "President to Craig," March 26, 1954, *Eisenhower Papers*, 15:980–81.

54 See, for example, Greenstein, *The Hidden-Hand Presidency*, 155–227.

55 "President to Hauge," September 30, 1954, *Eisenhower Papers*, 15:1322.

56 Ambrose, *Eisenhower*, 218; see "Straining for Party Gain," *Washington Post*, November 1, 1954.

57 "Text of President Eisenhower's Talk Urging Election of Republican Congress," *New York Times*, October 29, 1954; see also "To Clifford Roberts," October 7, 1954, in *Eisenhower Papers*, 15:1335–36; and "To Clifford Roberts," October 30, 1954, in *Eisenhower Papers*, 15:1368–69.

58 See *Eisenhower Papers*, 15:1336 n. 2.

59 "Diary," November 20, 1954, *Eisenhower Papers*, 15:1402–5.

60 James C. Hagerty and Robert H. Ferrell, *The Diary of James C. Hagerty: Eisenhower in Mid-Course, 1954–1955* (Bloomington: Indiana University Press, 1983), December 7, 1954; Ambrose, *Eisenhower*, 220–21.

61 "To Paul Hoffman from Sherman Adams," November 22, 1954, RNC, Box 709, WHCF Official File, DDEL.

62 Ibid., and see "To Paul Gray Hoffman," November 23, 1954, in *Eisenhower Papers*, 15:1411–12.

63 "President to Adams," December 4, 1954, Adams, Sherman (5), Box 1, Whitman File, DDEL.

64 Ibid.

65 Ibid.

66 Walter Williams and Mary Lord Oral Histories, DDEL. Bone, *Party Committees*, 29–31.

67 "Paul Hoffman, December 1, 1954," Whitman notes, in *President Dwight D. Eisenhower's Office Files, 1953–1961, Part I: Eisenhower Administration Series, 64 Microfilm Reels*, ed. Robert E. Lester (Bethesda, Md.: University Publications of America, 1990). Henceforth *Office Files*.

68 "Willis to Adams," February 10, 1955, RNC, Box 709, WHCF Confidential File, Subject, DDEL.

69 "Willis to Adams," March 4, 1955, RNC, Box 709, WHCF Confidential File, Subject, DDEL.

70 "Willis to Adams," May 20, 1955, RNC April–June '55, Box 466, WHCF General File, DDEL.

71 Press Release, Citizens 1955, Box 3, Whitman Campaign Series, DDEL.

72 Ibid.

73 "Division: Enrollment of New Republicans," Citizens 1955, Box 3, Whitman Campaign Series, DDEL.

74 Ibid.

75 "President to Flenniken," December 3, 1953 in *Eisenhower Papers*, 15:727–28.

76 Ibid., and also see, for example, "President to Alcorn," March 4, 1958, in *Eisenhower Papers*, 19:751–52; see also "President to Hall," April 26, 1956, in *Eisenhower Papers*, 16:2137.

77 "President to Alcorn," March 4, 1958, in *Eisenhower Papers*, 19:751–52; see also "President to Alcorn," April 1, 1959, in *Eisenhower Papers*, 20:1436. Eisenhower's efforts to invigorate the party through the recruitment of young Republicans were many. For a sampling, see "President to Alcorn," March 4, 1958, *Office Files*; "President to McKay," June 4, 1956, in *Eisenhower Papers*, 17:2180–81; "President to Summerfield," June 13, 1957, in *Eisenhower Papers*, 18:258–59; "President to Whitney," March 12, 1956, in *Eisenhower Papers*, 16:2063–64.

78 See "President to Lampe and Fort," draft, November 24, 1958, *Office Files*.

79 "President to Lampe and Fort," in *Eisenhower Papers*, 19:1217–18. See a similar sentiment expressed to Lucius Clay, noted in "Diary, secret," November 20, 1954, *Eisenhower Papers*, 15:1402–5.

80 "Diary, secret," October 8, 1953, *Eisenhower Papers*, 14:568.

81 Sherman Adams, *Firsthand Report: The Story of the Eisenhower Administration* (New York: Harper, 1961), 28–29.

82 "Memorandum for the Record," November 20, 1954, *Office Files*; also in Dwight D. Eisenhower and Robert H. Ferrell, *The Eisenhower Diaries* (New York: Norton, 1981), November 20, 1954; also in "Diary, secret," November 20, 1954, *Eisenhower Papers*, 15:1402–5.

83 "President to Alcorn," August 30, 1957, in *Eisenhower Papers*, 18:396–97.

84 "President to Jones," November 25, 1958, Republican Party, Box 708, WHCF Official File, DDEL.

85 William F. Buckley Jr., "Reflections on Election Eve," *National Review*, November 3, 1956, 7.

86 Andrew, *Other Side of Sixties*, 15–16.

87 "What If He Doesn't Run?" *National Review*, June 27, 1956, 5.

88 George H. Nash, *The Conservative Intellectual Movement in America since 1945* (New York: Basic Books, 1976); Rick Perlstein, *Before the Storm: Barry Goldwater and the Unmaking of the American Consensus* (New York: Hill and Wang, 2001); Niels Bjerre-Poulsen, *Right Face: Organizing the American Conservative Movement, 1945–65* (Copenhagen: Museum Tusculanum, 2002).

89 Cited in Reinhard, *Republican Right since 1945*, 133–35.

90 Ibid., 138.

91 Ibid., 133. "The way we did it," Meade Alcorn explained, "was to ask them to do a lot of things that they hadn't been asked to do before, and when they either didn't do them or said that they were not in a position to do them, it ultimately brought about the resignations or retirements of quite a few of them. And as a consequence, we got the average age on the National Committee rather dramatically reduced." Meade Alcorn Oral History, DDEL, 86.

92 Paul Hoffman estimated in 1956 that "forty-two new state chairmen of the Republican Party are new, solid, Eisenhower men. Eighty-five of the 146 members of the National Committee of 1952 have been replaced by new faces. In state after state, the young men and women we first brought into politics through the Citizens for Eisenhower movement have begun to occupy commanding posts in the regular structure." Hoffman, "How Eisenhower Saved the Republican Party," *Collier's Magazine*, October 26, 1956.

93 Cotter, "Eisenhower as Party Leader," 273–74.

94 "President to Hazlett," November 2, 1956, in *Eisenhower Papers*, 17:2353–55.

95 "President to Paley," November 14, 1956, in *Eisenhower Papers*, 17:2392–93.

96 "President to Landers," November 23, 1956, Modern Republicanism, Box 21, Whitman Name Series, DDEL.

97 "Regional Conference Plan," March 11, 1957, 1954–1959-RNC–Campaign Director, Box 12, Humphreys Papers, DDEL.

98 Ibid.

99 "President to Alcorn," February 27, 1957, *Office Files*.

100 Ibid.

101 Godfrey Sperling Jr., "The Real Eisenhower Plan," *Christian Science Monitor*, May 21, 1957.

102 "Alcorn Sees Good Coming from GOP 'Differences,'" *Washington Post*, June 3, 1957.

103 Robert C. Albright, "Goldwater Hits 'Modern' GOP," *Washington Post*, April 9, 1957.

104 Lee Edwards, *The Conservative Revolution: The Movement That Remade America* (New York: Free Press, 1999), 84.

105 Reinhard, *Republican Right since 1945*, 140–42.

106 "Remarks by Alcorn, Republican National Conference: June 7, 1957, Washington, D.C.," *PRP*.

107 Godfrey Sperling Jr., "GOP Rift 'Approved,'" *Christian Science Monitor*, May 18, 1957. See also "Address by the President, Republican National Conference, June 7, 1957, Washington, D.C.," *PRP*.

108 See "Alcorn to the President," March 13, 1959, Alcorn, H. Meade, Box 1, Whitman Administration Series, DDEL.

109 "Memorandum for the Record," December 6, 1958, Political Committee 1959 (1), Box 26, Whitman Name Series, DDEL.

110 Ibid.

111 Ibid.

112 Eisenhower personally telephoned Percy on January 13 to convey his desire that he assume the chairmanship of the new committee, which was set to launch in February 1959. See "President to Dart," January 19, 1959, in *Eisenhower Papers*, 19:1305. Also see "President to Roberts," December 19, 1958, Doc. no. 983, in *Eisenhower Papers*, vol. 17, esp. n. 5.

113 "Straight Telegram," January 21, 1959, Alcorn, H. Meade, Box 1, Whitman File, DDEL.

114 William M. Blair, "President Urged to Set Example for Active GOP," *New York Times*, January 23, 1959.

115 "President Tells GOP to Wake Up," *Los Angeles Times*, January 23, 1959.

116 See "Remarks by Alcorn," March 13, 1959, Alcorn, H. Meade, Box 1, Whitman Administration Series, DDEL.

117 "RNC Executive Committee, Executive Session," January 21, 1959, Des Moines, Iowa, *PRP*.

118 Press Release, Folder 6, Box 41, TMP; Edward T. Folliard, "GOP Seeks Philosophy Restatement," *Washington Post*, September 26, 1959.

119 Republican Committee on Program and Progress, *Decisions for a Better America* (Garden City, N.Y.: Doubleday, 1960).

120 "Excerpts from Remarks by Thruston Morton," May 1, 1959, Folder 6, Box 41, National Republican Committee Series, TMP.

121 Cited in Andrew, *Other Side of Sixties*, 37.

122 Ibid., 39.

123 "President to Percy," November 3, 1959, *Eisenhower Papers*, 20:1719–20.

124 Quoted in Andrew, *Other Side of Sixties*, 40.

125 Ibid., 41.

126 Ibid., 47.

127 Thelen, *How Institutions Evolve*, 36–37.

128 Gould, *Grand Old Party*, 167; see also Key, *Southern Politics*, 292–97; Vincent P. De Santis, *Republicans Face the Southern Question: The New Departure Years, 1877–1897* (Baltimore: Johns Hopkins Press, 1959).

129 Earl Black and Merle Black, *The Rise of Southern Republicans* (Cambridge: Belknap Press of Harvard University Press, 2002), 209, 257; Numan V. Bartley, *The New South, 1945–1980* (Baton Rouge: Louisiana State University Press, 1995), 101–2.

130 "Committee on the South," Southern Situation 1953–54, Box 166, RNC Office of the Chairman Records, DDEL.

131 Anderson served as Eisenhower's deputy secretary of defense and then later Treasury secretary. See Ambrose, *Eisenhower*, 222; and *Eisenhower Papers*, 14:229 n. 16 for background.

132 "Committee on the South"; see also "Wisdom to Hall," September 26, 1953, Southern Situation 1953–54, Box 166, RNC Office of the Chairman Records, DDEL.

133 "To Herbert Brownell, Jr., Personal and Confidential," March 13, 1953, in *Eisenhower Papers*, 14:97.

134 Ibid.; "Committee on the South"; "Memorandum," 1954–1959-RNC–Campaign Director (1)–(9), Box 12, Humphreys Papers, DDEL. Wisdom wrote, "We cannot muff this opportunity by making it too attractive for Eisenhower supporters to remain Democrats; yet, we are in a transitional period, where we must exploit support from Republican-minded Democrats. It is a tight-rope type of operation." See "Wisdom to Hall," September 26, 1953, Southern Situation 1953–54, Box 166, RNC Office of the Chairman Records, DDEL.

135 "McKillips to Jones," October 19, 1953, and "Willis to Brownell," October 27, 1953, in Republican Party, Box 708, WHCF Official File, DDEL.

136 "Memorandum for the Record," August 19, 1953, RNC (1)–(5) [1953–57], Box 30, Whitman File, DDEL.

137 "Report on the Southern Committee Meeting," and "McKillips to Chairman," November 24, 1953, in Southern Situation 1953–54, Box 166, RNC Office of the Chairman Records, DDEL.

138 See "Diary," July 24, 1953, in *Eisenhower Papers*, 14:415; see also "President to Byrnes," July 22, 1953 in *Eisenhower Papers*, 14:408–9.

139 Ibid.

140 Karl A. Lamb, "Under One Roof: Barry Goldwater's Campaign Staff," in *Republican Politics: The 1964 Campaign and Its Aftermath for the Party*, ed. Bernard Cosman and Robert J. Huckshorn (New York: Frederick A. Praeger, 1968), 14–15. See also Alan L. Otten, "GOP in Dixie," *Wall Street Journal*, October 1, 1958.

141 "GOP in Dixie," *Evening Star*, May 13, 1957, in Misc., 1957, Box 7, MAP.

142 Otten, "GOP in Dixie."

143 Meade Alcorn Oral History, DDEL, 89–90.

144 Ibid., 91.

145 "Alcorn to Bermingham," July 26, 1957, Correspondence: 1957, Box 1, MAP; and see, for example, "Potter to Alcorn and Alexander," July 23, 1957, in 1957 P-W, Box 5, MAP.

146 "RNC Budget and Expenses," Budget and Expenses of RNC Divisions, Box 2, MAP.

147 See, for example, "Potter to Alcorn and Alexander," July 23, 1957, in 1957 P-W, Box 5, MAP.

148 Meade Alcorn Oral History, DDEL, 92.

149 "GOP in Dixie," *Evening Star*, May 13, 1957, in Misc., 1957, Box 7, MAP.

150 "Potter's report," RNC Executive Committee, January 30, 1958, *PRP*.

151 Ibid.

152 Meade Alcorn Oral History, DDEL, 98.

153 Ibid.

154 Earl Mazo, "GOP in Dozen States Plans Southern Bloc," *Washington Post*, April 27, 1959; Staff Reporter, "Republicans Banking on Help from South," *Washington Post*, July 21, 1960; "Operation Dixie," *Wall Street Journal*, June 24, 1960.

155 Klinkner, *The Losing Parties*, 53–55.

156 Ibid.

157 Otten, "GOP in Dixie."

158 See also Perlstein, *Before the Storm*, 167–69.

159 Meade Alcorn Oral History, DDEL, 89.

160 Ibid., 98–99.

161 Ibid., 120; Hedrick Smith, "G.O.P. Is Attacked for Its Aid to Segregationists in the South," *New York Times*, November 26, 1962; Klinkner, *The Losing Parties.*

162 Ibid., 69.

163 Handwritten notes, 1952—Campaign and Election (1)–(4), Humphreys Papers, DDEL.

164 See, for example, "Hall to Adams," November 2, 1955, Staff Headquarters 1955-26, Box 103, RNC Office of Chairman Records, DDEL; "Republican National Finance Committee: Special Solicitation Drive," 8, 1958, Folder 8, Box 2; and "Memorandum," April 23, 1958, Folder 14, Box 5, MAP.

4 | Building the New Majority: Richard Nixon

1 Richard M. Nixon, *RN: The Memoirs of Richard Nixon* (New York: Grosset and Dunlap, 1978), 764; Nixon quoted in Monica Crowley, *Nixon Off the Record* (New York: Random House, 1996), cited in Robert Mason, "'I Was Going to Build a New Republican Party and a New Majority'": Richard Nixon as Party Leader, 1969–73," *Journal of American Studies* 39, no. 3 (2005).

2 In 1968, third-party candidate George Wallace garnered 14 percent of the popular vote; Nixon's share of the two-party vote was just over 50 percent.

3 "President's News Conference," December 10, 1970, *PPP*; see also "A Political Strategy for the '70s," HRH—1972 Political Strategy, Box 298, White House Special Files (WHSF)-Staff Member and Office Files (SMOF)-Haldeman, NLCP.

4 Klinkner, *The Losing Parties*, 41–87.

5 Ibid., 78–87; see also John F. Bibby and Robert J. Huckshorn, "Out-Party Strategy: Republican National Committee Rebuilding Politics, 1964–1968," in Cosman and Huckshorn, *Republican Politics.*

6 Milkis, *The President and the Parties*, 230; Lowi, *The Personal President*, 77.

7 David A. Crockett, *The Opposition Presidency: Leadership and the Constraints of History* (College Station: Texas A&M University Press, 2002), 162–63. For an extended discussion, see Theodore White, *The Making of the President, 1972* (New York: Atheneum, 1973).

8 Schlesinger, *The Imperial Presidency*, 254–55.

9 Walter Dean Burnham, "Rejoinder to 'Comments' by Philip Converse and Jerrold Rusk," *American Political Science Review* 68, no. 3 (1974): 1057. Political scientists Sidney M. Milkis and Jesse Rhodes similarly argue that the Republican Party organization "suffered at the hands" of Nixon because like other modern presidents, Nixon "considered partisanship an obstacle to [his] ambition." His self-serving "political goals," Paul Frymer and John Skrentny agree, "often worked to the detriment of the Republican party as an organization." Milkis and Rhodes, "George W. Bush," 465; Frymer and Skrentny, "Coalition-Building," 132–33 n 6.

10 In 1974, Republicans lost control of twelve state houses, sxi governorships, forty-three House seats, and four Senate seats.

11 See, for example, reports of 23 and 24 percent party ID reported by the Gallup poll in 1974: Christopher Lydon, "Nixon's 'New Majority' Seems Shattered for Him and the G.O.P.," *New York Times*, January 21, 1974; and R. W. Apple Jr., "Woman Elected Chairman of G.O.P. National Panel," *New York Times*, September 17, 1974.

12 Gould, *Grand Old Party*, 395.

13 With the exception of recent work by Robert Mason. See Robert Mason, *Richard Nixon and the Quest for a New Majority* (Chapel Hill: University of North Carolina Press, 2004); Mason, "I Was Going to Build."

14 Nixon, *RN*, 764.

15 Barber has described Nixon as a compulsive strategist, ever willing to recalibrate his political tactics in order to achieve his larger ends. *The Presidential Character*, 463.

16 Moe, "The Politicized Presidency."

17 David E. Rosenbaum, "Klein Says Nixon Will Help Party," *New York Times*, November 18, 1968.

18 James Boyd, "Harry Dent, the President's Political Coordinator," *New York Times*, February 1, 1970.

19 "Dent to the President," October 10, 1969, The President, Box 2, HDP; see also Boyd, "Harry Dent."

20 "Dent to Harlow," February 13, 1969, 1969 Southern GOP, Box 8, WHSF: Dent, NLCP.

21 "Dent to the President," March 5, 1969, and "Dent to Sears," March 19, 1969, 1969 Southern GOP, Box 8, WHSF: Dent, NLCP.

22 Ibid.

23 "Dent to the President," June 28, 1969, The President, Box 2, HDP.

24 Boyd, "Harry Dent."

25 Harry Dent speech at RNC Executive Session, June 28, 1969, *PRP*.

26 Ibid.

27 Ibid.

28 See, for example, "Dent to State Chairmen," August 11, 1969, 1969 Southern GOP, Box 8, WHSF: Dent, NLCP.

29 Harry Dent speech at RNC Executive Session, June 28, 1969, *PRP*; also see "Chapin to Dent," October 17, 1969, Memos to the President 1969, Box 2, WHSF: Dent, NLCP.

30 "Dent to the President," June 28, 1969, The President, Box 2, HDP; "Dent to Ehrlichman," July 26, 1969 to July 7, 1969, 6A-26-47, *PNWH*.

31 Ibid.

32 "Dent to the President," October 13, 1969, The President, Box 2, HDP.

33 Ibid.

34 Ibid.

35 "Dent to Cole," October 28, 1969, WHSF: Dent: 1969 Staff Memos, no. 1, Box 5, NLYL.

36 "Dent to Allison," November 4, 1969, Staff Memos, Box 3, HDP.

37 "Dent to the President," November 17, 1969, WHSF: Dent: 1969 Southern GOP, Box 5, NLYL.

38 "Nixon Aides, Dixie GOP to Confer," *Washington Post*, November 22, 1969.

39 "From the President," December 2, 1969, Folder 3, Box 202, RMP.

40 "Dent to the President," December 8, 1969, Memos to the President, Box 2, WHSF: Dent, NLCP.

41 See, for example, "Morton talking points," Folder 3, Box 202, RMP; "Dent to Allison," November 4, 1969, and "Dent to Cole," November 4, 1969, Staff Memos, February–December 1969, Box 3, HDP; "Dent to the President," June 11, 1971, Political Analyses—Rumsfeld, Dent, Box 302, SMOF-Haldeman, NLCP; "Limehouse to Colson," August 27, 1970, RNC, SMOF-Haldeman, NLCP.

42 "Brown to Dent," December 11, 1969, Memos to the President, SMOF-Dent, NLCP.

43 Ibid.

44 "Dent to Sears," February 10, 1969, 1969 Southern GOP, Box 8, WHSF: Dent, NLCP.

45 "Dent to Morton," April 1, 1969, Folder 6, Box 204, RMP.

46 "Dent to Morton," August 22, 1969, 1969 Southern GOP, Box 8, WHSF: Dent, NLCP.

47 "Nixon to Haldeman," December 30, 1969, WHSF-SMOF: H. R. Haldeman: HRH Memoranda G-M March 1970, Box 6, NLYL.

48 Frymer and Skrentny, "Coalition-Building," 139, 141.

49 "Haldeman Political Action Memo," August 7, 1972, Haldeman Action Memos 8, 1972, Box 7, NLYL.

50 "Parties-in-service" is from Aldrich, *Why Parties?* See also Xandra Kayden and Eddie Mahe, *The Party Goes On: The Persistence of the Two-Party System in the United States* (New York: Basic Books, 1985).

51 Goldman, *National Party Chairmen*, 566. See also Milkis, *The President and the Parties*; Cornelius Cotter and John F. Bibby, "Institutional Development of Parties and the Thesis of Party Decline," *Political Science Quarterly* 95, no. 1 (1980); Cornelius P. Cotter and Bernard C. Hennessy, *Politics without Power* (New York: Atherton Press, 1964).

52 "Meeting of the President with H. R. Haldeman, Max Fisher, and Henry Kissinger in Oval Office," January 30, 1969, 5-1-58, *PNWH*.

53 "Meeting of the President with H. R. Haldeman, Bryce Harlow, and John Ehrlichman in Oval Office," February 7, 1969, 5-1-77; "Haldeman to Ehrlichman," February 17, 1969, 4-35-50, *PNWH*.

54 "Remarks by Morton," RNC, April 14, 1969, RCBM Acceptance Speech, April 14, 1969, Box 198, RMP.

55 Ibid.

56 "Mission '70s Manual and Workbook," 1970, Folder 2, Box 441, RMP; "The Chairman's Report," 1969–1970, Folder 1, Box 217, RMP.

57 Norman C. Miller, "Rogers Morton, Nixon's Party Builder."

58 "Remarks by Rogers C. B. Morton on Mission 70's Party Organization Program," at RNC Executive Session, January 15, 1971, *PRP*.

59 Ibid.

60 Ibid.

61 "Notes," Southern Regional GOP Conf., Box 202, RMP.

62 "Chairman's Report, 1970," Box 262, RMP.

63 "Morton to the President," May 5, 1970, WHSF-SMOF: H. R. Haldeman: June 4, 1970 Political Meeting, Box 18, NLYL.

64 Ibid.

65 "Dent to Haldeman," May 8, 1970 (and attachments); "Dent to Haldeman," May 11, 1970, and "Higby to Haldeman," May 27, 1970, all in WHSF-SMOF: H. R. Haldeman: June 4, 1970 Political Meeting, Box 18, NLYL.

66 "Haldeman to Dent," October 31, 1969, WHSF-SMOF: H. R. Haldeman: Memos/Harry Dent, Box 6, NLYL; "Dent to Cole," October 28, 1969, WHSF-SMOF: Dent: 1969 Staff Memos, no. 1, Box 5, NLYL; "Brown to Dent," December 19, 1969, Catholics, Box 1, HDP.

67 "To Ehrlichman from Staff Secretary," December 2, 1969, 4-35-27, *PNWH*.

68 H. R. Haldeman, *The Haldeman Diaries: Inside the Nixon White House* (interactive multimedia) (Santa Monica, Calif.: Sony Imagesoft, 1994), December 2, 1969.

69 Ibid., November 7, 1970.

70 Ibid.

71 Ibid., November 8, 1970 and December 14, 1970.

72 R. W. Apple, "Dole Confirmed as Head of G.O.P.," *New York Times*, January 16, 1971.

73 Ibid.

74 "Haldeman Memo," January 23, 1971, 71-1-17:B11, *PNWH*.

75 "Evans to Bush," December 22, 1972, Papers from RNC 12, 1972–79, 1974 [1], Box 1, Personal Papers: RNC, GBL.

76 "Morton to Butterfield," May 5, 1969, 1969 RNC, Box 6, WHSF-SMOF: Dent, NLCP.

77 "Evans to Bush," December 22, 1972, Papers from RNC 12, 1972–79, 1974 [1], Box 1, Personal Papers: RNC, GBL.

78 Ibid., and David S. Broder and Don Oberdorfer, "A '72 Head Start for Nixon," *Washington Post*, June 13, 1971.

79 "Evans to Bush," December 22, 1972, Papers from RNC 12, 1972–79, 1974 [1], Box 1, Personal Papers: RNC, GBL.

80 Ibid.

81 David S. Broder, "GOP News Machine Grinds Away," *Washington Post*, August 19, 1972.

82 "Evans to Bush," December 22, 1972, Papers from RNC 12, 1972–79, 1974 [1], Box 1, Personal Papers: RNC, GBL.

83 "President to Haldeman," November 22, 1970, WHSF-SMOF: President's Office Files: Beginning November 22, 1970, Box 49, NLYL.

84 See "Remarks at a 'Salute to the President' Dinner in New York City," November 9, 1971, *PPP*.

85 "Evans to Mitchell," December 4, 1971, WHSF-SMOF: Staff Secretary: RNC Budget, Box 53, NLYL.

86 "Remarks at the Dedication of the Dwight D. Eisenhower National Republican Center," 15, 1971, *PPP*.

87 *Haldeman Diaries*, January 15–17, 1971.

88 "Memo from Andrews, John," February 19, 1971, 71-2-14:A12, *PNWH*.

89 "Meeting of the President with John Ehrlichman and Henry A. Kissinger," February 20, 1971, 3-27-F01, *PNWH*.

90 "Klein to President," March 4, 1971, 6A-125-17, *PNWH*.

91 "Colson to Haldeman," December 3, 1971, WHSF-SMOF: H. R. Haldeman: Dole Telecoms, Box 7, NLYL.

92 "Dent to the President," August 9, 1971, 71-8-8:A04, *PNWH*.

93 Warren Weaver Jr. "Nixon Recruiting G.O.P. Candidates for Senate Bids," *New York Times*, September 28, 1969; and Stuart H. Loory, "Nixon Starts Last Drive to Aid GOP Candidates," *Los Angeles Times*, October 28, 1970.

94 Ibid.

95 *Haldeman Diaries*, December 11, 1969; see also "Factual Situation," Folder 3, Box 25, HDP.

96 Timothy S. Robinson, "Ex-Nixon Aide Guilty in Fund-Raising Case," *Washington Post*, November 16, 1974; Timothy S. Robinson, "Dent Pleads Guilty on Funds," *Washington Post*, December 12, 1974; Morton Mintz, "Kalmbach Funds Inducement," *Washington Post*, July 20, 1974.

97 Robinson, "Ex-Nixon Aide Guilty."

98 Ibid.

99 Ibid.

100 Jack Anderson, "Loophole May Allow Fuel 'Shortages,'" *Washington Post*, November 22, 1974. See, for example, "Dent to Haldeman," June 18, 1970, HRH-Political-1970, Box 292, WHSF-SMOF-Haldeman, NLCP.

101 Robinson, "Dent Pleads Guilty."

102 See "RNC Finance Manual," 1970, Folder 4, Box 440, RMP; "Stans to Morton," February 2, 1970, Folder 12, Box 261, RMP; "Milbank to Jones," July 6, 1970, Folder 10, Box 258, RMP; "Chairman's Report," 1971, Folder 12, Box 261.

103 "Chairman's Report," 1971, Folder 12, Box 261; "Knox to Morton," March 17, 1970, Folder 14, Box 249, RMP; "Limehouse and Curry to Allison re: Campaign Management School," August 31, 1970, Folder 3, Box 262, RMP; "Mission 70's Training Session, Rochester, NY," September 30, 1970, Folder 8, Box 253, RMP; "Campaign Manager's Guideline," 1970, Folder 3, Box 262, RMP.

104 For a detailed contemporary history of the election campaign, see White, *Making of President, 1972*.

105 "Nixon to Mitchell," June 6, 1972, WHSF-SMOF: H. R. Haldeman: HRH 1972 Memoranda from the President, Box 8, NLYL.

106 White, *Making of President, 1972*, 278–79; Joel M. Gora, "Campaign Financing and the Nixon Presidency: The End of an Era," in Leon Friedman and William F. Levantrosser, *Richard M. Nixon: Politician, President, Administrator* (New York: Greenwood Press, 1991), 300–302.

107 R. W. Apple Jr., "Nixon Gives the G.O.P. Chairman More Authority," *New York Times*, March 27, 1973.

108 Broder and Oberdorfer, "Head Start for Nixon."

109 "Meeting of the President with H. R. Haldeman, Robert Finch, John Ehrlichman, John Mitchell, and Donald Rumsfeld at Key Biscayne," November 7, 1970, 5-35-53, *PNWH*.

110 On the pilot projects, see "DeBolt to Dent," February 24, 1972, March 10, 1972, May 1, 1972, August 24, 1972, Folder 1, Box 14, HDP.

111 "State Chairman's Organization Manual, Committee for the Re-Election of the President," Box 348, WHSF-SMOF-Haldeman, NLCP.

112 "DeBolt to Dent," October 6, 1972, Folder 2, Box 14, HDP.

113 Ibid.

114 *Haldeman Diaries*, October 10, 1972.

115 Lou Cannon, "Bush Remolds GOP Committee into Adjunct of White House," *Washington Post*, March 19, 1973.

116 *Haldeman Diaries*, November 8, 1972.

117 Ibid., April 22, 1972.

118 Ibid., September 18, 1972.

119 "Brock and Rietz to the President," October 30, 1972, WHSF-SMOF: H. R. Haldeman: The New Majority, Box 23, NLYL.

120 Ibid.

121 Ibid.

122 *Haldeman Diaries*, November 1, 1972.

123 Ibid., December 1, 1972; see also December 5, 1972.

124 Mason, *Richard Nixon*.

125 Conversation Number 819-2, December 11, 1972, Oval Office, Nixon White House Tapes: December 1972, NLYL.

126 "Meeting of the President with John Ehrlichman and George Bush at Camp David," November 20, 1972, 3-54-D13, *PNWH*.

127 Ibid.

128 *Haldeman Diaries*, November 20, 1972.

129 Conversation Number 34-35, December 11, 1972, Oval Office, Nixon White House Tapes: December 1972, NLYL.

130 "November 25, 1972," Diary Entry, Personal Notes: October 1973–August 1974 [1], Personal Papers: RNC, GBL.

131 "Timmons to the President," November 28, 1972, 72-11-26:A03, *PNWH*.

132 *Haldeman Diaries*, January 11, 1973; see also *Haldeman Diaries*, January 7, 1973; "Press Conference of Senator Bob Dole, Chairman, Republican National Committee," December 11, 1972, Papers from RNC 12, 1972–79, 1974 [1], Box 1, Personal Papers: RNC, GBL.

133 Conversation Number 822-06, December 13, 1972, Oval Office, Nixon White House Tapes: December 1972, NLYL.

134 "Remarks by Republican National Committee Chairman-Elect George Bush," January 19, 1973, *PRP*.

135 Ibid.

136 "Bush to the President," February 13, 1973, White House Memos—Outgoing, Box 1, Personal Papers: RNC, GBL.

137 "Handwritten notes, from the desk of George Bush," White House—Presidential Visits; also "Bush to the President," March 6, 1973, White House Memos—Outgoing, Box 1, Personal Papers: RNC, GBL.

138 "Parker to Bush," March 6, 1973, and "Parker to Bush," March 19, 1973, White House Memos—Outgoing, Box 1, Personal Papers: RNC, GBL.

139 See, for example, Bob Woodward and Carl Bernstein, "McCord Charges Backed," *Washington Post*, March 27, 1973.

140 "April 19, 1973," Diary Entry, Personal Notes: October 1973–August 1974 [1], Personal Papers: RNC, GBL.

141 "May 11, 1973," Diary Entry, Personal Notes: October 1973–August 1974 [1], Personal Papers: RNC, GBL.

142 Ibid.; and "May 21, 1973," Diary Entry, Personal Notes: October 1973–August 1974 [1], Personal Papers: RNC, GBL.

143 "Bush to Haig," May 29, 1973, White House Memos—Outgoing, Box 1, Personal Papers: RNC, GBL.

144 "Bush to the President," July 16, 1973–August 7, 1973, 6A-294-35, *PNWH*. See also "Bush to the President," July 23, 1973, White House Memos—Outgoing, Box 1, Personal Papers: RNC, GBL.

145 "Bush to Nixon," March 1, 1973, White House Memos—Outgoing, Box 1, Personal Papers: RNC, GBL.

146 "Bush to the President," March 6, 1973, and "Chairman to Key Staff and Department Heads," July 16, 1973, White House Memos—Outgoing, Box 1, Personal Papers: RNC, GBL.

147 "Evans to Bush," December 22, 1972, Papers from RNC 12, 1972–79, 1974 [1], Box 1, Personal Papers: RNC, GBL.

148 See, for example, "Dent to Mitchell," September 20, 1971, 1972 Elections, March–December 1971, Box 9, HDP.

149 "White to Bush," May 23, 1973, and "Bush to Haig," May 29, 1973, and "Bush to the President," February 13, 1973, in White House Memos—Outgoing, Box 1, GBL; "May 11, 1973," Diary Entry, Personal Notes: October 1973–August 1974 [1], Personal Papers: RNC, GBL.

150 "Bush to the President," May 9, 1973, White House Memos—Outgoing, Box 1, Personal Papers: RNC, GBL; "Remarks by Edward Mahe, Jr.," RNC meeting, September 10, 1973, *PRP*.

151 "Campaign Management College Training Professionals for '74," *First Monday*, December 1973, 7.

152 "'Mary Louise Smith, Co-Chairman of the RNC,' GOP Nationalities News," May 1974, RNC (1), WHCF Name, GFL.

153 "Smith to the President," July 17, 1974, and attachment, "Grassroots '74—Fact Sheet," July 17, 1974, Political Affairs—Republican Party (Ex): September 1, 1974–September 14, 1974, Box 1, WHCF, GFL.

154 Ibid.

155 "Remarks by Bush," RNC meeting, September 10, 1973, *PRP*.

156 "Remarks by Edward Mahe, Jr.," RNC meeting, September 10, 1973, *PRP*.

157 "New Majority Workshops Draw Wide Support," *First Monday*, December 1973, 14.

158 "Bush to Wardell," February 19, 1974, White House—Presidential Visits, Box 1, Personal Papers: RNC, GBL.

159 "March 20, 1974," Diary Entry, Personal Notes: October 1973–August 1974 [1], Personal Papers: RNC, GBL.

5 | The Politics of Addition: Gerald R. Ford

1 "Remarks of the President," March 7, 1975, RNC (2), WHCF Name, GFL.

2 "Poll Finds G.O.P. at Lowest Point," *New York Times*, July 18, 1974; R. W. Apple, "For Democrats, a Problem; For G.O.P., Still a Nightmare," *New York Times*, August 11, 1974.

3 "Schweiker Voices Fear on Future of the G.O.P.," *New York Times*, November 7, 1974; personal interview with Mary Lukens, former political director of Market Opinion Research, June 15, 2005, Ann Arbor, Mich.

4 Yet as it turned out, like every other minority-party president, Ford still ran ahead of most Republican congressional candidates in 1976. He received a larger share of the vote than the Republican congressional candidates in 58 percent of all congressional districts.

5 Nelson W. Polsby, "The Vice Presidency and the GOP's Future," *Washington Post*, August 16, 1974.

6 Personal interview with Eddie Mahe Jr., February 16, 2006.

7 Alfred J. Preston, "Republican Setback in Michigan," *Los Angeles Times*, April 24, 1974; David S. Broder and Jules Witcover, "Ford Staff Mapping Transition Plan," *Washington Post*, August 8, 1974.

8 Ford's comments at the Midwest Republican Leadership Conference on March 30, 1974, are repeated in Gerald Ford, "Lessons of Watergate," *First Monday*, May 1974.

9 "August 12, 1974," "August 22, 1974," "August 26, 1974," "August 28, 1974," Diary Entries, Personal Notes: October 1973–August 1974, Personal Papers: RNC, GBL. Throughout her tenure, Smith was referred to as "Chairman Smith," as the more appropriate, gender-neutral term *chair* was not yet used.

10 "Ford to Smith," September 10, 1974 and "Jones to Haig," August 21, 1974, both in PL-Republican Party (Ex): September 1, 1974–September 14, 1974, Box 1, WHCF PL: Republican Party, GFL; also see "Ford to Smith" September 10, 1974 and "Smith to Ford," October 15, 1974, Box 41, MLS.

11 See sources in preceding note.

12 "Talking Points for the President," September 13, 1974, RNC (1), Box 7, Burch Files, GFL.

13 "Remarks of the President at the Republican National Committee Luncheon, Mayflower Hotel," September 16, 1974, RNC (1) WHCF Name, GFL. Also see Apple, "Woman Elected Chairman."

14 The documents are too many to list, but see, for example, the collections in WHCF: Name: Smith, GFL; WHCF (PL): Republican Party, GFL; and Boxes 34, 35, 41, and 72, MLS.

15 Until late in Clinton's presidency; see chapter 11.

16 "Smith to Burch and Rumsfeld," October 10, 1974, and "Smith to Ford," October 30, 1974, RNC, Box 7, Burch Files, GFL; also "Smith to Burch and Rumsfeld," November 22, 1974, White House Memos, Box 72, MLS.

17 Gerald Ford, "President Offers Total Support for New Program," *First Monday*, November 1974; for staff edits to Ford's column, see RNC (2), Box 7, Burch Files, GFL.

18 "Mahe Brings Long Record of Professional Experience to Executive Director Post," *First Monday*, December 1974.

19 "Smith to Ford," October 30, 1974, RNC (2), Box 7, Burch Files, GFL.

20 Aldrich, *Why Parties?*

21 "Thaxton to RNC Staff," December 31, 1974, Fieldmen, Box 6; "Mahe to RNC Staff," September 17, 1975, RNC Memos, Box 68, MLS.

22 "Expanded Political Operation Envisioned as RNC Gears Up to Meet Challenges of 1976," *First Monday*, November 1974.

23 "Opening Remarks, Executive Committee," December 6, 1974, Box 41, MLS.

24 "Mrs. Smith Relinquishes Chairmanship of RNC," *First Monday*, December 1976.

25 "Remarks by Smith," September 16, 1974, *Papers of the Republican Party.*

26 "Chairman Makes New Staff Appointments, Reorganizes National Committee Structure to Meet Demands of 1976," *First Monday*, November 1974.

27 "Remarks of the President," September 8, 1975, RNC Reception, Box 28, Hartmann Files, GFL.

28 "Interview with RNC Chairman on the Challenge of '76," *First Monday*, November 1974.

29 "Additional Services Will Be Provided State and Local GOP Units by Restructured Political/Research Division," *First Monday*, November 1974.

30 Ibid.

31 "RNC Fund Raising Off to Good Start," sidebar, *First Monday*, May 1975.

32 "CMC Interest Greater Than Previous Year," *First Monday*, September 1975.

33 Ibid.

34 "CMC Offers Broad Base Curriculum," *First Monday*, August 1975.

35 "CMC Interest Greater Than Previous Year," *First Monday*, September 1975.

36 "Training and Programs Division Schedules Seminars for State, County, City Republican Leadership," *First Monday*, November 1974.

37 "RNC Training Program Part of New Momentum," *First Monday*, May 1975.

38 "CR Fieldmen School Trains Students as GOP Campaigners," *First Monday*, March 1976.

39 "Schedule Proposal for the President," April 7, 1975, PL: Republican Party (Ex): April 1, 1975–April 31, 1975 and "Greeting: The National Teen Age Republican Leadership Training Conference," June 18, 1975, PL: Republican Party (Ex): June 18, 1975–June 30, 1975, Box 2, WHCF PL: Republican Party, GFL.

40 "RNC's School of Politics Adds Five Summer Sessions," *First Monday*, May 1976.

41 "RNC Waging Biggest Effort," *First Monday*, October 1976.

42 Timothy Clark, "The RNC Prospers, the DNC Struggles as They Face the 1980 Elections," *National Journal*, September 27, 1980, 1617–21; Klinkner, *The Losing Parties*, 139–41; Bibby and Huckshorn, "Republican Party in American Politics"; M. Margaret Conway, "Republican Political Party Nationalization, Campaign Activities, and Their Implications for the Party System," *Publius* 13 (Winter 1983).

43 "Anderson to Hartmann," December 9, 1974, RNC Executive Committee, Box 3, Calkins Files, GFL.

44 "G.O.P. Tells Plans to Rebuild Image," *Chicago Tribune*, January 26, 1975; "Fall Registration Drives: The Key to Victory in '76," *First Monday*, September 1975.

45 "Ford to County Chairman," September 16, 1975, PL: Republican Party (Ex): September 10, 1975–October 31, 1975, Box 2, WHCF PL: Republican Party, GFL; for background on Ford's participation in the effort, see "Calkins to Buchen," September 17, 1975, RNC, May–December 1975, Box 3, Calkins Files, GFL.

46 "Remarkable Results Noted in GOP Registration Drive," *First Monday*, November–December 1975.

47 "Fall Registration Drives: The Key to Victory in '76," *First Monday*, September 1975.

48 "RNC Training Program Part of New Momentum," *First Monday*, May 1975.

49 "August 26, 1974," Diary Entry, Personal Notes: October 1973–August 1974, Personal Papers: RNC, GBL.

50 "Obenshain to Marsh," August 12, 1974, and "Marsh to Obenshain," August 15, 1974, RNC (1), Box 7, Burch Files, GFL.

51 "Remarks of the President," September 16, 1974, RNC (1), WHCF Name, GFL; "Qs & As / Republican National Committee," August 1974, RNC (1), Box 7, Burch Files, GFL.

52 "Meeting with Republican Southern State Chairmen," November 9, 1974, PR 7-1, November 6, 1974–November 11, 1974, WHCF, GFL; see also "Agenda, To: The President, From: Dean Burch," November 9, 1974, PL: Republican Party (Ex): November 1, 1974–November 30, 1974, Box 2, WHCF PL: Republican Party, GFL.

53 "'Best Program Ever,' State Chairmen Say," *First Monday*, February 1975.

54 Rowland Evans and Robert Novak, "Reagan 13, Ford 0," *Washington Post*, April 20, 1975.

55 Jerald F. ter Horst, "Bo Brings Back Southern Strategy," *Chicago Tribune*, June 22, 1975.

56 "Smith to Ford," October 30, 1974, RNC (2), Box 7, Burch Files, GFL; "1976 Program," Box 66, MLS.

57 See sources in preceding note and "RNC Fund Raising Off to Good Start," sidebar, *First Monday*, May 1975.

58 "Smith to Hartmann and Whitman," February 12, 1975, and "Calkins to Connor, et. al.," February 27, 1975, RNC 1-April 75, Box 3, Calkins Files, GFL.

59 "Mrs. Smith Relinquishes Chairmanship of RNC," *First Monday*, December 1976.

60 "Buchen to Calkins," October 2, 1975, RNC 5-12/75, Box 3, Calkins Files, GFL.

61 "RNC Statement of Sources and Uses of Funds," January 1–May 31, 1976, Box 42, MLS. Also see "RNC Fund Raising Off to Good Start," *First Monday*, May 1975.

62 "RNC Cash Flow Statement," January 1–December 17, 1976, Box 60, MLS.

63 Clark, "RNC Prospers"; Bibby and Huckshorn, "Republican Party in American Politics"; Conway, "Republican Political Party Nationalization."

64 "GOP Reception," June 30, 1976, PL: Republican Party (Ex): June 1, 1976–June 30, 1976, Box 3, WHCF PL: Republican Party; "Drop-By Briefing for the Republican Eagles," February 26, 1976, Republican, A–K, WHCF Name File; "Reception for Republican National Associates," June 24, 1975, Republican National Association Reception, Box 27, Hartmann Files; all from the GFL.

65 Aldo Beckman, "Ford Shows Republican Fund-Raisers in Texas How It's Done, Gets $2 Million," *Chicago Tribune*, September 14, 1975.

66 See, for example, James N. Naughton, "Suddenly the Questions Are as Far-Reaching as Ford's Travels," *New York Times*, September 19, 1975. Internal memos evidencing Ford's efforts are many. See, for example, "Anderson to Ford," October 15, 1975, RNC, Finance Committee, Box 3, Calkins Files, GFL.

67 "Anderson to Ford," November 12, 1975, White House Memos, Box 72, MLS.

68 "Remarks of the President," September 8, 1975, RNC Reception, Box 28, Hartmann Files, GFL.

69 "Ford Tells RNC Party Building Priority of '76," *First Monday*, October 1975.

70 James M. Naughton, "Ford Vows Unity for Republicans," *New York Times*, April 1, 1976.

71 "Anderson to Ford," with attachment, April 28, 1975, Hartmann-Memos-President (1), Box 131, Hartman Files, GFL.

72 Burns, *Running Alone*.

73 "Anderson to Ford," with attachment, April 28, 1975, Hartmann-Memos-President (1), Box 131, Hartman Files, GFL.

74 "Burch to Smith," and attachment, November 21, 1974, RNC (3), Box 7, Burch Files; "Anderson to Smith," April 17, 1975, RNC 1-April 75, Box 3, Calkins Files; both GFL.

75 "Fee to Bennett," June 25, 1975, RNC (4), WHCF Name, GFL.

76 Ibid.

77 "Reception for the Members of the RNC," September 8, 1975, SO 6, July 28, 1975–September 30, 1975, WHCF, GFL; see also David S. Broder, "Ford Warns His Party against Divisiveness," *Washington Post*, September 9, 1975.

78 "Hartmann to Ford," September 10, 1975 and "Callaway to Rumsfeld," August 29, 1975, PL: Republican Party (Ex): September 10, 1975–October 31, 1975, Box 2, WHCF PL: Republican Party, GFL.

79 "Connor to Hartmann, November 7, 1975, RNC (5), Box 28, and "Hartmann to Ford," August 16, 1976, Box 131, Hartman Files, GFL; also "Smith to Hartmann," July 11, 1975, and attachment, RNC (3), Box 28, Hartmann Files, GFL.

80 "Smith to Ford," December 15, 1975, RNC (2), Box 20, Anderson Files; also see Box D14, PFC Records; both GFL; also "Smith to Ford," January 15, 1976, Meetings with the President, Box 35, MLS.

81 Ibid.

82 Warren Weaver Jr., "G.O.P. Chiefs Meet in Chicago; Discuss Unity for '76 Campaign," *New York Times*, January 17, 1976.

83 "Mrs. Smith Relinquishes Chairmanship of RNC," *First Monday*, December 1976.

84 "RNC Phonebank Program," RNC Phonebank Program–General, Box C28, PFC Records, GFL. Also see "RNC Fund-Raising on Target for Ford, Congress Races," *First Monday*, September 1976, 11.

85 "RNC Role in Campaign Set by Rules," *First Monday*, September 1976.

86 "Remarks of the President," September 8, 1975, RNC Reception, Box 28, Hartmann Files, GFL.

87 Rowland Evans and Robert Novak, "The Ford-Reagan Summit," *Washington Post*, November 4, 1974; and clippings from PL: Republican Party (Ex): April 1, 1975–April 31, 1975, Box 2, WHCF, GFL.

88 "Hartmann to Bakshian," November 11, 1975, "Williams to Ford," March 14, 1975; and "Ford to Williams," March 28, 1975 in PL: Republican Party (Ex), Box 2, WHCF PL: Republican Party, GFL.

89 "Meeting with Irving Kristol," November 15, 1974, PR 7-1, November 12, 1974–November 16, 1974, WHCF, GFL.

90 "Meeting with Senator James Buckley," April 16, 1975, PL: Republican Party (Ex): April 1, 1975–April 31, 1975, Box 2, WHCF, GFL.

91 Lou Cannon, "Third-Party Speculation Worries GOP," *Washington Post*, February 23, 1975.

92 "National Leadership Conference Needs You," *First Monday*, February 1975.

93 "Rustand to Rumsfeld," February 25, 1975, Smith, Mary Louise (1), WHCF Name, GFL.

94 "Remarks of the President," March 7, 1975.

95 Ibid.

96 R. W. Apple Jr., "Reagan Rejects Ford Plea to G.O.P. to Broaden Base," *New York Times*, March 9, 1975.

97 Jon Margolis, "Ford's Unity Plea Supported," *Chicago Tribune*, March 2, 1975.

98 "Friedersdorf to Ford," and attachment, Political Affairs (1), Box 36, Presidential Handwriting File, GFL.

99 "White House Republican Reception," Speech Draft, March 6, 1975, RNC (2), Box 27, Hartmann Files, GFL.

100 "Rustand to Rumsfeld," February 25, 1975, Smith, Mary Louise (1), WHCF Name, GFL.

101 "Training Seminars Slated for GOP Workers," *First Monday*, April 1975.

102 "Scott to Rustand," August 24, 1974, PL: Republican Party (Ex): August 9, 1974–August 29, 1974, Box 1, WHCF PL: Republican Party, GFL.

103 "Black Republican Councils Organized in 21 States," *First Monday*, August 1975; "NBRC Sets Meeting in Kansas City," *First Monday*, April 1976.

104 "Meeting with Key Black Republicans," and attachments, September 11, 1974; "Scott to Marsh," September 12, 1974 and PL: Republican Party (Ex): September 1, 1974–September 14, 1974, Box 1, WHCF PL: Republican Party, GFL.

105 "GOP Ethnic Leaders Have Political Seminar, WH Briefing," *First Monday*, March 1974.

106 "Hartmann to Ford," September 10, 1975, "Callaway to Rumsfeld," August 29, 1975, PL: Republican Party (Ex): September 10, 1975–October 31, 1975, Box 2, WHCF PL: Republican Party, GFL.

107 "Heritage Groups Received by Ford," *First Monday*, June 1975.

108 "Hispanic Assembly a New Bridge to GOP," *First Monday*, April 1976.

109 "Meeting with the Leadership of the Republican National Hispanic Assembly," December 10, 1975, Republican, L–Z, WHCF Name, GFL.

110 "RNC Role in Campaign Set by Rules," *First Monday*, September 1976.

111 "Armstrong to Smith," September 26, 1974, Republican, A–K, WHCF Name, GFL.

112 "Meeting with Major City Republican Leaders' Conference Attendees," May 21, 1975, PL: Republican Party (Ex): May 1, 1975–May 31, 1975, Box 2, WHCF PL: Republican Party, GFL.

113 "Republican Mayors Establish Conference," *First Monday*, June 1975.

114 "GOP Mayors Dominate Conference," *First Monday*, August 1975.

115 "Hanzlik to Cannon," September 9, 1976, and "Meeting with Republican Mayors," January 18, 1977, Republican, L–Z, WHCF Name, GFL.

116 Mahe, personal interview.

117 See PL: Republican Party (Ex): November 21, 1976–January 20, 1977, Box 4, WHCF PL: Republican Party, GFL.

118 "Ford Hosts Parley," *Chicago Tribune*, December 10, 1976.

119 "Ford to Smith," January 12, 1977, Political Affairs (3), Box 36, Presidential Handwriting File, GFL.

120 On Brock's Regional Political Directors (RPDs), see Klinkner, *The Losing Parties*, 141–42.

121 "Brock to Ford," January 3, 1977, PL: Republican Party (Ex): November 21, 1976–January 20, 1977, Box 4, WHCF PL: Republican Party, GFL.

122 Klinkner, *The Losing Parties*, 137–46.

123 Paul S. Herrnson, "National Party Organizations at the Dawn of the Twenty-First Century," in *The Parties Respond*, ed. L. Sandy Maisel (Cambridge: Westview Press, 2002), 52, 61. Also see Klinkner, *The Losing Parties*, 138.

6 | Building the Republican Base: Ronald Reagan

1 Frank Fahrenkopf, "Republican Party Strives for Majority Status—'84 and Beyond," *First Monday*, November–December 1983.

2 Ronald Reagan, "Inaugural Address," January 20, 1981, and January 20, 1985, *PPP*. See, for example, Skowronek, *The Politics Presidents Make*, 409–46; John W. Sloan, *The Reagan Effect: Economics and Presidential Leadership* (Lawrence: University Press of Kansas, 1999); Larry Berman, ed., *Looking Back on the Reagan Presidency* (Baltimore: Johns Hopkins University Press, 1990).

3 Especially in the South, where the GOP had been making significant electoral gains for more than a decade. As early as May 1981, Lee Atwater, deputy director of the White House Office of Political Affairs, observed that "the principle [*sic*] impact of the 1980 election was that this region [the South] must now be categorized as a competitive two-party area. This prediction has been made many times in the past and was the central thesis of Kevin Phillips' 1969 book, *The Emerging Republican Majority*. Phillips was a prophet." See "Atwater to Dole," May 31, 1981, "Dole Memo," Box 2, Atwater, Series I, RRL. Kevin P. Phillips, *The Emerging Republican Majority* (New Rochelle: Arlington House, 1969).

4 National Election Studies. In 1988, the NES found 47 percent Democratic identification and 41 percent Republican identification (three-point scale).

5 As the appendix elaborates, the documentary evidence of president-party interactions in the newer presidential libraries (Reagan and beyond) is much thinner than that which can be found in older libraries. This chapter relies on available documents at the Reagan Library and is supplemented by party publications, newspaper articles, and personal interviews. While many of the existing Reagan

Library documents prove to be invaluable, the best evidence has yet to be released. Evidently, the collection of documents considered "political" has been processed but still awaits permission from the Reagan family to be released. Nevertheless, there is sufficient material on hand to advance our analysis of presidential party building. See the appendix for a fuller discussion of sources and methods.

6 Neustadt, *Presidential Power*, 276, 280.

7 Sheingate, "Political Entrepreneurship"; Elisabeth S. Clemens and James M. Cook, "Politics and Institutionalism: Explaining Durability and Change," *Annual Review of Sociology* 25 (1999): 452.

8 Martin Schram, "Reagan Backs Utah Pol for RNC Chairman," *Washington Post*, December 17, 1980; "Party's Organizational Man," *New York Times*, January 18, 1981.

9 Adam Clymer, "New G.O.P. Chairman Criticizes Party's Right Wing," *New York Times*, January 18, 1981; Richard Richards, "The Job Ahead," *First Monday*, February 1981.

10 "A Conversation with Richard DeVos," *First Monday*, June 1981.

11 This model is sometimes called multilevel marketing. Its influence in the Republican Party has evidently persisted. See Bai, "Multilevel Marketing."

12 Cited in Frederic A. Birmingham, "The Amway Dream," *Saturday Evening Post*, 11, 1979.

13 Ibid.

14 DeVos was fired after he described the economic recession as a "cleansing process" in June 1982 and then added that he had "never seen anyone unemployed who wanted a job." DeVos went on to join the advisory council of the National Conservative Political Action Committee (NCPAC), then the largest donor to Republican candidates. See Lou Cannon, "Mike Curb Will Replace Richard DeVos at RNC," *Washington Post*, August 14, 1982; and Thomas B. Edsall, "Money, Technology Revive GOP Force," *Washington Post*, June 17, 1984.

15 "A Conversation with Richard DeVos," *First Monday*, June 1981.

16 "Shareholders Conventions Planned for RNC Sustaining Members," *First Monday*, August 1981.

17 "When Shareholders Go Home, RNC Goes Back to Work," *First Monday*, April 1982.

18 Ibid.

19 "Finance Chairman DeVos Introduces New RNC Membership Clubs," *First Monday*, April 1981.

20 Paul Taylor, "RNC Can't Spend Its Money as Fast as It's Pouring In," *Washington Post*, November 13, 1981.

21 "1982 Chairman's Report," *RNC*, 1, 1982; "The Chairman's Report—1982," *First Monday*, January–February 1983.

22 Ibid.

23 Alex P. Hurtado, "Achieving Majority Status," *First Monday*, August 1981.

24 "The Chairman's Report—1982," *First Monday*, January–February 1983.

25 The RNC Political Division defined "majority status" in the following way: "Majority status will only be achieved when Republicans control the U.S. Senate, the U.S. House of Representatives, the Governors' Mansions, the State Legislatures, the County Courthouses and the City Halls across the country." See Hurtado, "Achieving Majority Status."

26 Ibid.

27 "Campaign '82: CMC Turning Out Pros," *First Monday*, March 1982.

28 "The Chairman's Report—1982," *First Monday*, January–February 1983.

29 Ibid.; and Hurtado, "Achieving Majority Status."

30 Laura Broderick, "Drawing the Battlelines: Redistricting," *First Monday*, June 1981.

31 James Druckman and Lawrence R. Jacobs, "Segmented Representation: The Reagan White House and Disproportionate Responsiveness." Paper presented at the Annual Meeting of the Midwest Political Science Association, Chicago, April 12–14, 2007 .

32 Dom Bonafede, "As Pollster to the President, Wirthlin Is Where the Action Is," *National Journal*, December 12, 1981.

33 Richard Richards, "Republicans United," *First Monday*, March 1981; S. J. Masty, "Toward Majority Status," *First Monday*, October 1981.

34 Dom Bonafede, "Can the DNC Adjust to Being a Minority? Can the RNC Reverse 50 Years of History?" *National Journal*, September 5, 1981.

35 Personal interview with former RNC chairman Richard N. Bond, June 26, 2007, Washington, D.C.

36 Ibid.

37 Dom Bonafede, "Part Science, Part Art, Part Hokum, Direct Mail Now a Key Campaign Tool," *National Journal*, July 31, 1982.

38 Ibid.

39 Personal interview with former RNC chairman Frank Fahrenkopf Jr., February 9, 2006, Washington, D.C.

40 On incremental processes of institutional change, see Thelen, *How Institutions Evolve*.

41 "Recommended Telephone Call to Senate Majority Leader Howard Baker, House Republican Leader Bob Michel, House Republican Whip Trent Lott," November 6, 1982, Presidential Telephone Calls, PR007-02, RRL.

42 "Remarks of the President at Reception for Richard Richards," January 27, 1983, Drop-by Reception for Richard Richards, Box 72, White House Speechwriting Office, RRL.

43 Fahrenkopf, personal interview.

44 Ibid.

45 Ibid.

46 Frank Fahrenkopf, "Republican Goal: Translating '84 Win into Long-Term Gains," *First Monday*, February 1985.

47 Fahrenkopf, personal interview.

48 Fahrenkopf, "Republican Party Strives."

49 Ibid.

50 "Herlihy to Reagan," November 21, 1983, November 1983, Box 2, Tutwiler Files, RRL; and "Reagan Scheduled to Address GOP Regional Meetings," *First Monday*, June–July 1983.

51 Fahrenkopf, personal interview.

52 Fahrenkopf, "Republican Party Strives."

53 David Burnham, "Have Computer, Will Travel the Campaign Trail," *New York Times*, September 22, 1983.

54 Fahrenkopf, personal interview.

55 "Tutwiler to Jenkins," January 31, 1984, January 1984 (1), Box 2, Tutwiler Files, RRL.

56 Fahrenkopf, personal interview.

57 "Presidential Support: Greening the GOP Grassroots," *First Monday*, March–April 1983.

58 "Tutwiler to Baker and Deaver," March 14, 1984, White House—Baker, Box 7, Tutwiler Files, RRL.

59 Fahrenkopf, personal interview.

60 Ibid.

61 Ibid.

62 "Puttin' on the Blitz!" *First Monday*, February 1985.

63 "Tutwiler to Baker and Deaver," April 16, 1984, White House—Deaver, Box 7, Tutwiler Files, RRL.

64 "Reagan and Bush Make History in Landslide Victory," *First Monday*, December 1984–January 1985.

65 Carolyn Leubsdorf, "Registration Drives: GOP Recruits New Voters in Record Numbers," *First Monday*, May–June 1984; Fahrenkopf, personal interview.

66 "Rollins to Outreach Working Group," April 15, 1983, Staff Memoranda: Political Affairs, Box 5, Baker Files, RRL. For an excellent discussion of how Reagan sought to transform social groups into new members of his Republican coalition, see Ginsberg and Shefter, "Presidency and Organization of Interests."

67 "Talking Points: Organizational Efforts," October 24, 1984, Political Affairs, Box 10, Baker Files, RRL.

68 Leubsdorf, "Registration Drives."

69 "Talking Points: Organizational Efforts," October 24, 1984, Political Affairs, Box 10, Baker Files, RRL.

70 Ibid.

71 Ibid. Also see "Reagan-Bush '84 Get-Out-The-Vote Program," Political Affairs, Box 10, Baker Files, RRL.

72 "ACTV: The Two Party Platforms' Position on Traditional Values," "The ACTV Network 1984 Board of Governors Directory," and "ACTV: Who We Are and What We Stand For," in Engagements, Appointments, Interviews 279000–280599, Box 24, PR, RRL. See also Bruce Nesmith, *The New Republican Coalition: The Reagan Campaigns and White Evangelicals* (New York: P. Lang, 1993), 4–5.

73 A. James Reichley, "Religion and the Future of American Politics," *Political Science Quarterly* 101, no. 1 (1986).

74 Nesmith, *New Republican Coalition*, 95.

75 Ibid., 98.

76 Rob Gurwitt, "1986 Elections Generate G.O.P. Power Struggle," *Congressional Quarterly Weekly Report* 44, no. 15 (1986), also cited in Nesmith, *New Republican Coalition*, 98.

77 "ACTV: The Two Party Platforms' Position on Traditional Values," and "The ACTV Network 1984 Board of Governors Directory," and "ACTV: Who We Are and What We Stand For," in Engagements, Appointments, Interviews 279000–280599, Box 24, PR, RRL.

78 Haynes Johnson and Thomas B. Edsall, "North Carolina Contests Spark Registration War," *Washington Post*, September 30, 1984.

79 "LaHaye to Ryan," November 1, 1984, and "Jarmin to Donatelli," October 31, 1984, in Engagements, Appointments, Interviews 279000–280599, Box 24, PR, RRL.

80 Thomas B. Edsall, "GOP Fund-Raiser Plans 'Nonpartisan' Vote Drive," *Washington Post*, June 6, 1984.

81 James M. Wall, "Lazy Churches and Voter Registration," *Christian Century*, June 20–27, 1984, clipped in Engagements, Appointments, Interviews 279000–280599, Box 24, PR, RRL. For commentary on Reagan's participation with the letter, see Anthony Lewis, "Abroad at Home: Cross and Flag," *New York Times*, October 8, 1984.

82 "Tutwiler to Baker," and "Dear Christian Leader," White House—Deaver, Box 7, Tutwiler Files, RRL.

83 Kenneth L. Woodward, "Playing Politics at Church," *Newsweek*, July 9, 1984, clipped in Engagements, Appointments, Interviews 279000–280599, Box 24, PR, RRL.

84 "American Coalition for Traditional Values," Speech copy, July 9, 1984, 300, Box 16, Presidential Handwriting File, RRL.

85 Ibid.

86 "LaHaye to Baker," August 1, 1984, White House—Baker, Box 7, Tutwiler Files, RRL.

87 Lewis, "Abroad at Home"; "Jarmin to Donatelli," October 31, 1984, Engagements, Appointments, Interviews 279000–280599, Box 24, PR, RRL.

88 Kimberly H. Conger and John C. Green, "Spreading Out and Digging In: Christian Conservatives and State Republican Parties," *Campaigns and Elections*, February 2002. Though not without controversy: see Gurwitt, "1986 Elections."

89 Dan Balz, "Vote Turnout Increased in November," *Washington Post*, January 8, 1985.

90 "An Interview with RNC Chairman Fahrenkopf," *First Monday*, December 1984–January 1985; also see the Committee for the Study of the American Electorate's study of the election: Curtis B. Gans, *Non-voter Study '84–'85* (Washington, D.C.: Committee for the Study of the American Electorate, 1985).

91 Thomas B. Edsall, "GOP Seeking Converts in Four Key States: $500,000 Program to Court Democrats," *Washington Post*, May 8, 1985.

92 "Telephone Call to Frank J. Fahrenkopf, Jr.," November 29, 1984, Presidential Telephone Calls (273000–279000), PR 007-02, RRL.

93 Fahrenkopf, "Republican Goal."

94 Neustadt, *Presidential Power*.

95 Fahrenkopf, personal interview.

96 "Republicans Launch a Campaign to Court Disenchanted Demos," *First Monday*, Spring 1985.

97 Gerald M. Boyd, "White House Is Seeking Converts to G.O.P. Chiefly in Statehouses," *New York Times*, March 19, 1985.

98 Fahrenkopf, personal interview.

99 Although the administration recognized, as early as May 1981, that gains were slowly being made at the local level. See "Atwater to Dole," May 31, 1981, "Dole Memo," Box 2, Atwater, Series I, RRL.

100 Fahrenkopf, personal interview.

101 Frank Fahrenkopf, "Republicans Reach Out to Disenchanted Demos: Come Join Our Party," *First Monday*, Spring 1985.

102 Phil Gailey, "G.O.P. Opens Drive for 100,000 Voters," *New York Times*, May 8, 1985.

103 "Remarks at a White House Reception for New Republicans," *PPP*, June 10, 1985.

104 Paul Taylor, "Party-Switchers Stir High Emotions at Atlanta RNC Meeting," *Washington Post*, June 29, 1985.

105 Bill Peterson, "GOP Extends Recruitment of Democrats," *Washington Post*, August 16, 1985; Bill Peterson, "GOP 'Open Door' Deemed Success Despite Shortfall," *Washington Post*, August 23, 1985.

106 "Republicans Launch a Campaign to Court Disenchanted Demos," *First Monday*, Spring 1985.

107 "Democrats Find New Home in Republican Party," *First Monday*, September–October 1985.

108 "The RNC '1991 Plan' for Victory," *First Monday*, December 1984–January 1985.

109 Fahrenkopf, personal interview.

110 Ibid.; and "Fahrenkopf to Reagan," January 29, 1986, 221, Box 14, Presidential Handwriting File, Records, RRL.

111 "Laxalt to Baker, Deaver, Fahrenkopf," May 20, 1983, Staff Memoranda: Political Affairs, Box 5, Baker Files, RRL; "National Forums: GOP Women Bridge the News Gap," *First Monday*, September–October 1983; "Viva '84: Republicans Court Hispanic Voter Support," *First Monday*, September–October 1983.

112 Interview with Frank Fahrenkopf in *Leadership in the Reagan Presidency, Part Two: Eleven Intimate Perspectives*, ed. Kenneth W. Thompson (Lanham, Md.: University Press of America, 1993), 35.

113 "Achievement '86 and Grassroots Politics," *First Monday*, November–December 1986.

114 Ronald Brownstein, "Eye on 1991 in States," *National Journal*, December 7, 1985.

115 Dick Kirschten, "Testing the Waters," *National Journal*, July 20, 1985.

116 "State Parties Recruit Volunteers," *First Monday*, January–February 1988.

117 Fahrenkopf, personal interview.

7 | Leveling the Playing Field: George H. W. Bush

1 President George Bush, "Remarks at the Annual Republican Congressional Fundraising Dinner," June 14, 1989, *PPP.*

2 Bush ran ahead of the Republican congressional candidate in 60 percent of districts, not including uncontested races.

3 President George Bush, "Remarks to New Members of the Republican Party," June 26, 1989, *PPP.*

4 "President-Elect Remarks to Republican National Committee Luncheon," Federal News Service, January 18, 1989.

5 As noted in the previous chapter, the documentary evidence of president-party interactions in the newer presidential libraries (Reagan and beyond) is much thinner than in older libraries. Consequently, this chapter draws upon available primary source documents but is more heavily reliant upon party publications, newspaper articles, and personal interviews conducted by the author. A full discussion of methods and data sources can be found in the appendix.

6 "President-Elect Remarks," January 18, 1989.

7 "Lee Atwater, RNC Summer Meeting," Federal News Service, June 16, 1989.

8 President George Bush, "Remarks at the Annual Republican Congressional Fundraising Dinner," June 14, 1989, *PPP.*

9 Ibid.

10 "Lee Atwater, RNC Summer Meeting," Federal News Service, June 16, 1989.

11 "Press Conference with Frank Fahrenkopf and Lee Atwater," Federal News Service, November 17, 1988.

12 "Redistricting: Battle Lines Are Drawn for 1991," *First Monday*, Fall 1989.

13 James Barnes, "Reports: Drawing the Lines," *National Journal*, April 1, 1989.

14 Ibid.

15 Ibid.

16 "Redistricting: Battle Lines Are Drawn for 1991," *First Monday*, Fall 1989.

17 David S. Broder, "For GOP's Statehouse Recruiters, 'Bait-and-Switch' Takes on New Meaning," *Washington Post*, October 8, 1989.

18 Lee Atwater, "Predetermined Elections Must End," *First Monday*, Fall 1989.

19 "Lee Atwater, RNC Summer Meeting," Federal News Service, June 16, 1989.

20 Ibid.; "Legislative Task Force Targets Republican Wins," *First Monday*, Summer 1989.

21 "Redistricting: Battle Lines Are Drawn for 1991," *First Monday*, Fall 1989.

22 "Prepared Remarks of Lee Atwater," January 19, 1990, Political Affairs (Wray/Rogers [5]), Box 97, Sununu Files, GBL.

23 Bond, personal interview.

24 Broder, "GOP's Statehouse Recruiters."

25 Lee Atwater, "Manning the Battle Stations at the RNC," *First Monday*, Spring 1989.

26 Ibid.

27 "Report on 1989 Mass Mailings Signed by the President," December 27, 1989, Richard N. Bond Personal Paper Collection.

28 "Report on 1989 Fundraising Events Involving the President" and "Report on 1989 Mass Mailings Signed by the President," December 27, 1989, Richard N. Bond Personal Paper Collection.

29 Janet Hook, "Republicans Looking to Bush to Spread Coattails in 1992," *Congressional Quarterly Weekly Report*, August 17, 1991.

30 "Jackson to Wray," May 1, 1990; and "Bates to the President" and "Report on Cabinet Domestic Travel," April 27, 1990, both in Richard N. Bond Personal Paper Collection.

31 "Alexander to Wray," March 5, 1990; and "Winkeljohn to Card," May 7, 1991, and attached "Carney to Sununu, Card, and Rogers," and "Baker to Sununu," April 22, 1991, all in Political Affairs (Wray/Rogers [5]), Box 97, Sununu Files, GBL; also "Atwater to Sununu," August 13, 1990, FG006-01, Box 79, White House Office of Records Management (WHORM), FG, GBL. Also see "The President's Club," *First Monday*, Spring 1990.

32 President George Bush, "Remarks at a Reception for Supporters of the Annual Republican Congressional Fundraising Dinner," June 12, 1990, *PPP*.

33 Atwater, "A Grand New Beginning."

34 The congressional "switchers" were Representatives Tommy Robinson of Arkansas and Bill Grant of Florida.

35 Broder, "GOP's Statehouse Recruiters."

36 President George Bush, "Remarks to New Members of the Republican Party," June 26, 1989, *PPP*.

37 "Roemer to Bush," May 3, 1991, Political Affairs (Wray/Rogers [5]), Box 97, Sununu Files, GBL.

38 "Lee Atwater," *First Monday*, Winter 1989.

39 Atwater, "A Grand New Beginning."

40 Renee Loth, "GOP Teaming Up with Minorities," *Boston Globe*, May 19, 1991.

41 Thomas B. Edsall, "Atwater and the Politics of Race," *Washington Post*, March 13, 1989.

42 Ibid.

43 John Dillin, "GOP Seeks More Black Candidates," *Christian Science Monitor*, May 29, 1990.

44 "GOP Chief Makes Pitch to Mayors," *St. Louis Post-Dispatch*, June 20, 1989.

45 "Carney to Demarest," May 29, 1990 and "McDuffie to Thurmond," May 7, 1990, Documents 4901–50, Open P2/P5, GBL; also see Juan Williams, "Why Blacks Like Bush," *Washington Post*, January 28, 1990.

46 Perry Lang, "GOP Luring Blacks Away from Democrats," *San Francisco Chronicle*, November 5, 1990; Brian Duffy et. al., "Now Willie Horton Stalks the GOP," *U.S. News & World Report*, March 20, 1989.

47 On "breach of faith," see Skowronek, *The Politics Presidents Make*, 429–42.

48 Stephen H. Wildstrom and Richard Fly, "How Bush Is Keeping the Radical Right Inside the Tent," *Business Week*, June 19, 1989.

49 "Prepared Remarks of Lee Atwater," January 19, 1990, Political Affairs (Wray/ Rogers [5]), Box 97, Sununu Files, GBL.

50 Robin Toner, "Atwater Urges Softer Abortion Line," *New York Times*, January 20, 1990.

51 "Shortley to Bush," January 18, 1990, and "Ebauer to Bush," March 5, 1990, and "Kuttner to Ebauer," April 10, 1990, WE003 [098343–109458], Box 36, WHORM Subject WE, GBL; and also see Toner, "Atwater Urges Softer Abortion Line"; Paul Taylor, "Chairman Urges GOP to 'Defy History,'" *Washington Post*, January 20, 1990.

52 Richard L. Berke, "G.O.P., in Revolt on Taxes, Steps Up Criticism of Bush," *New York Times*, June 28, 1990; Richard L. Berke, "Shouts of Revolt Rise Up in Congressional Ranks," *New York Times*, October 1, 1990; Thomas B. Edsall and E. J. Dionne Jr., "Democracy at Work: The Tax Revolt of the Masses," *Washington Post*, October 14, 1990.

53 Robin Toner, "G.O.P. Conservatives Take Grass-Roots Road," *New York Times*, May 20, 1990.

54 "Bennett's New Deal," *National Review*, December 17, 1990.

55 Ronald D. Elving, "Bennett Decides RNC Chair Won't Fit After All," *Congressional Quarterly Weekly Report*, December 15, 1990.

56 "Biography: Clayton Yeutter," Moran Files, WHOPA: Yeutter, GBL; "Presidential Remarks: Republican National Committee Briefing," January 25, 1991, Documents 1451–1500, Open P2/P5, GBL. And see Ronald D. Elving, "Republican Party: Search for an RNC Chairman Takes Root in Yeutter," *Congressional Quarterly Weekly Report*, January 5, 1991; and Ronald D. Elving, "Republicans: GOP Ducks Intraparty Fights, at Least for Time Being," *Congressional Quarterly Weekly Report*, January 26, 1991.

57 Elving, "Republicans: GOP Ducks"; Jack W. Germond and Jules Witcover, "Yeutter Will Be a Team Player at RNC," *National Journal*, January 12, 1991.

58 Richard Benedetto, "Election '92: Top Parties Map Their Strategies: GOP Goal Is Congressional Gains," *USA Today*, June 24, 1991; Clayton Yeutter, "Incumbents Will Stop at Nothing!" *Washington Post*, May 9, 1991.

59 "Remarks of Clayton Yeutter, National Grocers Association," Federal News Service, June 24, 1991.

60 "Remarks of Clayton Yeutter, National Federation of Republican Women Political Briefing," Federal News Service, May 21, 1991.

61 Bond, personal interview. Also: "Bond to President Bush," March 9, 1992, Richard N. Bond Personal Paper Collection. "Reapportionment has gone *very* well for us," Bond wrote to Bush, and predicted major gains in California and Illinois.

62 John Yang and Tom Kenworthy, "Tax Hearings to Give Democrats a Forum," *Washington Post*, November 28, 1991.

63 "GOP Sponsors Televised Workshop," *First Monday*, Spring 1990.

64 "Gingrich to the President," October 8, 1991, Politics—1991, Box 82, Sununu Files, GBL.

65 Ibid.

66 Ibid.

67 Tony Freemantle, "Convention '92: Buchanan Is Ebullient about New Role in GOP," *Houston Chronicle*, August 19, 1992.

68 Patrick J. Buchanan, "1992 Republican National Convention Speech, Houston, Texas," August 17, 1992. http://www.americanrhetoric.com/speeches/patrick buchanan1992rnc.htm.

69 Howard Kurtz, "A Decidedly Muddled Message of Sound Bites: Amid Jumble of Images, Even Bush Has Trouble Articulating Themes," *Washington Post*, August 20, 1992.

70 Ibid.

71 Atwater, "A Grand New Beginning."

72 John W. Mashek, "GOP Rewards in 1988 Campaign," *Boston Globe*, February 12, 1990; Sidney Blumenthal, "House Afire," *New Republic*, December 24, 1990.

73 James A. Barnes, "Politics: Seasoned to Perfection," *National Journal*, May 23, 1992.

74 Douglas Harbrecht, "Mary Matalin: The GOP's Secret Weapon," *Business Week*, May 21, 1990.

75 Barnes, "Politics: Seasoned to Perfection."

76 Malek resigned his RNC post in 1990 after it was revealed that he had drawn up, at Nixon's request, the names of all the Jews who worked at the Bureau of Labor Statistics. Tom Squitieri, "Ousted GOP Activists Back in Favor," *USA Today*, February 2, 1990; Thomas B. Edsall, "Bush Campaign Plans Major Change at RNC," *Washington Post*, August 3, 1988.

77 Barnes, "Politics: Seasoned to Perfection."

78 Ibid.

79 Martin Tolchin, "New Chairman Installed to 'Invigorate' G.O.P.," *New York Times*, February 2, 1992.

80 Charles Trueheart, "The GOP's VIP: Party Chief and Bush Loyalist Rich Bond, Taking the Heat," *Washington Post*, March 12, 1992.

81 Bond, personal interview.

82 Ibid.

83 Ibid.

84 Ibid.

85 "Bond to President Bush," March 9, 1992, Richard N. Bond Personal Collection.

86 Ibid.

87 Bond, personal interview.

88 Personal interview with Frederic V. Malek, July 17, 2007.

89 Maureen Dowd, "What Went Wrong, and Right," *New York Times*, November 5, 1992.

90 "1993 Chairman's Report," *Republican National Committee.*

91 Ibid.

92 I find no concrete evidence that Bush sought to enhance the party's capacity to mobilize voters, but this does not mean it did not happen. As discussed in note 5, at the time of this writing most political documents from the Bush presidency have yet to be released. It is quite likely that the RNC was engaged in voter mobilization efforts as part of the 1992 campaign, and Bush may have supported the effort in some manner. But without the evidence, it must remain a "neutral" finding.

93 David S. Broder, "Barbour: The GOP's 'Third B,'" *Washington Post*, February 3, 1993.

94 Gary C. Jacobson, "The 1994 House Elections in Perspective," *Political Science Quarterly* 111, no. 2 (1996): 222. Also see Dan Balz, "A Historic Republican Triumph: GOP Captures Congress," *Washington Post*, November 9, 1994.

95 For summaries of Barbour's tenure, see Ron Faucheux, "The Many Sides of Haley Barbour," *Campaigns and Elections*, August 1996; Alan Greenblatt, "Barbour: A Tough Act to Follow," *Congressional Quarterly Weekly Report*, January 25, 1997.

8 | Operation Support: John F. Kennedy

1 Transcript, Lawrence O'Brien Oral History, V, Internet Copy, LBJL, 19.

2 Not including uncontested districts (where either the Democratic or Republican House candidate received 100 percent of the vote).

3 Kernell, *Going Public*, 4.

4 "Dutton to Sorensen," November 21, 1961, PL October 1, 1961–February 20, 1962, Box 680, WHCF, JFKL. See also "Brightman to Sorensen," and Sorensen handwritten notes, DNC Publications, Miscellaneous, Box 32, Sorensen Files, JFKL.

5 "Report by Price," May 27, 1961, DNC Papers 1963–64, Box 20, MPP.

6 "Basic Action Kit," Operation Support, Box 21, MPP.

7 Ibid. Also see "11 States Act on 'Operation Support,'" *The Democrat*, April 27, 1961.

8 "Dutton to Burns," March 24, 1961, PL January 4, 1961–September 30, 1961, Box 680, WHCF, JFKL; "Dutton to Sorensen," November 21, 1961, PL October 1, 1961–February 20, 1962, Box 680, WHCF, JFKL; "Feldman to Price," November 30, 1961, PL October 1, 1961–February 20, 1962, Box 680, WHCF, JFKL.

9 "Price to Collins," May 6, 1961, Correspondence, April–May 1961, Box 4, MPP.

10 "Remarks by Price," May 21, 1962, Press Releases, March–December 1962, Box 8, MPP.

11 "Remarks by Price," January 20, 1962, Box 23, DNC Clippings File—Press Releases, JFKL.

12 Ibid.

13 "1962 Advance Report from Chairman Bailey," January 1, 1962, Box 23, DNC Clippings File—Press Releases, JFKL.

14 "Dutton to Sorensen," November 21, 1961, PL October 1, 1961–February 20, 1962, Box 680, WHCF, JFKL.

15 DNC Press Release, May 6, 1962, Box 24, DNC Clippings File—Press Releases, JFKL.

16 "An Information Program," Politics—Prior 1964 Campaign July 1962–February 5, 1963 and undated, Box 36, Sorensen Files, JFKL.

17 "An Information Program."

18 Ibid.

19 DNC Press Release, April 30, 1962, Box 24, DNC Clippings File—Press Releases, JFKL.

20 Ibid.; DNC Press Release, June 28, 1962, Box 24, DNC Clippings File—Press Releases, JFKL.

21 Ibid.

22 DNC Press Release, August 1, 1962, Box 25, DNC Clippings File—Press Releases, JFKL.

23 DNC Press Releases, June 28, 1962, July 16, 1962, Box 24, DNC Clippings File—Press Releases, JFKL. See also "Confidential Memorandum No. 2," January 12, 1962, Papers on 1962 Campaign, Box 21, MPP; and "Dutton to Bailey," November 21, 1961, PL 2, May 1, 1961–March 25, 1962, Box 692, WHCF, JFKL.

24 Democrats lost only four seats in the House and gained two seats in the Senate.

25 DNC Press Release, May 5, 1961, Box 22, DNC Clippings File—Press Releases, JFKL; and "Open Biggest Sustaining Member Drive," *The Democrat*, May 11, 1961, in DNC Publications: *The Democrat*, March 16, 1961–June 15, 1961, Box 32, Sorensen Files, JFKL.

26 Transcript, Lawrence O'Brien Oral History, V, Internet Copy, LBJL, 19.

27 Herbert E. Alexander, *Financing the 1964 Election* (Princeton, N.J.: Citizens Research Foundation, 1966), 77.

28 Transcript, Arthur B. Krim Oral History, I, Internet Copy, LBJL, 12–13.

29 Alexander, *Financing the 1964 Election*, 10, 79; Arthur B. Krim Oral History, I, LBJL, 12–13.

30 Arthur B. Krim Oral History, I, LBJL, 12. Also see "Criswell to Krim," January 21, 1967, Name File: Arthur Krim, LBJL.

31 Ronald Brownstein called this practice an "epochal shift of political power." Ronald Brownstein, *The Power and the Glitter: The Hollywood-Washington Connection* (New York: Vintage, 1992), 192.

32 Alexander, *Financing the 1964 Election*, 80.

33 Robert S. Allen and Paul Scott, "Democrats Put Price Tag on Talk," *Los Angeles Times*, March 11, 1963.

34 Ibid.

35 James MacGregor Burns, *John Kennedy: A Political Profile* (New York: Harcourt Brace, 1960); Sean J. Savage, *JFK, LBJ, and the Democratic Party* (Albany: State University of New York Press, 2004); Richard H. Bradford, "John F. Kennedy and the 1960 Presidential Primary in West Virginia," *South Atlantic Quarterly* 75 (1976): 161–72; Theodore H. White, *The Making of the President, 1960* (New York: Atheneum, 1961).

36 "Benedict to Goemans, Kennedy, and Spelar," January 8, 1961, PL 2 Elections—Campaigns, January 8, 1961–February 28, 1961, Box 691, WHCF, JFKL.

37 Ibid.

38 White, *Making of President, 1960*.

39 "Benedict to Goemans, Kennedy, and Spelar," January 8, 1961, PL 2 Elections—Campaigns, January 8, 1961–February 28, 1961, Box 691, WHCF, JFKL.

40 Dutton served as deputy national chairman of the Citizens for Kennedy and Johnson group in 1960.

41 "Benedict to Goemans, Kennedy, Spelar," January 8, 1961, PL 2 Elections—Campaigns, January 8, 1961–February 28, 1961, Box 691, WHCF, JFKL.

42 Ibid.

43 Richard P. Hunt, "Kennedy at Work on '64 Race Here," *New York Times*, April 6, 1963.

44 Ibid.

45 Edward T. Folliard, "See In-Law Smith Hard at Work in JFK 'Army,'" *Washington Post*, March 8, 1963; Tom Wicker, "The Name Is Smith," *New York Times*, July 28, 1963.

46 Wicker, "The Name Is Smith."

47 Ibid. Wicker boasted of his privileged access to Kennedy: see Transcript, Thomas G. Wicker Oral History, JFKL, 156.

48 "Harris to the President," September 3, 1963, Part I, 3, *KOF.*

49 "Harris to the President," Part I, 3, *KOF.*

50 See "JFK and Louis Harris," Cassette F (side 1), 17B.3, April 3, 1963; Cassette I (side 1), 26C.3 and 26D.1, August 23, 1963, JFKL Presidential Recordings. Also see Theodore C. Sorensen, *Kennedy* (New York: Harper and Row, 1965), 333; Kenneth P. O'Donnell and David F. Powers, *"Johnny, We Hardly Knew Ye": Memories of John Fitzgerald Kennedy* (Boston: Little, Brown, 1972), 222.

51 "Kennedy to Bailey," February 17, 1961, Part IV, 3, DNC Members for May 26, 1961, Reception, *KOF.*

52 Transcript, Matthew A. Reese Jr., Oral History, JFKL, 29.

53 Ibid.

54 Ibid.

55 "Bailey to Congressmen and Senators in 12 Priority States," (loose material 1 of 2), Box 83, DNC Collection, LBJL.

56 DNC Press Release, July 9, 1962, Box 25, DNC Clippings File—Press Releases, JFKL.

57 "Proclamation 3489 National Voter Registration Month," 6, 1962, *PPP.*

58 "Statement by the President Upon Signing Order Establishing the Commission on Registration and Voting Participation," March 30, 1963, *PPP.*

59 "Reese to O'Donnell," July 12, 1962, PL 2 Elections March 26, 1962–August 20, 1962, Box 692, WHCF, JFKL.

60 Stephen Skowronek, *Presidential Leadership in Political Time: Reprise and Reappraisal* (Lawrence: University Press of Kansas, 2008) 46, 57.

61 Transcript, Matthew A. Reese Jr., Oral History, JFKL, 29.

62 Transcript, Lawrence O'Brien Oral History, XVI, Internet Copy, LBJL, 19.

63 "Reese to Chairman Bailey," December 13, 1963, and December 19, 1963, in EX PL November 22, 1963–August 6, 1964, Box 1, WHCF, LBJL; "Reese to Maguire," December 31, 1963, Box 83 DNC Collection, LBJL.

64 Ibid.

65 "Maguire to O'Donnell," July 9, 1963, and "COPE" PL 2 Elections—Campaigns, December 1, 1962–end, Box 692, WHCF, JFKL; "Remarks to Delegates to a Conference on Voter Registration Sponsored by the AFL-CIO's Committee on Political Education," September 18, 1963, *PPP*; "Taylor to Fluet," September 17, 1963, PL 2 Elections—Campaigns, December 1, 1962–end, Box 692, WHCF, JFKL.

66 "10 Subcommittees Will Work to Strengthen the Party," *The Democrat*, June 2, 1961, DNC Publications *The Democrat*, March 16, 1961–June 15, 1961, Box 32, Sorensen Files, JFKL.

67 Savage, *JFK, LBJ*, 153.

68 DNC Press Release, December 22, 1961; also see "DNC Subcommittees"; both in Box 23, DNC Clippings File—Press Releases, JFKL.

69 DNC Press Release, January 26, 1962, Box 23, DNC Clippings File—Press Releases, JFKL.

70 DNC Press Release, February 23, 1962, Box 24, DNC Clippings File—Press Releases, JFKL.

71 "Roche to Maguire," and attachments, February 21, 1962, PL Political Affairs February 21, 1962–August 31, 1962, Box 680, WHCF, JFKL.

72 Ibid.

73 "Operation Know-How," 1962, Papers on '62 Campaign, Box 21, MPP.

74 DNC Press Release, June 12, 1962, and "DNC Operation Know-How," both from Box 24, DNC Clippings File—Press Releases, JFKL. At an Operation Know-How meeting in mid-March 1962, for example, Bailey devoted his entire keynote speech to an attack on the American Medical Association for its opposition to Kennedy's medical care for the aged proposal. "DNC Operation Know-How," March 28, 1962, Box 24, DNC Clippings File—Press Releases, JFKL.

75 "DNC Press Release," June 18, 1962, Box 24, DNC Clippings File—Press Releases, JFKL.

76 Transcript, Lawrence O'Brien Oral History, XX, Internet Copy, LBJL, 6.

77 Ibid., X, 3–4.

9 | The President's Club: Lyndon B. Johnson

1 Lawrence O'Brien Oral History, XXVI, LBJL, 20–21.

2 Skowronek, *The Politics Presidents Make*, 325. Sean Savage calls LBJ's approach a "suprapartisan, non-ideological, unifying consensus politics." Savage, *JFK, LBJ*, 159.

3 Doris Kearns Goodwin, *Lyndon Johnson and the American Dream* (New York: Harper and Row, 1976), 374; George Tames Oral History, HSTL, 19.

4 Quote from Al Barkan, director of the Committee on Political Education (COPE), in Savage, *JFK, LBJ*, 174.

5 Broder, *The Party's Over*, 62; Theodore White, *The Making of the President, 1968* (New York: Atheneum, 1969), 120; Milkis, *The President and the Parties*, 179; Skowronek, *The Politics Presidents Make*, 352.

6 White, *Making of President, 1968*, 120; Skowronek, *The Politics Presidents Make*, 352; Milkis, *The President and the Parties*, 179; Savage, *JFK, LBJ*, 158.

7 Doris Kearns Goodwin, "Lyndon Johnson's Political Personality," *Political Science Quarterly* 91, no. 3 (1976): 386, 388; Robert Dallek, *Flawed Giant: Lyndon Johnson and His Times, 1961–1973* (New York: Oxford University Press, 1998), 281.

8 Dallek, *Flawed Giant*, 281.

9 As in the well-documented case of DNC staffer Paul Corbin. Ibid., 58, 135–36; Michael R. Beschloss, *Taking Charge: The Johnson White House Tapes, 1963–1964* (New York: Simon and Schuster, 1997), 236–38.

10 Goodwin, *Lyndon Johnson*, 372.

11 Dallek, *Flawed Giant*, 125.

12 Robert A. Caro, *Master of the Senate* (New York: Knopf, distributed by Random House, 2002), 427–29, 632–33.

13 Arthur Krim Oral History, I, LBJL, 13.

14 Ibid., 8–9. Robert S. Allen and Paul Scott, "Johnson's Rapport with Business Undermined by Actions of Aides," *Los Angeles Times*, May 5, 1964; Tom Wicker, "Johnson and Business Find That Tie Still Binds," *New York Times* January 17, 1966.

15 Arthur Krim Oral History, I, LBJL, 11–12.

16 Ibid., 10. Also see "Jenkins to Weisl," December 18, 1963, Name File: Arthur Krim, LBJL.

17 Ibid., 21

18 Thomas Buckley, "President Here for Dinner Given by 1,000 Donors," *New York Times*, May 23, 1965.

19 "Watson to the President," July 8, 1965, PL June 29, 1965–October 18, 1965, WHCF PL, LBJL; and see, for example, Buckley, "President Here for Dinner"; "Johnson Going to Houston to Open Party's Fund-Dinner Campaign," *Washington Post*, April 27, 1966.

20 "Marvin to Mr. President," February 15, 1966, January 1966–April 1966, Name File: Cliff Carter, LBJL.

21 "Marvin to Mr. President," November 18, 1965 (attachment), DNC/Miscellaneous [3 of 3], Box 19, Aides: Watson, LBJL.

22 Ibid., 164. Arthur Krim Oral History III, LBJL, 3.

23 "Criswell to White," November 16, 1967 and "Criswell to Watson," November 18, 1966, in DNC/Financial Reports, Box 19, Aides: Watson; "Marvin to Mr. President," December 17, 1965, EX PL October 19, 1965–January 15, 1966, Box 1, WHCF PL, LBJL.

24 "Marvin to Mr. President," June 14, 1965, EX PL August 7, 1964–June 28, 1965, Box 1, WHCF PL; "Kintner to Moyers," August 29, 1966, Name File: Arthur Krim; "Report of John Criswell," DNC/Financial Reports [1 of 4], Box 19, Aides: Watson, LBJL. Also see Herbert E. Alexander, *Financing the 1968 Election* (Lexington, Mass.: Heath Lexington Books, 1971), 151.

25 See "Price to Cater," July 5, 1966, PL 3 November 27, 1965–April 25, 1966, Box 110, WHCF PL, LBJL; also "1966 Dollars for Democrats Drive," and "Democrats Launch National Fund Drive," July 17, 1966, Papers Concerning 1964 Presidential Campaign, Box 22, MPP.

26 The influential Unruh was a stalwart Kennedy family friend; in addition to seeking his organizational help during the campaign, Johnson also wanted to ensure that he did not support Robert Kennedy for the presidential or vice presidential nomination at the convention.

27 Philip Warden, "$1,000-or-More Johnson Club Reports," *Chicago Tribune*, October 23, 1964.

28 See, for example, "Bailey to the President," October 3, 1964, November 1, 1963–December 31, 1964, Name: John Bailey, LBJL; "Criswell to Watson," March 8, 1967, DNC/Financial Reports [1 of 4], Aides: Watson, LBJL.

29 Arthur Krim Oral History, V, LBJL, 4.

30 "From the desk of Marvin Watson," EX PL September 12, 1966–January 19, 1967, Box 1, WHCF PL, LBJL. On the separate bank accounts used, see, for example, "Criswell to Krim," January 21, 1967, Name File: Arthur Krim, LBJL.

31 Thomas P. Ronan, "Democrat's Bill in Albany to Seek List of Gifts to President's Club," *New York Times*, November 25, 1966. See also Rowland Evans and Robert Novak, "Birch Money Burns Hole," *Washington Post*, September 4, 1966; George Lardner Jr., "GOP Tops Democrats in Election Financing," *Washington Post*, Oc-

tober 30, 1966; Rowland Evans and Robert Novak, "Inside Report," *Washington Post*, July 6, 1966.

32　Goodwin, *Lyndon Johnson*, 256.

33　"Watson to the President," July 28, 1965, and "Watson to Carter," July 30, 1965, in PL 2 August 15, 1964–August 25, 1964, Box 83, WHCF PL, LBJL.

34　See, for example, "Watson to Clark," October 21, 1965, PL 3 July 12, 1966–December 25, 1966, Box 110, WHCF PL, LBJL.

35　"Operation Support," Operation Support, Box 21, MPP.

36　See, for example, "Colgate to Chewning," November 2, 1964, Correspondence, November 1964, Box 5, MPP.

37　"Operation Support for the Great Society," PL 3 November 27, 1965–April 25, 1966, Box 110; also see "Criswell to Watson," September 2, 1967, PL 7 August 25, 1967–November 15, 1967, Box 123, in WHCF PL, LBJL.

38　"Bush to Watson," July 19, 1965, EX PL June 29, 1965–October 18, 1965, Box 1, WHCF PL, LBJL.

39　"Watson to the President," April 13, 1965, EX PL August 7, 1964–June 28, 1965, Box 1, WHCF PL; "Carter to Mr. President," December 21, 1963, PL 2 Elections—Campaigns November 22, 1963–January 3, 1964, Box 81, WHCF PL; "Marvin to Mr. President," December 12, 1966, January 1, 1966–December 31, 1966, Name: Bailey; "Marvin to Mr. President," October 5, 1967, DNC/Miscellaneous [1 of 3], Box 19, Aides: Watson; "Criswell to Watson," September 20, 1967, PL 6-2 Democratic Party November 23, 1963–March 8, 1967, Box 16, WHCF PL; "Roche to the President," March 7, 1967, and "Bailey and Criswell to Watson," March 28, 1967, and "Criswell to Watson," March 4, 1967, in EX PL January 20, 1967–March 31, 1967, Box 1, WHCF PL, LBJL.

40　Each man arrived at different times: Criswell largely assumed Carter's responsibilities; Krim took some responsibilities from Watson; each man's role was somewhat fluid. See W. Marvin Watson and Sherwin Markman, *Chief of Staff: Lyndon Johnson and His Presidency* (New York: Thomas Dunne, 2004), 163; also Arthur Krim Oral History, III, LBJL, 5.

41　Edward T. Folliard, "Registration Lead Claimed by Democrats," *Washington Post*, October 4, 1964.

42　"Criswell to Watson," December 1, 1966, and attachments, PL 6-2 Democratic Party November 23, 1963–March 8, 1967, Box 116, WHCF PL, LBJL.

43　Watson and Markman, *Chief of Staff*, 163.

44　See, for example, "Reese to the Chairman," March 17, 1964 (loose material 1 of 2), Box 83, DNC Collection, LBJL.

45　Ibid.

46　"Valenti to the President" with attachment, January 31, 1964, PL 2 Elections—Campaigns November 22, 1963–January 3, 1964, Box 82, WHCF PL, LBJL.

47　"Bailey to Congressmen and Senators in 12 Priority States" (loose material 1 of 2), Box 83, DNC Collection, LBJL; see also O'Brien's analysis that "among those who declare a party affiliation, the edge has been 2-1 Democratic," "O'Brien to the President," October 8, 1964, PL 2 October 8, 1964, Box 85, WHCF PL, LBJL.

48　"Reese to the Chairman," November 5, 1964; also see "Reese to Bailey," December 12, 1964, in Name: Matt Reese, LBJL.

49　"Watson to Mr. Vice President," February 15, 1965, January 1, 1965–December 31, 1965, Name: John Bailey, LBJL.

50 On Reese's departure, see "Manatos to Byrd," April 5, 1965, and June 1, 1965, and "Rowe to Reese," June 17, 1965, in Name: Reese, LBJL. On the nonpartisan drive, see "Cater to the President," November 29, 1965, and "Cater to Watson," December 6, 1965, May 11, 1965–January 17, 1966, Box 85 and "Marvin to Mr. President," January 6, 1966, PL 3 November 27, 1965–April 25, 1966, Box 110, WHCF PL, LBJL.

51 "Marvin to Mr. President," August 5, 1966, Name: Arthur Krim, LBJL.

52 "Criswell to Watson," December 1, 1966 and attachments, PL 6-2 Democratic Party November 23, 1963–March 8, 1967, Box 116, WHCF PL, LBJL.

53 Ibid. The American Heritage Foundation conducted national nonpartisan voter registration drives.

54 Greenstone, *Labor in American Politics*, 323–24.

55 Milkis, *The President and the Parties*, 206–7.

56 See, for example, "Carter to the President," December 21, 1963, PL 2 Elections—Campaigns November 22, 1963–January 3, 1964, Box 81, WHCF PL.

57 Arthur Krim Oral History, III, LBJL, 4–5.

58 Johnson's refusal to replace the team he inherited was due to his public promise to continue along the path charted by his fallen predecessor, which he described in valiant terms: "Rightly or wrongly, I felt from the very first day in office that I had to carry on for President Kennedy. I considered myself the caretaker of both his people and his policies. He knew when he selected me as his running mate that I would be the man required to carry on if anything happened to him. I did what I believed he would have wanted me to do. I never wavered from that sense of responsibility, even after I was elected in my own right, up to my last day in office." Lyndon B. Johnson, *The Vantage Point: Perspectives of the Presidency, 1963–1969* (New York: Holt Rinehart and Winston, 1971), 19.

59 "Campaign Organization," November 16, 1964–December 25, 1964, Box 85, WHCF PL, LBJL; Watson and Markman, *Chief of Staff*, 56–66, 249.

60 Robert S. Allen and Paul Scott, "Johnson Strengthens His Control of Party before Convention Opens," *Los Angeles Times*, June 5, 1964.

61 O'Brien Oral History, IX, LBJL, 2.

62 Ibid., VIII, LBJL, 11.

63 Ibid., X, LBJL, 1–2.

64 See, for example, "O'Brien to the President," October 8, 1964, October 9, 1964, in PL 2 October 8, 1964, and PL 2 October 9, 1964, Box 85, WHCF PL, LBJL.

65 O'Brien Oral History, X, LBJL.

66 Ibid., 2.

67 Ibid., XX, April 23, 1987, LBJL, 2.

68 Ibid., X, June 25, 1986, LBJL, 2–3.

69 Watson and Markman, *Chief of Staff*, 249.

70 James Rowe Jr. Oral History, LBJL, 47; and "JV (Jack Valenti) to the President," July 1, 1964, PL 5 November 22, 1963–August 19, 1964, WHCF PL, LBJL.

71 Rowe Oral History.

72 O'Brien went back to his post as special assistant to the president for congressional relations and personnel, and in 1965 was appointed by LBJ to be postmaster general. Carter went to work as Johnson's personal representative and political director of the DNC, and James Rowe returned to his Washington law practice.

73 O'Brien Oral History, XXI, LBJL, 8.

74 "A White Paper for the President on the 1968 Presidential Campaign by Lawrence F. O'Brien," September 29, 1967, DNC/Rowe-O'Brien-Crooker-Criswell Operation, Box 20, Aides: Watson, LBJL. For O'Brien's discussion of the White Paper and the discussions surrounding it, see Lawrence F. O'Brien Oral History, XXI, LBJL.

75 "A White Paper," 29.

76 "Notes and Comments on 'A White Paper …' by James Rowe," undated, DNC/Rowe-O'Brien-Crooker-Criswell Operation, Box 20, Aides: Watson, LBJL. See also "O'Brien to Rowe," November 7, 1967, and "O'Brien to the President," November 3, 1967, in O'Brien, Larry, Box 25, Aides: Watson, LBJL.

77 Watson and Markman, *Chief of Staff*, 165–66.

78 O'Brien Oral History, XX, LBJL, 2.

79 "Bailey and Criswell to Watson," March 16, 1967, January 1, 1967–December 31, 1967, Name: John Bailey; "Criswell to Watson," September 3, 1967, EX PL August 1, 1967–September 14, 1967, Box 2, WHCF PL; and "Regional Meetings to Focus on Issues of '68 Campaign," *The Democrat*, 12, 1967, PL 7 November 16, 1967–January 9, 1968, Box 123, WHCF PL, LBJL.

80 "DNC Press Release," March 7, 1968, Democratic Regional Conferences, Box 22, Aides: Watson, LBJL.

81 See, for example, "Criswell to Watson," March 16, 1968, Democratic Regional Conferences, Box 22, Aides: Watson, LBJL.

82 "Report from Watson to the President," December 15, 1967, Democratic State Chairmen, Box 22, Aides: Watson, LBJL.

83 "Criswell to Watson," February 3, 1968, January 23, 1968–February 6, 1968, Box 88, WHCF PL; also see "Daniel to Watson," January 16, 1968, and "Criswell to Watson," February 6, 1968, Johnson-Humphrey, Box 24, and "Crooker to Watson," February 9, 1968, DNC/Rowe-O'Brien-Crooker-Criswell Operation, Box 20, Aides: Watson, LBJL.

84 "Citizens for Johnson-Humphrey," March 16, 1968, DNC/Rowe-O'Brien-Crooker-Criswell Operation, Box 20, Aides: Watson, LBJL.

85 On the state of the party apparatus during Humphrey's ill-fated campaign, see, for example, Carl Greenberg, "Humphrey's Calif. Drive Lags," *Los Angeles Times*, September 18, 1968. The new DNC treasurer during Humphrey's campaign, Robert E. Short, noted that the President's Club money had dried up. He said: "The committee was about even—no bills and no money." David R. Jones, "Humphrey Seeks $1,000 Supporters," *New York Times*, October 25, 1968. For a good discussion, see Savage, *JFK, LBJ*, 173–81.

86 See Caro, *Master of the Senate*, 403–13. For more on how Johnson's background experiences informed his future presidential behavior, see, in particular, Savage, *JFK, LBJ*, chap. 2; Dallek, *Flawed Giant*; Goodwin, *Lyndon Johnson*.

87 O'Brien Oral History, IX, LBJL, 15–16.

88 Watson and Markman, *Chief of Staff*, 166–67.

89 Ibid.

90 Ibid.

91 "Fact Sheet, 1964 Democratic Congressional Candidates' Conference," PL 2 Elections—Campaigns June 15, 1964–July 23, 1964, Box 82, WHCF PL, LBJL.

92 "Congressional Services," February 5, 1965, Papers, 1963–64 of DNC, Box 20, MPP.

93 "Marvin to Mr. President," June 19, 1965, EX PL August 7, 1964–June 28, 1965; also see "Cliff Carter to the President," October 14, 1965, EX PL June 29, 1965–October 18, 1965, Box 1, WHCF PL, LBJL.

94 "Watson to Mr. President," February 2, 1966, EX PL October 19, 1965–January 15, 1966, Box 1, WHCF PL, LBJL.

95 Clifton Carter Oral History, LBJL, 30.

96 O'Brien Oral History, XVI, LBJL, 21. See, for example, "Bill Moyers to the President," May 2, 1966, January 18, 1966–May 23, 1966, Box 85, WHCF PL; "Carter to the President," May 24, 1966, May 1966–August 1966, Name: Cliff Carter; "Watson to the President," July 8, 1966, DNC/Miscellaneous [2 of 3], Box 19, Aides: Watson, LBJL. "LBJ to JRJ" with attachment, August 28, 1967, EX PL August 1, 1967–September 14, 1967, Box 2, WHCF PL, LBJL.

97 "Kintner to the President," September 6, 1966, EX PL June 10, 1966–September 11, 1966, Box 1, WHCF PL, LBJL.

98 Watson and Markman, *Chief of Staff*, 56–66.

99 Recording of Telephone Conversation, Johnson and Cliff Carter, June 23, 1964, 1:36 pm, Citation no. 3826, LBJL.

100 Rowland Evans and Robert D. Novak, *Lyndon B. Johnson: The Exercise of Power* (New York: New American Library, 1966), 465; and Savage, *JFK, LBJ*, 227.

101 Watson and Markman, *Chief of Staff*, 62.

102 Carl Albert Oral History, IV, LBJL, 8–9.

103 Ibid., 9–10.

104 Charles S. Murphy Oral History, LBJL, 9.

105 "Reedy to the President," November 10, 1966, November 2, 1966–December 3, 1966, Box 87, WHCF PL, LBJL.

106 "Martin to Watson," November 30, 1966, DNC/Miscellaneous [2 of 3], Box 19, Aides: Watson, LBJL.

107 "Criswell to Watson," December 1, 1966, EX PL September 12, 1966–January 19, 1967, Box 1, WHCF PL, LBJL.

108 Ibid.

109 "Criswell to Watson," December 1, 1966 and attachments, PL 6-2 Democratic Party November 23, 1963–March 8, 1967, Box 116; also see "Criswell to Watson," February 1, 1967, EX PL January 20, 1967–March 31, 1967, Box 1, WHCF PL, LBJL.

110 See sources in preceding note and "Marvin to Mr. President," January 18, 1967, and attachments from Criswell, DNC/Financial Reports [1 of 4], Box 19, Aides: Watson, LBJL.

111 "Criswell to Watson," February 3, 1968, 1967 July—3 of 4, Name: John Criswell, LBJL.

112 "Criswell to Watson," February 17, 1968, 1967 July—3 of 4, Name: John Criswell, LBJL.

113 "Criswell to Watson," March 29, 1968, DNC/Miscellaneous [2 of 3], Box 19, Aides: Watson, LBJL.

114 "Criswell to Watson," July 19, 1967; "Criswell to Watson," June 2, 1967; "Jones to Criswell" with attachment, September 4, 1967; "Criswell to Watson," October 23, 1967; "Criswell to Watson," October 10, 1967; Box 2, WHCF PL, LBJL.

115 "Kintner to Mr. President," December 2, 1966, November 2, 1966–December 3, 1966, Box 87, WHCF PL, LBJL.

116 Recording of Telephone Conversation, Johnson and Kintner, December 5, 1966, Tape WH6612.05, 7:57 am, LBJL.
117 "Markman to Watson" and LBJ dictation, December 20, 1966, December 4, 1966–December 22, 1966, Box 87, WHCF PL, LBJL.
118 O'Brien Oral History, XX, LBJL, 3.
119 "West's Demos Press Party's Rebuilding," *Salt Lake Tribune*, January 15, 1967, EX PL September 12, 1966–January 19, 1967, Box 1, WHCF PL, LBJL.
120 "Marvin to the President," January 17, 1968, EX PL September 12, 1966–January 19, 1967, Box 1, WHCF PL, LBJL.
121 "O'Donnell to Carpenter," December 18, 1963, Correspondence, November–December 1963, Box 5, MPP; "Colle to Valenti," March 25, 1966, January 1966–April 1966, Name: Clifton Carter, LBJL.
122 "Price to Carter," July 5, 1966, PL 3 November 27, 1965–April 25, 1966, Box 110, WHCF PL, LBJL.
123 "Marvin to the President," January 9, 1967 and "Price to Watson," January 9, 1967, EX PL September 12, 1966–January 19, 1967, Box 1, WHCF PL, LBJL.
124 "Liz to the President and Mrs. Johnson," September 29, 1966, DNC/Women [1 of 2], Box 21, Aides: Watson, LBJL.

10 | Alternative Priorities: Jimmy Carter

1 President Jimmy Carter Oral History, November 29, 1982, Carter Presidency Project, Miller Center, 43.
2 Klinkner, *The Losing Parties*, 88–132.
3 "A Suggested Carter Administration Agenda," Political Problems—Political File, August 1976–January 1977, Box 3, Office of Staff Secretary, JCL. Also see Rudy Abramson, "Memo Suggested Techniques," *Los Angeles Times*, May 4, 1977.
4 "A Suggested Carter Administration Agenda"; also see "Caddell to Carter," December 21, 1976, Caddell [December 1976–January 1977], Box 1, Staff Secretary, Handwriting File, JCL.
5 Carter said: "I got the nomination without the help or support of the Democratic National Committee members or executive officers. And I won the nomination on that basis by taking my case directly to the people and running to some degree as an outsider, not only from the Congress in Washington, but also from the Democratic National Committee" (Jimmy Carter Oral History, 43). Charles O. Jones notes that "political party often is available as a resource … however, the outsider president serving as a trustee is unlikely to depend on this resource." Charles O. Jones, *The Trusteeship Presidency: Jimmy Carter and the United States Congress* (Baton Rouge: Louisiana State University Press, 1988), 8.
6 On Carter's formative political experiences in Georgia politics, see Erwin C. Hargrove, *Jimmy Carter as President* (Baton Rouge: Louisiana State University Press, 1988), chap. 1; Carter was, of course, more of a party outsider than Ford, Nixon, and Johnson. But he was hardly a novice when it came to party affairs. In March 1973 he was appointed by DNC chairman Robert Strauss to be the national campaign chairman for all Democratic congressional and gubernatorial elections in 1974. In that role, Carter represented the party establishment and built relationships with Democratic officials across the country. By the time he reached the presidency, he certainly had more experience in party politics than Dwight

Eisenhower in 1953, yet the two men could not have approached their party more differently. See Jones, *The Trusteeship Presidency*, 24–25.

7 On the distance between Carter and his fellow partisans, see Skowronek, *The Politics Presidents Make*, 361–406.

8 Skowronek, *Presidential Leadership*, 71.

9 Jimmy Carter Oral History, 17.

10 Ibid., 26, 27.

11 Hamilton Jordan Oral History, Carter Presidency Project, Miller Center of Public Affairs, 9.

12 David Broder, "Carter Takes Complete Control of Democratic Party Machinery," *Washington Post*, January 22, 1977; Warren Weaver, "Carter Campaign Aides Leading Democrats' Staff," *New York Times*, January 19, 1977.

13 Broder, "Carter Takes Complete Control."

14 "Curtis Elected as Democratic Party Leader," *Los Angeles Times*, January 21, 1977.

15 "A Suggested Carter Administration Agenda," Political Problems—Political File, August 1976–January 1977, Box 3, Office of Staff Secretary, JCL.

16 "Democratic National Committee: Goals and Structure," March 15, 1977, DNC January 5, 1977–March 28, 1977, Box 96, Butler, JCL.

17 Ibid.

18 Ibid.

19 Ibid.; "Curtis to Jordan" February 8, 1977, DNC January 5, 1977–March 28, 1977, Box 96, Butler, JCL.

20 "Lipshutz and Jordan to the President," April 6, 1977 and "McCleary to Jordan," March 22, 1977, and "Hendrix to Falk," March 25, 1977, DNC [2], Box 2, Rafshoon, JCL. On the fund-raiser, see "Jordan to Carter," May 23, 1977, President-DNC "Birthday Party," 5, 1977, Box 34, Chief of Staff, JCL.

21 "Siegel to Jordan," March 29, 1977, Memoranda [1977], Box 55, Chief of Staff, JCL.

22 David Broder, "Party Politics," *Washington Post*, April 6, 1977.

23 "Siegel to Jordan," Memoranda [1977], Box 55, Chief of Staff, JCL.

24 "Democratic National Committee Work Program," May 19, 1977, DNC, April 11, 1977–October 27, 1977, Box 96, Butler, JCL. The "President Has Seen" stamp indicates that Carter personally read the work program.

25 "Meeting the Challenge," *Political Report*, June 1977, DNC, April 11, 1977–October 27, 1977, Box 96, Butler, JCL.

26 "Curtis Says Money Was Top Headache as DNC Chairman," *Washington Post*, December 9, 1977; and Terence Smith, "Democratic Leader Denies White House Forced Him to Quit," *New York Times*, December 9, 1977.

27 Robert Shogan, "Democratic Party Chief Resigning," *Los Angeles Times*, December 8, 1977.

28 "Jordan to Carter," DNC-President, 1977–79, Box 34, Chief of Staff, JCL.

29 "Democratic National Committee Remarks at a Special Meeting of the Committee," January 27, 1978, *PPP*.

30 Terence Smith, "Carter, Apologizing for Neglect, Makes Up with Party Committee," *New York Times*, January 28, 1978.

31 Jimmy Carter Oral History, 43–44.

32 "Confidential," December 14, 1977, DNC-President, 1977–79, Box 34, Chief of Staff, JCL.

33 "Carter to Galbraith," December 28, 1977, PL October 1, 1977–February 28, 1978, Box PL-1, WHCF, JCL.

34 "White to the President," April 14, 1978, White, Democratic Partnership, Box 82, Staff Offices, Press: Powell, JCL.

35 Ibid.

36 "White to DNC Member," February 21, 1978, DNC, January 6, 1978–February 17, 1978, Box 5, Speechwriters—Subject File, JCL.

37 Judith Frutig, "Western Governors Wary of Carter Help," *Christian Science Monitor*, June 21, 1978; "Democrats in the West Express Concern at Republicans' Ascent," *New York Times*, July 25, 1978.

38 "White to the President," April 14, 1978, White, Democratic Partnership, Box 82, Staff: Powell, JCL.

39 For example, see Bill Peterson, "Democratic Chairman Escalates Attempt to Head Off Carter Foes," *Washington Post*, May 25, 1979.

40 Frutig, "Western Governors Wary"; "Democrats in the West Express Concern at Republicans' Ascent," *New York Times*, July 25, 1978.

41 See, for example, "Rendon to White," November 3, 1978, DNC [7], Box 239, Hutcheson, JCL. Note the bare-bones "work plan" initiated by the DNC Political Division in mid-1979 in "Democratic National Committee Political Division July 1979/Work Plan," DNC [8], Box 239, Hutcheson, JCL. Also see the singular emphasis on meetings, resolutions, and future party proceedings to the exclusion of organizational development in "Rendon to Kelly," October 31, 1979, DNC [9], Box 239, Hutcheson, JCL. For a fascinating examination of Rendon's later political career, see James Bamford, "The Man Who Sold the War," *Rolling Stone*, November 17, 2005.

42 "Kraft to Jordan," May 24, 1978, DNC, Box 44, Chief of Staff, JCL.

43 Ibid.

44 "Meeting with Democratic State Party Chairs and Vice Chairs," October 3, 1979, DNC—State Chairs, Box 78, Chief of Staff, JCL; and see also "Weddington to Voorde and Wise," November 26, 1979, PL September 1, 1979–January 31, 1980, Box PL-2, WHCF, JCL.

45 Godfrey Sperling Jr., "Carter Lays '80 Campaign Plans," *Christian Science Monitor*, August 21, 1978.

46 "Confidential," December 14, 1977, DNC-President, 1977–79, Box 34, Chief of Staff, JCL.

47 Ibid.

48 Ibid.

49 Margaret McManus, "Political Stardom Predicted for Wexler," in Kraft, Tim [Misc. Communications—April 18, 1977–June 28, 1978], Box 1, Staff Offices: Tim Kraft, JCL; Godfrey Sperling, "Carter Acts to Improve Standing with Party Leaders across U.S.," *Christian Science Monitor*, May 3, 1978; David Broder, "Kraft to Be Carter's Campaign Chief," *Washington Post*, August 11, 1979.

50 "Jordan to Nelson," November 11, 1977, Box 2: DNC [1], Rafshoon, JCL; "Gianni to Kite," November 11, 1977; and "McGee to Poston," November 4, 1977, in DNC [1], Box 2, Rafshoon, JCL; see also David Broder, "President's Yule Cards Aimed at Garnering Support," *Washington Post*, December 6, 1977.

51 Broder, "President's Yule Cards."

52 Terence Smith, "It's Carter Folk vs. Regular Democrats," *New York Times*, December 11, 1977.

53 "Fallows and Nesmith to the President," January 19, 1978, DNC, January 6, 1978–February 17, 1978, Box 5, Speechwriters—Subject File, JCL. See "Remarks at a Reception for Georgia Campaign Volunteers," 20, 1978, *PPP*.

54 Smith, "Carter Folk."

55 "Moore and Kraft to President," August 24, 1978, July 1, 1978–December 31, 1978, Box PL-1, WHCF, JCL.

56 "DNC Data Bank Program, Democratic National Committee," DNC—1978 Campaign Notebook, Box 96, Butler Subject File, December 7, 1976–January 6, 1981, JCL.

57 Ibid.

58 "Direct Voter Contact Proposal, Democratic National Committee, by NTA National, Inc.," June 1977, DNC [4], Box 238, Hutcheson, JCL.

59 Klinkner, *The Losing Parties*, 171.

60 "Confidential," December 14, 1977, DNC-President, 1977–79, Box 34, Chief of Staff, JCL.

61 "Moore and Kraft to the President," September 22, 1978; and "Presidential Appearances in 1978," Elections 1978, Box 2, Rafshoon; and "1978 Campaign Photo Opportunities," July 1, 1978–December 31, 1978, Box PL-1, WHCF, JCL; see also Edward Walsh, "Carter Aides to Stump for Democrats to Build Hill Support," *Washington Post*, February 22, 1978.

62 After the elections, Democrats still held 277 House seats, fifty-eight Senate seats, 64 percent of state legislative seats (and controlled thirty-one state legislative chambers), and thirty-two governorships; Democratic Party identification rose two points to 54 percent.

63 "Kamarck and Murray to Donilon," February 28, 1980, DNC [9], Box 239, Hutcheson, JCL; "Rendon to Kelly," October 31, 1979, DNC [9], Box 239, Hutcheson, JCL.

64 Ibid.

65 "Finchem to Kraft, Smith, and Donilon," March 6, 1980, DNC [9], Box 239, Hutcheson, JCL.

66 Francis X. Clines, "About Politics: A Lift for Party Unity," *New York Times*, July 23, 1980.

67 "Finchem to Kraft, Smith, and Donilon," March 6, 1980, DNC [9], Box 239, Hutcheson, JCL.

68 "Weddington to Wise and Voorde," May 20, 1980, PL February 1, 1980–January 20, 1981, Box PL-2, WHCF, JCL.

69 Clines, "About Politics."

70 See, for example, "Plan to Simplify Voter Registration Is Slated by Carter," *Wall Street Journal*, March 21, 1977; Congressional Quarterly, "'Instant' Voter Registration Splits Democrats, GOP," *Christian Science Monitor*, January 6, 1977.

71 In a memo to Carter in December 1977, for example, Jordan argued that the DNC should concentrate on "voter registration and turnout" in 1978 and beyond as the best way to benefit Carter in 1980. He acknowledged, however, that voter mobilization was a "complex and massive organizational job" that required considerable funding, manpower, and planning, and the party's debt would need to be retired "before we can hope to have the resources for a really effective DNC operation." See "Confidential," December 14, 1977, DNC-President, 1977–79, Box 34, Chief of Staff, JCL.

72 "Voter Registration," DNC Material, Box 33, Martin, JCL; "White to Carter," June 23, 1978, and "White to Carter," July 14, 1978, DNC [3], Box 2, Rafshoon, JCL.

73 Jimmy Carter Oral History, 44.

74 Robert Shogan, "Democratic Charter Unit Begins Work," *Los Angeles Times*, July 22, 1973.

75 Warren Weaver Jr., "Democratic Leaders Vote to Cut Size of '78 Midterm Conference," *New York Times*, June 11, 1977.

76 Helen Dewar, "Democratic Committee Agrees to Hold a 'Mini-Convention,'" *Washington Post*, June 11, 1977.

77 "Siegel and Jordan to the President," May 19, 1977, Siegel, Mark, Memoranda [1977], Box 55, Chief of Staff, JCL.

78 "Weekly Political Report to the President from Hamilton Jordan," February 28, 1977, DNC January 5, 1977–March 28, 1977, Box 96, Butler, JCL.

79 "Hutcheson to Curtis and Jordan," May 19, 1977, DNC April 11, 1977–October 27, 1977, Box 96, Butler, JCL.

80 Weaver, "Democratic Leaders Vote."

81 See, for example, "Rendon to Gallagher," June 25, 1978, DNC [5], Box 238, Hutcheson, JCL.

82 David Broder, "New Rules for Democrats," *Washington Post*, December 8, 1978.

83 "Workshop Panelists at Midterm Conference, by Rick Hutcheson," October 13, 1978, DNC, 1978, June 19, 1978–March 20, 1979, Box 96, Butler, JCL.

84 David Broder and Bill Peterson, "Kennedy Warns of a Party Split by Arms Outlays," *Washington Post*, December 9, 1978.

85 Ibid.

86 Adam Clymer, "Carter Aides Favor Shift in Primary Rule," *New York Times*, August 31, 1977.

87 "Jordan to the President," September 6, 1977, Delegate Selection Rules for 1980, September 1977, Box 34, Chief of Staff, JCL.

88 Ibid.

89 "Hutcheson to Jordan," September 7, 1977, Delegate Selection Rules for 1980, September 1977, Box 34, Chief of Staff, JCL.

90 For example, see "Hutcheson to Jordan," April 25, 1978; "Talking Points for Phone Call to John White," Winograd Commission 1977–78 [2] Box 251, Hutcheson, JCL; and see "Hutcheson to Moe," May 31, 1978, DNC [4], Box 238, Hutcheson, JCL.

91 "Hutcheson to Jordan," September 13, 1977, DNC—General, Box 78, Chief of Staff, JCL. See also David Broder, "Democratic Unit Backs 12-Week Primary Season," *Washington Post*, September 11, 1977.

92 "Hutcheson to Jordan," April 25, 1978; "Talking Points for Phone Call to John White," Winograd Commission 1977–78 [2] Box 251, Hutcheson Files, JCL.

93 "White to Carter," June 15, 1978, DNC, 1978, June 19, 1978–March 20, 1979, Box 96, Butler, JCL.

94 "Hutcheson to White," April 14, 1980; and "White to Carter," April 14, 1980, DNC—General, Box 78, Chief of Staff, JCL.

95 "Jordan to the President," April 14, 1980, DNC—General, Box 78, Chief of Staff, JCL.

96 William Schneider, "Have Conventions Become Beastly Burdens?" *Los Angeles Times*, August 17, 1980.

97 Jimmy Carter Oral History, 43–44.

98 Klinkner, *The Losing Parties*, 164.

99 Ibid.

100 Dom Bonafede, "Politics: Democratic Party Takes Some Strides Down the Long Comeback Trail," *National Journal*, October 8, 1983.

101 Klinkner, *The Losing Parties*, 164.

102 Bonafede, "Politics."

11 | Culmination and Reversal: Bill Clinton

1 Personal interview with former DNC chairman Donald Fowler, June 14, 2007, Columbia, SC.

2 See, for example, Kenneth S. Baer, "Life after Clinton," *New Democrat*, January 1, 2000.

3 Political documents from the Clinton White House are not yet available at the Clinton Library at the time of this writing. This chapter therefore relies on personal interviews conducted by the author, party publications, memoirs, and newspaper and journal articles to identify president-party interactions and deduce Clinton's motives within a changing political context.

4 Ceci Connolly, "Developing the Sales Pitch for the Overhaul Plan," *Congressional Quarterly Weekly Report*, July 10, 1993; Ceci Connolly, "DNC Aims to Approach Hill from Ground Up," *Congressional Quarterly Weekly Report*, October 16, 1993.

5 Connolly, "DNC Aims to Approach Hill."

6 Ibid.; James A. Barnes, "Politics: Double Identity," *National Journal*, November 27, 1993.

7 Ceci Connolly, "Clinton's Health-Care Cheerleader," *Congressional Quarterly Weekly Report*, October 16, 1993.

8 Barnes, "Politics: Double Identity."

9 Ibid.

10 Richard L. Berke, "Clinton Moving to Avoid Losses in '94 Elections," *New York Times*, February 22, 1994.

11 Barnes, "Politics: Double Identity."

12 Connolly, "DNC Aims to Approach Hill."

13 James A. Barnes, "Politics: Double Identity."

14 Ibid.

15 Ibid.

16 Ibid.

17 James A. Barnes, "White House Notebook: Clinton's 1994 Political Machine," *National Journal*, February 12, 1994.

18 Julie Kosterlitz, "Health: The Democratic Steamroller That Wasn't," *National Journal*, May 14, 1994.

19 Ibid.

20 "Campaign Notes: Coelho Becomes DNC Adviser as Wilhelm Announces Exit," *Congressional Quarterly Weekly Report*, August 13, 1994; Stephen Engelberg, "Democrats' New Overseer Is Everybody's Mr. Inside," *New York Times*, August 19, 1994; "Inside Washington: McAuliffe's Leaving DNC," *National Journal*, August 20, 1994; James A. Barnes, "Politics: Gore and Coelho: How Good a Fit?" *National Journal*, May 22, 1999.

21 Bob Woodward, *The Agenda: Inside the Clinton White House* (New York: Simon and Schuster, 1994).

22 Bill Clinton, *My Life* (New York: Alfred A. Knopf, 2004), 631.

23 Ibid., 632.

24 Hillary Rodham Clinton, *Living History* (New York: Simon and Schuster, 2003), 288.

25 Fowler, personal interview.

26 Edward Walsh, "State Democrats Retreat in Search of Answers," *Washington Post*, November 19, 1994.

27 Ibid.

28 Al From and Will Marshall, "Editorial," *The New Democrat*, January–February 1995, 5.

29 Personal interview with Al From, March 24, 1999.

30 Dick Morris, *Behind the Oval Office* (New York: Random House, 1997), 34–41, 80–85; Clinton, *My Life*, 660; Stephanopoulos, *All Too Human*, 334–36.

31 Edwards, "Campaigning Is Not Governing," 40–48.

32 Barnes, "Politics: States of Repair," *National Journal*, September 16, 1995.

33 Richard L. Berke, "Aides Say Clinton Will Choose Dodd to Lead Democrats," *New York Times*, January 10, 1995.

34 Fowler, personal interview.

35 The story of Clinton's 1996 campaign strategy is now well known. See, for example, Alison Mitchell, "The Fund Machine: A Special Report," *New York Times*, December 27, 1996; Bob Woodward, *The Choice* (New York: Simon and Schuster, 1996); Morris, *Behind the Oval Office*.

36 Personal interview with former White House political director Craig Smith, June 25, 2007, Washington, D.C.

37 James A. Barnes, "Politics: Along the Campaign Trail," *National Journal*, January 20, 1996; James A. Barnes, "Campaign Spending: Party Favors," *National Journal*, May 11, 1996; James A. Barnes, "Campaign Notebook: The Great 'Soft'-Money Flood of '96," *National Journal*, June 1, 1996; James A. Barnes, "Politics: Along the Campaign Trail," *National Journal*, September 7, 1996; James A. Barnes, "Politics: Along the Campaign Trail," *National Journal*, October 12, 1996.

38 Fowler, personal interview.

39 Ibid.

40 Ibid.

41 See Ruth Marcus, "DNC Acknowledges Inadequate Checks on Donors," *Washington Post*, November 2, 1996.

42 "Congressional Facts and Figures: Party Money Just Keeps On Growing," *National Journal*, January 18, 1997.

43 President Bill Clinton, "Remarks to a Democratic National Committee Meeting," January 21, 1997, *PPP*.

44 Arthur H. Rotstein, "Vice President Urges Democratic Chairmen to Build Party's Base," Associated Press, December 6, 1996.

45 Personal interview with former DNC chairman Steve Grossman, June 11, 2007, Boston.

46 Ibid.

47 Smith, personal interview.

48 Richard L. Berke, "Debate Aside, Fund-Raising Doesn't Stop," *New York Times*, October 3, 1997; "Inside Washington: No Tricks Please," *National Journal*, October 11, 1997; James A. Barnes, "Administration: No Rest for the Fund Raiser in Chief," *National Journal*, November 22, 1997; Smith, personal interview.

49 Katharine Q. Seelye, "Clinton Follows the Money from Boston to New York," *New York Times*, July 1, 1997.

50 David Shribman, "Hillary Fills the Trough," *Fortune*, April 13, 1998; James A. Barnes, "Administration: The Appeal of Paula Jones," *National Journal*, April 4, 1998.

51 James A. Barnes, "Politics: Campaign Circuit," *National Journal*, July 18, 1998.

52 Alexis Simendinger, Peter H. Stone, and Richard E. Cohen, "Presidency: Impeachment Improv," *National Journal*, October 10, 1998; Peter H. Stone, "Politics: The Politics of Survival," *National Journal*, October 24, 1998.

53 See sources in preceding note.

54 Grossman, personal interview.

55 Ibid.

56 Woodward, *The Agenda*, 165.

57 Clinton, *My Life*, 892.

58 David Broder, "Person to Person in Indiana," *Washington Post*, December 9, 1998.

59 Andrew J. Glass, "Campaign 2000 Internet," *Atlanta Journal and Constitution*, August 6, 1999.

60 Personal interview with former DNC chairman Joe Andrew, June 26, 2007, Washington, D.C.

61 Ibid.

62 Ibid.

63 "America 2000," *Democratic National Committee*, March 1999.

64 "DNC National Chair-Designate Joe Andrew, Keynote Address, DNC Full Committee Meeting, Washington, D.C., March 19, 1999," in "America 2000," *Democratic National Committee*, March 1999.

65 Ibid.

66 Andrew, personal interview.

67 Ibid.

68 "America 2000," *Democratic National Committee*, March 1999.

69 Ibid.

70 Andrew, personal interview.

71 "America 2000," *Democratic National Committee*, March 1999.

72 Ibid.

73 Melinda Henneberger, "Democratic Chairman Plays Humble Hoosier Effortlessly," *New York Times*, August 14, 2000.

74 Andrew, personal interview.

75 Ibid.

76 "Interview: DNC Co-Chair Urges Party toward New Political Thinking," *CNN AllPolitics*, June 1, 1999.

77 Ibid.

78 "DNC National Chair-Designate Joe Andrew, Keynote Address, DNC Full Committee Meeting, Washington, D.C., March 19, 1999," in "America 2000," *Democratic National Committee*, March 1999.

79 "Statement of DNC Chair Joe Andrew on Strong State of Party Finances," DNC Press Release in *Presidential Campaign Press Materials*, July 1, 1999; and see *PPP.*

80 Andrew, personal interview.

81 "Joe Andrew Holds Post-election News Conference," *FDCH Political Transcripts*, November 8, 2000.

82 Ibid.; also see "Statement by DNC National Chair Joe Andrew on Al Gore's Concession," DNC Press Release in *Presidential Campaign Press Materials* (Washington, D.C.: Congressional Quarterly), December 14, 2000.

83 Terry McAuliffe and Steve Kettmann, *What a Party! My Life among Democrats: Presidents, Candidates, Donors, Activists, Alligators, and Other Wild Animals* (New York: Thomas Dunne, 2007), 281, 285, 385.

84 Ibid., 374

85 Ibid., 285.

86 Brian Reich, "Please Standby ... The DNC Is Still Experiencing Technical Difficulties," *Personal Democracy Forum*, April 18, 2005.

87 McAuliffe and Kettmann, *What a Party!* 298, 374; Kamarck, "Dean's Fifty State Strategy"; Bai, "The Inside Agitator."

88 Kamarck, "Dean's Fifty State Strategy"; Bai, "The Inside Agitator."

89 McAuliffe and Kettmann, *What a Party!* 303.

90 Matt Bai, "The Framing Wars," *New York Times*, July 17, 2005.

91 Kathy Kiely, "'New Direction' Is New Theme for Democratic Plan," *USA Today*, June 14, 2006.

92 Howard Kurtz, "Making a Left at the Mike," *Washington Post*, March 21, 2004.

93 David Paul Kuhn, "DNC Blunts GOP Voter Targeting Efforts," *Politico.com*, May 23, 2008; "On the Download: DNC Launches Vote Builder," *The Hotline*, May 3, 2007.

94 Ibid.; Press Release, "DNC Launches McCain Ad and New National Field Organizing Effort," Democratic National Committee, April 21, 2008.

95 Kamarck, "Dean's Fifty State Strategy."

96 Bai, "The Inside Agitator."

97 See, for example, Adam Nagourney, "Dean and Party Leaders in a Money Dispute," *New York Times*, May 11, 2006; Dan Gilgoff, "Dean's List," *U.S. News & World Report*, July 24, 2006; Kamarck, "Dean's Fifty State Strategy"; and Galvin, "Grow a Democratic Majority."

98 Bai, "The Inside Agitator."

99 Transcript, *The Situation Room*, CNN, May 11, 2006.

100 Paul Begala, "Bringing a Knife to a Gunfight," *HuffingtonPost.com*, May 19, 2006.

101 John Dickerson, "The Doctor Is In: Howard Dean Isn't Getting Tossed from the DNC," *Slate.com*, November 22, 2006.

102 Mike Madden, "Obama's Debt to Howard Dean," *Salon.com*, 11-12-08; Berman, "The Prophet."

12 | Conclusion: Presidents, Parties, and the Political System

1 It is equally important not to conflate the intent of presidential actions with their effects: Eisenhower designed a "southern strategy," but he did not design *the* southern strategy. New party forms rarely reflect their founder's intent.

2 Broder, *The Party's Over*; Burns, *Running Alone*; Lowi, *The Personal President*; Milkis, *The President and the Parties*; Milkis, *Political Parties*.

3 Wilson, *Constitutional Government*, 60; E. E. Schattschneider, *Party Government* (New York: Rinehart and Winston, 1942); A Report of the Committee on Political Parties, American Political Science Association, "Toward a More Responsible Two-Party System," *American Political Science Review* 44, no. 3 (1950); James MacGregor Burns, *Presidential Government: The Crucible of Leadership* (Boston: Houghton Mifflin, 1966); Broder, *The Party's Over*.

4 American Political Science Association, "Toward a More Responsible Two-Party System," 13, 89–90.

5 Ibid., 30.

6 Ibid., 17–18.

7 Regarding the "integrative" function, see the excellent discussion in King, "Political Parties in Western Democracies," 123–28. King writes: "The problems that confront the political scientists are to ascertain whether political integration and mobilization are taking place at all and, if so, to what extent and with respect to whom" (124).

8 Stephen Skowronek has queried, for example, whether the GOP under George W. Bush became simply "whatever the president needs it to be," a mere "tool of presidential management" (Skowronek, "Leadership by Definition," 829). Sidney M. Milkis agrees that if we were looking for evidence that "party organization has become a vehicle for the White House's objectives," the RNC under George W. Bush would seem to offer a case in point. Sidney M. Milkis, "George W. Bush and the 'New' American Party System," *Clio* 16, no. 1 (2005–6): 44; also see Milkis and Rhodes, "George W. Bush."

Afterword | George W. Bush and Beyond

1 Senator James Jeffords of Vermont switched his party affiliation from Republican to Independent and began to caucus with the Democratic Party on May 24, 2001. James M. Jeffords, *My Declaration of Independence* (New York: Simon and Schuster, 2001).

2 Charlie Cook, "Bush Mines for Gold as GOP Fundraiser," *National Journal*, April 6, 2002; Harold F. Bass, "George W. Bush, Presidential Party Leadership Extraordinaire?" *The Forum* 2, no. 4 (2004); Milkis and Rhodes, "George W. Bush"; Skinner, "George W. Bush."

3 Kornblut and Shear, "Architect Envisioned GOP Supremacy." Also see Peter Baker, "Rove Remains Steadfast in the Face of Criticism," *Washington Post*, November 12, 2006.

4 See, for example, Nicholas Lemann, "The Controller."

5 R. H. Melton and Thomas B. Edsall, "Bush Taps Gilmore as RNC Chairman," *Washington Post*, December 22, 2000.

6 CNN transcript, "George W. Bush Taps Governor Jim Gilmore as Head of Republican National Committee," December 22, 2000.

7 Ralph Z. Hallow, "GOP in March Raises a Record $6.8 Million," *Washington Times*, April 20, 2001.

8 R.H. Melton and Dan Balz, "Gilmore Resigns RNC Post, May Run Again in VA," *Washington Post*, December 1, 2001.

9 President George W. Bush, "Remarks Following a Meeting with Republican National Committee Chairman Marc Racicot," December 5, 2001, *PPP.*

10 President George W. Bush, "Remarks at a Republican National Committee Dinner," May 14, 2002, *PPP.*

11 Gillespie, *Winning Right*, 262–63.

12 Bai, "Multilevel Marketing."

13 Ken Mehlman, "Republicans and the Future," *Washington Times*, January 25, 2005.

14 "Special Elections Confirm the Importance of Grassroots Turnout Efforts," RNC Press Release, May 23, 2005.

15 Cillizza, "Martinez Will Reach Out."

16 "RNC Chairman Ken Mehlman Remarks to RNC Winter Meeting," RNC Press Release, January 19, 2005.

17 See, for example, James Dao, "Republican Party Is Backing Black Candidates in Bid to Attract Votes," *New York Times,* July 1, 2005; "GOP, Bush Continue Wooing Black Pastors," *Christian Century,* February 22, 2005.

18 "RNC Chairman Ken Mehlman Takes 'Conversations with the Community' to Jewish Leaders in Pittsburgh," RNC Press Release, June 9, 2005; Cindy Arora, "GOP Courting O.C. Hispanics," *Orange County Register,* June 3, 2005; "RNC Chairman Ken Mehlman Announces Hispanic Advisory Committee," RNC Press Release, May 4, 2005; "RNC Chairman Ken Mehlman Announces African-American Advisory Committee," RNC Press Release, March 10, 2005.

19 Greg Pierce, "Inside Politics: Candidate Training," *Washington Times,* February 16, 2006.

20 Jim VandeHei, "Democrats Scrambling to Organize Voter Turnout," *Washington Post*, August 2, 2006.

21 Baker, "Rove Remains Steadfast."

22 Ibid.

23 Mike Duncan, "Reelect Mike Duncan, Republican National Committee Chairman," http://www.mikeforchairman.com/PDF/PlanForTheFuture.pdf.

24 Cillizza, "Martinez Will Reach Out"; Karl Rove, "A Way Out of the Wilderness," *Newsweek*, November 15, 2008; Tom Bevan and John McIntyre, "Interview with President George W. Bush: Part One," *Realclearpolitics.com,* December 16, 2008; Perry Bacon Jr., "Bush Tells His Party to Be 'Open-Minded,'" *Washington Post,* January 12, 2009.

25 "See How They Run," *New York Times*, May 16, 2008.

26 Ryan Grim, "Bush Fundraising Down by $40 million," *Politico.com*, October 21, 2008.

27 Jill Lawrence and Judy Keen, "To Dems, Rove 'More Dangerous' Outside West Wing," *USA Today*, August 14, 2007; see also Joe Hadfield, "The RNC Keeps on Rollin," *Campaigns and Elections,* April 2005.

28 Karl Rove, "Lincoln's Rule: Organization Matters," *Wall Street Journal,* June 5, 2008.

29 Alexander Burns, "A Guide to the RNC Chairman Race," *Politico.com,* December 18, 2008; "Americans for Tax Reform RNC Chairman Debate," January 5, 2008, http://www.yourrnc.com/videos/.

30 DiMaggio and Powell, "The Iron Cage Revisited."

31 Sam Stein, "Obama and Dean Team Up to Recast the Political Map," *Huffington Post,* June 5, 2008.

32 Ben Smith, "Obama Moves DNC Operations to Chicago," *Politico.com,* June 12, 2008.

33 Berman, "The Prophet."

34 Ben Smith, "Obama's Aim: 14 Bush States and Local Races," *Politico.com,* June 5, 2008.

35 Quote is from respected party leader Donna Brazile: "Dean helped Obama and other Democrats prepare for this day.... While others lamented our loss in 2004, Dean got to work in devising a 50-state strategy that eventually laid the groundwork for Obama and others to harvest votes in 2008." Quoted in Mike Madden, "Obama's Debt to Howard Dean," *Salon.com,* November 12, 2008.

36 Berman, "The Prophet."

37 Lisa Wangsness, "A Changed Strategy Preceded a Changed Electoral Landscape," *Boston Globe*, November 6, 2008.

38 Ari Berman, "The Dean Legacy," *The Nation*, February 28, 2008. Berman, "The Prophet."

39 "Obama Announces Kaine as New DNC Chair," *The Office of the President Elect*, January 8, 2009, http://change.gov/newsroom/entry/obama_announces_kaine_as_new_dnc_chair/

40 Ibid.

41 John Heilemann, "The New Politics: Barack Obama, Party of One," *New York*, January 11, 2009; Berman, "The Prophet"; Peter Wallsten, "Retooling Obama's Campaign Machine for the Long Haul," *Los Angeles Times*, January 14, 2009; Tim Kaine, "Tim Kaine Answers Questions about Future of Party," http://www.democrats.org/page/invite/questionsvideo, January 16, 2009.

42 David Plouffe, "Before Anything Else," *Obama for America email*, November 12, 2008.

43 Gaspard, political director for the Obama campaign, previously served as political director for 1199 SEIU (the largest health care workers union in the nation) and as national field director for America Coming Together (ACT), a technically nonpartisan 527 group that worked at the grassroots level to get out the vote for Democratic candidates during the 2004 election cycle. Perhaps no group symbolized the Democratic tradition of relying on outside groups for campaign support better than ACT. Thus, symbolically, bringing Gaspard "in-house" appeared to signal a dramatic shift in the party's priorities.

Kaine was applauded for his party-building work as governor of Virginia—the Democratic state party chairman of Virginia called Kaine as "focused at party building as any governor that we've ever had," citing Kaine's willingness to help raise money, "professionalize the operations of the Democratic Party," and "recruit highly qualified candidates" (Greg Giroux, "Kaine Readies for Multitasking in Governing and Politics," *Congressional Quarterly*, January 8, 2009). Jennifer O'Malley Dillon served as director of battleground state operations during the Obama campaign. Obama called her "a tireless organizer, a beloved manager, and … a trusted advisor. She will ensure that state parties, DNC members, elected officials, and candidates have the full attention of the DNC over the next four years, and that we will continue to build our grassroots movement from the ground up in all 50 states" ("President-Elect Obama Announces Virginia Governor Tim Kaine as DNC Chair: Jennifer O'Malley Dillon to Serve as Executive Director," *PR Newswire*, January 8, 2009).

44 Marc Ambinder, "Obama 2.0: Axelrod Gives Up Stakes, Gris Joins AKPD; Dillon Is Dep. Pol. Director," *The Atlantic*, January 16, 2009, http://marcambinder.theatlantic.com/archives/2009/01/obama_20_axelrod_lives_up_stak.php.

45 Mark Ambinder "The Organizing DNC; The Future Of Obama's Campaign," *The Atlantic*, January 5, 2009, http://marcambinder.theatlantic.com/archives/2009/01/the_organizing_dnc.php.

46 Wallsten, "Retooling Obama's Campaign Machine"; Tim Kaine, "Tim Kaine Answers Questions about Future of Party," http://www.democrats.org/page/invite/questionsvideo, January 16, 2009.

47 Chris Bowers, "Life and Death of the Fifty-State Strategy, Update," *Openleft.com*, November 18, 2008, http://www.openleft.com/showDiary.do?diaryId=10017. Bowers explains that the "state party program," the centerpiece of the fifty-state

strategy, used DNC funds to pay for largely autonomous activities at the state and local levels. The degree of autonomy local party leaders would be granted in the future was uncertain.

48 "Partisan Trends," *Rasmussen Reports*, January 5, 2009, http://www.rasmussen reports.com/public_content/politics/mood_of_america/party_affiliation/partisan_trends. State legislative data from "2008–09 (Post-Election) Partisan Composition of State Legislatures," December 1, 2008, http://www.ncsl.org/state vote/partycomptable2009.htm.

49 It is worth noting, however, that the Democratic Party's competitive standing appears slightly weaker for Obama than it was at the beginning of the Clinton and Kennedy presidencies, and a good deal weaker than at the beginning of the Johnson and Carter presidencies.

50 Berman, "The Prophet."

51 Transcript, "Barack Obama's New Hampshire Primary Speech," *New York Times*, January 8, 2008; "Blueprint for Change: Obama and Biden's Plan for America," Obama '08, www.barackobama.com.

Appendix | Methods and Sources

1 I have omitted only those episodes that are plainly trivial or clearly redundant.

2 These actions vary so widely in their scope and intensity that I do not attempt to present them as event-count data. To be sure, it would be *possible* to provide an event count, but not necessarily *desirable*: such data would likely be more misleading than helpful. The main difficulty lies in expressing the intensity and significance of president-party interactions. If a president launches a massive nationwide training initiative of lengthy duration in a single action, for example, but makes a dozen minor changes at different times and for different reasons to the communications processes, staffing routines, and other such activities at the National Committee, it would seem rather unfair to count the former instance as one and the latter as twelve. Related president-party interactions can be treated as "episodes," but all episodes are not of equal significance.

3 Being agnostic about the effects is important because it ensures that variations that emerge from the data are not the result of selection bias in the data collection.

4 See below for a discussion of the six dimensions of party activity.

5 This is not to say that that neglect, exploitation, and undercutting are the same. Indeed, the substantive chapters in Part II have elaborated at length upon the different faces of party "predation" (see, especially, chapter 10). But the effect of any nonconstructive effort is the same; hence, the single grouping.

6 The relationship established between the president and his national chairman is therefore of the essence. Some party chairmen were demonstrably empowered to undertake party-building initiatives on behalf of the president (Hall, Alcorn, Evans, Bush, Smith, Fahrenkopf, Atwater, Bond, and Andrew), and others were clearly not (Bailey, Dole, Curtis, Wilhelm, and Fowler).

7 For an excellent discussion of the selection process for every chairman in each party's history, see Ralph Morris Goldman, *The National Party Chairmen and Committees: Factionalism at the Top* (Armonk, N.Y.: M. E. Sharpe, 1990).

8 Quotes from ibid., 561, 566. See also Cotter and Bibby, "Institutional Development of Parties"; Cotter and Hennessy, *Politics without Power*.

9 Every older library contains voluminous collections of "political" papers; the archivist of the United States noted in August 2001 that "presidents who served before 1981, except for President Nixon, were free to limit access to any and all of their White House papers, because their papers were considered their personal property. However, all of them since Herbert Hoover, except Nixon, have donated those papers to the Federal Government with very few restrictions, except for records dealing with national security, personal materials, and materials that would be embarrassing to other individuals or otherwise invade personal privacy" (http://www.archives.gov/presidential-libraries/laws/access/reagan.html). In the summer of 2007, Nixon's "political" papers were declassified in their entirety and made available for research at the Nixon Library in Yorba Linda, Calif.

10 Some of the more prominent works consulted include Cornelius P. Cotter et al., *Party Organizations in American Politics* (New York: Praeger, 1984); Leon D. Epstein, *Political Parties in the American Mold* (Madison: University of Wisconsin Press, 1986); Paul S. Herrnson, *Party Campaigning in the 1980s* (Cambridge: Harvard University Press, 1988); Joseph A. Schlesinger, *Political Parties and the Winning of Office* (Ann Arbor: University of Michigan Press, 1991); Philip A. Klinkner, *The Losing Parties: Out-Party National Committees, 1956–1993* (New Haven: Yale University Press, 1994); John J. Coleman, "Resurgent or Just Busy? Party Organizations in Contemporary America," in *The State of the Parties*, ed. John C. Green and Daniel M. Shea (Lanham: Rowman and Littlefield, 1996).

Index |

Princeton Studies in American Politics
Historical, International, and Comparative Perspectives

Edited by Ira Katznelson, Martin Shefter, and Theda Skocpol